Cloud Computing Strategies

IT MANAGEMENT TITLES
FROM AUERBACH PUBLICATIONS AND CRC PRESS

The Executive MBA in Information Security
John J. Trinckes, Jr
ISBN: 978-1-4398-1007-1

**The Decision Model: A Business
Logic Framework Linking Business
and Technology**
Barbara von Halle and Larry Goldberg
ISBN: 978-1-4200-8281-4

The SIM Guide to Enterprise Architecture
Leon Kappelman, ed.
ISBN: 978-1-4398-1113-9

Lean Six Sigma Secrets for the CIO
William Bentley and Peter T. Davis
ISBN: 978-1-4398-0379-0

**Building an Enterprise-Wide Business
Continuity Program**
Kelley Okolita
ISBN: 978-1-4200-8864-9

Marketing IT Products and Services
Jessica Keyes
ISBN: 978-1-4398-0319-6

**Cloud Computing: Implementation,
Management, and Security**
John W. Rittinghouse and
James F. Ransome
ISBN: 978-1-4398-0680-7

**Data Protection: Governance, Risk
Management, and Compliance**
David G. Hill
ISBN: 978-1-4398-0692-0

**Strategic Data Warehousing: Achieving
Alignment with Business**
Neera Bhansali
ISBN: 978-1-4200-8394-1

**Mobile Enterprise Transition
and Management**
Bhuvan Unhelkar
ISBN: 978-1-4200-7827-5

The Green and Virtual Data Center
Greg Schulz
ISBN: 978-1-4200-8666-9

The Effective CIO
Eric J. Brown, Jr. and William A. Yarberry
ISBN: 978-1-4200-6460-5

**Business Resumption Planning,
Second Edition**
Leo A. Wrobel
ISBN: 978-0-8493-1459-9

**IT Auditing and Sarbanes-Oxley
Compliance: Key Strategies for
Business Improvement**
Dimitris N. Chorafas
ISBN: 978-1-4200-8617-1

**Best Practices in Business Technology
Management**
Stephen J. Andriole
ISBN: 978-1-4200-6333-2

**Leading IT Projects:
The IT Manager's Guide**
Jessica Keyes
ISBN: 978-1-4200-7082-8

**Knowledge Retention:
Strategies and Solutions**
Jay Liebowitz
ISBN: 978-1-4200-6465-0

The Business Value of IT
Michael D. S. Harris, David Herron,
and Stasia Iwanicki
ISBN: 978-1-4200-6474-2

**Service-Oriented Architecture: SOA
Strategy, Methodology, and Technology**
James P. Lawler and H. Howell-Barber
ISBN: 978-1-4200-4500-0

Service Oriented Enterprises
Setrag Khoshafian
ISBN: 978-0-8493-5360-4

Cloud Computing Strategies

Dimitris N. Chorafas

CRC Press
Taylor & Francis Group
Boca Raton   London   New York

CRC Press is an imprint of the
Taylor & Francis Group, an **informa** business
AN AUERBACH BOOK

CRC Press
Taylor & Francis Group
6000 Broken Sound Parkway NW, Suite 300
Boca Raton, FL 33487-2742

© 2011 by Taylor and Francis Group, LLC
CRC Press is an imprint of Taylor & Francis Group, an Informa business

---

Library of Congress Cataloging-in-Publication Data

Chorafas, Dimitris N.
  Cloud computing strategies / Dimitris N. Chorafas.
     p. cm.
     Includes bibliographical references (p.   ) and index.
  ISBN 978-1-4398-3453-4 (hardcover)
  1. Web services. 2. Cloud computing. I. Title.

  TK5105.88813.C492 2011
  006.7'6--dc22   2010018872

Visit the Taylor & Francis Web site at
http://www.taylorandfrancis.com

and the CRC Press Web site at
http://www.crcpress.com

Contents

SECTION IV   CASE STUDIES ON CLOUD COMPUTING APPLICATIONS

Foreword

Over the last few years daily papers as well as weekly and monthly magazines and the media have been heralding "digital U.S.," "digital Europe," and "digital Asia." America and most countries of the European Union are already wired. They score highly on access to broadband, while *Internet* has become a household word. But this is only part of the new environment that is evolving.

In the five and a half decades since the first commercial applications of digital computers at General Electric's factory in Louisville, Kentucky, we have passed the stone, copper, and steel ages of computer technology. We have developed at a rapid pace successive generations of hardware but at the same time hardly reached adolescence in software development. Consequently, many user organizations have found themselves in the midst of the software snarls.

Now we are entering into the *software age*. Programming products available as commodity packages came to the market in the late 1960s and brought computer applications out of boyhood. Twenty years later, in the late 1980s, software was in its teens, thanks to the Internet. However, all this is past. Today, another two decades down the line, adulthood may come to applications programming through onDemand facilities, also known as software as a service (SaaS).

OnDemand is a generic issue in cloud computing; *cloud computing* is a strategic inflection point in information technology. Not only applications software but also platforms, infrastructure, and enabling services—in short, all four pillars on which the cloud rests—may be onDemand, as contrasted to the *onPremises* practice, which has dominated IT so far.

***

Written for information technology (IT) professionals, IT departments, consultancies, and company managements contemplating cloud computing, this book also addresses itself to senior management. Apart from presenting the facts, the text examines the strategies available in regard to cloud computing from as many perspectives as the divergent opinions heard during my research.

To enable the reader to make his or her own judgment, the text defines cloud computing strengths and weaknesses—therefore, its assets and liabilities. Could this strategic inflection point in information technology become a poisonous gift? And will companies massively migrate to cloud computing when they realize that there is no way to own and control the end-to-end network?

As chapter after chapter documents, there are security concerns about cloud computing, reliability issues, response time worries, and many uncertainties regarding costs. There are, as well, some fake hopes; for instance, that it can act as the twenty-first century's penicillin, curing a company's problems that are strategic, tactical, or organizational—and many of them have nothing to do with technology.

One thing that negatively impressed me during the research is that companies are very secretive about their cloud computing plans and views. Some even characterized them as "company confidential," which speaks volumes about their quality of governance. Their CEOs and CIOs have probably not read the dictum by Louis Brandeis, U.S. Supreme Court justice, who once said: "Sunshine is the best disinfectant."

***

The research brought good news and bad news. Quite disquieting has been the finding that some user organizations look at cloud computing as a way to preserve their batch procedures and legacy software. That's patently wrong, negating all benefits a company might get from the cloud. In a globalized market characterized by unprecedented competition:

- the crucial issue in information technology is being ahead of the curve, and
- dreaming to stay behind is no recipe for business success.

The good news is that what companies are presently confronting is not just a matter of new IT features but also of new concepts requiring a culture quite different from the one that reigned for over half a century. Cultural change is welcome, but as some experts have suggested, that may also be the reason why universal acceptance of the cloud is not yet on call.

The pros are saying that the ability to store sprawling databases on giant servers managed by providers and accessed on request is an important added value in IT. Critics answer that this appeals to technophiles, but benefits are not clear-cut, the risks associated with it are opaque, there are unanswered queries in a system sense, and cost-effectiveness is not self-evident.

Beyond that, significant investments need to be made to improve outdated wired and wireless networks. Moreover, security measures have not been properly studied so far, and thorough reliability studies did not precede the cloud computing announcements. Companies worldwide are worried about the challenge presented by the rapid growth in networked data traffic and the fact that it is exposed to terrorist attacks, let alone war conditions.

Concomitant to these worries is the fact that while onPremises solutions have been characterized by lots of patchwork, companies can profit from an onDemand strategy *only if* they seriously and effectively reengineer their systems and procedures. The phenomenal rate of change experienced by business and industry with globalization must be finally reflected in the organization and in IT's implementation.

Competitiveness mandates that approach. A large number of enterprises today operate in a market that increasingly requires a global view of products, customers, and competition. This has greatly influenced the direction of capital investments (capex). In 1980 only 30 percent of capex was IT related. In 2009 this zoomed to 54 percent. It needs no explaining that these statistics are propelled by fundamental reasons.

Software has been a key beneficiary of this surge. In 1980 software's share in IT-related capital expenditures was about 12 percent. Today, software's share of a much bigger market for computers and communications equipment is nearly 50 percent. This rapidly growing dependence on software is one of the reasons why the acquisition of onDemand programming products has become a must.

There is another issue of which to take notice. A positive aftereffect of so many decades of IT experience is that user organizations have been maturing in terms of IT management. The days are past when a manufacturer could use gimmicks and slick talk to sell computing machinery. Through costly mistakes, a lot of users learned to become less dependent on promises that engage only those who listen to them.

However, not all the blame can be put on vendors. Too often, user organizations have been apathetic, not knowing well their problem and having paid scant attention to how to solve it. Computers in many companies became expensive "glory boxes" or status symbols, rather than profitable, problem-solving information processing installations. Could cloud computing change all that?

The answer is not obvious. Turning computing into a utility *might* provide a solution. There is no lack of challenges in the way. The best that can be presently said is that

■ information technology has come to a strategic inflection point, and
■ what follows will largely depend on how well user organizations reengineer themselves.

As the research that underpins this book has documented, the die is not cast for the time being. Rather, the message about cloud computing and its deliverables is akin to an oracle given by the ancient temple of Delphi: "You do it you benefit not you live in cloud cuckoo land."

The oracle by Delphi given to a Spartan who asked if he comes back victorious from the war is "*Ixis afixis uk en to polemo thnixis*," which translates: "You go you come not you die in the war." It all depends where you put the comma: before or after *not* (*uk*). The same is true with cloud computing. An honest answer today is *ixis afixis*.

There are limits to technology's reach and risks associated with these limits. As the Epilog explains, it is high time that people and companies pay attention to them.

***

In conclusion, the book's aim is to present to the reader cloud computing's opportunities and challenges, as well as to serve as devil's advocate in matters regarding cloud strategies and motives that management should consider before passing the point of no return in regard to commitments being made.

I am indebted to many knowledgeable people, and organizations, for their contributions to the research that made this book feasible. Also to several senior executives and experts for important suggestions and constructive criticism during the preparation of the manuscript. Dr. Heinrich Steinmann and Dr. Nelson Mohler have been of great help in evaluating the risks and opportunities of IT's strategic inflection point.

Let me thank John Wyzalek for suggesting this project, Andrea Demby for seeing it all the way to publication, and Sheyanne Armstrong for editing the manuscript. To Eva-Maria Binder goes the credit for compiling the research results, typing the text, compiling the index, and suggesting valuable insights.

Dimitris N. Chorafas
April 2010
Valmer and Vitznau

About the Author

Dr. Dimitris N. Chorafas has, since 1961, advised financial institutions and industrial corporations in strategic planning, risk management, computers and communications systems, and internal controls. A graduate of the University of California, Los Angeles, the University of Paris, and the Technical University of Athens, Dr. Chorafas has been a Fulbright scholar.

Financial institutions that sought his assistance include the Union Bank of Switzerland, Bank Vontobel, CEDEL, the Bank of Scotland, Credit Agricole, Österreichische Länderbank (Bank Austria), First Austrian Bank, Kommerzbank, Dresdner Bank, Demir Bank, Mid-Med Bank, Banca Nazionale dell'Agricoltura, Istituto Bancario Italiano, Credito Commerciale and Banca Provinciale Lombarda.

Dr. Chorafas has worked as a consultant to top management of multinational corporations, including General Electric-Bull, Univac, Honeywell, Digital Equipment, Olivetti, Nestlé, Omega, Italcementi, Italmobiliare, AEG-Telefunken, Olympia, Osram, Antar, Pechiney, the American Management Association, and a host of other client firms in Europe and the United States.

He has served on the faculty of the Catholic University of America and as a visiting professor at Washington State University, George Washington University, University of Vermont, University of Florida, and the Georgia Institute of Technology. Additionally, these educational institutes include the University of Alberta, Technical University of Karlsruhe, Ecole d'Etudes Industrielles de l'Université de Genève, Ecole Polytechnic Fédérale de Lausanne, the Polish Academy of Sciences, and the Russian Academy of Sciences.

More than 8,000 banking, industrial, and government executives have participated in his seminars in the United States, England, Germany, Italy, and other European countries, and in Asia and Latin America. Dr. Chorafas is the author of 153 books, some of which have been translated into 16 languages.

CLOUD TECHNOLOGY AND ITS USER COMMUNITY

I

Chapter 1

The Cloud Computing Market

1.1 For and against Cloud Computing

No two people will completely agree on what *is* and *is not* cloud computing* or even on the origin of the term. To some the concept looks too general, the domain too broad and too dependent on the Internet, and the competitors too diverse in their business background and even more so in their size.† Not all of the people expressing such reservations are the cloud's critics.

For the pros cloud computing is the solution, the borderless information utility they have always wanted. To their judgment it will enable companies to cast away their legacy core systems that are technologically outdated and are restricting the development of business opportunities—and therefore of profits.

Not everybody, of course, agrees with the statement that existing core systems do not have the flexibility needed to meet organizational requirements as well as customer needs and expectations. Many chief information officers (CIOs) like their legacy systems so much that they already plan to duplicate them in a cloud, and some vendors are ready to oblige.

In this environment, much more than just novelty is at stake, particularly so when the experts' opinions do not converge. There is no general agreement even on

---

* Defined in terms of its component parts and services in Section 1.3.
† A snapshot of cloud vendors is given in Section 1.4 and details on their wares in Chapter 6.

the origin of the label *cloud computing*. An often heard argument is that it sprung from the graphical presentation of a cloud frequently used in reference to the Internet. But it is also true that the term *cloud* came into use nearly two decades ago, in the early 1990s, in identifying large ATM networks.

The roots of cloud computing's functionality are also open to debate. According to one definition, which is not generally accepted, it should be found in advances in grid computing, used for scientific calculations. The term *grid computing* evolved in connection to shared high-performance computing facilities, which have been *multitenant*. Database clustering for multiple users from different firms has been instrumental in evolving features like dynamic resources scheduling and load balancing, which:

- increased resource utilization, and
- eventually led to the cloud computing concept.

These advances have enabled information technology providers to use relatively low-cost commodity servers to wring out computing and data storage power. Moreover, the combination of commodity software and easy online access allowed user organizations to pool and allocate programming resources onDemand, rather than dedicating stacks of onPremises software to specific tasks, the old legacy way.

Etymologically, the terms *onDemand* and *onPremises* can be used not only for software and different types of services but also for infrastructure. It has been a deliberate choice in this text to employ these two words strictly in connection to programming products on the cloud, as the developing general practice warrants, but the terms are much more generic and can apply to all four pillars of the cloud discussed in Section 1.3, namely:

- applications,
- platforms,
- infrastructure, and
- enabling services.

The pros say that the wide possibilities these four component parts offer can best be exploited by companies with a record of innovation. Laggards don't need to apply. Some critics answer that while onDemand applications may offer distinct advantages compared to onPremises, onDemand infrastructural facilities encompass risks and can bring the user organization to the bleeding edge.

Security and reliability are two leading reasons behind this statement. Loss of control over the basic infrastructure is a third factor. Still, for companies searching to reposition themselves into a changing information technology environment, the aforementioned distinction between onDemand and onPremises provides a fast and dirty definition of the cloud (we will see more polished definitions in Sections 1.2 and 1.3):

- Cloud computing is onDemand, and this is true of applications, platforms, infrastructure, and enabling services.
- By contrast, the information technology facilities that we have known so far, from mainframes to minis, PCs, and client-servers, have been onPremises.

The reader should be aware that around cloud computing revolve some terms that, to say the least, are misleading. A case in point is *ecosystem*. This word is inappropriate in the Internet context because with computers and communications there is nothing "ecological," as we will see later. Therefore, ecosystem is a misnomer and it will not be used in the context of this book, even if *ecology* is a popular word these days.

Gone is the time when the motto "communicate, don't commute" made the headlines. Ecology and IT don't go hand in hand. If anything closely associates itself with cloud computing, it is the technical requirements cloud computing poses, which are far from heralding environmental protection. Data centers containing the cloud cannot be built just anywhere. They need:

- dry air,
- chilly climate,
- cheap power,
- fiber optic cables,
- high security, and
- right political conditions.

Neither are privacy and cloud computing good bedfellows. Personal information will be everywhere, and online crooks can easily jump jurisdictions. This is the alter ego of the fact that cloud computing is a borderless utility. Theoretically, it does not matter where your data and programs are stored.

Practically, geography matters a great deal. Good sites are scarce, and secure good sites are even more rare. Cloud environments must be controlled, which consumes a great deal of energy, and nobody will ever underwrite an insurance policy that no hacker will infiltrate the distributed database (hackers are people who like to tinker with technology).

There is as well a paradox that cloud computing inherited from the Internet. The services the Internet provided are now widespread, but classical concepts about pricing them did not hold water. Companies active on the Internet have come to appreciate that it is not only an equalizer but also an opportunity to get something for free.

- As an equalizer, it makes it difficult to distinguish one's product from the next.
- By offering some services free of cost, it creates the challenge of how to make money to continue being active.

Hence the need to find out what one can do that one's competitors cannot, betting on that difference or alternatively capitalizing on other people's inefficiencies.

For instance, vendors of onDemand customer relationship management (CRM; Chapter 11) software stress the savings resulting from its efficiency. They estimate it could trim 75 percent of the cost incurred by a user organization to maintain a legacy customer handling service that measures up to what is available as an online commodity.

It is essentially this efficiency that leads people who look at cloud computing as a *strategic inflection point* (Chapter 3) in information technology to the statement that it will dramatically rearrange the pecking order of companies in many fields. In their opinion, it will help those willing and able (not every firm) to make the leap from laggard to "leader.

This hypothesis tests the notion that just like in a recession,* companies will use the online facilities offered by cloud computing to squeeze their IT costs and win market share from their competitors by being ahead of the curve. As this text will document, however, while this is indeed possible for the majority of companies, it does not constitute a self-evident truth.

1.2 OnDemand vs. OnPremises IT

Some people challenge the notion that there is something "new" with cloud computing. Oracle's Larry Ellison was quoted in the *Wall Street Journal* as having said: "The interesting thing about Cloud Computing is that we've redefined (it) to include everything that we already do. ... I don't understand what we would do differently in the light of Cloud Computing other than change the wording in some of our ads."†

This is not an accurate statement, and the same is true of comments made by other people about "jumping on the cloud bandwagon." Even if there was nothing else but the distinction between onDemand and onPremises software (Section 1.1), there would have been something new and important in the road information technology has been following: The term *onDemand* software has wide implications all the way to the information utility concept, even if in this text it is used to identify applications routines rented online from providers, which some people call software as a service (SaaS).

Because onDemand software is the most positive development of cloud computing, and along with onDemand platforms a truly new departure in information technology, this book dedicates a quarter of its text to it. Chapter 11 explains the concept of open-source software and its precedents. Chapter 12 is a case study on

---

* Thirty percent of banks and two-fifths of big American industrial firms dropped out of the first quartile of their industries in the recession of 2001–2002. Quite interestingly, two out of three companies that came up from under during the previous recession preserved their gains during the subsequent boom.

† *Wall Street Journal*, September 26, 2008.

logistics and supply chain management. Chapter 13 is a case study on cloud programming products for private banking and asset management. An onDemand solution contrasts with onPremises and its sense of proprietorship, including routines coming from in-house development or bought off-the-shelf—whether or not the latter have been (incorrectly) massaged to fit the user organization's internal procedures (more on this later).

This book will demonstrate that the first alternative is far superior to the second, not only because it is much more cost-effective but also because software on rent cannot be altered by user organizations. All things being equal, this lack of interference sees to it that onDemand has a much higher dependability (Chapter 11).

Not everybody appreciates that the in-house and commissioned routines widely used today are not so reliable. Glitches can create havoc. On October 3, 2009, a computer glitch delayed dozens of flights from British airports.* A few years earlier, another software malfunction sent the luggage of thousands of passengers to the wrong destination. Mine went to Tokyo, while I was flying to Chicago.

If current trends are an indication of future conditions, *then* onDemand information technology services are the shortest and best definition of cloud computing. The alternative definition, which emphasizes the storing of information and applications in remote data centers instead of on one's own PC, client-server, or other equipment, is much more restrictive.

This global size warehousing has further implications. With telecommunications charges in free fall, the pros predict that hard drives on most devices—from workstations to handheld—will become obsolete, and in a few years computer manufacturers will make and sell the majority of PCs, laptops, and other gear without them. Some Internet providers already offer centralized storage services of end user e-mails, but the results are not so convincing.

One of the strengths of technology is that in the longer run it avoids tunnel vision. Over the years, servers have evolved with the capability to share multiple applications, while *virtualization* (see Chapter 2) became a most relevant development—and more recently, the basic notion in cloud computing. At the same time, the need to share information between widely varied applications has grown, and this resulted in an increased demand for networked storage capabilities. In short, there has been a simultaneous exponential rise in three directions, as shown in Figure 1.1:

■ exploding number of online users,
■ petabytes to accommodate the growth of databases,† and
■ teraops for information processing and in-depth analytics.

Also fast increasing has been the demand for resource sharing, which transcends onPremises systems. Theoretically, resource sharing enables companies and

---

* CNN, October 3, 2009.
† Metrics for database sizes are described in Table 1 in the Epilog.

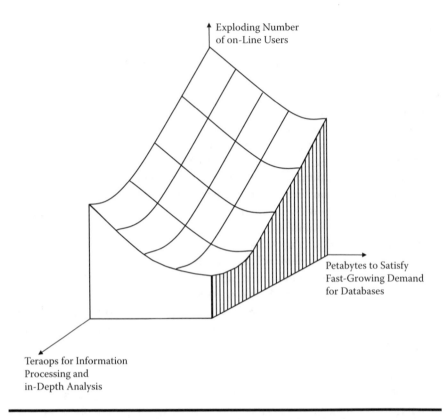

Exploding Number
of on-Line Users

Petabytes to Satisfy
Fast-Growing Demand
for Databases

Teraops for Information
Processing and
in-Depth Analysis

Figure 1.1   Information technology is confronted with a simultaneous exponential rise in all axes of its frame of reference.

individual users to cut costs by handing over the running of their e-mail, databases, sales orders, CRM, enterprise resource planning (ERP; Chapter 12), asset management (Chapter 13), accounting, and other software (more on applications) to the care of someone else, then accessing programs and data over the Internet. Practically, such matters are going to be neither so simple nor so linear; we will see why.

These have been some, but not all, of the opinions heard during the research. According to other opinions, cloud computing is more than what was stated in the foregoing paragraphs; while still others think that it offers less. An interesting thought, contributed by an expert, has been that it is not the *cloud* practice per se but the *style* of computing that matters the most—specifically, the dynamically scalable virtualized resources provided as a service over the Internet.

The pros add with a certain amount of optimism that users don't need to really know (let alone appreciate the fine print of) the underlying technological infrastructure, because this will be provided as a utility—just like the software will be a service accessible from a web browser. This argument of computing as a utility is long held but it is not ironclad.

- Computing has associated with it too much personal involvement, because it is an active enterprise.
- By contrast, the use of electricity, which is a true utility, is passive. For instance, plug in and tune to your preferred radio station.

Neither is it true that cloud computing will provide infinite computing resources available on demand, eliminating the need for user organizations to plan far ahead for provisioning or doing away with up-front commitments. People (and certain vendors) who make such statements are living in the clouds.

According to still other opinions cloud computing is the twenty-first century's reinvention of telephony, in both an allegorical and a technical sense. Until a little over two decades ago most data circuits were hardwired and switched between destinations. But in the 1990s telephone companies began offering virtual private network (VPN) services, with guaranteed bandwidth, at low cost—a practice that has been based on virtualization (Chapter 2).

Other experts answer that argument by saying that while indeed cloud computing relies greatly on virtual machine (VM) concepts, its origin is not found in virtual circuits but in virtual operating systems—a development of the late 1960s. The way still other people look at cloud computing is that no matter what the exact definition may be, the important issue is the benefits derived from online delivery of personal services.

The personal services to which reference is made range from e-mail and word processing to graphics, calendars, accounting, relationship management, human resources, and business productivity applications. More than personal, these are really *interpersonal*, and benefits are achieved by sharing resources like bandwidth, storage, processing, platforms, and onDemand routines, rather than one owning these resources, as had been the case with sixty years of information technology (see also Chapter 3).

Along a similar line of reasoning, other experts choose as number one deliverables from cloud computing the relatively new method of software services from shared servers. Evolving over a number of years, this not only contrasts with the classical process of software loaded onto a personal computer, server, or mainframe but also revolutionizes programming concepts that are six decades old.

In the background of this consideration, and the greater efficiency it makes possible, lies the swamping of costs. "Turning most of the aspects of computing into onDemand services and virtualized shared resources is a matter of economics rather than of braking technical limits," said one of the experts during our meeting. In his opinion, cloud computing is a paradigm for greater cost-effectiveness.

According to critics, however, while shared data centers might provide users with economies of scale as storage supply is consolidated, there are also negatives associated with that practice, such as reduced security (Chapter 9), no matter what the vendors may be saying. By contrast, automating an intensively manual IT activity like programming is a real gain.

With so many interpretations and definitions of cloud computing, as well as its conceivable risks and benefits, the reader might feel at a loss. He or she should not be, because even if these partial views superficially seem disconnected (though they are not outright contradictory), they are in reality complementary. Cloud computing can best be defined as everything that has been stated and more. The difference in views is largely due to the fact that people and companies may see it:

■ from a narrow perspective, as a way to reduce IT budgets and headcounts; or
■ from a broader perspective, as a strategic IT solution that requires a great lot of reengineering (Chapter 6) and rearchitecturing (Chapter 8) to offer real advantages.

In conclusion, the pros say that cloud computing is the long-dreamed-of "information at your fingertips" approach, which has promoted *software as a service* and an *open data* movement. They point out that in 2001 IBM already detailed these concepts in the computing manifesto,* which described advanced automation techniques such as self-monitoring, self-healing, self-configuring, and self-optimization in the management of complex IT systems.

The pros are also impressed by the fact that in March 2009 a group of technology firms published the *Open Cloud Manifesto*, which has since received the support of more than 150 different entities. Critics answer that this sort of enthusiasm by computer vendors for cloud computing hides dangers. Computer services delivered from vast warehouses of shared machines run by the vendors have efficiency, reliability, and security problems—sometimes serious ones. We will study each of them in the appropriate chapter.

1.3 The Four Pillars of Cloud Computing

While there is no general agreement on the exact definition of cloud computing, there exists little doubt about its main component parts and their functionality. As shown in Figure 1.2, the cloud computing landscape rests on four pillars:

■ applications,
■ platforms,
■ infrastructure, and
■ enabling services.

Among them, these sustain the armory of the new IT, whether we talk of private clouds or public clouds (Chapter 2). The concept and practice of virtualization constitutes the inner core of the system, and all productized services are delivered

---

* Which had much to do with motherhood and apple pie.

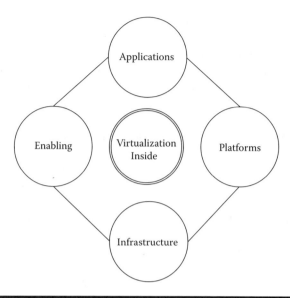

Figure 1.2   The four pillars of cloud computing.

through the Internet, bringing into the cloud computing market many more players and their wares than the bigger computer vendors.

The four pillars are in no way distinct market segments, as they correlate two by two and three by three. This is the case of onDemand software (productized applications delivered online) and platforms (for applications development); platforms and infrastructure (networks, computers, databases); platforms, infrastructure, and enabling services; and so on. Big providers will not limit themselves to segments of the cloud. They will try to dominate all of it.

This is not impossible. IBM and Hewlett-Packard have bought and fairly well integrated into their operations huge IT consulting companies. Dell recently did the same. Before slimming down its manpower, IBM featured some fifty thousand consultants. Cisco does not have that army of enablers, but it teamed up with Accenture in a cloud partnership (Chapter 7).

It would be wrong, however, to believe that everybody looks favorably at the outcome. One of the cloud's critics is Richard Stallman, of the Free Software Foundation, who said that it endangers liberties because users sacrifice their privacy and personal data to a third party. These days personal privacy and identity are under attack from all sides, not just from the cloud. In 2008 in France, two hundred thousand people were subject to identity theft.*

The boss of the Free Software Foundation characterized cloud computing as a trap aimed at forcing more people to buy in to locked, proprietary systems that would cost them more and more over time. "It's stupidity. It's worse than stupidity:

---

* M6, October 6, 2009.

it's a marketing hype campaign. Somebody is saying this is inevitable—and whenever you hear somebody saying that, it's very likely to be a set of businesses campaigning to make it true," Stallman said, as quoted by *The Guardian.**

I don't believe Stallman is 100 percent right, but neither is he 100 percent wrong. Whether the scales lean toward one side or the other, it will largely depend on the user organization's wisdom and the cloud computing vendors behavior toward their clients, as well as on the quality of services they offer. *If* user organizations fall blindly into the arms of vendors because cloud computing becomes a fashion, *then* they will be in a trap, and they will deserve it.

It would seem to me that some of the user organizations are all too happy to follow the path traced for them by their preferred vendor in the name of cloud computing. This is imprudent at best. Here is, as an example, a letter that I received while conducting my research from one of the largest and best-known companies:

> Dear Prof. Chorafas,
>
> Thank you for your latter dated August 3rd, 2009. We feel honored by the fact that you chose (our firm) as a partner for your research project on Cloud Computing.
>
> It is our policy not to share information of certain sensitivity with external parties outside of. … Unfortunately the data on request is classified within this category, thus we ask for your kind understanding that we won't be able to participate in your research project for the time being.
>
> We wish you all the best with your project.
>
> Sincerely,

Secrecy is precisely what one should not do. When confronted with uncharted territory, like the cloud computing landscape is today, by far the best policy is open communications leading to exchange of (the still limited) experience—getting critical input and learning from other people's mistakes. One must keep all doors and windows open to let fresh air come in; otherwise, the company will suffocate.

Fifteenth- and sixteenth-century explorers provide an example. Christopher Columbus made the mistake of trying to keep his discovery more or less a well-guarded secret. Amerigo Vespucci not only positioned the new world as a separate continent but also wrote extensively of his discoveries. One of Vespucci's letters was translated into forty different languages and in the mind of people positioned him as the discoverer of the New World. Thus, *America* is the name of the whole western hemisphere, while *Colombia* is just a country whose name is closely linked to drug cartels.

---

* *The Guardian*, September 29, 2008.

One of the most important benefits a company can gain by sharing with other parties its cloud computing hypotheses, moves, and projects is their experience in avoiding the deadly embrace of one cloud vendor. (The risk of a lock-in by the provider is discussed in Chapter 5.) Stallman may be right when he warns that an open cloud architecture is not in the books—at least not at present (Chapter 8).

Some experts think that against a market dominance (similar to the one experienced in the 1960s, 1970s, and early half of the 1980s with mainframes) works the fact that cloud computing services depend on the Internet, which is the most open, cost-effective, and fast way to deliver software and other functions. That's true, but the application programming interfaces (APIs), other interfaces, data formats, and protocols are the providers' own.

That the Internet is an open network (and an equalizer) is no recent awareness. It dates back to the mid-1990s. Somewhat less appreciated is the fact that the services provided by the net increased by leaps and bounds not only because access became nearly seamless but also because of giveaways, which is precisely the opposite strategy of the proprietary approach.

A great deal of credit should be given to Netscape, which, as a start-up, found new and more efficient ways to deliver than what was then the status quo with client-servers, mainframes, and private networks. Its *Navigator* browser and e-mail *Messenger* have shown the way, providing the companies who capitalized on them with leverage in the IT market.

The established computer companies' reaction was an assertion of weakness. In October 1997 Microsoft's *Explorer* could be accessed from the vendor's home page, and users liked the idea. But while Microsoft said (at the time) that more than 1 million copies were downloaded, experts pointed out the downside. This Internet-based delivery was:

■ more prone to bugs and
■ less stable than what classical software distribution had supported.

I bring this as evidence of a paradigm of problems that may be presented with more recent cases of software as a service. Microsoft's cure was to ask the user community to post on the web the bugs that it found in the released programming product. This was a smart for the vendor, but:

■ it is utterly unacceptable if it becomes general practice, even for software distributed free of cost; and
■ apart from the fact that it casts user organizations in an ambiguous sort of responsibility, quite often new bugs are introduced because of the old one's repair.*

---

* Years ago, an IBM study had found that changing one instruction in a program affects seven or eight other instructions, though not all cases turn into bugs.

The aforementioned paradigm should also serve as a warning. It is by no means true (as some vendors suggest) that people, companies, and other user organizations can employ cloud computing with the same ease with which they (today) send and receive e-mails. (As a reminder from earlier advances and their problems, it should be recalled that things were not so simple in the late 1970s and early 1980s when electronic mail became available. Four decades of usage have practically eliminated the rough edges, but security issues continue to be a major concern, and as already mentioned, cloud computing is not alien to such worries; Chapter 8.)

These are, in a nutshell, the opportunities and challenges connected to the four pillars of cloud computing, using past IT experience as food for thought. We will examine each of them in greater detail in subsequent chapters, particularly so the applications available on demand (Chapters 11 to 13). Adopting Sherlock Holmes's maxim, when one eliminates the impossible, whatever remains, however improbable, must be the truth.

1.4 A Bird's-Eye View of Cloud Computing Vendors

A long list of companies compete for a piece of the action in the cloud computing marketplace. We will take a deeper look at them, their products, their services, and their challenges in Chapter 7. The purpose of this section is to provide the reader with an overview so that the discussion that follows in Chapter 2 on public and private clouds, as well as that in Chapter 3 on information technology inflection points, is more meaningful.

Some of the competitors have been long-established computer hardware providers, who in the 1990s and early years of this century morphed into hybrid software and hardware firms with consulting on the side. IBM and Hewlett-Packard are examples. Others started their life as software providers; for instance, Microsoft. Still others are Internet success stories, like Google and Amazon. And there is as well a list of competitors that would fit under the start-up label, even if they have been in the market for some time; for example, Salesforce.com.

A general observation is that several of these competitors are, so to speak, in the business of cross-market offerings. Take Cisco as an example. Routers are an important part of cloud computing infrastructure. Servers and other hardware can be *virtualized*, with physically separate systems acting as one thanks to:

- powerful chips and
- intelligent software.

Another reason for promoting cross-market competition in cloud computing is the polyvalence of new equipment: a server can function as a router, and vice versa. Like a sophisticated traveler influences in some way the country he or she visits, the different backgrounds, experiences, and sales practices of these firms leave a footprint in cloud computing.

Here is a snapshot of the main competitors and what they provide.* The list is written in the vendors' alphabetic order without regard for company size or cloud market share:

> *Amazon.com* has established itself with a long list of clients. Its *Amazon Web Services* (AWS) permits small businesses and developers to access its infrastructure. It offers storage through its *Simple Storage Service* and markets a cloud computing environment known as *Elastic Compute Cloud* (EC2). It also provides support for offerings by IBM, Microsoft, and Oracle.

> It has been a deliberate choice to place *Apple Computer* in this short list of vendors, even if there is no unanimous opinion that it is active in cloud computing. Those who say yes point out the company's highly innovative hardware/software packages with great appeal to the consumer market (Chapter 4), as well as the fact that it is building a $1 billion data center in North Carolina, which may be the world's largest by the time it goes into operation.

> Contrarians to the positioning of Apple among cloud vendors say that iTunes stores music and video, nothing comparable to what other operators offer,† and most particularly, Apple is not in the mood to adopt an open architecture or open OS. Indeed, the company's software environment imposes restrictions, but Apple also has:
> - AppStore for mobile applications, boasting eighty-five thousand applications with over 2 billion downloads;
> - MobileMe, for online services, which seems to be gaining market share; and
> - more than 30 million iPhones sold, which is significant in terms of mobile/fixed convergence.

> Since *convergence* is the domain where one of the biggest cloud computing battles will be fought, it is interesting to compare the three companies that (by all evidence) will be the main players: Google, Microsoft, and Apple. Based on published statistics, Table 1.1 suggests that Google is the most cost-effective of the three in terms of revenue per employee (closely followed by Apple) and also in profit per employee (where Apple and Microsoft are at a roughly equal level).

> *Cisco* initiatives to increase its exposure to the cloud revolve around its *Unified Computing System* (UCS), a data center platform integrating networking, virtualization, and network management technologies. It also offers *Unified Service Delivery* (USD) for cloud providers, as well as virtualization, and it

---

* A more detailed discussion on their wares, marketing thrust, and alliances, along with reference to more companies than the sample in this section, will be found in Chapter 7.
† Apple accounts for nearly 70 percent of online music sales in the United States.

Table 1.1 Google vs. Microsoft vs. Apple[a]

Criterion	Google	Microsoft	Apple[b]	Mean Figure
Revenue, in billion $	22.3	58.4	34.6	
Profit, in billion $	4.6	14.6	5.2	
Profit as % of revenue	20.6	25.0	15.0	20.20
Employees, in thousands[c]	20.0	93.0	32	
Revenue per employee,[d] in million $	1.12	0.62	1.08	0.94
Profit per employee	0.23	0.16	0.16	0.18

[a] Basic statistics by *The Economist*, October 17, 2009.
[b] Google controls 83 percent of search, its key market; Microsoft, 93 percent of OS for PC; Apple, nearly 70 percent of digital music.
[c] As of June 30, 2009.
[d] Rounded up to three digits. What is important in this case is the order of magnitude.
[e] Google claims that there are nearly two hundred thousand developers using its App Engine.

works in partnership in cloud computing with BMC, EMC, Intel, Microsoft, and VMware.

EMC offers a cloud storage product known as *Atmos*, whose objective is to leverage commodity hardware and highly parallel software. It provides services such as manageability, fault tolerance, and secure information flow across multiple devices (EMC is also 86 percent owner of VMware, one of the leaders in virtualization).

Google is rated as one of the most powerful entrants in cloud computing. Its services provide consumers and enterprises access to infrastructure and internally developed technology. It has released a full suite of productivity applications, including the Google *App Engine*, giving developers a cloud computing environment. Google's *Gmail* targets the market of Microsoft's Exchange. Google works in partnership with Salesforce.com.

With its *Dynamic Cloud Services Hewlett-Packard* takes a somewhat different approach than other vendors, placing particular emphasis on platforms that assist on applications personalization, infrastructure, and enabling. The guideline seems to be "everything as a service." With its acquisition of EDS, HP aims for leadership in consultancy. It has also teamed up with a much smaller firm, Cast Iron Systems, to make onDemand software more appealing to small and medium enterprises (SMEs).

Compared to the thrust of other players with its *Blue Cloud*, *IBM* has rather timidly started to offer small and medium enterprises cloud computing solutions. Part of its services is a platform for backups; other products are *CloudBurst* (advertised as "cloud computing in a box") and a *Websphere*-based appliance.

Big Blue also collaborates with Google on developing the next-generation technologies for the Internet. Some experts suggest that IBM's processor technology and expertise in system design, software, and services positions it rather well for a shift toward cloud infrastructures. However, contrarians say that IBM's main strategy in the cloud is to protect its base of installed mainframes, rather than to cut new ground.

Microsoft bets on its *Azure* platform to promote a software and enabling strategy, betting on it to position itself as a leader in the cloud computing environment. Behind this strategy is the hypothesis that desktop software and applications will continue to be demanded in their current form, which suggests that Microsoft, too, is most interested in protecting its installed base. The software company also delivers, on top of Azure, Windows Live for consumers, Office Live for SMEs and other enterprises, as well as services like SharePoint Online and Exchange Online.

Like Apple, Microsoft invests heavily in data centers to position itself as provider of infrastructure for cloud computing services. In September 2009 it opened two data centers that between them contain more than five hundred thousand servers.

Salesforce.com specializes in OnDemand applications, with its major thrust being its *Force.com* cloud platform with extendable web-based functionality. Its best-known product is CRM; it also offers enabling services. Its *Sites* product permits customers to expose their Force.com applications on public and private websites. The company has a partnership agreement with Google, Amazon.com, and Facebook.

Symantec started in cloud computing by concentrating on consumers with online backup facilities, then entered the market of enterprise offerings like *Veritas Operations Services*, including products like Veritas Installation Assessment and Veritas Storage Foundation Health Check. It has also launched the *Symantec Protection Network* (SPN) to provide online backup capabilities as a web offering adjunct to its SME backup product, Backup Exec.

VMware can be seen as key player in virtualization, enabling emulation of physical servers and pooling of resources. Its *vCloud* initiative acts as an enabler in porting server workloads between off and on premises. Its *vSphere* is designed to tighten its relationship with companies in networking, semiconductors, and other product lines.

Yahoo's strategy has been to capitalize on its users of Internet services (which run in the millions) and on its fairly extensive IT infrastructure. It employs this infrastructure to enhance its present consumer Internet business and attract more online advertising, but experts think it is unlikely that it would aggressively launch cloud computing applications in the medium term. However, Yahoo's current expertise permits it to compete with other players in at least part of the cloud market.

This is only a sample of companies presently active in cloud computing (more on the ongoing competition in Chapter 6). Many analysts believe that the aforementioned firms are well launched in the Internet environment to benefit from cloud computing, but it is too early to have an opinion about who will be the winners. Figure 1.3 positions these companies along a frame of reference based on the four pillars of the cloud, which we examined in Section 1.3.

1.5 A New Industry Is Being Born

Section 1.4 brought to the reader's attention a dozen cloud computing competitors, briefly describing each of them. It also underlined that companies active in the cloud have chosen a strategy of partnerships and alliances, which leads to the first law of modern *technodynamics*: you can't take the road alone and win.

Alliances mean sharing know-how but also business opportunities and therefore profits (see also the discussion on virtual companies in Chapter 4). As the domain of information technology expands in all directions and the technology market gets widely diffused, no company, no matter how big and powerful, can put its arms around the domain all alone.

This is particularly true for the first-time vendors in the computers and communications industry who are aggressively commercializing infrastructural services they have already developed or are in the process of developing for themselves. Google operates a global network with 1 million servers, and it is also expanding its suite of cloud-based offerings. Hewlett-Packard is replacing eighty-five data centers the world over, with six in America.* Microsoft is looking for a site in Siberia where its servers can chill.†

Some countries, too, take advantage of technology's strategic inflection point (Chapter 3). They are capitalizing on their cold climate to attract infrastructural investments for cloud computing. Iceland is marketing itself as a prime location for data centers. Hitachi and Data Islandia built a huge data storage facility underground on Iceland. Eventually colossal data centers in Iceland, Canada's Northern Territories, and Siberia will be serving companies and private citizens in the United States, Brazil, India, and Australia.

There is another important issue raised by the cloud vendors' eagerness to commercialize their widely distributed infrastructure: capital investments (capex) are

---

* Probably having in mind sales of cloud infrastructure and services to the U.S. government.
† *The Economist*, May 24, 2008.

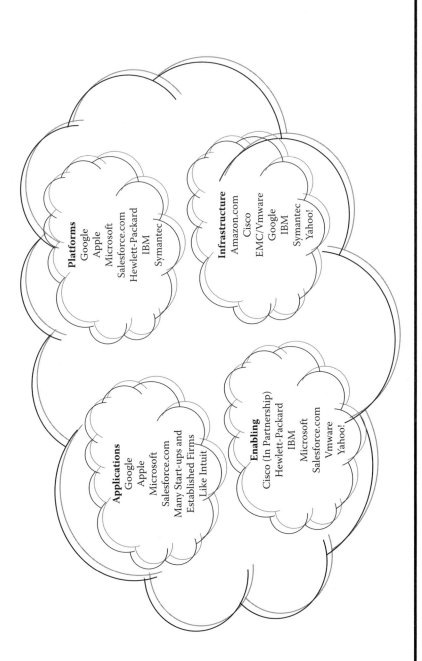

Platforms
Google
Apple
Microsoft
Salesforce.com
Hewlett-Packard
IBM
Symantec

Infrastructure
Amazon.com
Cisco
EMC/Vmware
Google
IBM
Symantec
Yahoo!

Applications
Google
Apple
Microsoft
Salesforce.com
Many Start-ups and
Established Firms
Like Intuit

Enabling
Cisco (In Partnership)
Hewlett-Packard
IBM
Microsoft
Salesforce.com
Vmware
Yahoo!

Figure 1.3 Incumbents from IT and new entrants are competitors in cloud computing.

not one tantum. They are steady and heavy, and they are unsustainable if companies don't make good profits out of them—but neither can these firms afford to use old technology, which sometimes is last year's. This leads to the second law of technodynamics: you cannot fall behind in technology and break even.

As these references suggest, a new industry is being born, quite different from those that preceded it in information science. While Sections 1.1 to 1.3 brought to the reader's attention that cloud computing is still lacking a generally agreed-upon definition, the business war of the mammoth data centers has started. It is motivated by estimates that in 2009 all sorts of companies will have spent some $100 billion on infrastructural services to provide a home for their sprawling data (see also Chapters 4 and 5).

In a way, this is a dual fight: for survival and for self-renewal. Back in the 1950s I had a professor at the University of California who taught his students that the characteristic curve of the life of persons, companies, and nations is lognormal:

- rise,
- peak, and
- decline.

That's the pattern in Figure 1.4. Physical entities like people try to avoid the decline by keeping active until they give up their souls. For companies and nations, the recipe is different. They must reinvent themselves. This leads to the third law of technodynamics: you cannot stay put without losing much of your power.

IBM tried to stay put on mainframes in the late 1980s and found itself next door to oblivion. Going ahead, however, takes not only vision and guts but also a torrent of money (see Chapter 3 on strategic inflection points). To stay in the game, players must keep on increasing their thrust and investment.

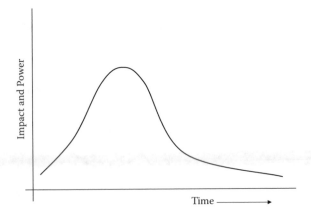

Figure 1.4 Every phenomenon in life, and life itself, has a characteristic curve.

It needs no explaining that this involves risks. The information technology market will continue to grow but not fast enough to return a profit on escalating investments for an increasing number of competitors. The evident way out of this narrow margin of maneuver is to get the other companies' market share where it counts most, which is in new market drives. That's the strategy of practically all twelve cloud providers briefly discussed in Section 1.4.

The landscape in which a golden horde of computers and communications entities compete for each other's turf and for the user organizations' IT budgets is known as *Web 2.0*. That's a Silicon Valley term that is not just network and software. It also describes a collection of other services, including processing, databasing, and metalevels in infrastructure. As such, it allows wired* consumers and companies a much greater interaction through the Internet, as well as:

■ transition from a collection of websites to a fully fledged computing utility and
■ fat online service agreements meeting the ever-changing needs of end users.

As we have already seen in the preceding section, cloud computing's pros say that such onDemand services will replace desktop computing and alter the perception of data processing. And they also add that Web 2.0 is the first real application of *service science*.†

One may accept or refute these claims, but there is no argument that the developing trend is cross-industry and that service science is near the heart of it. On March 16, 2009, Cisco moved into selling servers. Its unified computing system (see Section 1.4) is essentially a private cloud (Chapter 2) in a box. The vendor says that instead of having to wire up servers, storage devices, and networking gear, companies can build and reconfigure online virtual computers.

In terms of an overall concept, this is also what Hewlett-Packard offers. In addition to positioning itself in the *enabling* cloud market, HP acquired EDS. IBM wanted to buy Sun, but at the end of the day Oracle carried the prize.‡ Microsoft has also entered this cross-industry rush, offering, among other goodies, to run the computer systems of user organizations for them—inside its own giant cloud.

The careful reader will also recall that aside from hardware and software vendors there are Internet companies, the survivors of the 1990s' tsunami, who have built huge infrastructural facilities with services that can be sold. Section 1.4 presented as an example Amazon.com, the $19 billion e-tailer that has quietly developed a nice sideline providing computing and storage facilities on rental:

---

* *Wired* is the term currently used, but it is imprecise because connectivity is increasingly wireless.
† D. N. Chorafas, *IT Auditing and Sarbanes-Oxley Compliance* (New York: Auerbach/CRC, 2009).
‡ Though at the time this text is written this is still pending because of opposition by the European Commission.

- Amazon's products are now competing with Google's, and
- Google's products, whose online applications like Gmail and Google Docs have built a following, are competing with Microsoft's.

Amazon Web Services, for instance, claims more than fifty thousand corporate customers, ranging from big to small. Infrastructural onDemand services are piggybacking on Amazon's other facilities, such as handling of e-commerce orders, which integrate with its clients's internal cloud services (Chapter 2). And Amazon can claim infrastructural expertise documented by its handling of its own heavy workload of the parent company.

The message the reader should retain from this discussion is that the current strategic inflection point in information technology is in the process of creating a new industry through cross-fertilization and integration of many already existing business sectors. This is best demonstrated through practical examples (Section 1.6), and it is vastly promoted by means of new income sources like advertising (Section 1.7).

1.6 Competition in the Cloud Is Asymmetric

Not every company in the cloud competes on an equal footing. Examples of smaller firms that lack the clout of Amazon.com, Google, Microsoft, Hewlett-Packard, IBM, and other big players, but also have more to gain from their success as providers of cloud computing services, are Concur Technologies, Salesforce.com, and VMware.

- The baseline of the first is invoice software.
- That of the second is sales software.
- The remit of the third is virtualized engines.

All three smaller firms, and many more, provide a gateway to corporate intranets, and they seem to expand into sites and applications that help to position them as entrants. There is little doubt that the number of newcomers will increase, followed by a shakedown and by a success story for the survivors, who will take some time before becoming known.

For the time being, competition in the cloud is asymmetric, and any rush to name winners will be highly ill advised. Statistics suggest that in 2008 cloud computing companies averaged 23.8 percent growth, albeit most of them from a low base. Averages, of course, don't mean much. Growth numbers ranged from 43.8 percent for Salesforce.com and 41.8 percent for VMWare to 7.1 percent for Microsoft. Sun had a 5.1 percent negative growth.

In 2009 computing cloud players were expected to see a 3 percent growth in their revenue in spite of a 7.8 percent decline in information technology spending. People who like to prognosticate place in first position Amazon.com, with 19.3

percent, followed by Rackspace, with 17.3 percent, and Salesforce.com, with 17.0 percent. By contrast, Microsoft, IBM, Symantec, EMC, and Cisco are projected to have a negative growth in their cloud business, ranging from –3.7 percent for Microsoft to –15.1 percent for Cisco.*

There is as well reasonable justification to the argument made by some experts that certain software companies like Oracle, SAP, and probably Microsoft have moved into cloud computing not really because of their desire to participate to the action but for defensive reasons. As software vendors they also hope to capitalize on charges for technical support and upgrades.

Oracle is the world's biggest vendor of paid for onPremises database management systems (DBMSs), with a market share of nearly 50 percent. With Sun's acquisition, it is expecting to strengthen its position in the cloud. Sun owns MySQL, the most widely used open-source database software. The synergy is evident (it is as well the reason why the European Commission objected to the merger): *if* Oracle were to rein in MySQL, *then* the Internet's community of developers and users should be creating and promoting an alternative.

Oracle's dominance in DBMSs is another side of the cloud's asymmetric might of vendors. Handling it will require a meeting of minds between America's, Europe's, and probably Asia's trustbusters to ensure that cloud computing preserves its heralded but far from being assured open architecture (Chapter 8).

Monopoly in DBMSs, OSs, or major applications software routines can carry far and fast. The way some current estimates have it, DBMSs will only represent 5 percent of the onDemand market for programming products and enabling services (two of the four cloud pillars), while applications software will be a much higher percentage. This is, however, a near-sighted view because the DBMSs market share in the cloud will largely depend on how successful the *thin client* drive might be (Chapter 2).

What could be said with a fairly good degree of assurance is that before too long the lion's share of the cloud market will be taken by consulting (where Hewlett-Packard, IBM, and recently Dell are best positioned) because of their acquisitions. Another notable income source will be onDemand education:

■ both consulting and education will favor the vendors of onDemand software, and
■ this will eventually throw the dice to their favor, in regard to leadership in cloud computing.

By contrast, monolithic software companies don't have an ensured future in the cloud. It is the opinion of several industry watchers that the classical style of the big software vendors would have to change if these companies are to adapt to the changing perspective of software business as it transits from OnPremises to OnDemand.

---

* Bank of America/Merrill Lynch, "Technology," June 2, 2009.

■ As OnDemand software providers they take on the capital, implementation, and maintenance risk from the user organizations, which can present drawbacks to some of them.

■ This contrasts with the attitude of OnPremises players, where software licenses were sold to the client, and the vendor transferred the operational and implementation risk to the other party.

Mainly hardware vendors entering the cloud computing landscape also face challenges. Their motivation has been different from that of software firms. Technological advances have assisted and sometimes propelled their transition to the cloud. One example is broadband capacity at an affordable cost; another is low-cost commodity hardware that made possible fairly inexpensive virtualization.

This being said, as a general rule, whenever companies decided to move toward cloud computing, they did so on the premise that as mass providers they have a significant advantage over user organizations in building and deploying the cloud infrastructure. But those who think that cloud computing is a shift away from client-servers work under the wrong premises for two reasons:

■ by and large the huge database farms will be largely based on thousands of servers, not on mainframes, and

■ a large number of user organizations that are currently planning to adopt cloud computing are still living and laboring in the medieval age of mainframes, and hence, at least virtually, they will be moving out of them—not back to them.

It should as well be noticed that the better managed user organizations contemplating cloud computing services would like to see that the underlying architecture is at the same time open (Chapter 8) and transparent to the end user. The concept guiding their thinking is that, to be worth his salt, the service provider must be able to ensure:

■ fail-safe,

■ secure, and

■ OnDemand access to applications and their information elements stored somewhere in the cloud.

In this they will be probably be deceived, as we will see in Chapters 9 and 10. In addition, it is too early to say whether a collection of OSs, DBMSs, and applications from several vendors will maximize remote servers usage and will fit into margins allowing for seasonal peaks within a given distribution of resources.

A different way of looking at this very issue is that while theoretically cloud computing is turning hardware resources into a commodity that can be parceled out and sold, this notion is unstable. Down to its fundamentals, it is confusing the distinction between:

- commoditization of *computers* as the cloud's underlying gear and
- commoditization of *computing* as a process whose services are rented out.

It is easier to see that one sells computer devices off the racks, as practiced for so many years and which is the commoditization of computers, than parceling out and selling multitenant time sharing in hundreds of thousands or millions—and doing so in an effective manner. Yet, this is precisely what a virtualized machine composed of long arrays of computers should do.

At the level of hundreds of thousands or millions of tenants, the successful commoditization of computing depends on too many factors to be technically valid and economically viable *a priori*. Nobody can claim today to have all these factors under control, and neither is every cloud vendor presenting the user organizations with the same solutions. At the end user level, which is the most visible, there will be an asymmetric distribution of devices ranging from mobile to thin client (no local disk storage) to thick client, with web browsers like Google's Chrome and Microsoft's Internet Explorer.

Last but not least, all the competitors discussed in this chapter share a weak spot: the potential loss of brains. In "old times," which means some twenty years ago, at Silicon Valley it was said that the scare of a CEO when seeing his brilliant people taking the elevator and leaving for home was that tomorrow they may take another elevator in the next building and go to work for a competitor. The Internet radically changes the physical aspect of the scare.

A company's "best brains" don't need to take elevators to switch alliances. Everybody can be on the Internet any time during the day. There is no way to forbid mobility. Just like any consumer can buy on Sundays through the Internet, and no shopkeeper can keep up when his or her clients have access to lower-priced products at any time during the day or night, no company can put a net around its brains. Brains go online where they are appreciated.

1.7 The Multi-Billion-Dollar Opportunity: Internet Advertising

Besides the drive to be present and take part of the cake of a new industry, as well as for the defensive reasons mentioned in the preceding sections, companies are also motivated in entering the cloud computing market by the multi-billion-dollar business opportunity on the Internet. This is in direct proportion to the number of user organizations and consumers who, in one way or another, are on the cloud.

Even in times of an economic downturn, advertising means big money. If anything, the 2007–2009 economic and banking crisis* not only did not diminish Internet advertising but also brought a major switch away from newspapers and magazines (as well as, partly, from TV) toward online. Indeed, the Internet presents major advantages because it is

■ more direct,
■ more personal, and
■ less costly.

The downside is that this is no good for democracy because newspapers are a pillar of liberty and free expression. Good or bad, however, it is a fact that newspapers and magazines are dying. Advertising continues to shift to the net. The formerly formidable *Business Week* has been for sale for a nominal $1, town newspapers feel an earthquake, and even *The New York Times* has faced financial troubles.

The roots for Internet advertising were planted in the 1990s with browsers motivated by the fact they have been so user-friendly, easy to employ for surfing the Internet, and available practically free of cost. Browsers soon became communications devices by excellence specializing, in connecting all sorts of users among themselves.

Not too long after they came into existence, browsers went beyond just the basic Internet connection, integrating e-mail services, personal home pages, and other functions serving the user community. This made the Internet experience more enjoyable for many, while opening still more possibilities, like news and advertising.

It should also be noticed that as a process, advertising meshes well with other functions flourishing on the Internet, like direct sales. It is therefore no surprise that the business projected in the coming years is so promising that several large providers, like Google, plan to subsidize their cloud computing services with online advertising:

■ they look at motivating consumer access as a way to envelope their product brand, and
■ through it they try to maximize end users' experience, in a self-feeding cycle of increasing accesses and opportunities for more product sales.

The size of the online advertising market is already impressive. It generated over $40 billion in 2008 and will generate about $45 billion in 2009, as well as likely reach or exceed $50 billion in 2010. Some analysts think that from then on it will accelerate, going beyond $65 billion by 2012.

■ Roughly half that market is search.

---

* D. N. Chorafas, *Financial Boom and Gloom. The Credit and Banking Crisis of 2007–2009 and Beyond* (London: Palgrave/Macmillan, 2009); D. N. Chorafas, *Capitalism without Capital* (London: Palgrave/Macmillan, 2009).

- Nearly a third is branded products.
- The remaining is composed of different other services.

This money flowing toward Internet advertising drains other advertising budgets, as attested to by statistics that ads to local newspapers are fast declining. In Britain, Trinity Mirror shut twenty-seven local newspapers in 2008 and another twenty-two in the first half of 2009. According to Enders Analysis, a media consultancy, a third to half of remaining local papers in Britain may go in the next five years.*

Television stations, too, got clobbered in their advertising revenues. British statistics show that in the 2008–2009 time frame they lost 10 percent of their income from ads (vs. 25 percent for local newspapers and 15 percent for national newspapers). Not long ago, some pundits prognosticated that those services still separating TV and PCs on the Internet would merge. This is happening through the shifting domain of advertising.

If the siphoning out of advertising budgets by the Internet does not happen faster, it is primarily because not everybody in a local community is computer literate. Therefore, there are segments of the population who have not yet come around to e-mail and browsers as a means of mass communication. (This is particularly true of the middle-aged and older—a population slowly fading away.)

By contrast, for the new generation, which means from seven-year-olds (or even younger) and up, the Internet is limitless. When they find a site they like they are hooked up to it, and they return to it instantly when they have a free moment. That's the population Google and its competitors, as well as their advertisers, are targeting not just for now but for the long run.

Projections made for the next five years are based on the aforementioned facts and figures. Interpretations, however, vary. Two different schools of thought try to draw a thin red line between cloud computing and Internet advertising. The one says that in the future all searches should be considered cloud-based usage. The other would rather keep advertising separate as a different experience:

- Theoretically, these two opinions contradict one another.
- Practically, they are not so different because many users start making no distinction between cloud computing and the Internet at large.

Consumers, for example, are already using advertising-supported cloud applications like e-mail, as well as social networking and entertainment applications. Aside from lower costs associated with Internet advertising, this drive is a main reason why sponsors are switching out of magazines and newspapers and into the cloud.

In conclusion, the best way to look at cloud computing is as a market in full evolution in which many players, some old and others new, compete for a piece of

---

* *The Economist*, July 25, 2009.

the action. The majority of these contenders for cloud leadership have ambition, but this does not mean that their ambition will be satisfied or that everything will evolve smoothly. Chapter 2 explains what the cloud has to offer. Chapter 3 brings in perspective the challenges associated with strategic inflection points.

Chapter 2

What Cloud Computing Has to Offer

2.1 Public Clouds, Private Clouds, and Clients

The discussion in Chapter 1 mainly focused on markets and vendors for *public clouds* (also known as external clouds), their pillars, and their services. There is no reason why the bigger user organizations will not adapt this technology to develop *proprietary clouds* (private or internal clouds)* in a way similar to the policy followed with extranets and intranets. Proprietary clouds will have many of the public clouds' characteristics:

■ being Internet based and dynamically provisioned;
■ benefiting from onDemand software, platforms, and enabling services; and
■ billing their internal users on fine-grained computing and databasing resources being employed, as providers of external clouds do.

From an architectural viewpoint, this will create *hybrid cloud* environments consisting of multiple internal clouds that, at least in theory, are seamlessly connected to external clouds and their providers. As the concept of cloud computing

---

* Examples of user organizations that will prefer private clouds include governments, financial services, health care, and more.

gets wider market acceptance, the way to bet is that more and more companies may build in-house computing utilities, their private clouds, to:

- capitalize on onDemand software,
- attempt to simplify complex data centers,
- make a decent effort to cut costs, and
- develop a culture of pay-as-you-do inside the firm.

Progression toward that state of business is not going to be easy or without hurdles. Key to hybrid cloud computing is the adoption of an open architecture, and as Chapter 8 brings to the reader's attention, this has not yet been found, no matter what the providers may be saying.

An effectively implemented open architecture, if one emerges in the cloud environment, must see to it that different system solutions no longer have hard frontiers, as they currently do. In addition, definitions, formats, and protocols become homogeneous no matter who the vendor is; this is plain good sense, but:

- it is against commercial interests, and
- past IT history is not encouraging in this direction.

On the other hand, if cloud computing is successful and private clouds spread in the business landscape, pressure will be created by user organizations to harness the benefits of public clouds by pressing for *de facto* standards. This will promote hybrid solutions.

Because internal/external cloud computing will probably become an important market, some experts think that vendors will tend to provide cloud services with restricted access offered to a limited subset of users paying a premium for that service. Other things being equal, security, privacy, and reliability (Chapters 9 and 10) will be higher in the internal cloud—and they will probably justify such a premium.

Nevertheless, costs should be carefully studied and compared to risks associated with public clouds, which are easily accessible by all parties, including hackers. Another important design criterion is flexibility and adaptation of the private cloud, in a system sense. An advanced technological product must be flexible and adaptable to further developments from its conception, and the drafting board is the right place to put that principle to work.

- As Figure 2.1 suggests, a good example has been Boeing's 707 airframe series.
- A bad example has been the Anglo-French Concorde, which came only in one version and never lifted off the ground in a commercial sense.

Whether the solution a user organization chooses is public cloud, private cloud, or a hybrid, senior management (not only the IT department) will be well advised

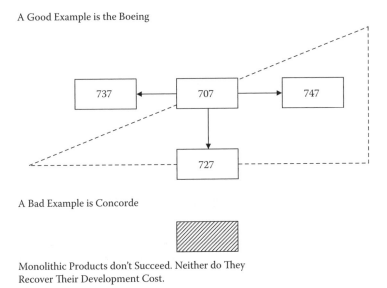

Figure 2.1 An advanced technological product must be designed to fit different markets and applications requirements.

to pay full attention to the business architecture. In so doing, it should always keep in mind that the *system architecture* is an expression of technical terms, but what is most important to the company is its *business architecture.*

As we will see in Chapter 8, a business architecture should never be bought off-the-shelf from some vendor. Ingenious choices and an effective solution to the user organization's business architecture will serve as *metalevel* to the hardware and software layers of the cloud:

■ qualifying through metadata access to information elements residing in hundreds of data nodes and

■ applying constraints while each node works independently, delivering information elements to cloud users or applications.

Constraints are restrictive conditions on the validity of object knowledge and associated actions. Descriptions of constraints must cover state changes caused by such actions, including environments, times, metrics, conditions for changes, patterns, and more.

■ The constraint mechanism is a good way to specify and supervise prevailing relations, including authorizations, and

■ its mechanics help in guaranteeing consistency in system functions and expected deliverables.

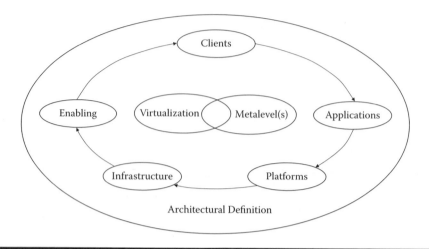

Figure 2.2 Extent of cloud computing architectural coverage from user organization's viewpoint.

Based on these notions, Figure 2.2 restructures the simpler form of cloud computing's pillars presented in Chapter 1, incorporating end user engines, or clients, as another pillar. A carryover from client-server solutions, the term *clients* stands for a growing variety and type of engines on the end user side. The three main types are

- workstations and PCs with hard disk, hence local storage capability at gigabyte level;
- the so-called thin clients without hard disk, promoted by some cloud providers who offer to map the end users' files into their infrastructural services; and
- a diversity of mobile clients, some with hard disk and others bare, whose accesses, queries, and transactions take place within the cloud environment.

The metalevel(s) in Figure 2.2 act as the alter ego of virtualization for operational purposes, and the whole is wrapped by the architectural definition of the cloud computing system. Except for the clients, all other components (including pillars and core functions) are transparent to the end user.

- Thin or thick, the client appears as a single point of access for all the computing needs, and
- cloud computing services are accessible anywhere by every device that has access to the Internet.

Whenever real time is not a competitive advantage or operational requirement, the better option is *asynchronous* operations, which permit minimizing costs and (among other benefits) avoid deadly embraces in database updates and access. The reader should not confuse asynchronous operations with *batch*. A remnant of the 1950s and 1960s that is still in use, batch is the mentality of IT's middle ages. Neither should asynchronous solutions be used to cover technical failures like:

- extending the life of batch software or
- making up for lack of real-time skills.

Because a growing number of clients will be mobile, whether we talk of an external or internal cloud, an architectural solution should as well pay attention to fixed-mobile convergence. Even if, so far, this has not been an unqualified success, its advent promises to transform system design. (Some analysts think that femtocells, which are smaller and less expensive than picocells, could help mobile operators resolve capacity and coverage problems, as well as provide a new way to offer more services via the home network.)

Architecturing for multitenancy gets more complex with fixed-mobile convergence, but this does not change the fact that in the coming years both fixed-mobile and multitenancy will become system design requirements, as they are more efficient than attending a single instance for each client. (However, in terms of design complexity, keep in mind that, by definition, clouds work with combinations of operating systems, databases, and applications software.)

Experts suggest that to really benefit from multitenancy user organizations need to fully devote themselves to that model from both a technological and an operational perspective. They also add that what we are really talking about is a fundamental change in conceptual models.

2.2 Cloud Applications and Platforms*

Vendors active in cloud computing have announced a broad set of applications and tools accessible from anywhere in the world by using an Internet connection. Applications for rental are mainly mainstream routines like customer relationship management (CRM), enterprise resource planning (ERP), accounting, and human resources—the stuff appealing to the broadest possible market. Platforms help user organizations develop their own programming routines.

Originally known as *software as a service* (SaaS) or *software on demand* (SoD), this inventory of applications emulated onPremises packages focusing on sales, bookkeeping, finance, planning, scheduling, productivity, and communications. (The terms SaaS and SoD are used practically interchangeably, and as the reader will recall, the term employed in this book is *onDemand*.)

---

* See also the discussion in Chapter 7 on the characteristics of platforms offered by cloud vendors.

An important point to bring to attention is that today a significant part of onDemand applications are rented—not sold. Tomorrow this practice may well be generalized. That's very good for the user organization because it means that it cannot manipulate the routines to make them fit its internal procedures, a common policy with bought onPremises commercial packages. (Practical examples with onDemand applications are given in Chapters 11 to 13.)

- Consumers and companies can access onDemand software fairly easily.
- The likelihood of contextually linked ads makes sense if it is associated with free-of-cost apps.*

Small and medium enterprises (SMEs) that are a target market (see Chapter 4) can purchase more advanced versions of these applications with no accompanying ads, for a fee. Typically onDemand routines are browser and operating system (OS) agnostic, which, however, should not be interpreted to mean that user organizations cannot be locked in to a cloud computing vendor's suite (Chapter 5).

Still, as long as onDemand software is operating system and browser agnostic, its online availability constitutes an interesting development in IT, which is sure to have long-term consequences. Standards have never been the forte of information technology companies, and without that agnostic feature there would have been an explosion of cloud computing versions—one or more by vendor—and with it the risk that:

- interfaces will be increasingly incompatible, and
- programming modules of similar functionality but different standards would be causing a lot of pain to both software developers and users.

Old hands in the computer industry remember that this has happened not just between vendors but also within vendor establishments and its wares. Programming products have been classically developed by different teams in competition with one another and without appropriate coordination in regard to protocols, operating systems, database management systems (DBMSs), and teleprocessing routine (TPR).

In the 1980s, for example, IBM had eight different and incompatible OSs in its product line. At that time, a user organization I was consultant to was totally at a loss as to how to make them work together, and the vendor was not of much assistance either in terms of providing a solution for an effective and dependable seamless interconnection.

- At headquarters IT had told the affiliates to keep with IBM procurement but failed to specify *which* basic software.
- Each affiliate chose a variety of IBM boxes and OSs without any plan or coordination, until incompatibilities became an unmitigated disaster.

---

* This is true for free-of-cost applications, as in the case of Google.

Another example of confusion due to unprincipled basic software choices is offered by Jennifer Edstrom and Marlin Eller by quoting Chris Guzak, who had worked on the Windows 95 shell: "When Windows 95 was out and NT 3.51 was the platform, things were screwed up." This was most likely repeated with Windows 98, as the same authors quote Lin Shaw, Windows 95 development manager, as having said: "Windows 98 is just trying to make it faster. In my opinion it's like a .1 release of Windows 95."*

Illusions, incompatibilities, and misunderstandings are very common in IT, particularly in regard to basic and applications software. Most evidently, this poses challenges to user organizations moving toward cloud computing. The way to bet is that they will have to do lots of work in the transition: *from onPremises* applications, including in-house developments and off-the-shelf routines that became the purchasing organization's asset, *to onDemand* applications accessed when needed by users but remaining the proprietorship of the cloud vendor.

If past experience is any guide, this transition has, and will continue having, many features in common with that which took place from classical proprietary computer programs developed in-house to programming product sold off-the-shelf. Over and above that, as Chapter 6 documents, to benefit from the cloud companies will have to do a great deal of reengineering of their systems and procedures.

As for cloud providers, their remit is that of a significant tightening of their project planning schedules and quality control procedures. In his excellent book *The Mythical Man-Month*, Fred Brooks documents why a programming product is an order of magnitude more complex in terms of project planning and control than the commonplace in-house applications routines.

Several important decisions must be reached before the product comes to the drafting board. To simplify software design and increase the user population's potential, the projected onDemand software should be stripped of excess features that are rarely used but require special skills when applied.

In addition, help features should also be incorporated since the drafting board. The usual help desk service (part of enabling) cannot take care of them postmortem, and user organizations, particularly SMEs, adopting cloud computing want to significantly reduce IT's headcount, not hire expensive specialists.

The good news is that a growing emphasis on the mass market, with "back to the fundamentals" as a common denominator, facilitates the adoption of common characteristic for onDemand routines—at least those aiming to become mainstream and successfully pass market tests. This is what has happened with CRM, ERP, and accounting programs, particularly those offered by the main vendors. These belong to the high-frequency main body of a normal distribution of applications, but there is also a need for serving the application's distribution long leg, where the market niches are.

---

* Jennifer Edstrom and Marlin Eller, *Barbarians Led by Bill Gates* (New York: Henry Holt, 1998).

Market niches are usually exploited by start-ups. The view of big vendors like IBM and Microsoft is that not all applications are suitable to be handled through cloud computing. For instance, those with high memory requirements are best when installed locally, temporarily uploaded onto a centralized service (emulating the concept of a cache) for cross-departmental collaboration. This is essentially a hybrid model: OnDemand plus OnPremises.

The alternative is *platforms*, the pillar of cloud computing next to applications software (Chapter 1). Platforms are largely intended to encourage the new generation of developers to add to the programming products made available on demand by the vendor. Indeed, cloud applications and platforms complement one another, which explains why the latter have attracted the interest of companies, in spite of the fact that large user organizations have already made investments in platforms from incumbents like Microsoft, IBM, and SAP.

Experts suggest that the cloud platform model of software development provides interesting economics, being in reality an offshoot of the provider's underlying infrastructure, including its database management system and operating system. User organizations can save money by capitalizing on the facilities platforms offer.

By all evidence cloud platforms will be particularly favored in the case of new application development reflecting the user's willingness to embrace a solution that allows for rapid and cheaper deployment of applications—particularly if the platform acquired is user-friendly. Large incumbents are aware of the risk this strategy carries to their base of revenue and develop strategies for responding to it.

For instance, Microsoft's Azure Platform has two layers: The base is proprietary hardware and software serving as a central point in managing switches, routers, server nodes, and connectivity. The upper layer is composed of building blocks like Live services, NET services, SQL services, SharePoint, and Dynamics CRM. All of these are designed for usage in conjunction with applications developed on the base layer, and can help in extending onPremises applications to cloud computing. (More on platforms will be discussed in Chapter 7.)

2.3 Providing the Cloud Infrastructure*

The discussion on onDemand software and platforms has given a glimpse on the *infrastructure* that hosts them. The cloud vendors sell time-shared facilities to their clients who consume computing, databasing, routing, and switching resources *as a service*. This way:

- ■ users pay a rental for only the facilities they employ, and

---

* Chapter 8 presents a holistic view of the cloud infrastructure, by examining the impact of system architecture on supported services.

■ the pay-as-you-do bill is calculated on the basis of a utility model that works in a way analogous to that of traditional utilities.*

Pay-as-you-do means invoicing as infrastructural services are consumed. The alternative is to pay on a subscription basis. Vendors of infrastructural services are still on the learning curve on how to reach a dual goal: maximize their profits and still be competitive in pricing.

The underlying assumption is that sharing computing, databasing, and networking resources improves their utilization rates. Computing engines and database servers are not left idle. At least theoretically, this reduces costs as resource usage rises—though not necessarily dramatically because the constraint is contention. Many *providers* claim that this way customers do not have to worry about peak load limits, but this is half true at best.

Arguments that suggest near miracles to be expected from a shared infrastructure are totally unrealistic, casting doubts on other claims made. As a recent research paper had it: "When Animoto made its services available via Facebook, it experienced a demand surge that resulted in growing from 50 servers to 3500 servers in three days, no one could have foreseen that resource needs would suddenly double every 12 hours for 3 days."†

That's not a spike that could be gracefully sustained by the provider of infrastructural services. *If* many spikes do occur simultaneously among its clients, *then* the vendor is unable to face the demand. Cost savings are a chimera when one must be positioned to respond to a very rapid step-up function, even if traffic afterwards falls below the peak. Surges in demand can totally upset the vendor's planning for rental resources.

■ Such events do occur and, as such, they do not document the cloud's so-called *elasticity*.‡
■ What they show is that honest vendors should explain to their clients that low cost and elasticity are two desirable factors contradicting one another.

Either the infrastructural resources run half empty to take care of unexpected peaks in demand, or somebody must pay for the elasticity. Miracles do not happen in IT, or in any other business. An improved solution, though by no means a miracle, is that of an intelligent infrastructure, by adding sensors, meters, and *agents* (mobile knowledge engineering artifacts). Section 2.4 elaborates on this issue. An intelligent infrastructure will help to:

---

* The algorithms being employed, however, are still in their infancy.
† A. Armbrust, A. Fox, et al., Above the Clouds: A Berkeley View of Cloud Computing, Technical Report UCB/EECS-200-28, UC Berkeley Reliable Adaptive Systems Laboratory, February 10, 2009.
‡ The ability to absorb higher loads without adverse effects on users.

- better forecast the need for new facilities,
- avoid wild outages by rebalancing the load, and
- eventually save energy and costs for both parties: the vendor and user organization.

One of the benefits to be derived by this strategy is better forecasting and planning by vendors of infrastructural services and their clients. Another benefit is the demolition of the simplistic belief that cloud computing services, which are upscale on the food chain, can be equated to electricity, whose bare wires and outlets are way down on the food chain.* The cloud has prerequisites. Two of the most evident are

- high-speed bandwidth for the Internet, making it feasible to receive very short response times from vendor-centered infrastructures and
- steady watch that this infrastructure is upgraded by the cloud computer vendor, to ensure enough capacity, avoid bottlenecks, support high reliability (at least 99.9 percent; Chapter 10), and provide first-rate security—all at a relatively low cost.

As these references demonstrate, and as should be expected, there exists a huge gap between theory and practice. It is alright to say that with cloud computing user organizations may avoid capital expenditures on hardware, basic software, and associated services and instead pay the provider only for the resources they use, but it is wrong to think that all these goodies will fall from heaven as the need arises, like biblical manna.

Prospective users must appreciate that there exist many challenges associated with very large-scale storage. As hard disk capacity has crossed the multipetabyte environment demanded by a cloud infrastructure, data management and availability, response time, deadly embraces, system failures, blackouts, backups, and plenty of other issues haunt cloud vendors. It matters little that consumption is billed on a utility or subscription basis often with minor or no up-front cost (this, too, being theoretical). What is important is to:

- know the downside connected to these expected benefits and
- gain enough knowledge about the cloud, well before being committed to "this" or "that" vendor, based on promises about "a broad range of IT services."

It may sound impressive to state that the god-size data center of the future will leverage storage as a service beyond anything known in the past, but this will not come easily. Neither is utility storage the only domain of concern. There is as well

---

* Though with power distribution networks, too, there is increasing emphasis on smart grids.

the ability for applications to invoke various common reusable functions across heterogeneous storage. Yet, this is necessary to perform functions like provisioning, replication, de-duplication, and more.

Vendors say that all this will be taken care of by their storage-oriented architecture and will be included in customer-specific service level agreements. When I hear such arguments in discussions about cloud computing or any other vendor wares, I interpret them as evidence that:

■ either the vendor plans to take his clients for a ride, or
■ it has not yet thought through all of the problems that need to be confronted with a massive and growing storage capability accessed by all sorts of users.

Existing systems have not yet effectively addressed such complexities. A fully distributed architecture (Chapter 8) with thousands of servers and automatic configurations benefiting from top availability, fault monitoring, and rapid resource redeployment capability is not available today. Many cloud providers say that they are working toward such a solution, but the results are still to come, and they cannot be judged before experience catches up with them.

What is more or less available in terms of present cloud computing infrastructure falls short of the outlined requirements and their projected evolution. It generally consists of a more or less scalable infrastructure that indeed allows fairly sophisticated searches (and has cost providers a good deal of money) but has not passed a *stress test*.

For instance, Google says that it has spent an estimated $8 billion building thirty-seven data centers worldwide that house more than a million interconnected low-end servers. These are very large systems of unprecedented proportions, addressed to a population of widely variable user profiles. They might be well managed, but they have not yet come under stress.

Even the question of the best-fit database management system is not yet settled. Google uses a proprietary distributed file management solution. Other infrastructural vendors bet on relational solutions.

Microsoft's *SQL Services* provides a relational database approach for working with structured, semistructured, and unstructured information elements. It is built on the company's synonymous database technology extending SQL Server capabilities to cloud computing. The evidence that this will perform under stress in a cloud environment is not on hand:

■ Microsoft's SQL Server was originally developed for relatively contained client-server solutions.
■ By contrast, with the cloud we are talking of requirements related to megasystems, and as experience teaches, big systems are not small systems that grew up.

Available evidence suggests that the design requirements posed by a cloud computing infrastructure still have to be properly settled. These have much to do with *macroengineering* (huge dams, coast-to-coast electricity networks, space travel) and very little to do with portals. Since 1998, Netscape's Netcenter, among other examples, Internet portals have made online interactive information and transactions so much easier, enabling full-service websites that are

- online launching pads,
- entertainment networks, and
- shopping malls rolled into one.

But what cloud computing vendors set out to achieve has no resemblance to daytime–nighttime web-based entertainment or consumer chores. It is requiring extensive expertise beyond that of Internet traffic, with routing utilizing proprietary algorithms in combination with techniques like caching, compression, route optimization, and load balancing (to automatically direct traffic through the best path). The cloud will severely penalize infrastructure providers who:

- fall behind in resource planning,
- for one reason or another start having dissatisfied customers,
- cannot run faster than their competitors all of the time, and
- employ old systems software in a futile attempt to bridge their cloud product line with their old one (for instance, the case of IBM and Microsoft).

Survival in the cut-throat, dynamic environment of a megasystem like the cloud infrastructure is in no way guaranteed by calling this or that systems approach dynamic. Just renaming the crust of the cake will be like betting on an empty shell, and it will constitute a good prescription for losing contact with the market. (From an architectural point, issues connected to the cloud infrastructure are discussed in Chapter 8.)

2.4 Cloud Computing, Spectral Efficiency, Sensors, and Perspiration

According to several opinions, the best applications in cloud computing will not be those coming from the conversion of old IT but from a domain still in its infancy: smart phones, personal assistants, mini-laptops—in short, the new generation of personal computers to be connected at almost anytime to anywhere. An infrastructural solution worth its salt must account for this option.

This requirement essentially means that it is wrong to look at cloud computing's infrastructure just as a vast array of interconnected machines managing the data and software that run on all sorts of IT equipment. The better way is to perceive it as an expanding combination of mobile and fixed technologies that:

- already pose a long list of challenging but fairly stochastic technical requirements and
- will shape up ongoing advances in the computing universe in the next decade.

To appreciate the meaning and reach of this evolution, it is necessary to turn back to the early 1970s and the developments associated with cell phones. Much of the credit for downsizing the volume and cost of cellular phones goes to Marty Cooper, who, confronted with what used to be unwieldy two-way radio devices built in to dashboards, conceived of the idea that they needed to be significantly redesigned and eventually made portable.

Cooper's concept developed into a tangible device, after Motorola put him in charge of its car phone division in 1972. It took just ninety days from idea to prototype as Cooper sponsored a design contest (among Motorola engineers). That led to the famous call on April 3, 1973, after a press conference to introduce the phone at the New York Hilton.

Called DynaTAC, the handset had thirty-five minutes of talk time and weighed 1 kilo. Cooper reduced DynaTAC's weight by half, and it was finally launched in 1983 with a price tag of $4,000. To appreciate the magnitude of the breakthrough, which must now be repeated with many engines entering the cloud structure, one should compare this to:

- present-day smart phones, and
- the advent of mobile Internet.

Smart phones have evolved into versatile handheld computers, an example being Apple's 3G iPhone. As the competition among different vendors intensified, hardware features became secondary to software. To succeed in the software-led race, their makers had to inspire third-party developers to write clever applications that attracted an army of end users.

Along with software, a crucial factor of market success has been bandwidth. Cooper's law says that *spectral efficiency* has doubled every thirty months since Guglielmo Marconi patented the wireless telegraph in 1897.* Present-day devices have a spectral efficiency of more than 1 trillion times greater than Marconi's original invention of the late nineteenth century:

---

* Which broadcast in Morse code over a wide frequency range.

- smart antennas will, most likely, ensure that Cooper's law continues to apply, and
- this will eventually permit cloud computing to encompass a vast array of applications from sensors to computers and social networking* (Chapter 4).

Sensors embedded in machinery currently in use can gather data in direct ways about the reliability of component parts as well as temperature, humidity, noise level, wear and tear, and more. Adding digital sensors and remote controls to the transmission and distribution of a power network, for example, and combining their input with data mining and expert systems, will turn it into a *smart grid* whose management is far more responsible and transparent than today's approaches, making it better able to:

- cope with new sources of renewable power,
- feature coordinated use of different sources of energy,
- provide information to consumers about their usage,† and
- permit utilities to monitor and control their networks more effectively.

In a fairly similar way, sensors and digital relays installed on other types of transmission and distribution will make possible a higher level of supervisory control by optimizing the employment of resources. They will also provide a new array of services that find precedence in the introduction of supply chain management a decade and a half ago.

The message to retain from these references is that, interesting as it may be, the current discussion on cloud infrastructure is in some aspects near-sighted. Beyond the cloud computing label, technology offers a wide range of possibilities, and benefits will depend on the players' preparedness to capitalize on new developments as they come out of the labs, sharing the resulting advantages with their clients.

System engineers, for instance, look forward to the day when sensors and mobile phones can provide a central nervous system for large-scale projects by combining a wide variety of data sources, such as from satellites, imagery, and seismic sensors to fieldwork in a mine or in deep-water oil exploration. Health care organizations study solutions networking patients in a health management system, making it possible to get a holistic view of their health and treatment.‡

Blue Cross of northeastern Pennsylvania started to use a cloud computing system aimed at allowing its three hundred thousand members to find medical

---

* Including areas of vital importance to an aging society, such as health care.
† Studies suggest that when people are made aware of how much power they consume, they reduce their use by roughly 7 percent.
‡ Typically so far, information tracking was oriented toward diseases or treatments rather than taking a holistic approach.

histories and claims information with their mobile phones. Other projects capitalize on the fact that consumers:

- tend to get away from the current concept of the cell phone, which implies talk and listen, and
- in so doing, they explore new applications based on sending data to and from mobile devices and databases.

Companies build systems that use handsets to sense, monitor, and predict environmental hazards and public health threats. These are the types of applications that can significantly benefit from mobile Internet. Nearly every day examples on how organizations may combine approaches with expert systems and cloud computing to improve the quality of their services and products are coming forward:

- pulling together pieces of vital information they did not have before and acting on it,
- reducing costs by identifying gaps in efficiency that they are correcting, and
- using analytics to size up the information as it changes, sending out alerts and checking on executions.

Companies whose management has decided to capitalize on new technology are turning inside out the systems of computers and communications platforms, including desktops, laptops, handhelds, and smart phones. Avon has embarked on a massive overhaul of the way it manages millions of sales representatives around the world equipping, as a start, 150,000 "sales leaders" with a cloud-based computing system accessible via smart phones and PCs. The concept is to:

- keep them up-to-date on the sales of each representative,
- alert them when orders have not been confirmed or clients have payments overdue, and
- control their performance in a real-time version of Thomas Watson Sr.'s quota system.

It comes as no surprise that some of the more imaginative developments originate with entities born and raised in the consumer world (see Chapter 4), where competition is toughest, as well as from firms whose management understands that simplicity and ease of use are essential to improving the sales of their products and size of their profit margins (see also Section 2.7).

One of the organizations ahead of the curve in using the new technology is Coca-Cola Enterprises, which equips its forty thousand mobile workers, including sales staff, merchandisers, and truck drivers, with portables to ensure that they are better connected to the home office while on the road. Salespersons can alert marketing

Project Management Metalayer
Design-to-Order Consultancy
Help-Desk Typically Internet Based

Figure 2.3   Three layers of enabling services for cloud computing.

instantly about problems they encounter, including shifts in demand. The after effect of this real-time input can be so much greater if combined with Six Sigma.*

Known as *reality mining* and employing *virtual doubles* (Chapter 4), this combination of facilities can x-ray entire organizations. Eventually the benefits from cloud computing will come from such business x-rays, but they will not flow automatically. Reengineering the organization is the key to opening the door to the benefits (Chapter 6). As Thomas Edison had it, the key ingredients of success are 5 percent inspiration and 95 percent perspiration.

2.5 The Technology of Enabling Services

The technology of the cloud's enabling services can be divided into three strata, as Figure 2.3 shows. The most common and least sophisticated is the *help desk*, currently offered by several cloud providers at the lower end (on a subscription basis). Salesforce.com is an example. The middle layer addresses itself to *consultancy* and what could be called design to order. This targets both internal and external cloud computing, with its deliverables still at an early stage of a fundamental definition.

Project management connected to the transition to cloud computing is at the higher level. Its principles, which evolved in the post–World War II years, are discussed in the second half of this section. While a user organization may have such skills available from its other business lines and previous IT projects, it may still require third-party input specific to cloud computing; for instance, in connection to:

- reengineering studies that are a prerequisite to a successful application (Chapter 6) and
- the distinction that must be made, in the most careful manner, between the cloud provider's system architecture and the user organization's business architecture (Chapter 8).

---

* D. N. Chorafas, *Integrating ERP, CRM, Supply Chain Management and Smart Materials* (New York: Auerbach, 2001).

Starting with the lower layer of enabling services, help desk activities are quite common these days (though in many cases they are not of satisfactory quality). As such, they don't need explaining in any detail. The reader's attention should, however, be brought to the fact that the quality of help desk services must be contractually guaranteed in the service level agreement (SLA; Chapter 5).

Vague promises are not acceptable, no matter who makes them, particularly so as the experience from help desk for e-mail and other Internet services is not the best. It is no secret that people manning help desks are not properly trained through simulators, and they often lack experience.* That's bad enough with e-mail, but it can be a disaster with cloud computing.

Consultancy services are, in general, of higher quality. As far as computer vendors are concerned (and evidently cloud outfits), services offered under the umbrella title *enabling* is their spearhead into the cloud market. Their deliverables can best be described as *design to order*, whose solutions should be tailored to the user organization's requirements but use commodity onDemand software.

It is essentially this duality that may call for expertise and support to see the project off the ground. But not all skill should be external. User organizations will need plenty of internal skills to be in charge of the quality and cost-effectiveness of what vendors are selling them and to ensure the latter don't engage in what is generally known as *vaporware*.

In use since the 1990s, the term vaporware describes the practice of public announcement of software products well before they are ready for sales (let alone for installation at client premises). The purpose of this more or less generalized practice is to cause user organizations not to buy a competitor's product that is either currently available or ready to enter the market.

Vaporware practices find their origin in the early twentieth century, in the infamous sales policy of the "broken down cash register" practiced by NCR. (At the time National Cash Register was a start-up eager to take market share away from established cash register companies, like Standard.) That practice consisted of first selling a machine under Standard's name, which was a fake, and then, after the merchant had enough with it because it was breaking down all the time, replacing it with an NCR cash register "at no extra cost to the customer."

I bring vaporware practices in perspective because there is a conflict of interest when the same cloud provider sells to a user organization all four business lines: onDemand applications, platform(s), infrastructure, and enabling services. Choices being made are open to conflicts of interest. And who is to say what is ready for use and what may be dead on arrival?

---

* When AT&T launched the Explorer credit card it developed a system that ensured steady online training of its agents by employing their idle time between customer calls. "We track everything that moves and everything that does not move," said the firm's executive VP for marketing during a London symposium at which we were both lecturers.

Provided that such conflicts do not exist, and that the right skills are available for the project, enabling services will invariably focus on reengineering the user's business architecture (the master plan must be made by the client), component optimization, custom-made add-ons to cloud applications, definition of scaling requirements, studies on growth trajectory, and (most importantly) engineering analysis for power and cooling.

User organizations will be well advised to be on guard for false claims. For instance, promises made by vendors to their clients that cloud computing is "ecological" are part of vaporware (Chapter 1). As we will see later, computers and communications are huge consumers of energy, and even an idle computer that is "on" uses roughly 65 percent of the power of a busy computer.

If experience from current (and past) computer projects is any guide, something similar will happen with large enabling teams by third parties. Charges will be billed even when these consultants are idle. This, too, is not 100 percent avoidable, but project management should see to it that it is minimized.

Part of the challenge comes from the fact that there is a long and growing list of issues needed to design a complete cloud solution able to capitalize on business opportunities. These range from reengineering and tailored deployment of cloud support services to early-life testing, design optimization, change management, addition of new facilities, and lifelong efficiency control.

Optimization studies is one of the domains where enabling services can make a contribution; energy consumption provides an example. Over several decades computers have been seen as the solution to the paper jungle, and since the early 1990s the Internet was heralded as the big change from commuting to communicating*—the way to save energy that is otherwise uselessly spent. Today they are both looked at as a problem, in terms of:

- energy consumption and
- environmental damage.

In 2000 worldwide energy consumption associated with information technology stood at about 66 billion kwh per year. For 2010 the estimate is that IT's energy consumption will reach 350 billion kwh, more than a 530 percent increase. This wholesome number is roughly divided between three big energy consumers:

- servers, the most hungry;
- cooling, next in line; and
- network and other gear.

---

* As a motto "communicate don't commute" lasted for nearly two decades.

In principle, general purpose servers consume more power and generate more heat as they are configured to run at maximum level for a specific workload, not the optimal one. Vendors say that by minimizing unnecessary features that create excess heat, and by appropriately provisioning power and cooling components, they will bring energy consumption under control. That, too, is vaporware.

Saving energy is necessary, but it is also more easily said than done, particularly since cost reasons see to it that clouds deploy commercial off-the-shelf gear that is far from being energy savings. If capital investments were no problem, this might have allowed us to take advantage of the latest technology, but cost optimization is not a recipe for minimizing energy usage. A balanced design would trade energy for cost, and vice versa.

Is it possible that a better project management will cut cost, swamp energy consumption, and increase quality of deliverables at the same time? Some people say so, and vendors promote the idea, but this statement shows people who either lack project experience or tell an outright lie.

The way to kill three birds with one well-placed stone has not yet been invented. Neither is this the goal of enabling assistance in project management, in the first place. A cloud project, and any other project, is a well-defined activity set up to produce *predetermined results*. As such, it involves the management of resources along four axes of reference:

- know-how, and hence personnel;
- money, and therefore budgets;
- time, projected in timetables; and
- computers and communications power.

As an organizational activity, the project is dedicated to the attainment of a precise, short- to medium-term goal. The best-ever concept of project management was written by Jean Monet, who had been an investment banker, the Anglo-French armaments boss in WWII, Churchill's personal delegate to President Roosevelt, and father of the European Union.

Monet's concept, shown in Figure 2.4, divides a project into milestones. Monet said that capable managers would start planning at the right end—the goal that must be reached after the last milestone (fifth one in this figure). Then, they will move backwards to the previous milestone until they reach the very beginning of the project. Execution will evidently be done by going from left to right.

If the enabling services to the user organization who gets ready for cloud computing apply Monet's principles, *then* they may be worth its salt. *If* project control is asleep at the wheel of governance and there are overruns, *then* the enabling assistance and the project itself will be a failure. Let me moreover add that the final responsibility for cloud project management should be with the CEO of the user organization, not with the vendor's consultants.

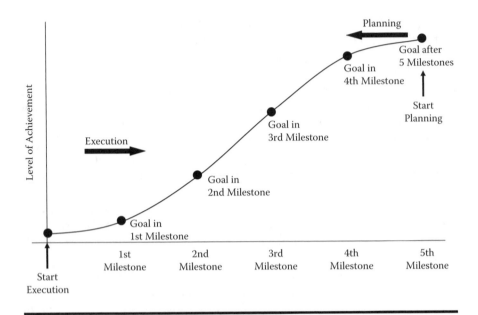

Figure 2.4 According to Jean Monet, planning for the future should start at the end results level and move toward the beginning.

2.6 At the Core of the Cloud Is Virtualization

One of the messages Section 2.5 brought to the reader's attention is that the slogan "communicate don't commute" is not so environmentally friendly as generally thought. Communicating intensity, which people and companies think is their right, and it is almost for free, has turned earlier hypotheses about environmental protection on their head.

Plenty of enabling studies will be needed to bend the curve of energy consumption—if this is at all doable. In reality it is not, because we continue adding more sophisticated services that consume energy, like virtualization. *Virtualization* consists of separating software functions from specific hardware devices. The goal is to share hardware capacity between software modules, in a way invisible to:

- end users,
- applications,
- platforms,
- storage systems,
- computing devices, and
- other infrastructural components.

Virtualization is at the heart of cloud computing. Through it resources are being shared while software and hardware facilities provide end users with seamless access to their specific applications and information elements they need for their work. It is doing so by recasting physical resources into logical facilities.

Each partition created through virtualization (more on this later) acts as an independent entity that can be assigned an OS and application supported by a given cloud. However, the act of separating logical from physical resources brings along challenges, costs, and energy requirements. On one hand, it is easier to dynamically add virtual files than to incorporate physical servers as nodes to the system. But on the other hand, crashes do happen, and recovery becomes more complex.

- Virtualization, which technically abstracts format and programs heterogeneity from the OS, is producing results but not miracles.
- Operating system heterogeneity limits the number of physical grid nodes available for productive work.
- The management of data centers becomes a demanding enterprise, as more applications are provisioned on a greater number of servers.

What is stated in the above list can be better appreciated by returning to the fundamentals. The *virtual machine* concept has been known since the 1970s. It started with IBM's VM operating system on mainframes, which permitted a processor to split itself into several virtual machines, sharing the (high-speed) memory. The twenty-first-century version of virtualization is that of:

- employing networked computers to provide a real-time infrastructure, assured through the *hypervisor*, and
- making use of the hypervisor to enable sharing access to software and hardware modules.*

In the background of virtual memory developments has been the concept of *paging*, which came to light in the late 1960s. Officially announced at the Bergen IT Symposium of 1968, paging became one of the pillars of information technology in the following years.

The best, but in no way exclusive, way to define a *page* is as a screenful of information on a video display.† The simpler way is to look at paging as a memory management approach used when a processor shares physical memory for all processes.‡

---

* VMware, Citrix, and XenSource are hypervisor vendors. VMware's vCloud initiative acts as an enabler in porting server workloads between off and on premises.
† Originally a page was a quantity of memory locations addressable with 1 byte. In the Viewdata system, for example, it was a unit of information accessed by the user through its page number or as a leaf of a tree.
‡ In the early incarnation of paging, an operating system kernel moved pages of memory between primary and secondary memory storage, as required.

The flexibility and adaptability of this approach are impressive and have led to other applications than the original VM. In 1979, for example, paging was reinvented and used with Prestel, the British interactive video text system, following the seminal work by Dr. Sam Fedida of the British Post Office. As years went by, designers recast virtualization into novel and more sophisticated forms. Pages are employed for backup of data, archiving, serving images and videos, storing secondary or static web-accessible information elements, and more. Paging, nevertheless, is not the biotechnology of computer systems.

"Our experience is that multiple Virtual machines can share CPUs and main memory surprisingly well in Cloud Computing, but that I/O sharing is more problematic. ... One opportunity is to improve architectures and operating systems to efficiently virtualize interrupts and I/O channels. ... Another possibility is that flash memory will decrease I/O interference," stated the University of California researchers who studied the issue.[*]

These are evident limitations that might turn into sources of future bad surprises with cloud computing. At stake is not just technical elegance but as well the ability to get better utilization out of shared server storage, I/O, and generally the cloud infrastructure.

- Optimization might happen when virtualization occurs in various places: desktop, servers, networks, channels, and switches.
- It should also be appreciated that for the time being, many of the technical challenges that lie ahead are opaque.

If everything goes well, then through virtualization cloud computing can run multiple applications on a single server, or a small group of servers, emulating a virtualized constellation of multiple devices. In this manner logical servers can be created, deployed, and cancelled regardless of location, which makes it feasible to optimize (up to a point) the handling of applications.

This case of physical space emulation has existed since the original virtual memory solution.[†] It started as a way to permit sharing, between applications, of a large central computer memory at reasonable cost—accomplished by paging on physical disk and rolling in or rolling out to central memory. Over the years, however, the virtual memory concept has gone through a radical transformation, which must be reflected in cloud-oriented design.

We no longer need to save central memory space, as significant technological advances brought a dramatic drop in cost. The way in which the VM concept is presently used is to create virtual machines. Physically, such machines that are

---

[*] A. Armbrust, A. Fox, et al., Above the Clouds: A Berkeley View of Cloud Computing, Technical Report UCB/EECS-200-28, UC Berkeley Reliable Adaptive Systems Laboratory, February 10, 2009.

[†] Virtual memory and virtual machine are both abbreviated by "VM." That's confusion, but it is far from being the only confusing issue in technology.

instantaneously born and die young seem to be impossible, while logically they are not only conceivable but also necessary components of large systems solutions.

As the perspectives of paging's applications expand, they facilitate scalable storage that is consumption based. They also enable publishing and distributing content through the cloud. The virtualization in storage has become an important ingredient of cloud computing because it helps to:

■ abstract physical objects and locations,
■ present their associated logical views,
■ manage multiple devices across vendors and protocols,
■ facilitate nondisruptively change in physical resources, and
■ make possible the so-called thin provisioning, which helps in reducing the margins of space typically allocated within a system.*

If we leave aside the challenges arising from scheduling virtual machines as well as the huge overhead associated with virtualization, which are far from having been overcome,† *then* we can celebrate a technical breakthrough. Virtual machine formats specify and encapsulate all components of an application, including operational instructions, and they port applications between clouds. (Some call this an ecosystem, which, as I have already underlined, is a misleading term.) In turn, this:

■ makes possible allocation and aggregation,
■ can lead to virtual machines used as specific appliances, and
■ helps to hold together a swarm of business partners until what the application specifies has been executed.

Further still, apart from ensuring applications mobility within and between clouds, virtualization helps in improving the usage of multicore processors (supposed to save energy). Such multicores are employed to provide more computing power per processor, and their growth has acted as a catalyst for the movement toward virtualization. The downside is that most application, database, and system software would have to be rewritten to fully optimize the power of multicore processors.

In addition, there is no reason why virtualization cannot be combined with other technological advances like data source *wrapper agents*, encapsulating various heterogeneous data sources, or broker agents sharing knowledge about, and transactions with, data source agents.

The wrapper agents enable plug-and-play third-party software, allowing one agent to communicate on a metalevel with other agents, while exploiting domain-specific software. The broker agents provide information that could answer more effectively user requests. For instance, brokers can accommodate single-occurrence

---

* Data de-duplication makes it feasible to compress data more efficiently.
† As well as the question of high energy consumption.

requests, service recurring behavioral objectives, and react dynamically to changes in goals. All this sounds great, but the reader should never forget that much of it is written in a future sense.

2.7 Strategic Products and Tactical Products

A subject that is seldom, or not at all, discussed in connection to cloud computing regards the most likely repetition of the strategy of selling old products as "strategic" prior to discontinuing them—well known from half a century of IT experience. For the time being, onDemand software and platforms are new. Hence, there is no reason for this stratagem. However,

- as they start aging and novel ones come to the fore, misinformation will start creeping up, and
- to protect themselves from buying the old technology, user organizations and consumers must appreciate what a strategic product really is.

Let's first look into this issue from the user organization's perspective. Because most firms are not technologically self-sufficient, strategic decisions must be made regarding which technologies are core to their business interests and which play a supporting role. With this comes the need to distinguish between strategic and tactical products, focusing on:

- how best to manage sourcing for core technology and
- whether to buy or make tactical software routines.

Starting with the premise that all sorts of products and services today require a good deal of software support to have market appeal and be profitable, the computer programs written or bought to support a company's strategic product line should themselves be strategic. Users will be well advised to examine whether this is the case or they are sold novel hardware run by obsolete software.

Typically, though by no means in every case, *strategic products* are longer range as well as key income providers. They are few but vital to the company's main business, and they must get most of management's attention. Often, but once again not always, they are the result of in-house R&D characterized by the fact that the company:

- has a commitment to their continuation,
- benefits from a degree of pricing freedom, and
- spends no money for subsidies to keep them on the market.

Typically strategic products have novelty, but not all innovative products become strategic. In the broader domain of engineering, about 5 percent of R&D's

output are products which become «winners», 15 percent just survive and the rest are failures, never reach the market and if they do so they fade away.

In the coming years, new languages stand good chance to become strategic. A new free programming language known as "*R*" assists companies in handling and visualizing big data sets (see the discussion on big data in the Epilog). Free software called *Hadoop* enables personal computers to analyze significant quantities of data, that previously required big expensive machines. It does so by parceling out the tasks to numerous computers.

- Visa, the credit-card firm, used it with test records amounting to 73 billion transactions and 36 terabytes of data.
- Allegedly, the processing time fell from one month with traditional methods, to a mere 13 minutes.*

Tactical products are shorter range and should be under steady profit and loss (P&L) evaluation as to whether they are continued. Some tactical products result from in-house R&D; others are bought licenses. In either case, they should answer low-cost production and distribution criteria (some may be sold at lower than production cost to lure clients to the firm and its strategic products, which means subsidized prices). Tactical products:

- are less affected by innovation than strategic products and
- are frequently outsourced to benefit from lower production costs.

These statements are generic in nature. They do not apply only to the cloud or (even less so) only to software. In their substance, they are particularly true in product lines with high competition. Though there exist some "me too" approaches, every company follows its own policies—and they vary widely among themselves.

Semiconductor industry policies, for example, range between those that maintain a large in-house manufacturing technology infrastructure and those that rely almost exclusively on external suppliers. In its heyday, General Motors was buying from outside the firm about 50 percent of the value of its products. Subcontracting or outsourcing, however, becomes touchy when the product is proprietary. The fate of OS/2, a co-development of IBM and Microsoft financed by the former, speaks volumes about the risks.

As Chapters 4 and 5 will bring to the reader's attention, sourcing decisions affect the fortunes of an enterprise in more than one way. Witness the results of IBM's decision in the 1980s to outsource the technology for its personal computer microprocessor and operating system to Intel and Microsoft, respectively. Before too long, this decision contributed to:

---

* *The Economist*, February 27, 2009.

- a major business reversal at IBM and
- dramatic growth at those two technology suppliers.

Within a half dozen years PCs ceased being a strategic product for IBM, and this happened at the very time PCs reached the summit of their popularity. The same can happen with a cloud vendor's strategic onDemand applications, platform, and infrastructure.

Bad decisions in business and industry are common currency. In other cases, supply chain relationships are characterized by conflicts of interest and in still others by interruptions in the promised or expected series of deliverables. A question not being asked in outsourcing as frequently as it should is the insourcer's ability to innovate and change—over and above its ingenuity in cutting costs. One who visits Wal-Mart's headquarters in Bentonville, Arkansas, is greeted by a large plaque in the lobby stating: "Incrementalism is innovation's worst enemy! We don't want continuous improvement, we want radical change."

These were the words of Sam Walton, Wal-Mart's founder, who radically changed the general store with his innovative approach to low-cost, high-volume supermarket retailing. Walton brought a merchandising innovation that in a few years made his company a global leader. (Walton had also said that he would never buy another person's or company's inefficiency by paying higher price for its goods and services. That's golden advice for those working on the cloud.)

Whether we talk of merchandising, of manufacturing, or of being busy with Internet transactions, the innovation culture of suppliers and insourcers is not just welcome but most necessary. Earlier on in this century, Procter & Gamble (P&G) looked into the life cycle of consumer goods in America, from 1992 to 2002, and found that it had fallen by half. That means two things for the impact on cloud computing:

- to be ahead of the game, a firm now needs to innovate twice as fast, and
- its suppliers, too, must be innovators, because otherwise the company will lose the competitive edge it has among its clients.

Remember this when dealing with a vendor of OnDemand software, platforms, infrastructure, enabling services, or anything else. It matters little if the vendor says that "this" or "that" took so many years in R&D and what it has to offer is its strategic product. *If* the product compares poorly with a similar strategic product(s) of its competitor(s), *then* it is not "for us."

Many innovative products are the result of an interdisciplinary research and development effort. A General Electric research project for jet fighters ended up with an invention that revolutionized the way doctors diagnose their patients' illnesses.

Scientists at GE's global research center in Niskayuna (upstate New York) were investigating how LCDs could improve the instrumentation of aircraft cockpits. One of them, who had worked in a related medical program, suggested applying the technology to x-rays. By the mid-1990s, GE was studying *digital x-rays*, which:

- require no film,
- do not need to be placed on light boxes, and
- give a more accurate view of organs and bones than was previously possible.*

Beyond this, the discovery of digital x-rays underlined the merits of having several fields of research under one roof. Something similar will probably happen with cloud computing. As Chapter 1 underlined, this domain is multidisciplinary, and this opens plenty of possibilities from concurrent software/hardware design to:

- integrated computing and communications developments and
- the merging of disciplines that so far have required a great deal of interfaces.

With interdisciplinary science becoming more widespread there is every reason to think that more and more inventions in information technology, communications, and intelligent software will find uses well outside their intended purpose. Industrial history teaches that developing innovative approaches and associated entrepreneurship rewards a company by differentiating it from its competitors.

The impact of innovation on a strategic product has after effects on education policies that should accompany a new technology. In February 1995, in a senior-level meeting at MIT in connection with the Industrial Liaison Program, most of the participating executives of firms sponsoring R&D told the university's administrators to:

- push Ph.D. programs toward industrial relevance and
- include subjects that enlarge a person's horizon.

Industrial liaison representatives also strongly advised stressing the need for *commercialization*. What the executives of sponsoring companies in the Industrial Liaison Program said should be written in block letters and be given a prominent place on the desk of every CEO of cloud providers and every CIO of user organizations.

---

* In 2000, GE began marketing the first digital x-ray machine, supplanting traditional equipment.

Chapter 3

Strategic Inflection Points

3.1 Strategic Inflection Points in Information Technology

A *strategic inflection point* (SIP) is a time in the life of a society, an economy, a company, or a person when the fundamentals of its existence, and therefore of its future fortunes, are about to change. The SIP can be a threat, but it also provides the opportunity to break out of the current status and thrust into a higher level of achievement. Precisely because it represents exogenous change, a SIP involves risks when it is not attended to:

- in time and
- in an able manner.

Information technology has gone through eight strategic inflection points in fifty-five years: in 1954, 1959, 1964, 1973, 1982, 1989, 1994, and 2010. These are indicative milestones, and therefore approximate, because a big change in business does not happen overnight; a SIP wave in IT can come from hardware, software, or a system change, and it takes time to build up. Table 3.1 summarizes some basic changes in hardware and software characteristics, as IT moved to a new epoch.

Over more than a half century, from 1954 to 2010, there have been many more basic IT developments worth noting, but each on its own did not create a strategic inflection point. At the end of the 1950s, however, the use of transistors altered the dynamics of computer design, while the first high-level languages, Fortran and

Table 3.1   Strategic Inflection Points in Information Technology

Approximate Year	Time Gap	Hardware	Software
1954		First industrial applications[a] Univac vs. EAM[b]	Symbolic programming language (by Grace Hopper)
1959	5 years	Transistors IBM-7090	Fortran (1957/8) Cobol (1959)
1964	5 years	Integrated design of a computer line[c] IBM 360	OS 360 Algol (1963)
1973	9 years	Microprocessors Minicomputers[d] Distributed information systems	Virtual Memory C language
1982	9 years	PCs, LANs	Expert systems Spreadsheets C+ Ethernet
1989	7 years	Client-servers	Shells Paint on video
1994	5 years	Wide adoption of Internet	Horizontal system integration Seamless access
2010	15 years	Cloud computing	Virtualization Metalevels Virtual integration

[a] At General Electric in Louisville, Kentucky.
[b] Electrical Accounting Machines, by IBM and Remington Rand.
[c] Which started vertical integration.
[d] While Arpanet was transferred from the U.S. military to academia in the late 1980s, it took about half a dozen years to be generally accepted as the basic, effective, and inexpensive solution.

Cobol, had a lasting impact on applications software (the term *software* was coined in 1958).

Developments in those early years were unrelenting. In 1963 IBM released IMS, the first ever DBMS, originally developed in 1958 for NORAD.* That same year Ramac 350 was marketed, the first disk storage ever. In late 1968 came SNA, the first system architecture released by a vendor (also by IBM). Both IMS and SNA were hierarchical, the technology of the 1960s, which is still in use.†

Among other important developments of the early to mid-1960s was the Multics operating system, developed at MIT (on whose notion Unix was based). Applications-wise, a breakthrough has been time sharing,‡ while on the hardware side of computing hard disks started to compete with magnetic tapes as the storage medium. All these references added up to the 1964 IT inflection point, particularly characterized by:

- upward compatibility in the 360 product line and
- Operating System 360, which integrated I/Os, housekeeping, and other routines—and whose design proved to be more complex than that of the new product line's hardware.

The eye-catcher of 1973–74 was the microprocessor by Intel and Texas Instruments. DEC's minicomputers, too, were a breakthrough leading to distributed information systems (DISs) over the following years. The early 1970s also saw a popularization of real-time applications, though the laggards remained faithful to mainframes and batch. (Chronologically real time saw the light in the late 1950s, when AT&T attached a nonintelligent terminal to a central resource, but it took more than a dozen years until applications started to become popular among the leading firms.)

A lesson to be learned from that time is that the companies at the leading edge of information technology in the 1960s and early 1970s were those who seriously studied the aftermath of developments connected to IT's strategic inflection point. They capitalized on them by projecting over the medium to longer term the most likely impact these SIPs would have on:

- their market,
- their customers, and
- their own organization.

---

* The North American defense system.
† SNA has practically disappeared from the IT applications landscape, but IMS is still kicking, used by companies too retrograde to update their technology.
‡ The joke at the time was that this concept did not qualify as a new invention, as it had been used by unfaithful wives through the ages.

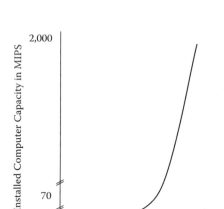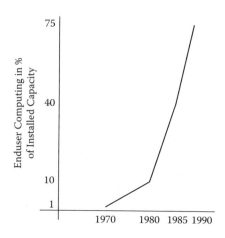

Figure 3.1 Forecasts made by a leading firm about technological evolution and its effects on the firm's operations.

The two graphs in Figure 3.1 encapsulate the results of a seminal study by Xerox, which was then a tier 1 company in technology thanks to its Xerox Park Research Center. In terms of prognostication, both graphs were prophetic. Capitalizing on the driving power of minicomputers and the early DIS concepts they brought along, the experts made two forecasts that (in terms of overall trend) proved to be right:

- computer power will increase exponentially, and
- three-quarters of the installed capacity will be in the periphery, near the end user—not at the center.

A third fundamental projection, this time from Intel, became the famous Moore's law (after the name of the firm's CEO, who prognosticated the microprocessor's conquest of the computer landscape). Moore's law predicts that densities of transistor technology will double every eighteen months. Several years later, it was matched by the *law of the photon*, which states that bandwidth will triple every year.

Another projection from the 1970s has been that peripheral and central computer resources will be architectured like a network. In fact, the network will be the computer. This emphasized the attention that has to be paid on the sharing of resources. The age of data communications had begun, but at the time it was mainly batch processing, even in teletransmission.

A breakthrough in data communications came in the late 1970s with X.25,* the layered public packed switching protocol (based on the Arpanet concept). For database management purposes, researchers at the University of California, Berkeley,

---

* X.25 was a breakthrough, while by contrast ISDN was just a marketing gimmick. There was good reason why in the late 1980s it was nicknamed "I See Dollars Now."

developed Ingres—the first relational DBMS. Its advent brought system designers, developers, and end users into a new era of flexibility in computer applications. (It was followed in the mid-1980s by object-oriented data management structures.)

These developments were soon joined by PCs and local area networks (LANs), culminating to the 1982 strategic inflection point, which was also characterized by a golden horde of artificial intelligence (AI) constructs. The era of expert systems divided IT users into two asymmetric populations:

- e-system users who were ahead of the curve and
- the laggards (the majority), who still kept with obsolete, ineffectual, inflexible, and highly costly Cobol programming.*

Those who by 1989 joined the client-server revolution in IT, which constituted a major strategic inflection point, have been among the doers of mankind. Board members, CEOs, CFOs, CIOs, and computer specialists will be well advised to study the life of the great *doers* to understand what it takes to be ahead of the curve. One of them was Andrew Carnegie, and another Henry J. Kayser, the American industrialist who in World War II built cargo ships in five working days each, when the best shipyards at the time required 210 days apiece.†

Kayser's motto was "You find your key men by piling work on them." This is exactly what a company should expect from its managers and all people working for it. Effectively applying new departures in information technology is imaginative and intelligent work rather than what slow-moving people call hard work—and it gives those who lead the effort the satisfaction of accomplishing something that the majority of their peers are unwilling or unable to reach.

The next strategic inflection point in IT came in the early 1990s with the Internet, but the client-server model continued strong, eating up the market from mainframes. Contrary to the preceding SIPs, in 1994 the Internet promoted client-server solutions rather than replacing them, giving client-servers a life cycle of two decades—the longest ever in IT's brief history.

In fact, as things presently stand, cloud computing—the SIP of 2010—integrates client-servers as megascale repudiates it, as some people like to think. Also, it *may* be that in this integration it is upgrading servers at the expense of clients. Time will tell whether this is a profitable switch and therefore whether it becomes effective.

What the reader should retain from these references is that they demonstrate that there is not one or two but plenty of developments that taken together over a given time frame create a strategic inflection point. Another lesson from the last six decades is that people and companies who see the SIP coming are able to position

---

* Many still do, but one can hope that cloud computing and onDemand software bring them out of this state of IT hibernation.
† Albert P. Heiner, *Henry J. Kayser, Western Colossus* (San Francisco: Halo Books, 1991).

themselves against its forces and gain from it. Ironically, however, the more successful one has been in the old structure, the greater is the difficulty one finds in making the switch.

Uncertainty also has something to do with this resistance to change, because an SIP leads into uncharted territory. Adapting to a new environment is, however, a responsibility, not an option—though there are strategic challenges to be faced by companies, IT professionals, and other technologists.

In conclusion, a basic question the reader will have to ask, and try to answer in a convincing way, is whether cloud computing is a fashion or a reflection of the times and therefore an SIP. To me it looks like a new paradigm that requires plenty of study, along with thorough identification of an organization's strengths and weaknesses and preparation. In principle, the more advanced and complex the technology we are planning to use is, the greater is the degree of necessary foresight, insight, know-how, and homework.

3.2 Cloud Computing and Its Slogans

Strategic inflection points are huge business challenges propelled by cultural forces, political currents, social movements, or technological strides. The latter change either the systems concept, as it has happened with client-servers, or some of the most fundamental components of the prevailing solution. Never in engineering does everything change at the same time. If it did, the result would be chaos, not progress.

In that sense, up to a point Larry Ellison might be right when he says that the interesting thing about cloud computing is that "we have redefined it to include everything that we already do" (see Chapter 1), but he should have added that the systems concept is different. The megascale of the cloud:

- ■ is something new and
- ■ may well bring along a mare's nest of unexpected consequences.

Without doubt, it will also feature new slogans to wrap up the commercial effort so that customers flock to "the latest solution," eager to share in its benefits but often unaware of the amount of effort that it involves or of its downsides. Slogans make the world go round until the next awakening.

Those of us who worked with computers since the early 1950s do recall that the first slogan was "faster and faster." But over the years of computer usage the leading concept changed, and with it the sugarcoating. With microprocessors a new notion dominated computer design: "smaller and smaller."

"Cheaper and cheaper" would have been a better motto, and it did not take long for the computer industry to discover that. First minicomputers and then PCs helped user organizations to swamp costs. But revolutionary architectural solutions did not come along until LANs matured and client-servers demonstrated that they can deliver a better and cheaper alternative than mainframes. (Until then, user organizations continued with practically the same architectures, though the ornaments attached to them were smaller and cheaper.)

The dual appearance of *business architectures* (Chapter 8), which have been a huge improvement over the computer manufacturers' system architectures, and expert systems brought along an interesting trend toward "newer and newer" solutions. Together with this came the realization that what was (then) thought to be large systems required a painstaking study that paid particular attention to the design and management of complex structures.

Cloud computing makes this requirement even more pressing because of the emphasis that has to be placed on the design, implementation, and administration of very large systems computers and communications systems. Experience from other significant departures from IT's beaten path suggests that the present strategic inflection point requires much more in terms of preparation than what was needed in order to:

- capitalize on the Internet or
- buy onPremises customer relationship management (CRM), enterprise resource planning (ERP), and other applications packages.

It is rather surprising, but not totally unexpected, that many companies are misjudging the effort and money that must go into reengineering in order to gain benefits from the cloud (mainly but not exclusively through onDemand software). The narrow view of somehow getting a "cheaper" solution seems to dominate. One of the major user organizations participating in the research that led to this book put it this way: "We see cloud computing as a valid option in saving costs by reducing the current IT infrastructure in-house, but it seems the cloud computing might still not be ready for enterprise class critical applications."

In other words, the choice is one of betting on the not-so-secure cloud infrastructure but leaving out the much more cost-effective onDemand software. Shortly thereafter the received response once again states: "The primary motivation is the reduction of costs down the line by reducing the in-house infrastructure."

It is always dangerous to place one's bet just on lower costs, because in IT (and in many other business propositions) projected lower costs have a nasty habit of not materializing. Even if they do, they are not sustainable over the longer term. (More on costs associated with cloud computing and the deceptions that they hide will be detailed in Sections 3.5 and 3.6.)

Competitiveness is a much better criterion when we are making investments, and the way to bet is that greater competitiveness will rather come from onDemand software and the cloud's platforms than from infrastructural services. The reader will be wise to remember that the latter are characterized by a lot of uncertainties (see Chapters 9 and 10). Just as advice, it makes really no sense to live on slogans, and "reduction of costs" is just a slogan.

Another one of the half-baked slogans heard about cloud computing is that it constitutes an ecosystem (see Chapter 1), which is a pure marketing dirty gimmick. IBM has carried out several corporate-wide brainstorms involving more than 150,000 people. The results encouraged it to put more emphasis on "green computing."* Other cloud providers, too, have come up with the same nonsense idea.

To put it mildly, this is preposterous. Companies should not be using a big lie to sell their wares. As Chapter 2 brought to the reader's attention, computers, and most particularly databases, have become huge consumers of energy. They are polluters, not environmentally friendly alternatives to paper and pencil.

Still another issue that tries to turn itself into a slogan is that of a *public utility* with unlimited resources at its disposal. Cloud computing, the pros say, will provide young firms with huge amounts of computer power. This is an argument for the birds, because young companies don't need such huge amounts. It is the big old companies, particularly those poorly organized, that need it—to feed their voracious entropy.

Having said so, it is proper to add that these *critiques* are not against cloud computing per se but against efforts to hide the facts and to mislead. Take as an example the foregoing reference by a cloud user (and often heard motto) that it "dramatically reduces costs." It does not, but it might improve them if the user organization:

- reengineers itself (Chapter 6) and
- reinvents its systems and procedures.

Slogans and wishful thinking will not solve the problem. Going ahead with the right preparation prior to committing oneself to the cloud is not an easy job. But the aftereffect of not doing so will most likely lead to a failure. Studying the IT miscarriages that have happened in the past, thereby avoiding repeating them, can be a rewarding exercise and a way of gaining future edge. Four of the most flagrant past mistakes with IT are relevant with cloud computing:

1. Lack of a strategic plan. Strategy is a master plan against an opponent. Are we planning to use the cloud to gain competitive advantages? Or are we drifting toward a life in the clouds because other people and companies are doing so?
2. Lack of skills. People and companies embedded in the old IT culture who refuse to change are unfit for the transition to cloud computing. Absence of appropriate skills results in an inability to focus and explore opportunities with the new technology.

---

* *The Economist*, August 29, 2009.

3. Confused objectives. The goals to be reached through cloud computing must be very few and very clear. A salad of ecology, public utility, low cost, and other blah-blah will leave a bitter aftertaste. Running after too many hares ends in catching none, and muddy goals are worse than none.

4. Keeping low technology alive. This is a very frequent and very costly mistake, for which people and companies present many justifications—none of them valid. One of the most often heard is that they have legacy applications that they have to continue running, a sort of sacred cow. To put it mildly, this is a silly excuse that in one stroke negates every reason for getting on the cloud.

Another justification, which has some rationale but not enough to justify keeping legacy applications alive, is the inability of cloud providers to ensure standardization for the full spectrum of utility computing. For instance, the ways (and the will) of leading cloud providers to distribute software to match standardized application programming interfaces (APIs) vary significantly from one firm to the next. In this respect, the user community must take the initiative, by contractually requiring:

– norms and standards for APIs based on open-source efforts and
– compliance to them by all providers of onDemand software, platforms, and infrastructure.

In addition, an integral part of a sound contract should be high security (Chapter 9) with severe penalties associated with breaches. Quality assurance clauses (see Chapter 10) are another must. Uptime of 99.99 percent, with 99.9 percent a minimum under stress conditions, is a reasonable goal. Another must is contractually guaranteed subsecond response time for more than 90 percent of systems responses—as well as bug-free onDemand software and tier 1 enabling services. As Figure 3.2 suggests, up to a point lower price and lower quality correlate.

In conclusion, people and user organizations who understand the implications of the management of change and know that they will be faced with organizational resistance are not overly enthusiastic about cloud computing. Three themes are dominating the doubters' thinking:

■ whether the cloud is really a strategic inflection point in IT or a fad,
■ how complex data security issues that loom menacing are going to be, and
■ the risk of reappearance of customer lock-ins, known since the mainframes epoch (Chapter 5).*

Advancements in technology and the rapidly growing importance of large databases, including their impact on operations—not just the generation of hackers— have turned privacy and security into a wide area of concern. The Internet has

---

* When switching to a rival was difficult and expensive.

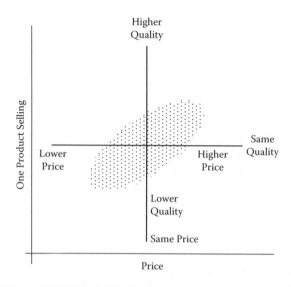

Figure 3.2 Quality and price correlate, but in a weak way; good management makes the difference.

added to the reasons of lack of security, and cloud computing promises to reinforce it. This looks like a pessimistic view, but it is realistic.

3.3 User-Centered Solutions and Cloud Computing

In today's global markets, enterprises succeed or fail based on the speed with which they can respond to changing conditions. Properly chosen and correctly used information is a vital ingredient of rapid response to market drives. Therefore, business solutions must be developed and deployed faster than ever before, reaching online the ultimate end user for input, output, and interactive communications purposes. Speed and quality of delivery see to it that:

■ in many cases it is no longer practical to build new business applications from the ground up, and
■ neither is it viable to deploy the classical off-the-shelf onPremises software, keeping the responsibility for upgrades and maintenance in-house because the package has been massaged.

Where business competitiveness is at stake, the answer is rapid prototyping and fast track or, alternatively, software onDemand, which is a user-centered approach. Assembling a business application from software components is like employing ready-made parts to build a car or house. Over and above what is commercially available online, a more sophisticated layer can be built by painting on video.

By contrast, opting for labor-intensive alternatives for programming and other IT services that have become a commodity is like reinventing the wheel. Clear minds have stated so several years ago. "It Does Not Matter" is the title of a seminal article by Nicholas Carr published in 2003 in the *Harvard Business Review*. In its time, it rose eyebrows, but Carr's concept has been proven by the facts in the seven years following its publication. His concept was that information technology became:

- an infrastructure rather than a differentiator;
- a utility, like railroads, highways, telegraph, and telephone;
- a cost to be managed and not an edge over rivals; and
- a risk to business continuity, not a guarantor of it.

Therefore, the article in the *Harvard Business Review* urged CIOs to spend less on their data centers; opt for cheaper commodity equipment; go for commodity software, like ERP; and focus more on IT vulnerabilities, from viruses to terrorism and data thefts. Behind this advice is the fact that computers and networks, most particularly the Internet, altered the attitudes of people and companies—all the way from daily life to the workplace.

Rare is the case of people who now think "technology does not affect me." Increasingly, there is evidence of an evolution in basic assumptions people make about their industry and their profession. Any-to-any instantaneous telecommunications have seen to it that the whole definition of what a service is and is not is being turned inside out:

- This has a tremendous effect on how products and services are designed, made, and sold.
- The ongoing change, particularly the inflection point of which we spoke in Section 3.1, punishes the laggards as never before because they are no more able to compete.

In engineering terms, the search for user-centered solutions is no more confined within what has been in the past considered a normal distribution of events. More and more designers are confronted with exceptional cases of technology convergence, which find themselves at the fringes of research and have to be brought together to capitalize on their synergy. The pattern is shown in Figure 3.3.

An example was provided in October 2009 as Google extended the reach of its Android software for mobile phones when Verizon Wireless, America's biggest mobile operator, backed the technology. Moreover, with the market for smart phones heating up, AT&T opened access to its wireless network to iPhone applications, enabling cheap Internet calls. These are the further-out spikes in the Figure 3.3 pattern.

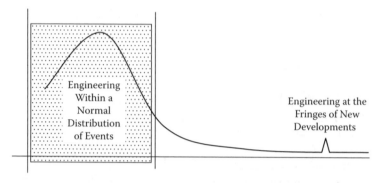

Figure 3.3 The need for engineering user-centered solutions goes well beyond what has been considered as the normal distribution of events.

In terms of management, steady watch over the effectiveness of user-centered solutions requires that the chief information officer is at the same time business innovator, service level designer, and agent of disruption and renewal. Such a triple functionality is demanding, but it is also a personal opportunity because it makes the CIO a *process innovation officer* whose clients are no more the different departments but the end users.

This raises the question about whether one of the main objectives of cloud computing is to provide user-centered solutions. The answer is neither simple nor linear. Theoretically, user-centered approaches are a worthy goal for a strategic inflection point. Practically, whether this happens or not depends a great deal on the CIO's preparedness and ability to employ his time* in:

■ thinking hard about all company processes,
■ analyzing the extent to which their upgrade furthers the firm's competitive position, and
■ projecting new IT solutions that bring personalized, intelligent information (not just data) to the end user.

CIOs don't have the luxury of falling back and letting things "take care of themselves" because the cloud's strategic inflection point may also take care of their career by eliminating the IT department—if it insists in providing precloud services. It is totally wrong to think of a swinging pendulum that shifts back the company's information technology from client-servers to mainframes or more generally centralized computing. Neither will this make life easy for the CIO.

Innovation, not just in IT but in any human enterprise, does not consist of looking to the future through the rearview mirror but of capitalizing on the fact

---

* Essentially, the big chunks of time he or she should save by employing cloud facilities.

that with broadband Internet, optical networking, and advances in storage, computing power, and networking:

■ it has become less relevant where the servers are located,
■ but it is highly important where the end users are and what they need in IT support today—not in three years.

As every good manager and professional knows, the key to winning in business is to operate at a faster tempo than your adversaries. That's part of being in charge of the time cycle loop. Cloud computing may provide the raw stuff for it but surely not the detailed solution. Any valid solution has to be specific to the user organization—and therefore is the CIO's responsibility.*

It is also interesting to observe that the present strategic inflection point is part of a twenty-year cycle that influences significantly the job CIOs have been doing. This does not happen for the first time. From the late 1950s mainframes to the late 1970s DISs the elapsed time was two decades, and another decade went by as DISs morphed into client-servers. Each of these periods redefined what chief information officers should accomplish.

Seen under a different perspective, rebundling and renaming products and processes like content, communications, collaboration (CCC), which is addressed to personal productivity, is not going to provide the end user with anything better than he or she already has. Neither are user-oriented solutions focusing on online secretarial assistance or middle management. Wang solved the problem of computer-aided secretarial duties back in the 1970s, and plenty of middle management as well as professional support has been provided:

■ in the early 1980s through computer-aided design (CAD), and
■ in the early 1990s through routines that evolved into CRM, ERP, and generally supply chain management (see Chapter 11 on logistics).

The real need for real-time user-centered solutions that are rich and analytical is at the senior management level, including members of the board, the CEO, and executive vice presidents. This has been a missed target of IT over nearly three decades. Though there exist some exceptional accomplishment dating back to the 1970s and 1980s, these continue to remain as exceptions. *If* cloud computing is not solving the executive information problem that persists,† *then* it will fail in providing the user organization with a real user-centered solution, no matter what its proponents may be saying.

Everything counted, the greater risk to the implementation of cloud computing services, and most specifically to the satisfaction of end user needs, comes from

---

* CIOs who think they can relegate that job to the cloud vendor will be bitterly deceived.
† D. N. Chorafas, *The Real-Time Enterprise* (New York: Auerbach, 2005).

the holdovers of mainframe mentality—which in the late 1980s and early 1990s filtered into the client-server model and is preparing itself to do the same with the cloud. CIOs who try to follow the (irrational) policy of supporting two cultures that bite each other will live to regret it.

Another bad policy that hopefully will be put to rest with cloud computing is to ask every year for more IT money, essentially to cover inefficiencies. Cash-strapped companies, particularly small to medium enterprises (SMEs), cannot afford big budgets, and their CIOs must appreciate that there are limits to IT expenditures (see Sections 3.5 and 3.6 on prices and costs with cloud computing).

In conclusion, cultural changes always accompany strategic inflection points because the before and after realities are so different. A basic prerequisite of cultural change is that our attitudes, policies, and procedures must change. This will not be provided in a miraculous way by the cloud but through reengineering, which is the user organization's responsibility. User-centered approaches are by no means an empty label, but expectations will not be fulfilled just by altering the crust of the cake.

3.4 For Cloud Vendors an Inflection Point Is Risk and Opportunity

"Suddenly there is an overnight success of the power of Internet in altering the perspective of the computer market and of the vendors," said one of the contributors to the research that led to this book. Another one, however, pointed out that this is by no means the first time a broad new perspective opens up in computers and communications, but as experience has shown, many companies are not capable of taking advantage of it.

Personal computers in the 1980s, and global network of computers and communications in the 1990s, have been instrumental in increasing the information-carrying capacity of systems. In line with Moore's law for more than two decades, costs fell fast; then intelligence-enriched global telecommunications networks provided the ingredients for a major leap in system solutions, but not every company profited from it.

Yet, there has been plenty of opportunity for doing so as research and development at both the very big and the very small end of technology's spectrum became the mover and shaker of innovative products and processes. "Nanotechnology is in our watches, cars, hospitals and it shuffles information around. But it's also about therapies and new ideas—the next big thing that's going to change the world in 20 years," says Jim Gimzewksi.[*] The problem with several computer vendors and many of their clients is that they have a short time horizon—that of the next three years in their policies.

---

[*] *UCLA Magazine*, Fall 2004.

Three years may be good for profits but not for sustaining a leadership position. According to some estimates, cloud spending will be $100 billion by 2013. This is the high end. A forecast on Bloomberg News on August 14, 2009, put it at over $40 billion in 2012, which may give somewhat over $50 billion in 2013. But even $50 billion is a very lucrative market—one no IT vendor would want to miss. In fact, it may be even more important if one counts the consulting and other enabling services client organizations will require to:

■ make user-centered solutions work properly and
■ reengineer a huge volume of legacy applications, some of which were written before the people who daily use their output were born.

Not only is the size of the projected cloud market appealing but also the growth of some segments of it surpasses what can be remembered from the fat years of the computer industry. Table 3.2 provides the reader with projections that explain why so many software and hardware companies have put their cloud at the core of their strategic plans.

While, as it will be discussed in Chapter 7, for some of them the number one motivation for joining the cloud is to defend a franchise, many others see business opportunities in enlarging their market, selling innovative applications, and providing enabling services. They also see an opportunity to help existing customers migrate to the cloud environment.

Being ready to reap the business opportunity the cloud might present also has another rationale. No company ever knows from where will come its next major challenge, its up-start competitor. In the early 1980s American Airlines commissioned

Table 3.2   Revenue from Internet Clouds and Other IT Services: Current Base and Projected Growth to 2013[a]

	Share of Current Base	*Projected Growth*
Communications and current type content	29%	15–20%
Customer relationship management (CRM)	25%	20–25%
Enterprise resource planning (ERP)	19%	14–18%
Supply chain management	13%	8–10%
Office sites and digital content	9%	90–100%
Other	5%	

[a] As of mid-2009.

a study to Booz, Allen, and Hamilton about its business future during the next ten years (to early 1990s). The consultancy answered that the challenge will come from telecommunications networks—not from another carrier.

For other firms, the prime motivation for entering the cloud computing market is the leveraging of customer relationships. Google, for example, will not be able to grow nearly as fast as it did thus far without new and appealing service offerings. Properly managed cloud computing offerings can help in opening up a new market, as well as strengthen existing customer relationships.

On the hardware side, both reasons seem to motivate Cisco. In early 2000, just before the punching of the dotcom bubble, the company's market capitalization peaked at nearly $550 billion, and it was briefly the world's highest. A year later it was hit by what John Chambers, its CEO, calls the "hundred-year flood." Its stock market value was swept away, settling in the range of $100 to $200 billion. Cisco did not drown, and it recently pushed into computer territory while at the same time joining the cloud computing market. This is part of a strategy:

■ to become key supplier of the essential elements of an increasingly connected economy and
■ to be a prime corporate example of how to effectively use the assets the company developed over the years.

On Wall Street, analysts worry that Cisco is stretching itself too thinly and that it could rip itself apart. My opinion is that a greater risk lies in the company's organizational model invented to keep it wholesome. While wishing Cisco success, organization-wise this is an example of what not to do. The company's most recent structure is on the lines of business held together through an elaborate system of committees. These are made up of managers from different functions, with one of their main responsibilities to tackle new markets.

■ "Councils" are in charge of markets that could reach $10 billion.
■ For "boards" that number grows to $1 billion.
■ Both are supported by "working groups," which are created "as needed."*

Henry Ford, the genius who built up the empire, had said that a committee cannot drive a company just like a committee cannot drive a car. Neither does a committee have a soul to blame or a body to kick. That's a kind of reinvention of matrix management (a darling of the late 1980s/early 1990s) that has failed. In fact, it is a merger of matrix and theory Y,† which has also been a disaster.

To position itself against cloud computing's strategic inflection point, Cisco is said to have set up fifty boards and councils, with around 750 members, and to

---

* *The Economist*, August 29, 2009.
† Of Douglas McGregor.

have given up counting the working groups, because they come and go so quickly. All this is done in an effort to combine:

- a functional structure and
- cross-functional working groups.

It is supposed to produce a culture of collaboration from top down, but in reality it is an example of how, by trying to reach all corners of the market, companies risk undoing themselves. Complex organizational structures often hide entropy and with it a snakepit of risks.

The message the reader should retain from this reference is that joining cloud computing—as a vendor or as a user organization—is by no means a safe strategy. To enter a new industry, GM paid $500 million to acquire EDS (and much more to buy out Ross Perot's share in GM equity when he correctly criticized a do-nothing board). The deal failed for the same reason GM went bankrupt in 2009: notorious lack of leadership at the top, in spite of Perot's efforts to make the company reinvent itself.*

Some experts say that, the lure of a new market aside, the reason that led some players into cloud computing is leveraging existing investments. Amazon.com falls into this class. Such services can be added without major problems, particularly if they are offered barebones on existing infrastructure. At the end of the day, this helps in amortizing large investments made in data centers initially developed for the company's other product lines.

It needs no explaining that the spirit of competition, too, has played a major role in the decision to offer cloud computer services. Companies with the requisite applications software and platform(s), as well as a deeper experience of the Internet, are well positioned to profit from the cloud market, while attacking incumbents is a great motivation for start-ups.

The other side of the coin, however, is that while on one hand technology contributes to the opening of new and important markets, on the other it impacts on business strategy and structure in a way that some firms get destabilized. Nobody should indeed doubt that while new technology usually brings advantages, its adoption and implementation present challenges to vendors and user organizations alike.

In addition, as Section 3.3 brought to the reader's attention, one of the big questions still to be answered with cloud computing is where the cost savings will be found. If one thing is certain, it is that plenty of cost-related issues that are today opaque will reveal themselves in the next few years, bringing along with them a roster of unexpected consequences.

---

* In the early 1970s Exxon bought one of the better business systems firms, also for diversification reasons. After some years of agony in trying to meet its new owner's stiff management rules, the free-wheeling office business firm failed.

In conclusion, solutions to be given to system challenges associated with cloud computing will provide both opportunities and risks to vendors and to users. Enrico Fermi, a physicist, used to draw a hazy cloud at the center of his diagram of the atom, with the label "Cui sono I draghi"*—the wild frontier that had to be explored. The dragons will come as problems associated with cloud computing continue to increase until the new implementation perspective and associated business architecture finally settle.

3.5 Cost Is One of the Dragons

Positioning a company against the forces of strategic inflection points does not come cheap. It takes skill, money, and undivided management attention to steer the firm through the high seas of innovation, toward a believable objective at destination.

Sometimes people are taken by the bandwagon syndrome, or by the projected size of a given market, without counting the costs involved in being a player. A recent financial analysis by a major U.S. broker put it in this way: the cloud opportunity will continue to be subsidized by the $65 billion online advertising industry, with a portion of the ad market being driven by cloud applications (see also Section 1.7).

This is, of course, true for cloud players, not for user organizations, and on paper it sounds great. I have no doubt that Internet advertising will siphon lots of money from other media (we have already discussed how it puts newspapers and magazines under stress). But as the results of my research reveal, user companies switching into cloud computing have poorly estimated (if at all) the cost they will incur in:

- capital expenditures (capex),
- operational expenditures (opex), and
- the resulting profit and loss figures.

Judging from responses I have received to my queries, there is no evidence that risk, cost, and return have been analyzed in a pragmatic way. *Risk is a cost* and it has to be aggregated with capex and opex in a break-even analysis, chapter by chapter, of the budget in a cloud computing setting.

- Averages and summaries, let alone hopes, are of no help to management decision.
- If anything, average figures are a disservice because they may lead to wrong paths and blind alleys in terms of commitment.

---

* "Here are the dragons."

One of the important contributions of analytics is that it motivates dissent in opinions, provided that dissent is permitted by the organization's culture. This is the only way to flush out the dragons and judge the damage they can make if costs and risks start running wild.

At the other side of the coin, if I were a vendor of cloud services I would like to see a realistic market segmentation and positioning for my cloud products, along with an estimate of the extent to which my current core onPremises products might be marginalized. Product cannibalization due to cloud computing:

- is a challenge for all established companies becoming players in that market, and
- this challenge may carry with it significant vulnerabilities in strategic products.

Whether they are active primarily in software or hardware, incumbents will be faced with pressure to develop cloud services that need a lot of consideration for how they integrate with their existing product line. Among the challenges is the cost of building bridges and interfaces to legacy products, at a level of elegance appealing to the client base.

Another important query whose solution a cloud provider should regard as a salient problem is the internal unbundling of expenses associated with cloud products and services. This is important for cost control even if the clients are presented with a bill for bundled services (Section 3.6). Theoretical opinions and pronouncements on how to go about it abound, but in practical terms they have little value to both providers and users.

For instance, one of the cloud pricing theories says that organizations that perform "batch analytics"* can use *cost associativity* and apply the following algorithm: "Using 100 machines (of a given type) for 1 hour costs the same as using 1 machine for 100 hours." That's a hypothesis that is preferable not to use because it is patently wrong.

Even if the algorithm were right, the pricing of IT services is in no way a linear proposition. While it is true that costs and billing should be proportional to user hours, data processing applications have many other cost factors—from I/Os to distributed data storage and disk accesses—and algorithms that do not account for them are going to give poor and misleading results.

I do not believe in the argument that because cloud computing "lends itself well" to markets that are horizontal and large, infrastructure costs will eventually take care of themselves because they can be shared easily. Infrastructural costs can be king-size. Yahoo! is reportedly spending some $800 million per year in infrastructure. That's not petty cash to leave its far-reaching implications out of the pricing equation. In addition, with cloud computing, demand is unknown in advance when capex decisions are made.

---

* Which, to say the least, is a curious label and a reminder of IT practices dating back to the 1960s.

Such an uncertainty makes cloud economics totally uncharted territory, as infrastructure providers will have to support spikes in demand. The cost of spikes will become even more relevant if and when cloud services become popular.

Bottlenecks will be quickly followed by customer dissatisfaction; end users will not take contention lightly (Chapter 10). Therefore, offering infrastructural services will not be the best idea for start-ups. By contrast, they may do well in selling onDemand software, as Salesforce.com does (Section 3.7). In addition, infrastructural cloud services demand a vast amount of expertise, which also must be costed and billed.

Not only do the projected very large data centers need to purchase thousands of servers, vast network bandwidth, and unprecedented amounts of electric power, but they must also face fixed costs of basic software development and deployment, which is better written as operational expense rather than something that can be amortized over many years.*

Big companies like Google, Microsoft, IBM, Hewlett-Packard, and some others have the capital to do huge investments, though whether they get their money back and make a profit is a different matter. Small companies will disappear under the weight of infrastructural capex. Economies of scale, the usual argument, will benefit the larger infrastructure provider, not the smaller one.

Indeed, it is not just a sufficiently large company but also one with a significant market share that could leverage its capex and opex because of economies of scale. Good governance, too, makes a difference because such a cloud provider must also be able to offer a pricing schedule well below the costs that might have been incurred in a medium-size user organization. Even so, its hope to come out of this experience wholesome is only a hope. There will be plenty of shakedowns in the sector of cloud infrastructure, including the ranks of the bigger cloud providers.

The structuring of the product line evidently plays a critical role in pricing decisions. For a software company entering the cloud computing market the cost of designing, programming, and upgrading interfaces may be a totally new experience. With onPremises software this issue was rather subdued and "specials" were charged to the customer (usually by system integrators).

For the typical off-the-shelf applications software vendor, once a product was developed and put on the racks, most other costs were traditionally variable, relating to sales and commissions (some of them occult). Cloud computing does not work that way. *If* a software company wants to invade its competitors' territory, *then* bridges and interfaces are unavoidable, and as special engineering items they may capsize the whole profit and loss (P&L) picture.

This will evidently be reflected in the bills cloud user organizations will have to pay. Quality, reliability, and seamless operations don't come cheap. As the vendors'

---

* A very bad budgetary practice adopted by poorly managed user organizations since the 1960s.

costs for infrastructural services rise, the dollars written in their bills will rise too. There will be no shortage of reasons for higher prices.

One of the subjects that unexpectedly came up in my research is that several user organizations contemplate having cloud computing on the side—over and above current IT expenditures—because "it is so cheap." This does not show good management.

At UCLA, one of the professors taught his students that "economy does not consist in putting aside a piece of coal, but in using the heat while it burns." If I were chairman of the board, I would like to know: Are we using the heat with cloud computing? Able businessmen see that point and, day in and day out, they use a sharp knife to cut costs. Sam Walton, founder of Wal-Mart, had a principle: "Never buy somebody else's inefficiency."

Quantitative benchmarks help, because they ring alarm bells when excesses take place. Walton's quantitative benchmarks were that, taken together, administrative costs should never exceed 2 percent of business—and expenses associated with business trips should never exceed 1 percent of purchases done. Expenses associated with cloud computing need similar benchmarks, which should be etched in a plate to be put on the desk of every company president, whether cloud vendor or user organization.

Every expense item should be scrutinized. Here is an example. While on the board of GM Ross Perot remarked: "In Pontiac (Michigan) GM executive parking garages are heated. It costs $140,000 a year to heat one parking garage. I would shut that thing down. It has nothing to do with (making) cars."

Closer to cloud computing, I will never buy the so often heard argument that benefits will accrue to both cloud providers and customers at the expense of traditional software and hardware vendors. That's a statement without any meat. Instead, I would like to have answers to specific issues. For instance, how are users supposed to protect themselves in the case of interruptions in cloud services because of:

- power failures,
- phasing out of satellite links,
- storms and other environmental effects, and
- plain terrorist acts?

A cloud study published not long ago* made the argument that to improve dependability and "save on costs," *full backups* can be moved weekly by shipping physical disks, while compressed daily incremental backups are sent over the network. Adjunct to that was the suggestion that cloud computing might be able to offer an affordable off-premises backup service (essentially reinventing the user organization's data center).

---

* Which I choose not to identify because in some of its aspects it was good.

I was flabbergasted. Those of us who in old times had to keep father/grandfather generations for backups know from firsthand experience what sort of rat hole is the daily shipping of tapes and disks. Now it is supposed to happen again under cloud computing. (The study in question further suggests that *à la rigueur* whole computers, not just disks, could be shipped through special delivery.)

Here is another great suggestion: "Once archived data is in the Cloud, new services become possible that could result in selling more cloud computing cycles, such as creating searchable indices of all archival data or performing image recognition on all (one's) archived photos to group them ... etc." All this not without even a mention of the size of the tab or who pays it. It sounds worst than GM's heated executive garages.

3.6 The Problems of Opaque Pricing*

The pricing of products and services has never been a simple, let alone linear, problem. The leader in a given market has a pricing freedom that his challengers lack. But he does not have an absolutely free hand in pricing, unless there is a monopoly—as happened from the late 1960s to the late 1970s with mainframes, until DEC's Vaxes turned IBM's pricing list on its head.

Existing evidence suggests that pricing and costing associated with cloud computing services is still in its infancy, particularly for products other than onDemand software (see Section 3.7). True enough, basic services have their metrics, which, however, tend to vary from one provider to the next. Typically,

- *storage* is charged at $x.x per Gbyte/month,
- *network*, at $y.y per Mbit/second/month,
- *administration*, at $z.z per 100 servers/DB manager, and so on.

There is as well overhead, of which, at least for the time being, cloud providers are not talking about. They probably include it as a flat rate to charged services, but for their own cost control purposes they should handle it separately. A similar statement is valid about local taxes, which are going to be a great diversity given the nature of the cloud's globalized operation.

Pricing and billing based on *usage* should not be confused with *renting*, which involves paying a negotiated price to have access to the resource over a period of time—whether this is a flat fee, hence an average, or is computed on effective time. A billing system truly based on usage involves effectively metering and charging

---

* The theme of this section is cloud services charged to the customer because of the challenge posed by other services that are free of charge. Since the late 1990s Internet companies have had a hard time making a buck when their competitors make their products available free of charge—as Google plans to do with basic spreadsheets.

based on actual employment of every resource available on the system. As a matter of principle:

- *pay-as-you-do* service charges must be detailed and well documented, and
- this means that prices and billing cannot be indifferent to incurred costs (Section 3.5).

There is no major problem in measuring time of usage as a basis for charges with office suites, CRM, ERP, and popular productivity tools. "Content" is more complex because so many things come under that heading, including communications and collaboration. But computing, and most particularly frequent multi-tenant accesses for accounting, scheduling, deliveries, and other business chores, is a different matter—requiring greater accuracy in monitoring and measuring.

It needs no explaining that plenty of issues must be reflected in a factual and documented service costing and pricing. Past practices of cutting the edges of prices established and demanded by industry leaders, like IBM was in mainframes and GM in autos, no more apply because no single firm will have nearly half the cloud market in the foreseeable future.

Here is an example of what I mean by cutting the corners of another party's price list. At a 1953 graduate seminar at UCLA colleagues asked Ralph Barnes, professor of production management and former senior executive of Ford, how Ford established its customer prices. Barnes answered that his former company did not really establish prices. It read the price list of General Motors and came up with a trimmed one. Otherwise, it would not sell cars.

Ten years later, in the 1960s, as consultant to Gordon Smith, the boss of Univac in Europe, we followed a similar pricing strategy. We controlled our costs and offered to the clients a lower price than IBM for reasonably better-quality products. This strategy worked and made good profits for Univac. But our margins were good because of cost swamping through internal reengineering. In a way similar to that of Ford, as number two in the computer market Univac had no pricing power.

None of the vendors in cloud computing are going to have pricing power over the next five years, and therefore reading in some price lists detailed formulas on costing and pricing based on bytes, accesses, movements of disk arms, and other technical details makes me laugh.

Only theorists who lack practical experience can write things like that. By contrast, each infrastructure vendor should develop and use reasonably good costing formulas—if it can develop them—for internal cost accounting reasons, profitability, and sustainability analysis. The latter is a cornerstone for the vendor reaching a decision on whether to stay in the cloud infrastructure market or lick its wounds and close shop. This being said:

- By all likelihood, pricing of large-scale infrastructural services will start as a matter of seat-of-the-pants feeling.

■ It will then enter the phase of analyzing the pricing cloud of competitors for better focusing, as well as taking advantage of anomalies.
■ It will proceed with a near normalization of price lists, as experience accumulates and both the infrastructure vendors and the market for such services mature.

The above list raises the question of how clients can choose one cloud computing vendor over another in terms of deliverables associated with infrastructural services, platforms, and other costs. The best answer is to follow the strategy we established for Ubinet in the late 1980s, at Union Bank of Switzerland (UBS), when I was consultant to the board.* We made a model for our implementation environment and data load (current and projected); specified topology, reliability, availability, response time, security, and quality of service criteria; and gave a copy of that study to five reputable telcos† who responded to our request for offers.

■ The UBS study set pragmatic requirements for Ubinet services.
■ Each vendor was required to come up with a qualitative and quantitative proposal, including pricing.

The choice we made in terms of supplier was not necessarily the lowest bidder, because cost was one of the key variables but not the only one. As a matter of principle, every factor that enters the algorithm of a wholesome service and its functionality has its price. Therefore, equations like the one twice quoted in a recent paper are lightweight, even if altogether the paper is rather good (but too academic):

$$\text{UserHours}_{\text{cloud}} \times (\text{Revenue} - \text{Cost}_{\text{cloud}}) \geq \text{UserHours}_{\text{datacenter}} \times$$
$$(\text{Revenue} - \text{Cost}_{\text{datacenter}}/\text{Utilization})‡$$

Apart from the fact that the left side of the equation should also feature *utilization* of each resource as a variable,§ because if it exceeds 80 percent or so contention will bring the infrastructure to a halt, an algorithm wholly based on costs is half baked. Where are the factors of reliability, availability, response time, quality of service, privacy, security, and more? Of penalties in case the cloud vendor breaks contractual targets? Each one of these quality factors weighs heavily on service

---

* The bank's large-scale global private network.
† Four out of five were already the bank's suppliers in different parts of the world. Hence, we had internal information on each one's dependability.
‡ A. Armbrust, A. Fox, et al., Above the Clouds: A Berkeley View of Cloud Computing, Technical Report UCB/EECS-200-28, UC Berkeley Reliable Adaptive Systems Laboratory, February 10, 2009.
§ The level of each resource utilization at the provider's premises. Indeed, cloud computing users should ask what the vendor's infrastructure utilization factor is. This should be specified in the service contract, reported to the user organization weekly, and have associated penalties if it exceeds a guaranteed factor.

costs, and when they are included in the algorithm, they may well make the adoption of cloud computing unwise.

Another critical factor that must enter the costing and pricing equation at the infrastructure vendor's side is that of synchronous vs. asynchronous operations (Chapter 1). Some services will be real time, and their guaranteed response time (on an escalation clause) is vital (see Chapter 10). Others can be asynchronous to benefit from lower costs. "Overnight delivery" is not the only option, though it may appeal to companies on Paleolithic technology characterized by mainframes and batch.*

To benefit from lower prices while still accepting an asynchronous mode, more alert users may require that deferred time is limited to one, two, or three hours. This still allows the vendor to optimize the use of his computing facilities, data centers, and network, while time-wise the user organization accepts a compromise. Such an approach, however, poses two prerequisites.

At the user side, workstations cannot be *thin*; i.e., deprived of their disk storage. They have to have embedded disk storage to accept and hold deferred data transmissions. This does away with the argument of just plugging unintelligent devices in the socket of an information utility, sort of an electric socket allegory promoted by theorists (Chapter 1).

In addition, as far as the infrastructural services vendor is concerned, it must get written guarantees with penalties from its suppliers that their computers, switches, and basic software can reliably ship information elements over the globe.† A four 9s (99.99 percent) requirement is advisable (Chapter 10). The alternative of shipping disks through couriers with redundant or updated data makes fun of the advantages the cloud is supposed to have, and therefore it should be discarded.

3.7 Salesforce.com: A Case Study on Pricing onDemand Services

Sections 3.5 and 3.6 provided evidence that costing and pricing are major challenges associated with strategic inflection points, because so many unknowns are at play. This pricing challenge is relatively eased in connection to onDemand applications software and associated services. Salesforce.com provides a practical example through its price list, which features additional functionality with every one of four editions:

■ group,
■ professional,

---

* Which cloud computing should help to eradicate rather than support.
† There is a significant difference in terms of restart and recovery between system interrupts on a single transaction and in the middle of a long file transmission.

- enterprise, and
- unlimited.*

The full range of applications the vendor offers includes CRM (available with all editions); custom programs, custom tabs, and custom objects, which are limited in number with lower-cost editions† but are full range with the unlimited edition; and premier support and administration, which cost more money with the first three editions but are free of charge with the unlimited one.

Also included in the bundle are API record types, workflow, and offline access available with the higher two editions but unavailable with the lower-level group edition. In a similar way, Force.com Sandbox is unavailable with the lower two editions, available at extra cost with the enterprise edition, and included in the price of the vendor's unlimited edition.

The pricing structure looks ingenious in motivating customers to move toward a higher edition after they gain experience (and satisfaction) with the lower one. There is moreover an original equipment manufacturer (OEM) edition allowing strategic partners and other third-party developers to build applications on top of the vendor's platform for $25 per user per month. Salesforce.com partners can market those products directly to their customers.

The vendor has done its homework in strategic thinking, including the case of alliances. While third-party applications do not offer core CRM functionality, they create a new addressable market that might have a need for core CRM. (Salesforce.com does not sell its own applications through the OEM.)

This is a good example of a sophisticated approach to the development of a price schedule, facilitated by years of experience with the marketing of off-the-shelf commodity software by myriad companies for onPremises applications. In fact, the cloud provider has also adopted a price differentiation between onPremises and onDemand applications. Over a five-year cycle:

- an onDemand business application in the cloud would cost a customer a third of an onPremises client-server application, and
- the customer can as well run personal productivity routines like e-mail, gaining a cost advantage.

This, too, is an interesting pricing approach because it induces cloud computing users to lighten up their labor-intensive chores in computer programming by switching from onPremises to onDemand. It also provides evidence that pay-as-you-do sits well with software provision even if there are problems in using it with storage and network bandwidth (Section 3.6).

---

* Costs range from $99 per year per user for the group edition to $3,000 per year per user for the unlimited edition.
† Though custom objects have an upper bound of $2,000.

Vendors of cloud infrastructure would say that the statement made in the second half of the preceding paragraph is wrong, as they take care of costing problems through *scaling*, charging cycles being employed and instances users occupy. Indeed, some vendors add that their machine routine learning, for both diagnostic and predictive reasons, allows dynamic scaling.

This argument is convincing in a laboratory environment but not in a real-life cloud with tens of thousands of servers and millions of users. The system is simply too big, too complex, and too unpredictable to be managed in an optimal way at a time when experience with pricing the cloud's infrastructural services is still thin—no matter what the models say. Neither is it true that if the vendor goofs with its cost estimates today, tomorrow that error will be erased because the cost of the cloud's components follows Moore's law. It does not.

■ Computing and storage costs continue to decline, though they do so at variable rates.
■ But wide area network costs are falling much slower, and they are a big chunk of the total expenditures in using cloud resources.

Today neat pricing solutions like that implemented for onDemand software by Salesforce.com are not easy with cloud infrastructure. A big, established computer company can say that it is willing to subsidize its entry into the cloud market by absorbing part of the cost, particularly overhead.* Or, it may adopt the policy that during the first few years it will not care about return on investment with its cloud computing infrastructure. Instead, it will use such an investment:

■ as a strategic weapon,
■ as a way to regain market leadership,
■ to innovate its product line,
■ to reach its clients online,
■ to enter new markets, and for other reasons.

All this is part of the so-called baby industry argument, and it makes sense provided subsidies don't last too long. If they do, then the company loses its entrepreneurship and the results expected from the new experience diminish to the level that it becomes counterproductive.

If subsidizing a new venture proves to be necessary, *then* this should be done in a fast cycle, based on a well-thought-out competitive strategy. This requires rapid, concise assessment of situations rather than being taken by a mirage.

---

* Manufacturers of servers, routers, and switches will also, most likely, write them on a direct labor and direct materials basis, which substantially reduces the cost basis of their cloud's infrastructure.

Avoiding Fata Morgana is vitally relevant in connection to benefits to be derived from the cloud.

To realistically appraise what they can and cannot expect from cloud computing, both providers and user organizations must be fully aware of technical, operational, and costing challenges. Take as an example virtualization (Chapter 2). This is an interpretation, not a compilation process, and at the cloud computing level it requires a very large-scale virtualizer that is voracious in its appetite for computer resources.

Few companies release the amount of required virtualizer overhead, as the whole experience is in its beginning and hard data are not generally available. But thinking by analogy from interpreters mapping one computer into another (for instance, a scientific machine into a data processor), the overhead cannot be less than 20 percent of available resources—and sometimes it is much more. This makes minced meat out of the cloud vendors' argument about economies due to scaling (the scaler itself has its overhead).

With its onDemand software Salesforce.com has a contained overhead, but with infrastructural services, the large overhead of virtualization presents serious problems to vendors, particularly as they project investments for proprietary data centers practically all over the globe. Another challenge is the widely varying telecom charges, from one jurisdiction to the next. In Europe, where telcos used to be government monopolies, telecommunications price structures are widely different from country to country. (For instance, it makes sense for a small firm to buy broadband in France but not in Switzerland.)

Neither are social costs the same in all jurisdictions, and total labor cost rather than only take-home pay should be budgeted with unbundled products. Last but not least, the user organizations should appreciate that cloud computing is *outsourcing* of facilities, and experience with outsourcing over the last dozen years suggests that the road can be rocky.

Chapter 4

User Organizations of Cloud Computing

4.1 Potential Customers of Cloud Technology

According to the broad definition of a user organization, anyone who so far has been benefiting from enterprise technology, not just IT, is a potential user of the cloud. This includes traditional data processing, office automation, computer-aided design (CAD),* productivity tools, social networking, scheduling, procurement, sales and marketing, applications software platforms, or other means employed to promote innovation, greater competitiveness, and profitability.

The better-focused definition looks individually at types of users, their sophistication and size, past experience with IT, as well as likelihood to use cloud computing facilities. This is the perspective taken by cloud computing vendors, and it is therefore marketing oriented. It also allows us to proceed in a more methodological sense than a general, all-inclusive definition.

Companies interested or potentially interested in being cloud computing users fall into two broad classes. The one is composed of large- to medium-size corporations with a long history in data processing, which have installed and been using the IT

---

* It was a deliberate choice not to include scientific computing in this list but to emphasize activities like CAD that benefit in a supply chain relationship.

vendors' wares—both tactical and strategic products—for many decades. These are much more likely to adopt the solution of private clouds (Chapter 2) and hybrids.*

By contrast, medium-size and small companies may be tempted to give up their IT operations (and head count) in favor of cloud computing, though it is still too early to have a clear opinion on this matter. Cost alone should not be used as the criterion for cloud decisions, as Chapter 3 has explained.

The way to bet is that large enterprises contemplating cloud computing will be guided in that direction by their current hardware vendors, and they will be getting a big quantity of it rather than cherry-picking cloud services as smaller companies now do (and should do). This will be a slow-going process for two reasons:

■ inertia coupled with the longer time necessary for reengineering, and
■ cloud computing will upset their IT organizations (Chapter 5), creating considerable resistance to change.

Therefore, according to at least some of the experts, in the near future wise vendors of cloud computing services should seek the best market for them, which is made up of *small and medium enterprises* (SMEs; Section 4.6). These have a major incentive in using onDemand products and services, because of their ongoing effort to change capex into opex. In addition, their applications are not as complex as those of big enterprises, which means that the necessary reengineering work (Chapter 6) will be easier to accomplish.

Next to the SMEs an interesting population of potential users may be that of *virtual companies* (Section 4.3). A virtual company typically outsources most of its products and services. It may have only a small head office combined with a sales office, letting third parties produce and deliver everything else—all the way from accounting records to manufacturing.

Still another population of potential cloud computing users will be consumers communicating through social networking (Section 4.7). Cloud vendors addressing the members of that group of users may offer scaled-down products appealing to the other classes of user organizations, as it happened with Facebook.

No matter in which of the aforementioned populations of computer users one belongs, the effect of the strategic inflection point described in Chapter 3 will not take long to be felt. As for the vendors, they will be confronted not only by a shift in demand for products and services they have been classically providing but also by novel risks and opportunities:

■ the cloud presents both *promises* and *threats* for which they must be adequately prepared, and
■ though their future course of action cannot be planned, as Peter Drucker once said, events can often be foreseen.

---

* Which in no way implies that they can skip reengineering (Chapter 6).

One of the foreseeable events to characterize the better-run enterprises in the next ten years is whether or not information is managed as a product. User organizations that have been active in IT and its evolution for more than five decades know that among financial and industrial organizations, let alone among governments and other state authorities:

■ for the most part, information is not well managed;
■ it is available in overabundance or not at all;
■ it is seldom accurate, timely, and complete; and
■ it is provided at a cost that cannot be determined with assurance.

What is more, to a very substantial extent today's approach to information management is based on yesterday's concept and technologies. In the majority of cases, the image of what can be done with present-day media steadily dates back to three or four decades ago and sometimes more. Watch the surprising popularity of Cobol, which is obsolete, cumbersome, inefficient, and of very low productivity— yet widely used.

This attitude that one pays for novelty but does not collect its fruits is widespread. General David Jones, former chairman of the Joint Chiefs of Staff and currently advisor to President Obama, has candidly acknowledged: "Although most history books glorify our military accomplishments, a closer examination reveals a disconcerting pattern: unpreparedness at the start of a war; initial failures; reorganizing while fighting; cranking up our industrial base; and ultimately prevailing by wearing down the enemy—by being bigger, not smarter."*

It is as if Jones had in mind the way IT has been (and continues being) used by most organizations. Optimists say that for those who employ it, the cloud will act as catalyst for abandoning their traditional, muddling-through approach to information technology. This is not at all sure, but it may happen in those firms that engage in reengineering (Chapter 6), provided that they understand the need for fast cycle times.

Much can be learned from Japanese companies who, in their heyday, achieved an enormous advantage in product development and in innovation through a process of steady, incremental improvements that kept them at least a step ahead of their competitors. Leadership is important, but leadership alone will not develop a system that gets and keeps ahead of the curve. This requires:

■ a decision to change,
■ superb organization, and
■ able, uninhibited use of high technology.

---

* *Forbes*, December 9, 1991.

New business models are needed to capture the pulse of the market, and these cannot be served through programming languages that are more than fifty years old. The language we use forms our mind, and something similar could be said of software. This is good news for vendors of onDemand applications who appreciate that capturing business opportunity requires:

- rapid identification of customer needs,
- swift product evaluation and brokering,
- on-time negotiation and confirmation of commitments, and
- a first-class after-sales product service (not just help desks).

Organizations choosing cloud computing will also be well advised to remember that in the coming competitive environment, dynamic markets, supply chains, and interactive distribution channels will obey the law of *volatility in returns*. Uncertainty about increasing or diminishing appeal of their products from one year to the next:

- will create a world of instability, not equilibrium, and
- will penalize those staying behind to the point of going bust.

One of the interesting statistics from the first years of onDemand software is that the top vendors in one year were not the same as those of the preceding and following years. The law, if there were one, would be that more successful companies were distinguished by their ability to keep on being on the run but not necessarily in first or second place year after year. This means that market leadership is still up for grabs.

After a strategic inflection point the doors of risk and return are adjacent and indistinguishable. Able management is anticipating change and identifying new opportunities. Still, if it wants to be one of the first exploiting and conquering a new commercial territory, it cannot wait for large amounts of evidence. By the time that is available, the market would have been de-creamed by someone else; hence the wisdom of distinguishing between strategic and tactical products (Chapter 1).

4.2 The Cloud Interests Small and Medium Enterprises

Companies can be generally classified as very large and usually global, medium to large, small and medium, and very small. The SMEs are typically those employing from ten to less than five hundred people and making roughly less than $160 million (110 million euros) per year.* In the New York stock market,

---

* According to a different classification, the mid-market features companies with one hundred to one thousand employees and small enterprises less than one hundred employees. There are no universal standards in regard to dichotomies.

there are three Russell indexes: for medium-sized companies, for small, and for very small.

I mention these indices because a better dichotomy than employment is to follow the Russell midcap, Russell 2000, and Russell microcap stock market indices, which divide the SMEs and very small firms not into two but three groups, each with its own characteristics, taking as a basis their capitalization. (Not all small to medium enterprises are quoted in exchanges, many being family companies. Those that are quoted constitute a better reference in the sense that their financial reporting permits us to know more about them.)

Not everybody realizes that the medium to small enterprises (and not the very big ones) are those that make the economy kick. They provide most of employment,* are faster to hire in an upturn, and (on average) are by far the best users of Internet services—and therefore also the best prospects for cloud computing.

Forrester Research says that in the coming years SMEs will drive 48 percent of the managed services market and will also be the most important insourcers/outcourcers. Specifically, in regard to the cloud, small and medium enterprises will require services for:

- developing and advertising new products;
- marketing B2B, B2C, C2B, and C2C†; and
- searching for means to reach their clients online.

This means great opportunities for onDemand software for B2B, B2C, C2B, and C2C, as well as to support online reporting services. Apart from external communications with business partners, many SMEs already use intranets for internal company communications, provide an information backbone and interactive staff support, care for interactive training chores, and are great believers in using technology for cost reduction.

Several vendors have been sensitive to these requirements. For example, Microsoft's Office Live Small Business (OLSB) offers SMEs a simple means for creating and managing websites, administering e-mail, handling accounts, implementing marketing campaigns, and managing documents and contacts with business partners.‡

Just as important is the fact that OLSB's cost is low. At $15 per year, its services provide a feature website; free web hosting with 500 MB of storage, expand-

---

* In the United States the Census Bureau estimates that mid-sized firms account for 23 million employees (20 percent of total) and one hundred thousand employers. Also, there are 6 million small firms accounting for 42 million employees. These represent 36 percent of employees and an impressive 98 percent of employers.
† Business to business, business to consumers, etc.
‡ Office Live Small Business is not a small-scale MS Office, and some of its tools come from traditional MS Office wares.

able to 5 GB for an additional fee; domain name registration with custom web address; up to a hundred e-mail accounts that match the domain name; online document storage and sharing; and contract management for sales, personnel, and customers.

A fairly sophisticated support is featured by Sun's Project Caroline, which is built around the development and deployment of Internet services. This is a utility computing initiative that acts as a portal for users, developers, and partners to enable building various application services.

Applications like sales force management, marketing, advertising, customer handholding, customer support, and public relations do not call for complex linkages to accounting systems. Therefore, they are a good market for platform usage by medium-size firms. They can also be enriched with standardized processes such as payroll, accounting, and the like. Other applications, by contrast, are rather customized. They include:

- financial settlement,
- order fulfillment,
- supply chain management, and
- the wider area of logistics, scheduling, and inventory control (Chapter 12).

While the attraction of cloud computing to the SMEs will most likely vary by the industry sector in which they operate, it is reasonable to expect that greater differences will be presented in terms of style of management rather than by product line. Alert managers push for client-oriented web applications that handle:

- the majority of transactions,
- content management,
- customer support,
- sales analysis, and
- campaign management.

Knowing the pattern of the SMEs' use of the web is important for cloud vendors because usually companies that have already adopted the Internet are more prone to go for cloud computing services, because their culture will not stand in the way when doing that transition, and the market these user organizations represent may be impressive as their numbers continue to grow.

For instance, not long ago the regional Chamber of Commerce and Industry of Provence-Côte d'Azur made a study among SMEs that involved 2,200 CEOs and their companies. Of these, 61 percent were found to be active on the Internet, and 39.6 percent confirmed having found new clients through the web.

Even more interesting has been the finding that the Internet-active population of SMEs might welcome enabling services. Many said that they lacked experience in maximizing their Internet exploits.* That is precisely where the opportunity for cross-sales lies: onDemand software, platforms, and enabling.

Indeed, at both sides of the Atlantic the potential size for onDemand software during the next few years can be impressive if current statistics are kept in perspective. In the United States, these statistics suggest that:

■ roughly 30 percent of total software spending is for off-the-shelf onPremises commodity offerings, and
■ the balance, 70 percent, is custom applications developed in-house or outsourced to contractors and system integrators.

Anecdotal evidence suggests that in Europe average figures (they vary by country) stand, respectively, at 26 and 74 percent. By contrast, in emerging markets, where there is less of an attachment to legacy code, the split tends to be even: 50-50.

There is really no reason why the United States and Europe should lag behind developing countries. If cloud computing providers bring the U.S. 30 percent to 70 percent distribution to a more even 50-50 by taking up 20 percent of new or thoroughly revamped applications through onDemand offerings, they will make for themselves a brilliant future. This will be tough but doable if vendors use their imagination.

The best example that comes to mind is the *bargain basement* idea. Its inventor, Edward A. Filene, was a department store owner from Boston who made his fortune in the early twentieth century by putting his idea into practice. As founder of the Good Will Fund and the International Management Institute, Filene's sensibilities had been attuned both to:

■ the needs of consumers and
■ sound inventory management.

Based on these two considerations he created the department store's famous Automatic Bargain Basement, whose prices dropped each week on unsold goods until the last unwanted shoes, shorts, and dresses were given to local charities. While manufacturers and industrial engineers worried about the cost of production, Filene focused on the cost of distribution of goods. Unsold inventories see to it that these costs skyrocket.

Some vendors may say (not without reason) that it is different with software, because once one copy has passed the tests, a million can be made from it. But Filene's concept can still be epoch making; it suffices to find the way to put it into practice in the cloud.

---

* The region established a budget of 18 million euros ($26 million) to close this gap, emphasizing five economic sectors: services, artisans, tourism, transport, and commerce.

4.3 Virtual Companies and the Cloud

A *virtual company** is a temporary consortium of independent member firms coming together, often on a limited time frame, to quickly exploit fast-changing national or worldwide business opportunities. Virtual enterprises share with their suppliers costs, skills, and core competencies that collectively enable them to:

- access global markets and
- provide world-class solutions each of them could not deliver individually.†

These are the basic concepts on which rest a virtual organization. At the same time, however, the notion underpinning a virtual organization is in flux, as the term tends to be interpreted in different ways by different people. Hence, it lacks a universally accepted definition (though in this book we will stick to the aforementioned concept).

Important in regard to cloud computing is the fact that the *temporary network* of independent business partners—customers, suppliers, even erstwhile rivals—is linked by information technology that enables its members to share data, management skills, R&D expertise, manufacturing capacity, marketing thrust, and costs. As such, it constitutes an excellent client base for vendors active in the cloud:

- The virtual company possesses *virtual resources* where and when they are needed.
- The result of ephemeral partnerships among firms is to effectively access one another's customer base in a way that is profitable to all of them.

Critics say that the usage of facilities that are not in-house—hence controlled—does not permit market exclusivity. This argument forgets that today no company has all the resources it needs at its fingertips in order to lead human, financial, products, and marketing. Furthermore, one of the consequences of virtual corporation alliances is psychological. Markets react to impressions.

In that sense, ephemeral alliances are made to satisfy requirements in a compressed time frame and to overtake other, similar virtual company efforts. In order to produce results quickly, such alliances depend to a very large degree on immediately available applications (hence onDemand software), platforms for added-value developments, broadband telecommunications, as well as fully distributed databases and effective any-to-any workstation connections—in short, the stuff cloud computing can offer.

---

* The term virtual company derives from a computing practice in the late 1960s when virtual storage described a way of making the machine act as if it had more central memory than it really possessed (see also Chapter 2 on virtualization). Likewise, the virtual company possesses more capabilities than its actual resources suggest.

† A challenge faced by virtual companies is taxation, because of conflicting international, federal, state, and local tax regulations, which vary significantly by jurisdiction.

What might be seen as common ground of virtual companies is a set of principles for metamanaging industrial and financial activities. These are undertaken by virtual teams—or groups of individuals that collectively possesses certain necessary skills but need to effectively communicate with one another in a way involving no misunderstanding or loss of time.

The resources virtual companies possess are left in place but are integrated to support a particular product effort for the way determined in advance or as long as this is viable. Such resources are selectively allocated to specific tasks, which becomes practicable because computers and communications provide the infrastructure, while optimizers make it possible to minimize the cost of switching among real companies as required by different activities.

For this purpose, virtual companies must be supported by virtual office systems, such as offered by several vendors on the cloud, to help expand the boundaries of each organization by providing a common ground. They do so by facilitating interactions with a broader business range than is possible under traditional approaches.

Because in a dynamic market intra- and intercompany resource availability can change almost minute to minute, advantages are accruing to parties able to rapidly arbitrage their resources. In addition, virtual organizations use information technology to supplement their cognitive capabilities, thereby providing themselves with an advantage given tight time constraints.

As the reader will detect between the lines of the preceding paragraphs, in the background of the advent of virtual companies lie both technological breakthroughs and the change of concepts about organization and structure. Culture, too, plays a crucial role.

To serve the virtual company, the virtual office cannot depend on a retrograde mainframe, the tyrannosaurus of the 1960s to 1980s, which found a way to survive with client-servers in at least the case of naïve communications protocols and obsolete Cobol programs. Totally new solutions are needed, and these started years ago. An example from the 1990s is the *Virtual Lab Notebook* (VILAN), which utilizes two types of software agents*:

- data source wrapper agents, encapsulating various heterogeneous data sources, and
- broker agents, which intermediate requests from users through knowledge about and transactions with data source agents.

The wrapper agents enable plug-and-play third-party software, making it possible that one agent communicates on some higher level with other agents while still being able to fully exploit domain-specific software. The broker agents find information that could enable the answering of user requests. Brokers accommodate

---

* Mobile knowledge engineering artifacts.

single-occurrence requests and service recurring behavioral objectives; they also react dynamically to changes in goals.

Virtual companies would not have been possible without knowledge-assisted artifacts. Technology has made them available since the mid-1980s, though only the best-managed firms have been effectively using them. Moreover, the synergy of deeper market changes and knowledge engineering made it possible to rethink many of the organizational principles of an entity, the majority of which date back to the 1920s.

For instance, as expert systems* replaced whole layers of middle management, the notion of the corporation as a structured hierarchical organization changed. The company, which in the past looked like an impressive monolith of sorts, has started to break into smaller pieces: the independent business units. More importantly, today new organizational theories advise that only a core of competencies should remain at the trimmed-down corporate center. The rest should be farmed out or performed through alliances, thus creating the *virtual company* we have been talking about.

Even huge office buildings, those citadels of the post–World War II era, are no longer considered impregnable. If anything, the concept that brought them to life started falling apart in the late 1990s, being replaced by the virtual office, to which reference was made in the preceding paragraphs.

Furthermore, the fall of General Motors, which sought protection from bankruptcy under Chapter 11, may well be the beginning of the end of the permanent and inflexible hierarchy that spreads fifteen layers down the line. Its place will probably be taken by a new, evolving corporate model that is purposely kept *fluid* and *flexible*, based on a group of collaborators who:

- quickly unite to exploit a specific opportunity and
- then disband once that opportunity has been seized.

When the virtual company restructures, this is often done in a different form and with other partners in order to meet new challenges. Alternatively, it has some old and some new business partners—even some who, a short while ago, were fierce competitors. This is the sense of shifting alliances that is becoming more and more prevalent in a modern economy—and a reason why onPremises software and proprietary IT establishments lose their appeal. The goal of a virtual company may be

- complementarity in a range of products and services,
- rapid engineering and development,
- unbeatable low-cost production and sales conditions,
- marketing muscle (to smash a market leader's hold),

---

* D. N. Chorafas, *Knowledge Engineering* (New York: Van Nostrand Reinhold, 1990); D. N. Chorafas and Heinrich Steinmann, *Expert Systems in Banking* (London: Macmillan, 1991).

- a level of quality competitors cannot emulate, or
- truly leading-edge technology.

An example on the first bullet is Google's alliance with Salesforce.com and other firms, creating the nearest thing to a virtual corporation with fairly well-defined core competencies. To be successful, this virtual company should concentrate on what it does best, leaving to its parent firms their sphere of competence.

Such multipartnerships will become current currency on the cloud, and they may be successful if each organization and its professionals know the strengths and weaknesses of their current skills—and appreciate their complementarity with the skills of business partners. The strength may be in design or marketing or in another function necessary to bring a successful product to market. The proper identification of the weaknesses is more important than that of strengths, because a basic aim of the virtual company is to use the strength of its members to swamp their weaknesses.

Last but not least, a major challenge for virtual companies, and for e-commerce at large, is the notion of *stable establishment*. The term comes from the time of brick and mortar but is still present. Is the server in a cloud's infrastructure a stable establishment? The answer is both yes and no at the same time. Online transborder trade changes the concept underpinning this term. A company (any firm, not just a virtual one) may have a stable establishment in one country, not in others, but:

- it trades over the Internet in many countries, and
- it uses a cloud computing infrastructure based in a far-away jurisdiction.

The stable establishments identification becomes even more complex with virtual companies, because they may have no brick and mortar at all. Nomadic computing adds another layer of uncertainty and there are, as well, other challenges. Bilateral agreements protect from double taxation. But there is no way to apply double-taxation agreements on the Internet. Hence, who should be taxing Internet commerce? And who will be taxing the cloud's infrastructure?

4.4 Virtual Networked Objects

Some years ago, in *The Real-Time Enterprise*,* I wrote that what we have available today, technology-wise, is only a forerunner of things to come. One of the premises was that computation will become freely available, accessible from something like power sockets and entering the everyday world at home and in business. This is happening with cloud computing, aided by imaginative projects run by major universities.

---

* D. N. Chorafas, *The Real-Time Enterprise* (New York: Auerbach, 2005).

Virtual Double

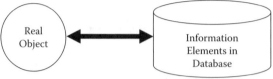

Virtual Customer

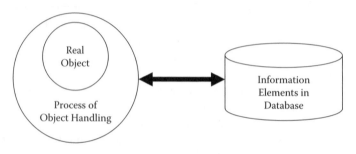

Figure 4.1 From the concept of virtual double to virtual customer identification.

A project that contributed a great deal to shaping up some basic aspects of new technology has been MIT's *virtual customer* (VC) Initiative,* a multidisciplinary approach that targeted significant improvements in speed, accuracy, and usability of customer input to a supplier's product design process. One of its deliverables was the *virtual double* (VD), which can be briefly defined as an information element:

■ mapping a real object and
■ open to qualification through a function (which may be another VD).

VDs are stored and retrieved as objects that are dynamically and seamlessly upgraded, updated, massaged, and reported to produce personalized ad hoc reports in real time. Figure 4.1 shows how easily a virtual double can create a virtual customer identification that becomes available at no time.

This virtual double may be the double of a customer, with the specific mission to instruct on execution of certain functions. As such, it will gather vital information over the life of the relationship and (if this is part of its objective) it will come up with a proposal. Dynamic insurance policies provide an example.

---

* MIT, "Innovation in the New Millennium," a conference program, March 2002.

Networked sensors can serve as online input devices to the virtual double. For instance, smart dust embedded into cars can help in tracking both the driver and the vehicle. Auto intelligence will be informing the driver "you crossed the speed threshold" but will also transmit to a control center that "this driver":

- goes too fast,
- talks on the handheld, and
- does not respect pedestrian crossings.

This is not daydreaming, it has already been happening for some time. Since the early 1990s Volkswagen's Audi and BMW cars have been equipped with fuzzy engineering chips that learn the driver and his or her habits to optimize gas consumption. More recently, Audi integrated the fuzzy chip into the car key, and as each driver has a key, the function of optimization is better focused.

In addition, with GPS becoming increasingly popular, there is no problem in supporting two-way transmission. Nor is there any challenge in keeping driver profiles on a virtual double. The technical solution, too, is far from being demanding. To be useful, data streaming from sensors requires:

- registration,
- integration,
- filtering, and
- analysis for insight.

Each of these steps can lead to messaging. Because of being an intelligent artifact, the VD of a real object has qualities the original object and its classical file are lacking. This greater sophistication helps to manage complexity. ABB, the big Swiss-Swedish engineering company, has been using virtual doubles for years, with every machine having its VD, which can provide information about the physical world that was not previously available.

South African Railways has a system with container intelligence tags. *If* a container is not tagged, *then* the system takes a photo of it and signals its existence. Executives from a major insurance company based in Trieste who were involved in this project* said that the system works well with one exception: too many containers coming into South Africa from neighboring Mozambique are not tagged. Therefore, this creates a bottleneck, and it also shows that:

- with globalization technological advances must be coordinated cross-border, and
- short of this, desired benefits will be limited and cost-effectiveness reduced.

---

* And participated in a seminar on high tech I was giving in Rome.

When the application is well planned, return on investment (ROI) can be impressive. In Britain, Marks & Spencer refitted all containers with sensors and got payback in twelve months. These sensors are tracking everything, everywhere:

- increasing accuracy and
- reducing handling time.

An American company planted sensors at the electricity distribution network coast to coast, and then it integrated and analyzed their inputs. The VDs created a pattern of electrical distribution that no electricity company had available prior to this implementation, and the pattern helped to optimize the company's power distribution operations.

Quite similarly, virtual doubles can be used to track customer profitability; analyze customer balances, loans, interest paid, and trading transactions; establish whether a person or company is profitable enough to qualify for waivers and white-glove treatment; and establish which profits stream (to the bank), which gives customers greater negotiating power. This information helps the bank's officers make decisions on fees and rates.*

Such information can be particularly valuable in strategic decisions, in repositioning the bank, and in marketing campaigns. Without the benefit of hindsight, sales programs fail to measure the potential value of a customer. Institutions that limit themselves to statistics from past transactions are usually very poorly informed about their depositors, borrowers, and investment partners.

The concept underpinning the use of virtual doubles is well suited to a cloud computing environment, particularly so as vendors must get to know their clients in a more fundamental way than through statistics—and onDemand software can handle the chores discussed in the preceding examples. There are, however, problems lying ahead and requiring able answers. Outstanding among them are security and reliability/availability.

Chapter 9 brings to the reader's attention the many concerns around *security*, particularly associated with the transfer of information elements in a global landscape not only their static access. Virtual customer files, indeed all virtual doubles, have significant privacy requirements, but cloud computing infrastructures currently provide a less transparent mechanism of storing and processing data than proprietary installations.

This makes many companies uncomfortable with their sensitive information being located somewhere in the cloud, outside of their direct control, particularly so because cloud computing services are multitenant. Beyond this, the regulatory environment

---

* Typically the top 20 percent of customers at a commercial bank generate up to six times as much revenue as they cost, while the bottom 20 percent cost three to four times more than they contribute to the bank's profit figures.

obliges companies to be very cautious with their data, as violations of the law can have serious legal, financial, and reputational consequences to the user organization.

Reliability, too, should be looked at in a most serious way, as Chapter 10 documents. There exist no reliability norms with cloud computing solutions. Theoretically service level agreements (SLAs) can be structured to meet reliability and availability objectives; practical SLAs printed by the vendor leave the door open to all sorts of failures. User organizations, therefore, should write their own contracts when negotiating infrastructural and other services (Chapter 5).

4.5 Consumer Technologies and the Cloud

Originally developed to capitalize on the web, consumer technologies brought along a revolution in information technology and, when successful, they morphed into business technologies. As such, consumer technologies replaced the federal government's large military handouts as number one supporter of the IT industry. One example is provided by Facebook, another by Google's New Services, which are

- offering corporate products free of cost,
- prodding a switch from traditional software to onDemand, and
- migrating applications, files, and service accounts on cloud servers.

As Figure 4.2 suggests, today business technologies and consumer technologies share a rapidly growing common ground, with the former benefiting from the latter. Therefore, information systems departments that reject consumer technologies as being beneath them increasingly find out that they made a big mistake.

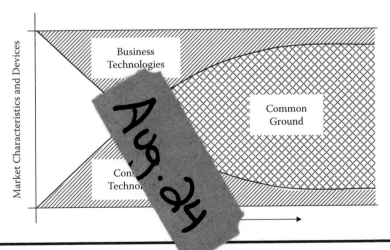

Figure 4.2 Business technologies and consumer technologies share a growing common ground.

This error or rejection took place first in the 1980s, when many corporate IT operations stuck to mainframes and dumb terminals, refusing personal computers as toys (and by consequence client-server solutions); continued programming in Cobol rather than by painting on video; and looked at knowledge engineering artifacts as academia's hobbies.

Companies that refused innovation in IT eventually found out the hard way that they lost a couple of decades in terms of competitiveness, along with the opportunity to cut their information technology costs with a sharp knife. What was intended to be another display of "professionals know best" turned into a major failure in judgment.

In a similar way today, companies that do not examine how they can benefit from consumer technologies are missing several potential benefits. One of them is resource flexibility, as the larger cloud computing providers can shift resource allocation among their servers, enabling customers to scale up capacity (subject to the constraints already discussed). Another is the cloud's pay-as-you-do pricing, which:

- helps in eliminating up-front expenditures and
- permits the converting of fixed costs into variable costs.

Besides dollars and cents, another after effect of capitalizing on consumer technologies is *empowering*. The biggest benefit of the Internet has been to empower the user, and this has shifted contractual power from the *sell side* to the *buy side*. It has also been an eye-opener for IT service providers who sensed a new business in the making.

Until recently most computers and communications companies typically considered as a market worthy of their attention the one that could be expressed in massive statistical terms. The Internet turned this argument on its head, by pricing emphasis to personalization—and cloud computing will, most probably, do even more in this direction. In the aftermath:

- technology leveled the playing field, giving consumers the means to be in control, and
- the Internet enabled them to get together and tell companies what to do in their product offerings.

This is not exactly in the interest of companies who would rather tell the consumer what "he needs" to buy. But as Walter Wriston, a former CEO of Citibank, once observed: "The information revolution has changed our perception of wealth. We originally said that land was wealth. Then we thought it was industrial production. Now we realize it's intellectual capital." One of the best expressions of intellectual capital is flexibility and adaptability.

Hands-on adaptability can capitalize on a mass market with global dimensions, exploiting a previously unthinkable number of possibilities to make a profit through the right product at the right time. The Internet, and by extension cloud computing, lowers the barriers to entry, promoting innovation and competition directly in the consumer landscape.

Computer capacity, including databases and telecoms, can be rented as needed—and novel products may become hotcakes. Chapter 1 made reference to consumer technologies by excellence: Apple's iTunes (for music and video), the iPhone (moving to business after having swept the consumer market), AppStore (for mobile applications), and MobileMe (a suite of online services).

Apple employed the Internet in the most intelligent manner to sell its hardware by means of value-added services. It also capitalized on the consumer market to reconquer the business market, after its hold of the 1980s waned.

Therefore, one of the surprises in my research has been the finding that not everybody is fully appreciating the fact that the Internet is a revolutionary technology, one of the three or four main forces driving the global business transformation.* The dynamics of global growth have changed as profoundly as they did with the advent of railroads, electricity, and auto transport. The evolution of an Internet-based supply chain meant that the two traditional factors of production and distribution—capital and skilled labor—are no longer sole determinants of an economy's power, because economic potential is increasingly likened to the ability to use information in an effective way. That's precisely where cloud computing is expected to make its mark among companies best prepared to catch the opportunity. (Only time will tell if they succeed by capitalizing on the fact that competitiveness is closely linked to the able use of information and knowledge.)

The Internet has promoted a better use of information by providing a framework for integrated distribution of products, services, and business support functions—with timely feedback. This permitted economies of scale traditionally associated with massive production, while supporting personalization made necessary by coexistence of multiple user communities.

The cloud has the potential to add to this transformation by supporting onDemand applications with diverse characteristics and quality of service requirements, as well as by providing multiple classes of service to user communities with a variety of underlying topology. The user communities in reference include end users, network services, applications, and their interfaces, which are providing:

- data services,
- voice services,
- image services, and
- video services.

---

* The others are innovation, globalization, and the switch to virtual assets, which has been friend and foe at the same time. See D. N. Chorafas, *Capitalism without Capital* (London: Palgrave/Macmillan, 2009).

One may look at the Internet as a consumer technology that is primarily a transport layer but should not miss the fact that this provides common application interfaces for reliable end-to-end multimedia transfers. One of the advantages is that it is shielding applications, applications making interfaces and protocols seamless to the users—a feat that, ironically, major computer vendors took years to materialize.

Because of such advantages, this consumer technology made feasible a diverse set of traffic characteristics and also offered potential solutions to other standing problems, permitting fairly well-defined service offerings and operational procedures. Based on the strength of these developments, cloud providers can say that the wares they offer are sufficiently flexible to support interconnection of components across heterogeneous user organizations while ensuring end-to-end connectivity.

Another little appreciated after effect of the development of Internet-based consumer technology is migration capabilities through a path, making feasible phased implementation of the next generation of applications. The net accommodates disparities in terminal equipment and software, thereby ensuring an evolutionary deployment characterized by:

■ an adaptable flexible framework as applications evolve,
■ enhancement of quality of service at an affordable cost,
■ expansion of network transport services and features as applications warrant, and
■ a balance between near-term pragmatic implementation realities and longer-term development goals.

This has become possible because consumer technologies developed on the Internet can be leveraged by all businesses and consumers. Applications interact with other applications across the network, as well as with external networks and applications in a dynamic environment that supports a wide range of service facilities.

While the passage from consumer technologies to a professional IT implementation brings up the need for certain improvements like configuration management, these are well within the range of a service structure based on components that are shared, like access gateways, value-added processes, and so on. Nevertheless, a global management view is necessary to directly control system functionality. (This is relatively small fries compared to the avoidance of having to reinvent the wheel.)

What the reader should retain from these references is that consumer technologies, and therefore the consumer market, have opened huge perspectives in business applications—rather than the other way around. Cloud providers plan to further capitalize on this fact, which, however, does not mean that there are no limitations. In technology, as in daily life, somewhere hidden are the constraints.

The most important constraint for business that I perceive today comes from the ever-growing *data center demand*, which becomes increasingly difficult to satisfy.

Global demand for data centers is projected to grow at an average of 12 to 15 percent per year over the next four years, surpassing supply growth by 300 percent.* (See also the discussion in Chapter 5 on this issue.)

Supply has lagged for several reasons. Data center construction is highly capital intensive and lead times are generally a year to year and a half. Data center building processes require design expertise and procurement of materials such as generators that are in short supply, and the 2007–2009 economic crisis has further reduced supply by:

- limiting access to capital and
- promoting demand, as SMEs chose to outsource their data center needs.

Another major factor limiting the supply of storage facilities comes from the fact that after having grown in an impressive way, the density of recording has stagnated. Counted in *bits per gram*, in antiquity the storage potential of cuneiform was 10^{-2}; that of paper, 10^3; microfilm, 10^5; and mag tape, 10^6. This grew with optical disks to 10^8. The difference from cuneiform to optical disks is ten orders of magnitude, but that's about where we are. Many research projects are promising but so far only on paper.†

4.6 Social Networks and Multimedia Messaging‡

Social networking is a label that, at least in some countries, has produced a high degree of excitement. Its definition is, however, ambiguous, as well as elastic. It can expand from chatting between members of social groups to the usage of the Internet by companies to help themselves in microtargeting consumer clusters.

Online social networks serve not just as ways of wasting time chatting but also as a communications tool for business purposes. Marketing people are eager to use fast-growing social networks to promote their products. For instance, Dell has made $3 million in sales from Twitter.§ Several experts now suggest that the social networking paradigm:

- is turning into a sought-out catalyst and
- permits us to take advantage to influence trends through self-help.

---

* Bank of America/Merrill Lynch, "U.S. REIT's," August 20, 2009.
† There is a double race toward higher density and longer record life cycle (Chapter 5). One way is through carbon nanotubes. Researchers at the University of California, Berkeley, have devised a method that will, they reckon, let people store information electronically for a billion years. By that time we shall see if they have been right or wrong.
‡ The Epilog further elaborates on social networking, its invasion of privacy, and contribution to the consumerization of IT.
§ *The Economist*, September 19, 2009.

Plenty of companies are harnessing the knowledge garnered from social networking. They are as well capitalizing on demographic change whereby a younger generation is more likely to use the web for service issues rather than the classical telephone. As an example, the integration with Facebook and Twitter by Salesforce.com helps companies to quickly research, anticipate, and resolve customer issues proactively.

There is a widely held belief that as social networking becomes more pragmatic its impact will increase, helped by the fact that its population of fans grows. In mid-September 2009 Facebook reported that 50 million people had joined its service since July, taking the total number of users to 300 million.*

Under these conditions, the reason justifying continuing use of the label *social networking* is that the social media is where it is happening. Another, more theoretical, reason is its characteristically easy accessibility, informality, and wider reach, mainly by bloggers who aim to chatter, make fun, provoke, inform, and engage in a way that cannot be effectively replicated offline—and buy goods and services. All this is another demonstration of consumer technology's impact.

To the opinion of many sociologists, the social and even ideological implications of social networking can be enormous. That may be true, but one can also exaggerate, as happened a few decades ago, when an opinion consistently heard was that man-made systems were less than thirty years away from giving managers, workers, bureaucrats, secretaries, shopkeepers, and farmers the opportunity of a new, direct stake in an economic welfare "propelled by intelligent machines."†

Three decades have passed by and these projections are still awaiting their (doubtful) fulfillment. On the other hand, as a service industry with wide appeal, IT stands to gain from social networking—if for no other reason because some of its wares:

- are designed to facilitate proximity of the participants to the social network, and
- as such, they find themselves in the mainstream of the information systems market.

Everything counted, the proximity brought by social networking has been unparalleled. Compared to it, the telephone is a limited way of taking our ears to another place, while what is called "presence" has become necessary to truly achieve interaction and understanding.

Social networking is in its formative years and has plenty of space to grow. Eventually, it will find its limits, as other events that preceded it suggest. Air travel

---

* Facebook also became cashflow positive, with plenty of revenue to cover its capex and opex.
† Another headline catcher from the 1980s has put it this way: "Experts agree that 'thinking' computers almost certainly will replace people in millions of jobs in many industries and offices. Currently, around 25 to 28 million people are employed in manufacturing in America ... to go down to less than 3 million by the year 2010." Ironically, this projection was validated not because of thinking computers but because of the deep economic crisis of 2007–2009, which hit not only manufacturing but also the service industries, leisure, research, and white-collar work.

brought us together physically but with great expenditure of natural resources and side effects of carbon dioxide and other pollutants. Even in the realm of travel, however, networking provides us with the ability to negotiate lower prices for airfares, hotel rooms, rental cars, and other items.

It is not without reason that people with broadband stay on the Internet four times longer than dial-up users—to an average of twenty-two hours per week vs. five hours for TV. They also tend to use networking during the day as opposed to evening hours.

An interesting contribution of social networking is that it has opened a market for group activities, family participation programs, and the chance to reinvent entertainment—beyond information, and communications formats necessary for multimedia messaging services (MMSs). Mobile operators had put a great deal of their hopes, and strategic plans, on market penetration and subsequent boom of multimedia messaging, though they are still struggling to position MMSs to users, as limited camera phone penetration, lack of interoperability, and other reasons have inhibited a take-off.

Costs matter. The expense associated with multimedia messaging services is turning off many potential users, forcing mobile operators to develop new business models around pricing and value-added services. MMS vendors have invested heavily in infrastructure to handle peak usage of thousands of messages a second, but so far they haven't found return on their money. Critics of cloud computing say that its vendors, particularly those spending hundreds of millions on infrastructure, may find themselves in similar situations.

There are as well other lessons to be learned from the fact that multimedia messaging did not take off as expected. A key point is lack of interoperability, which led operators to develop and promote content-based rather than interpersonal MMSs. This makes mobile operators nervous because it is very difficult to build a multimedia messaging business starting with content. And there are too many handsets on the market that cannot speak to each other because of lack of common standards.

The pros say that this standards snarl will not be repeated with cloud computing because of *netbooks*, the basic very low-cost laptops that have been selling like hotcakes. One of the problems, however, is that the more classical netbooks are being supplanted by myriad new gadgets, including tablets and increasingly computer-like mobile phones.

All these devices share a common idea: that a near-permanent connection to the Internet permits simpler technology and is more cost-effective. No wonder that this is the market also targeted by mobile Internet devices, which fit between smart phones and netbooks, like *net-tops* and *all-in-ones* with touchscreens instead of keyboards.*

---

* Something like tiny desktops. Several vendors now throw in free notebooks if subscribers sign up for a mobile broadband contract, putting further pressure on prices but also opening a larger new distribution channel for computer manufacturers—weakening some of them and strengthening others.

It is very good to have different alternatives, but the situation can get out of hand when there are too many with overlapping capabilities and incompatible standards. There are as well some technical issues that should have been solved long ago. An example is mobile number portability (MNP), which in Europe is still wanting, ten years after it was first introduced in some countries.

Other problems include high porting charges, cumbersome application procedures, and handset subsidies given by operators to tie in their customers. (These have impaired the success of MNP in many jurisdictions.) The fact that portability levels are low works against both social networking and the transfer of applications from a consumer to a business environment.

On the other hand, technology has its own dynamics. According to experts, the combination of the Internet, low-cost portable devices, and cloud computing will oblige mobile network operators to change their strategies toward consumers, and by so doing, it will give a big boost to social networking, which will benefit from converging technologies. However, as the Epilog documents, not everything is positive with social networking.

WHAT USER ORGANIZATIONS SHOULD KNOW

Chapter 5

Threats and Opportunities with Cloud Computing

5.1 The Computer Culture as We Know It Today May Disappear

Experts find it difficult to agree on many issues as far as what happens during the next five years is concerned. One of the issues looking for an answer is whether or not by 2015 everything having to do with IT resources will be Internet connected. Another, even more important, question is *if* and *when* the computer as we know it today may disappear, because:

- computing devices will integrate into other machines, and
- the IT culture itself will significantly change with the new generation of technologists.

As an example of the first, these days there are more electronics under the hood and in the body of tens of millions of vehicles than in computing devices in the classical sense of the term. This, however, does not mean that computing machinery, per se, has disappeared. Whether or not this might happen, and to what degree, will greatly depend on perceived threats and opportunities connected to cloud computing (Section 5.2).

What can be stated today with a certain level of assurance is that our notion of a computer the way it stood for more than half a century, as well as what is done with it, will change. This will happen not only because of cloud computing but also for other, extended reasons, such as:

■ pervasive networks, the so-called object Internet;
■ nanotechnology devices, which play a top role;
■ sensor technology, able to sense almost anything, becoming available at low price (Chapter 4); and
■ the fact that practically all content technologies will be digital and eventually smart.

As these developments take place, emphasis will be placed on much closer business partner integration, reengineering for greater efficiency in operations (Chapter 6), upgraded attention to compliance with regulations (which will be strengthened in the aftermath of the 2007–2009 deep crisis), and the replacement of the current generation of IT specialists by a new one that feels repulsion in regard to so-called legacy solutions.

This new generation of IT professionals will place a much greater emphasis on cost-effectiveness, and this is another reason why there will be significant changes in regard to the characteristics of an IT landscape, including skills and projects. This new culture should be welcome because every year companies are spending billions on information technology, but very few boardrooms:

■ know the value of hardware and software their firms acquire
■ or what's the contribution of IT investments to the success of the company's business.

These were the findings of a microfocus study published on October 1, 2007, based on a survey of 250 CIOs and CFOs from companies in five countries: the United States, Britain, Germany, France, and Italy, across all industries. The results of this study are eye opening, as nothing has really changed in the three years since in connection to at least three findings:

■ less than half the interviewed persons had ever valued their IT assets,
■ nearly two-thirds did not know the worth of their software libraries, and
■ 30 percent of respondents had no inkling how much money their companies spent on software each year.

According to another 2007 study, this one by the U.S. Department of Commerce, in spite of absence of cost-benefit analysis, lack of profitability evaluation, and misunderstanding of IT's contribution, spending by American corporations on hardware and software is rising steadily and by a two-digit number. The same mismanagement prevails in Europe as few boards, CEOs, and CFOs appreciate that spending money on IT without return on investment (ROI) is the worst possible solution. All this is happening because:

- the current generation of technologists focuses on acquiring new machines rather than on increasing the cost-effectiveness of installed gear, and
- CIOs and their people pay little attention to the benefit from, and better management of, IT assets—adopting new technology only when and where there is evidence of an excess of benefits over costs.

But as another survey has found, while only 37 percent of CIOs try to quantify and cost technology assets, over 65 percent of CFOs want them to do so. This means that nearly one out of three chief information officers will find themselves confronted with questions about cost-effectiveness of both:

- their present legacy operations and
- cloud computing solutions, which they will be ill-prepared to answer (see also the results of my research in Chapter 3).

The new generation of information technologists, particularly those with a business education, is expected to behave differently. This will be further promoted by the fact that practically all CIOs now confront threats posed by the cloud (Section 5.2)—including threats to their career—of which they are either unaware or unprepared to answer.

For instance, the fact that the infrastructure will be provided as a service will make redundant the computers and databases the CIO currently manages, as well as the people employed to operate them. By contrast, the CIO will be held responsible for two missions, which should have disappeared in the first decade of computer usage but didn't, because too little attention has been paid to organizational studies: *one entry, many uses* of information elements. This is still a dream in data processing.

A little more than a decade ago, it was not unusual to see the same information element input seven or eight times because it belonged to different procedures and had a different format for each of them. Today this number is cut in half but it is still inadmissible. With pay-as-you-do the user organization will be billed by the vendor three or four times for the same input, apart from the fact that such unwarranted redundancy is a major source of errors. Input data have never been 100 percent correct with legacy IT, and *error correction* continues to cost a fortune.

It is not for nothing that I/O costs have been eating about a quarter of the IT budget. Not only do too many people spend their time weeding out errors *after* data collection (which is totally silly business), but also time is spent on computers to catch them. This rotten policy would not be possible with cloud computing and, if done at all, it will bring along inordinate expenditures.

Program bugs, too, fall under a similar constraint. Catching the last bug is still a dream. Input error and program bugs share the fact that a tough challenge in cloud computing is removing and reversing malfunctioning that pops up in very large distributed systems.

Normally with software as a service platform bugs should not be on the radar screen, but they might show up unexpectedly as several onDemand providers developed their routines without using virtual machines either because:

■ they preceded the recent popularity of virtualization, or
■ they did not have internally available virtual machine experts.

Software that gets out of the environment for which it was designed has the nasty habit of coming up with surprises. Even the change in the release of an OS brings up bugs the previous release did not flash out. Problems that filtered through the grid of platform A may come up with a vengeance when platform B is used or when the processing environment is too different, as in the case of VM. (In fact, the interpreter may be stumbling on the bug.)

Hence, while we cannot be sure that the computer as we know it today will disappear, we should appreciate that several practices dating back to the 1950s and 1960s, like I/O bad policies and Cobol, which are pillars of legacy IT, will fade. If they don't, the heralded flexibility and cost containment of cloud computing will take residence in the cuckoo cloud and not in the Internet cloud.

5.2 The CIO's Career Is at Stake

There are two types of threats associated with cloud computing. The one is present with all new technologies and can briefly be stated as missing the chance that might have been. Being afraid to find oneself at the bleeding edge is the typical error made by many when it comes to a decision about adopting a novel solution. Rush without adequate preparation is the other way to mess up things (more on this later).

There are many reasons why traditionalists are set to *miss their chance*. The most frequently heard excuse is that "senior management did not yet make a decision," which usually hides a mixture of fear and ignorance about what the new technology is all about. Other reasons for missing the boat include:

■ lack of clear ideas on how to proceed,
■ inadequate or incomplete preparation, and
■ forcing the tool on the problem, which is itself ill-studied.

There is absolutely no reason to believe that all this will not be repeated with cloud computing. Subutilizing a novel technology is more or less a policy since day one of data processing. An example has been the ill-prepared transition to computers from electrical accounting machines (EAMs).

Studies able to produce commendable results in transition to a new technological environment must cross department lines, but people who want to do a neat job are often told, "Don't touch the fiefs of colleagues." This ends up with mismanagement and with general deception in regard to corporate expectations.

More than in any other time it will be wrong to repeat with cloud computing these past practices because careers are at stake, and this does not allow spending time to preserve the status quo. The coming generation of information scientists, now out of universities, has a different culture than those who preceded it:

- the new graduates are Internet-minded, and
- because of the economic crisis, company management is bent not just to reduce head counts but also to have younger people at lower salaries at the service departments.

Since the beginning of this century, something senior management has brought directly under its watch is profitability and return on investment in IT. This means that without a significant change in concept regarding organization and end user services, a company can be sure of one thing: it will miss the benefits that could be derived from a strategic inflection point, whether or not it adopts cloud computing. (The management of change is the theme of Section 5.3.)

Added to these references is the fact that from the viewpoint of user organizations, the financial advisability of cloud computing solutions is not at all self-evident. This is easily assessed from the uncertainty nowadays embedded in IT budgets.

Budgets are financial plans that, to be approved, require a lot of convincing evidence, and as of recently, they are tightly controlled (as Section 5.4 suggests). In addition, cloud computing essentially means outsourcing of services, and service level agreements (SLAs) often leave much to be desired (as Sections 5.5 and 5.6 document). Closely associated with that is the risk of a lock-in by cloud vendors, as it has happened with mainframes and protocols (Section 5.7).

Chief information officers who care about their careers and future employment are well advised to take notice of these issues. Today the computer is no more the glamour instrument that it used to be. Data processing and telecommunications have become services subject to ROI criteria like any other investment or expenditure.

This does not mean that the CIO must get everything about the cloud right from the start. What it means is that he or she should focus on the fundamental and be well informed in the study of opportunities, risks, and alternatives, which are nearly always around.

- "Me-tooism" is a sin, and this is also true of messing things up.
- By contrast, the careful study of competitive advantages and disadvantages is a virtue.

Here are a few examples on how other brilliant minds miscalculated important events before getting their sight right. "I think there is a world market for maybe five computers," said Thomas Watson Sr., IBM's founder, animator, and chairman, in 1943. "There is no reason anyone would want a computer in their home," suggested Ken Olsen, president, chairman, and founder of Digital Equipment Corp (DEC), in 1977.

Some judgments on IT's aftermath on corporate life are, quite often, tremendously optimistic. "By the turn of this century, we will live in a paperless society," predicted Roger Smith, chairman of General Motors, as late as 1986. Other prognostications regarding technology were very pessimistic. "There is not the slightest indication that nuclear energy will ever be obtainable. It would mean that the atom would have to be shattered at will," Albert Einstein said in 1932.*

Other examples of misjudgment by experts and by companies for which they work have been just startling. "This telephone has too many shortcomings to be seriously considered as a means of communication. The device is inherently of no value to us," stated a Western Union internal memo in 1876. Seven decades later, in 1949, the *New York Times* commented: "The problem with television is that the people must sit and keep their eyes glued on a screen; the average American family hasn't time for it."

These and more quotations from well-known people and firms document that there are no *self-evident truths* in information technology. Every advanced system has to be conceived, evaluated, designed, and tested for reliability, cost, and performance. And every study should be analytical, factual, and documented, which applies hand in glove to the challenge of reengineering the user organization for cloud computing.

As we will see in Chapter 6, an integral part of reengineering is turning systems and procedures out for reasons of simplification, streamlining, and adaptability to the new environment—and massive upgrade of skills. The obsolescence of human resources is nothing new with information technology. What is novel is that companies have at long last started to appreciate that they cannot afford anymore human obsolescence.

In addition, CIOs and IT departments must come to grips with the fact that not only individual skills and those of the organization as a whole wane, but also cloud computing may have unexpected consequences for which the company must have on-hand troubleshooters. For instance, the rising popularity of onDemand application may see to it that:

■ a large part of the cutting-edge software talent from colleges and universities ends up working for cloud companies, and
■ while user organizations will be reducing their head count, they will need some of the best graduates as troubleshooters working for their IT departments.

---

* *Communications of the ACM*, March 2001.

The competition for hiring these people will be tough because cloud computing providers are also facing similar challenges, and over and above them they will confront increasing legal risks. The assignment of legal liability is an example. Cloud providers evidently want legal liability to remain with the customer and not be transferred to them, but clients are not likely to accept that argument.

In addition, different vendors may try to pull the carpet from under their competitors' feet, which also tends to become a legal issue. In March 2007, Dell tried to trademark the term *cloud computing*. The notice of allowance it received in July 2008 was cancelled a week later, resulting in a formal rejection of its application. A different attempt has been to trademark *CloudOS* as an operating system managing the relationship between software inside the computer and on the Internet.

At an epoch when environmental subjects make headlines, two other issues confronting user organization and requirement troubleshooters are the huge amount of energy and cooling (particularly at the infrastructure side) and the so-called cloud computing paradox. The latter needs an explanation.

The paradox arises from the fact that cloud computing is defined as a borderless utility. Technically, it does not matter where the data and programs of the vendor and its clients are stored. But geography still matters (aside from legal constraints in different jurisdictions). Good sites are scarce. Data centers containing the cloud cannot be built just anywhere. They need:

■ dry air,
■ chilly climate,
■ cheap power,
■ fiber optic cables,
■ high security, and
■ right political conditions (and connections).

Part of the risk to be addressed, investigated, and settled in the service level agreement is technical. The cloud vendor cannot be permitted to store a company's data solely at its discretion. Another part of the risk is managerial, and a big chunk of it is legal. Legal risk can be far-reaching.

Personal information will be everywhere, and online crooks easily jump jurisdictions. Therefore, user organizations of cloud computing must think carefully about the pluses and minuses of the cloud's database globalization, which raises a mare's nest of geopolitical issues. With cloud computing the cyberspace is no more a distinct place having, so to speak, laws and legal institutions of its own.

Providers must satisfy complex regulatory environments in order to deliver service to a global market. And if there is a major failure, the CIO's job will be on the block even if it was not his or her fault. In no time cloud hurdles may turn into a no-win/no-win situation.

5.3 Centralization May Be a Foe, Not a Friend

In all classical tragedies, from Aeschyllos to Shakespeare, and from Sophocles to Schiller, the tragic failure of the leading figure has been his inability to change. This is seen, for example, in the destiny of Oedipus as well as in that of Hamlet and (nowadays) myriad companies that, by failing to reinvent themselves, have gone down the drain.

Every great classical tragedy moves an audience not because the latter has been deceived, as by tempting illusion, but because that audience is led to recognize the perils of immobility. The principle encountered in the majority of cases is that of discovery of a different way through intellectual activity, rather than by being submerged in the illusion that:

- nothing changes, and
- we can keep going on as in the past.

By extension, the greatest failure of senior managers (and of political leaders as well) is not in their violation of customs but in the inability or unwillingness to restructure existing concepts, products, and institutions. Their downfall is their lack of initiative to reconnect themselves and their entities to the evolution of their environment—thereby preventing decay and oblivion.

In IT, cloud computing may provide some of the ingredients necessary to change concepts and applications, test new ideas, develop better procedures associated with market opportunities, and serve customers in a way that involves people at all organizational levels. The bet on technology, however, should not be an asymmetric task favoring novelty but paying little attention to quality or failing to control present and future costs.

If this happens, then the user organization has been unable to manage change. IT's history is replete with such examples. The latest comes from Britain's National Health Service (NHS). In mid-August 2009 the Tories (the Conservative Party) said that if they win the next election, they will scrap national electronic patient records—one of the world's biggest civilian projects whose goals are fairly similar to those of the cloud.*

For starters, Britain has been one of the first countries to have fully digital imaging, replacing film x-rays and scans. The system NHS adopted also promoted a rapidly growing number of records being transferred electronically between family doctors' practices when patients move. On paper, this:

- avoided weeks and months of delays and
- weeded out duplicate records in doctors' offices, clinics, hospitals, and government offices.

---

* Moreover, as a case study, NHS's mishandling of information technology is a good example of what Obama's health care should avoid.

Eight years ago, in 2002, when the National Health Service project started, the idea of a full patient record, available anywhere instantaneously in an emergency, was big political selling stuff. The British government called it "the biggest civilian computer project in the world." Theoretically,

- this would have given some 50 million patients a fully electronic record *as if* it were in a cloud database, and
- altogether these records would have created a national database of patients, instantly available in an emergency from anywhere in the country.

Money was no problem, as the taxpayers were asked to contribute it. The NHS cloud database project (among with some other services) was wrapped up in a £12 billion ($19 billion) program that over years struggled to deliver and by 2010 was running more than four years late. Critics say that what went wrong was not too much ambition but:

- too much centralization and
- not enough study of alternatives and therefore choice.

This is highly relevant to all user organizations, including industrial and financial enterprises, contemplating to move their sprawling databases to the cloud. Mismanagement of change contributed to the project's downfall.* And the program's one-size-fits-all central offering did not make matters any better.

In a way replicating (but also preceding) the talk of cloud vendors, British government officials maintained that there were powerful arguments for "economies of scale" if the system was centrally established. The choice was one of multisourcing (sound familiar?), and assurances were given that all these systems would be able to talk to each other.

"Looking back, it was the wrong thing to do," said one of the experts, "It was right to centralize standards for communication and for what should be in the record. It was tight to use centralized purchasing power. But the next step, that the whole program had to be centralized, did not have to flow from that. It proved to be a mistake."†

Centralization of infrastructural and other services is a problem that both cloud computing vendors and user organizations have to confront—not "some time down the line" but now. A great deal in terms of quality results, and therefore marketability and profitability, will depend on how well service delivery coordinates and control at the vendor's side.

---

* Since it was created in the immediate post-WWII years, NHS had more than its share of IT disasters.
† *Financial Times*, August 20, 2009.

Coordination and control often leave much to be wanted. A few days ago a lady from SFR, the second largest telecommunications company in France (to which I am a subscriber), called. She wanted to sell me mobile services.* I told her I was not interested but did want to talk to her boss about the quality of line services, which was substandard. "Oh!" she answered, "that's not my problem" and closed the line. (Many requests have been made to other parties to improve the line but to no avail.)

The salesperson was wrong. Bad quality in line services was her problem because cross-selling is ineffectual when the client is already dissatisfied with one of the company's product lines. If the Googles, Microsofts, Amazon.coms, IBMs, and other vendors take that attitude with cloud computing, they can kiss their investments goodbye.

Precisely for this reason the huge British NHS centralized database fiasco is a warning for cloud vendors as well as for user organizations. When the rate of change inside an organization becomes slower than the rate of change outside, the two get unstuck.

■ Learning to live with change is an act of survival.
■ Change must always be seen as an opportunity, rather than a threat.

The opposite, however, is also true. When the opportunity does not materialize and the benefits become questionable, the fate of a project is sealed. Like individuals and organizations, projects are much more often destroyed from within, and in a more radical way, than from blows from the outside.

When the Tories say that, if elected, they will kill the British database cloud of medical records, they essentially confirm that its insiders have failed to deliver and that its usefulness could only be seen through a magnifying glass. Yet, behind it were some of IT's big names: Accenture, Fujitsu, and CSC BT.† But management was by all evidence wanting.

It is interesting to note that one of the critiques being made is that none of the aforementioned firms was a health IT specialist. But was one needed? The NHS was (theoretically at least) a health specialist. Its consultants and enablers were technology specialists.

What this and other similar experiences suggest is that managing change in an able manner requires a first-class ability to lead, the skill and will to deliver in a short time frame (so that business continuity is not lost), and the ability to communicate obtained results. Managers who wait for alarm bells to go off before they correct their path to reaching their target are not worth their salt.

---

* The holding to which this telco belongs is a huge conglomerate with construction and TV stations among its many activities.
† A decision to cancel the contracts will result in a blow to these firms and in mighty litigation.

In conclusion, managing change successfully begins with the ability to anticipate the future, develop foresight about risks and opportunities, and sell change as a product. Integral to the management of change is the guts to measure deviations that result from incompetence or misjudgments—and take immediate corrective action.

5.4 Budgeting for Cloud Computing

A budget is a formal written statement of management's plans for the future, expressed in quantitative terms. The financial allocations* the budget makes, and the statistics being derived from them, chart the course of future action. Provided that the budget contains sound, attainable objectives rather than mere wishful thinking, it serves as an excellent tool for planning and control.

- The budget is a *planning model*, and the means used for its development are planning instruments.
- *Budgetary control* works well when the company has proper methodology and solid cost data.

Fulfilling the premises of the second bullet will be rather difficult in the first years of cloud computing. The reason why a great deal of attention must be paid to costs is that the whole process of financial planning is based on them. Costing makes the budget an orderly presentation of projected activity for the next financial year,† based on the amount of work to be done.

Several of the knowledgeable people who contributed to the research leading to this book told me: "If you have the funding, you get the technology; and if you have the technology, you control the future."‡ That's true, but to pass the test of the first *if* one must have a plan. Money is no more spent on computers just for "me too" purposes, as it was fifty or even thirty years ago.

In a well-run organization, management appreciates that planning premises entering a budgetary process must serve to increase its ability to rely on fact finding, lessening the role of hunches and intuition in running the enterprise. A factual and documented budget for cloud computing makes possible effective management control, including:

- a profit and loss evaluation vs. the current IT solution, based on information derived from the financial plan and operating statistics, and

---

* According to General Electric rules, a budget allocates money but is not an authorization to spend money.
† Or rolling year, depending on the policy adopted for budgetary control.
‡ It's like the British recipe for cooking rabbits: "first catch the rabbit."

■ other management controls that, among themselves, provide the standards against which actual performance is evaluated and variances monitored.

This needs to be done both for each of the cloud computing services (onDemand software, platform(s), infrastructure, enabling) and for the project as a whole—hence in both a detailed and a consolidated way. An integrative view of accounts is necessary, starting at the system design level, translated into "bill of materials and services" and from there into budgetary premises.

The solution a user organization adopts must provide the basis for budgetary control. Short of this, the water will run under the bridge and nobody will notice. Actual relationships and linkages between individual budgetary elements determine the structure of such financial planning.

It needs no explaining that throwing money at the problem is not going to solve it. Let me use once again as a proxy the British National Health Service, whose cloud database misfired, as we saw in Section 5.3. NHS is one of the pillars of British entitlements, and the public's eyes are focusing on what it does and does not. The NHS is the closest thing the English have to a national religion, Nigel Lawson, a former chancellor, once observed.*

Successive British governments have thrown chunks of the economy at the health problem, to no avail. Even after a huge expansion of the NHS budget over the past decade (spending on health care in Britain now amounts to over 8.4 percent of the gross domestic product [GDP]),† there is a crying need for reforms to bring about better and cheaper care. Everybody wants that, but nobody knows how to do it.

This sort of deeply embedded mismanagement, with a horde of unfulfilled promises on the side, should not be allowed to happen with cloud computing. The way to avoid it is to pay particular attention not only to the money going to the cloud provider but also to the budget for *changeover* from current IT to the cloud—including all of its chapters. Don't ever believe vendors saying "the transition will be smooth and the costs will be easily recovered within a year by savings to be realized from the cloud."

■ It is unavoidable that there is going to be a transition, and this will cost money.
■ Over how long the changeover will spread—the time *t* in Figure 5.1—depends on many factors, from reengineering (Chapter 6) to the pricing of cloud services and the effectiveness of project management.

Astute business executives have found out, some of them the hard way, that ROI in information technology is at its best when planning for it goes hand in hand with organizational change. A study by MIT has looked into the effects of IT investment on the productivity and profitability of firms and found that return on IT investments

---

* *The Economist*, August 22, 2009.
† Which incidentally compares well with the 14 to 16 percent of GDP in America.

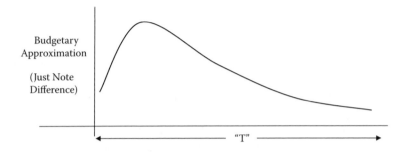

Figure 5.1   The time frame, *t*, of projected budget for changeover to cloud services depends on a great deal of factors, some of which trail in time.

is much bigger in companies that are also prepared to change work practices associated with the way they provide their products and services, as well as the manner in which they administer themselves. The principle is that:

- organizational investments complement IT investments, each feeding on the return of the other, and
- ROI depends most significantly on a culture that promotes flexibility and adaptation to the system changes being introduced.

A valid budget for cloud computing will see to it that organizational change is costed and provided with funds. The same is true of educational expenditures that assist in cultural change. *If* these chapters are skipped over, *then*:

- either the budget is incomplete, or
- nothing is done in reengineering and education, and therefore ROI will be a chimera.

As I will never tire repeating, organizational change, cultural change, flexibility, and adaptation have prerequisites. It is not enough for board members, chief executives, and their assistants to understand what has to be done. They have to make sure that change is forced through, and the funds to management change are available.

The worst return on investment is obtained when companies are using IT purely as a way of doing "more cheaply" the same old things in the same old ways. That's why the argument that "cloud computing will cost less" does not wash. The best ROI is obtained when companies are able to take things apart and find new solutions, which is the role of reengineering:

- turning the organization inside out and
- rethinking the way in which the firm communicates internally and with its business partners.

"It is better to see things once than to hear about them one hundred times," says an old Chinese proverb. If in the cloud computing budget possible savings heralded by the vendor and accepted by the CIO are written down as hard savings, senior management should not buy them. To confirm them, the CEO and CFO should ask to see them materialized next year.

Take the power budget for IT as an example. U.S. companies now spend 10 percent of their information technology budget on electricity consumption. This is expected to rise and equal expenditures made for hardware. To bend the curve, AMD, Dell, HP, IBM, Intel, Microsoft, and Sun launched some time ago the *green grid* consortium, but the deliverables lie at some unspecified time in the future.

Current technological fixes are multicore chips (two or four cores) by AMD and Intel with a criterion of *performance per watt*. These are using direct current (DC) rather than alternate current (AC). DC is more efficient, but there are no standards for a multisupplier policy. Hence, claims about energy savings are premature at best.

A similar statement about promises made today but which would not materialize until some unspecified time in the future is valid about the so-called onDemand use of cooling systems. Sensors, actuators, and expert systems can help. That's great; let them first help, and when they deliver results, we will talk about them in terms of ROI.

The purpose of any organization is to achieve output, says former Intel chairman Andrew S. Grove, whether it is widgets manufactured, bills mailed out, visas processed, or insurance policies sold. "Yet, in one way or another we have all been seduced by tangents and by the appearance of output," Grove suggests.[*]

In conclusion, good governance requires that the budget be used as the basic tool for separating real output from the imaginary. This needs measurements and metrics, precisely the function to be played by a *budget analyzer*, which will track in an objective manner projections that have been made, authorized expenditures, and obtained results. This is of capital importance with outsourcing of services—and therefore with cloud computing.

5.5 Outsourcing, Infrastructural Interdependencies, and the Cloud

In a cloud computing contract, the user organization is the outsoucer and the cloud provider the insourcer. *Outsourcing* is the delegation to another party—the insourcer—of the authority for the provision of services. This is done under a contract that incorporates service level agreements (SLAs; Section 5.6). An SLA must be precise and include quantitative measures and qualitative descriptions of:

- functionality,
- cost,

---

[*] Andrew S. Grove, *Only the Paranoid Can Survive* (New York: Currency Doubleday, 1996).

- quality, and
- timeliness of services

Insourcing is acceptance for rendering specific services, under the above conditions. The insourcer is faced with the challenge of getting it right and the cost of getting it wrong. (Outsourcing and insourcing are not necessarily the best policy for every entity and every service, but this is not the present book's subject.)* Four main problems exist with outsourcing:

1. Cultural. Leading to agency costs (frictions and their aftereffects), as well as subutilization of resources and inordinate expenses.
2. Technical. Technology moves fast, and so does obsolescence in skills, software, hardware, and systems solutions. Constant updating is a steady challenge with all technical issues.
3. Lack of proper methodology and conflicting methodologies. Because of heterogeneity in systems, methods, tools, and languages, as well as backgrounds and line of authority of people assigned to the project.
4. Absence of quality criteria. These should be both quantitative and qualitative, as well as precise and measurable. Moreover, they should be contractually defined between outsourcer and insourcer, which is very rarely the case.

The pros say that outsourcing IT to a cloud provider has the potential to transfer management responsibilities to this party while at the same time reducing costs. This long-haired argument is total nonsense. Risks and responsibilities cannot be delegated by the outsourcer to the insourcer. Instead, both of them are confronted by major risks:

- strategic,
- reputational,
- contractual,
- operational,
- counterparty, and
- exit (more on this later).

Other exposures are country risk and compliance risk.† All of them are present at the same time, because there exists a great lot of infrastructural interdependencies with cloud computing. Indeed, this infrastructural interdependence is critical in practically all applications involving computers, databases, and telecommunications.

---

* D. N. Chorafas, *Outsourcing, Insourcing and IT for Enterprise Management* (London: Macmillan/Palgrave, 2003).

† Basel Committee, "The Joint Forum. Outsourcing in Financial Services," BIS, August 2004.

Electric power is another risk present with both cloud computing and in-house IT. The absence of clean power (which to a substantial extent is not controlled by the cloud computing vendor) can break to pieces the cloud. Telecom equipment and computer facilities require uninterrupted electrical power, and vice versa. Electrical power systems depend on distributed control facilities supported by computers. *Power* is the alter ego of a sophisticated infrastructure, as well as an uncertainty because of its:

■ interdependencies and
■ associated risks.

Such infrastructural interdependence and risks associated with their outsourcing leads many experts to think that a one-sided emphasis on cloud computing is misplaced. It is necessary to study the whole system of in-house IT services and outsourced cloud computing services, judging each one by its costs and risks.

Contrary to what many user organizations and potential users tend to believe, outsourcing is not a relegation of responsibility. Most definitely, it is not a substitute to internal problem resolution. In fact, as in other areas of insourcing/outsourcing, the golden rule is

■ don't outsource a problem you have, and
■ if you have a problem, you fix it first.

The senior management of user organizations should appreciate that it is not possible to outsource its responsibility. The one-off discharge of management's duties and accountability has not yet been invented. Outsourcing is a situation where neither the supplier nor the customer is always right. Therefore,

■ painful decisions have to be made, in terms of outsourcing IT services, and
■ user organizations must appreciate that they cannot sign an outsourcing contract and walk away from it.

What could or would happen in a cloud meltdown is a good example of the challenges confronting the senior management of each company. A dozen years ago, because of a total computer failure of in-house IT resources at the Bank of New York (BNY), the Federal Reserve bailed out the credit institution with a $20 billion loan. That loan cost the commercial bank $50 million. In a 1998 speech, Dr. Alan Greenspan said:

■ *if* the loan could not have been supplied, and
■ *if* other banks simultaneously had the same problem,
■ *then* the entire banking system could have become unstable.*

---

* *Communications of the ACM*, June 1998.

With cloud computing, too, while minor information outages may be common, meltdowns can be very expensive and highly risky—wiping out whole corporations. This is one of the core problems with cloud computing. Reliability must be studied way ahead of any decision to outsource (see Chapter 10).

Other challenges come with multisourcing, which many user organizations consider the better strategy in connection to the cloud. True enough, companies that know how to put into effect a multivendor procurement have been reaping considerable benefits. But *multisourcing* is not a simple process, as it involves:

■ avoidance of duplicating the development and maintenance process,
■ challenges in effectively networking diverse computers and databases with diverse protocols and format,
■ allocation and scheduling difficulties in resource sharing within the user's total system, and
■ efficient operation in spite of differences in terms of support provided by multiple vendors and associated contractual clauses.

There is as well the very important issue of *exit clauses*, which most often is not properly addressed, as if outsourcing always delivers as expected and the outsourcer-insourcer partnership will last forever. A European survey by Gartner has shown that as many as *one in six* outsourcing contracts could be cut short because of unsatisfactory performance.* That's more than 16 percent.

Theoretically the instability of outsourcing/insourcing pays into the hands of the biggest vendors. Practically, big companies, too, may not perform. In the early years of this century, a financial analysis report indicated that Deutsche Bank was saving much less than it expected from its ten-year outsourcing contract with IBM, signed in 2002.† The expected 80 million euros of savings over the life of the contract was cut to 56 million euros, and even that was not sure.

From overly optimistic cost savings to poor deliverables, wanting quality of service, longer than contractual response times, and unacceptable cloud system reliability comes the day the outsourcing contract must end. If the SLA does not include detailed exit clauses, and if the user organization is not ready to take over for the insourcer, a multibillion disaster is the surest outcome.

5.6 Service Level Agreements

A service level agreement is a two-way contract that defines deliverables and their functionality, timing, quality, cost, and associated legal procedures. Because outsourcing contracts can be tricky, it is always advisable to check their clauses with

---

* *Total Telecom Magazine*, December 2003.
† Banca del Gottardo, Market Daily/Stock Market 342.

the user organization's lawyers prior to signing them. Legal issues should include guarantees in regard to:

- dependability of outsourced services;
- operational risk associated with these services;
- contract termination clauses and their reason;
- resolution of eventual conflicts, including conflicts of interest;
- penalties for noncompliance to contractual clauses; and
- the outsourcer's right to inspect facilities and staff of the insourcer.

The issues raised by the first four bullets have already been discussed. Let me explain why penalties for noncompliance are important. *If* penalties are nonexistent or are too low, *then* the insourcer may not care about whether or not it meets headline service levels. Therefore, most definitely:

- SLAs should incorporate an escalation of penalties and
- lead to the option to exit the entire contract for severe or repeated failure.

In addition, as the last bullet in the list points out, user organizations should definitely retain the contractual right to audit the vendor's premises and practices. In case they buy infrastructural services, this becomes an absolute must. The awareness about auditing the insourcers, its premises, and practices has not yet come to life with cloud computing, yet:

- it is important in absolute terms, and
- it is a good way to reduce the likelihood of having to use the exit clauses.

Regulators, too, should be active in auditing insourcers. In the late 1990s, in connection to year 2000 (Y2K) problem, examiners from the Federal Reserve, FDIC, and Office of the Controller of the Currency (OCC) audited all computer firms and service bureaus in the United States that served as insourcers of data processing services to the banking industry—and disqualified some of them.

The need for auditing cloud computing vendors and their premises is strengthened by the fact that such outsourcing-insourcing associations between user and vendor are not expected to be ephemeral and should be looked upon as a partnership. Good accounts make good friends. A prerequisite to auditing a cloud vendor's services, however, is that the user organization is clear about what it expects to *gain* from outsourcing, answering by itself and to itself questions like:

- What do we want to reach through the vendor's cloud computing services?
- Which conditions will bring us from "here" to "there"?
- How do we keep the outsourcing-insourcing partnership in control?
- How do we develop and maintain contingency plans and exit strategies?

Cloud vendors should welcome these clarifications, because they oblige CEOs and CIOs of user organizations to establish clear goals, evaluate risks and benefits from the cloud, review and document their existing operations, and set realistic expectations.

An integral part of a service level agreement for cloud computing must be the vendor's assistance to the user organization, in case the latter wants to transit to a *private cloud*. Such an option is part of an approach known as *surge computing*, which retains the public cloud for providing the extra tasks that cannot be easily run in the private cloud of the user organization due to end-of-month heavy workloads or other reasons. CIOs should nevertheless appreciate that surge computing:

- poses significant coordination problems and
- practically strengthens the probability of lock-ins (Section 5.7).

For all of the reasons presented in the preceding paragraphs, service level agreements should never be signed prior to examining the mistakes made in outcourcing by other user organizations and learning from them. Here is a short list of the most important I encountered in my experience:

1. Failure to focus on what exactly one needs to do in the short, medium, and longer term. For instance, which solution is cheaper *today* is important, but it only addresses part of the problem. The medium to longer term should also be part of a well-documented cost-benefit picture.
2. Decoupling cloud computing solutions from business strategy. Invariably, leaving aside the user organization's strategic goals or downplaying them leads to the wrong business model, which results in lost business opportunities and compliance and legal risks.
3. Overreliance by senior management on vendor promises. Examples are failure to look at the insourcer's support policies with other user organizations, survivability, methodology, level of technology, human resources, and more. The result is badly chosen criteria for cloud provider choice.
4. Failing to test stated advantages, beyond cost savings, and to account for pitfalls. Pitfalls are not just a nuisance. They have associated with them delays, costs, and risks that are important parts of the go/no-go picture. Failure to integrate them into a cloud decision is tantamount to going with the herd in outsourcing vital services. There is a snake pit of risks associated with such practices.
5. Little or no attention is paid to contract termination problems. The need for exit clauses has been discussed in Section 5.5. The shortfall resulting from their absence goes all the way from backup services to legal risk. Because the termination of SLAs for cloud computing is going to be a very painful exercise, I strongly recommend that the service level agreement also incorporate penalties for noncompliance, as has already been discussed.

In conclusion, the user organization should never give the cloud vendor, or any vendor for that matter, the feeling that the outsourcer-insourcer relationship is a blank check. This, for instance, happens when the vendor of cloud computing services, or its representatives, senses that the outsourcing organization is eager to transfer the *ownership* of a business process to the insourcer(s)—or that the user organization will consider the transfer of control.

5.7 Is Cloud Computing a Lock-In Worse than Mainframes?

The message of the previous two sections is that service level agreements should be explicit on both the threats and opportunities connected with cloud computing. One of the threats we have not spoken of so far is the risk that the cloud locks in the user organization to the vendor's wares. It has happened over several decades with mainframes, and it is likely to happen again.

Indeed, there are legitimate reasons to worry about this possibility. Who will be the cloud service providers most successful in locking in clients tells a great deal about who is going to eat whom at the cloud level; that is, at the very top of the food chain.

Far from being theoretical, questions regarding lock-in deserve a great deal of attention. Critics compare policies followed with cloud computing to those with mainframes in the 1950s, 1960s, and 1970s. Overwhelmed by a storm of proprietary protocols, data formats, and languages, users had no freedom to install new applications on more cost-effective equipment provided by other vendors. Recompilation overhead* and other expenditures:

■ limited their freedom of action and
■ increased in a significant way their costs.

One of the lock-in risks with cloud computing is connected to application programming interfaces (APIs). Because they have not been subjected to standardization, APIs for cloud computing are largely proprietary, with the result that user organizations cannot easily extract their programs and data in one process to run on another. This works to the user's disadvantage.

Anecdotal evidence suggests that concern about the difficulty of extracting information elements from one vendor's cloud to use in another's is preventing

---

* Even Cobol, supposedly a universal programming language, had versions tied to the vendor. For one vendor it was "data is," for another "data are." Compiling had to be done twice—in this particular case, once for IBM computers and again for Honeywell computers, and along with manual intervention, this increased the cost of in-house applications software by about 27 percent.

some organizations from adopting cloud computing. I think to this concern should be added another one, which is king size: policies urgently needed to deal with data decay on magnetic and optical supports (see also Chapter 4).

During the last decade computer user organizations, which practically means all companies, have been confronted with the challenge to keep a step ahead of data decay, over and above the fact that their databases have been exploding. Since the late 1990s they have been creating new databases just to decipher information on mag tapes, mag disks, and optical disks. Together with government agencies, many companies looked into:

- durability tests and
- standards for digital media, which did not come on-stream as expected.

The problems connected to data decay are not limited to time and cost associated with transcriptions. Information can be lost or corrupted as it is transferred periodically from one media or computer system to another. The better-managed companies have made *media preservation* a priority, when considering computer systems. But statistics are disquieting, as Table 5.1 shows.

Notice that superior quality estimates presented in this table are mainly based on assumptions concerning storage conditions and frequency of usage. For instance, that storage media is accessed infrequently while it is stored under optimal conditions, which is rarely the case. Typically, storage is awfully misused.

The message brought to the reader through the preceding paragraphs should also be interpreted by keeping in mind the amazing annual growth in data storage and the cost of managing it. In the United States, capital investment for databases stands at 80 percent or more of IT expenditures for hardware—a rapid step up over the last fifteen years, as shown in Figure 5.2.

Table 5.1   Decay of Storage Media

	Standard Quality	*Superior Quality*
Magnetic Tape Formats		
3480, 3490, 3490E types	5 years	20 years
Optical Disks		
CD-ROM	5 years	50 years?
Magneto-optical	2 years	30 years?
Microfilm		
Archival usage	50 years	100 years?

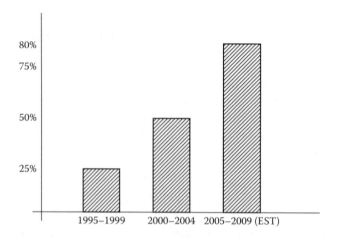

Figure 5.2 The rapid growth in spending for computer storage as percentage of bought hardware.

Some estimates bring the cost of managing online storage to over three hundred dollars per gigabyte per year, including tuning and backups. It needs no explaining that this is expensive, given that *petabyte* online memories are no more an undocumented hypothesis. The financial industry is leading the data storage explosion, but it is also the least likely to want to release its information elements to cloud providers because of:

- security,
- confidentiality, and
- probable legal cost reasons.

That's the case of what is called a double whammy: data decay problems multiply while the required amount of storage capacity explodes. Efforts to increase longevity are not uncommon, but still, the better policy is regeneration and reregistration. This confronts the management of user organizations considering cloud computing with two questions:

1. Should the cloud provider be asked to fulfill that task? If yes, what sort of guarantees does the user organization have that it will not become massively dependent on the cloud computing vendor? Data lock-in is a different but deeper issue than being constrained by using applications and enabling services that the cloud provider offers.

   In attempting to answer this query, the CEO and CIO of the user firm should factor in their equation that consumer lock-in is an attractive strategy to cloud computing providers—and specifically in the use of databases, customers become vulnerable to price increases. In fact, the greater the lock-in of its customers, the more the cloud services vendor will be inclined to increase his price list through different gimmicks presented as quality or service upgrades.

2. What kind of assurance is provided by the cloud vendor that decay of storage media is confronted in a dependable and cost-effective manner? This query brings squarely into the picture the need for auditing of the vendor's premises, systems, and procedures, legally guaranteed by clauses in the SLA contract (Section 5.6). The quality and persistence of a solution providing assurance from data decay matter as much as the price to be paid, if not even more. Therefore, user organizations should not go for the lowest cost but also consider the degree of data dependability guarantees provided by the cloud vendor.

The risks outlined in these paragraphs should not be confused with data security (Chapter 9), but they have a good deal to do with reliability (Chapter 10), in the broader sense of the cloud computing vendor–user organization relationship. Therefore, we will return to these issues, albeit from a different perspective.

Chapter 6

Reengineering the User Organization

6.1 Strategic Objectives and Reengineering

There is nothing permanent in strategic goals. In the 1960s the height of fashion in business was corporate diversification through mergers and acquisitions (M&A). Size was regarded as a criterion of excellence, and the drive was to grow fast. When the legendary Tex Thorton, CEO of Litton Industries, was asked why he aggressively bought other firms, he answered: "We don't buy companies, we buy time."

A decade later things changed, as even big corporations became prey to mergers and acquisitions. This gave rise to a different reason why companies engaged in M&As (along with "poison pills"): defense against predators. Size and diversification through acquisitions were no more the number one strategic goal; they became a form of insurance, with a second criterion of synergy-driven growth.

At the end, as it always happens with big size (whether we talk of empires or corporations), the warlords got tired or faded away and their very big entities became unmanageable.* By the 1980s mammoth size and wide diversification were no more in favor. The success of corporate raiders such as Carl Icahn and T. Bone Pickens has shown that many companies are worth more in pieces than as a whole.

In the (then) new culture, entrepreneurial managers organized leveraged buyouts (LBOs) and active shareholders encouraged senior executives to sell off

---

* It will happen with cloud computing as well, given its projected size.

businesses that were worth more to others. Far from being a friend, size suddenly become an enemy, and the better-managed conglomerates found it necessary to undertake defensive restructuring. In the 1990s, this was followed by the downsizing strategy and *reengineering*—the turning of the organization inside out with the dual goal to:

- slim down and
- find new synergies *within* the enterprise.

Sound governance followed Samuel Johnson's (1709–1784) advice, who once said: "I know not anything more pleasant, or more instructive, than to compare experience with expectation, or to register from time to time the difference between idea and reality. It is by this kind of observation that we grow daily less liable to be disappointed." In this way we also grow:

- wiser and
- better focused.

Focused business came into fashion in the last decade of the twentieth century, with some experts advising that diversification had done more to destroy shareholder value than to create it. Even former fans of giant corporations started to praise smaller firms. Having helped to train generations of middle managers in how to leverage, some companies practiced de-leveraging as a strategic decision.

All that did not last long. Leverage took off with the dotcoms in the late 1990s. After the year 2000 bust, both trends—"smaller is beautiful" and "leverage hurts"— have been reversed. The result has been the 2007–2009 deep economic crisis, where big banks fell on their swords, and it took an inordinate amount of public debt to pull them out of their self-engineered descent to the abyss.

With this, the concept of reengineering is back in fashion, appealing to executives who adopted the policy of rethinking and redesigning their enterprises and IT systems (Section 6.2). Well-governed entities developed new information technology paradigms as well as basic business practices like product development and customer service, and other lines of business required quick execution. Reengineering brought improvements in productivity, quality, cost reduction, and customer satisfaction. Some companies, however, missed the opportunity to regenerate their systems and procedures. Either they stuck with their crumbling structure or the reengineering job they did was ill-directed or half-baked.

The CEO, CIO, and their immediate assistants had a poor understanding of what reengineering meant. This violated the cardinal principle that change is impossible unless managers know how to organize, deploy, enable, measure, and reward value-added operations—as well as how to overcome resistance to change (Chapter 5).

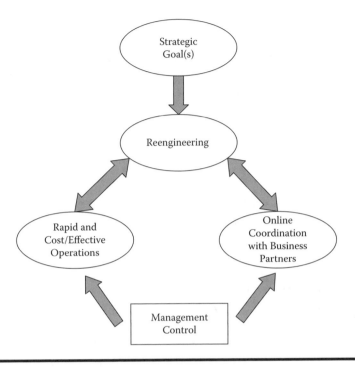

Figure 6.1 Able solutions supporting corporate strategy must have globality and benefit from reengineering and therefore from technology.

Companies that missed the opportunity to profit from new developments shared the wrong belief that throwing money at technology would produce miracles. That's a false premise. Technology is at the service of reengineering, which comes first, not vice versa. The simplified diagram in Figure 6.1 presents the reader with a method that has successfully passed real-life tests:

- reengineering serves specific strategic goals, and
- management control over reengineering's deliverables should practically know no pause.

Successful reengineering projects require clear-cut top management decisions as well as execution skills. The lack of either or both has been a stumbling block to nearly every initiative to gain the upper ground in competition. The challenge of corporate renewal is so much greater when we talk about reengineering in connection to a strategic inflection point—an example being the advent of cloud computing.

If the watch of senior management wanes, then the same mistakes of the past will be repeated time and again. This will do away not only with the competitive edge but also with cost reduction in IT. With cloud computing reengineering is not an option. It is a prerequisite. Migrating data from legacy applications into the cloud (Sections 6.5 to 6.7) is a tough job, and it is not a one-time task either, as some pundits say.

Though specific issues vary from one company to the next, the way to bet is that the amount of effort for streamlining systems and procedures will be significant, and the ability to do so should be a basic factor in deciding to use the cloud. True enough, this task is already spawning new opportunities for firms providing data integration across public and private clouds (Chapter 2), but relegating the mission of reengineering to insourcers (Chapter 5) without the company's own personnel playing an active part in it is highly unadvisable.

While teaching his students at UCLA the principles of statistical quality control (SQC), Ed Coleman made frequent references to Professor Uri of Columbia University, who led the quality assurance program of the Manhattan Project. Uri instructed his assistants, Coleman included, that they should not take the red carpet way in inspecting a factory working on atomic bomb parts and components but visit the back alley and study the rejects.

The same is true of reengineering and any other issue connected to the management of technology. As already mentioned, not all projects in restructuring and reengineering have been successful. In many cases money has been thrown at the problem—evidently with no results. That many reengineering efforts fail seems depressing—the reason being that not all CEOs and CIOs appreciate that success or failure is determined by:

■ a company's understanding of the process and its demands and
■ the ability to execute reengineering in a way that the whole firm is committed to it.

Achieving synergy requires an ingenious sales, rather than flat orders, effort coupled with the determination to overcome hurdles and show results. The primary causes of reengineering failures fall into four groups. One is what General Maxwell Taylor called "the uncertain trumpet": *if* the board and CEO do not know what they want to achieve through the cloud, *then* nothing will be achieved.

Whether or not cloud computing services should be used is a strategic decision—and the first to be made. Benefiting from onDemand software (Chapters 11 to 13) means abandoning the (wrong) past policies of massaging packages. Therefore, it makes sense to spend time and energy on analysis of the current organization. Since reengineering entails discarding current process designs, plenty of procedural detail is destined for the rubbish heap—the challenge is to decide which. It is easy to fall victim to a protracted analysis, postponing that fateful day when sweeping changes have to be made.

Part of protracted organization studies is the Santa Claus syndrome—trying to have goodies ready for everybody to sooth resistance or, alternatively, avoid stepping on toes. The clear result is timidity in redesign, stretching the reengineering program over a lengthy time frame while failing to focus on value-creating processes. Reengineering expertise is by itself not enough to guarantee success. It takes committed executive leadership to get results.

At the heart of the deadly sin of indecision is failure to appreciate that successful reengineering entails sweeping change to an organization—a job many companies try to avoid, just hoping that they can do without it. When the operating procedures are rethought, virtually every aspect of the company is up for reevaluation—that's reengineering's most basic premise. Reevaluation should regard the content of each job, deliverables it must produce, structure it should adopt, and mechanisms for reward if the effort is successful.

A thorough reevaluation will lead to new cultural norms that govern attitudes and behavior. As Chapter 5 brought to the reader's attention, an organization's culture must be consistent with the ways in which the mission of the firm, including everybody's daily work, can be performed more cost-effectively than under the present solution. That's where the cloud comes in—if it does.

6.2 Organizational Solutions Are No Sacred Cows

Any reengineering project targeting cloud computing, whether this concerns the internal or external cloud, must pay great attention to the fact that all sorts of applications are data intensive and continue becoming even more so. Not only does this significantly complicate reliability and security associated with data placement, access, and transport, but it also calls for the greatest care associated with:

- size of data storage and
- data traffic at nearly every level of the system functions.

If after adopting computing the company intends to continue expanding storage requirements at the currently prevailing levels discussed in Chapters 4 and 5, *then* surely what it needs is *not* a rush to the cloud. If I were given a choice, my first, second, and third choices would be reengineering and restructuring data storage needs at every layer of the organization without worrying about the cloud but concentrating on a thorough and deep restructuring.

These ever-growing trillions of information elements and files don't exist in the abstract or by an act of God. They are connected to departments and functions in the organization. That is exactly where the reengineering study should start making sense, by combining them and simplifying them. This should be done fast, like in an audit.*

---

* D. N. Chorafas, *IT Auditing and Sarbanes-Oxley Compliance* (New York: Auerbach/CRC, 2009).

- An IT audit challenges not just cost but also, if not primarily, lines of authority and responsibility—hence organizational solutions.
- Organizations are made of people; as people and functions change, chosen solutions become obsolete or outright wrong.
- The principle is that no organizational status quo or its details are a sacred cow to an audit and therefore to reengineering.

When a company asks me to conduct an audit of its technology status, my bet is that there is more than a 90 percent chance it has allowed both its headquarters and its operations worldwide to maintain separate, functionally duplicative systems supporting operational and reporting requirements for its various business components. This has two effects:

- it multiplies its files by a factor n, sometimes an order of a magnitude, and
- it makes up a highly heterogeneous environment in collecting, analyzing, and processing data.

Another educated guess dictated by experience, and supported by the facts, is that the company's management has asked for an audit if that consolidation of information elements never took place. Maybe the CEO or CFO asked for it, but never got it. Subordinate business units feeding information upstream—a job quite often done manually in spite of huge amounts of money spent on IT—just did not care to execute orders from headquarters, and they found the political clout to do away with orders from above.

Duplication and triplication of files cost dearly in expenses and delays. Even if costs are left aside, there is the problem of accuracy in stored data. Under these conditions, their consistency and accuracy become practically impossible to control—a situation that should definitely be corrected through reengineering prior to joining the cloud.

Many people say that the need to reengineer a major part of the company's database infrastructure is not self-evident. This is wrong, but it explains why one of the key questions facing companies today, to which there are no easy answers, is How long after a thorough restructuring of information elements and files should we go ahead with a new reengineering effort?

There is no universal answer to this query. The IT audit should provide a factual reply, within the realities of the environment within which it takes place. The only general remark is that practically every company today has, at least in some part of its operations, legacy data processing from the 1970s and even the 1960s.

- These have exhibited a crying need for restructuring, but typically the decision has been repeatedly postponed.
- With outsourcing infrastructural chores to the cloud, however, IT's inflection point works as a catalyst to finding what it takes in data organization.

There is simply no alternative to making the *organization of the company's database* state of the art through reengineering: weeding out duplicates, setting and using file standards, and making it integrated, highly functional, reliable, flexible, accessible in a seamless way, and able to be operated at reasonable cost.

Another crucial question that I have frequently encountered in my work is whether it is avoidable that the transition period to a new IT environment is inhibiting the IT personnel from performing its daily work. There is no doubt that there must be no interruption in services, and all end users should be guaranteed a seamless transition. This becomes difficult when the changeover project is not properly planned. In principle, the speed and expense associated with reengineering systems and procedures depend upon:

- how the work is organized and led,
- the skill of the people being employed,
- the ability to utilize relevant approaches attained by other firms, and
- linkages connecting older and newer systems until the former are weeded out.

The effort should be company-wide because historically, corporate information is kept in many places and in many forms. In addition, while a great wealth of data are stored on a company's computer system, there are also other media around, such as paper and microfilm.

Neither are all data on storage readily accessible and easy to find. With legacy software, data retrieval procedures are time consuming and not user-friendly. There may also be massive ongoing errors that should most definitely be identified and corrected through reengineering. *If* error sources are left as they presently stand in a cloud environment, *then* they will paralyze the user organization and bring its operation to a halt.

In addition, to provide a dependable picture in respect to data sharing requirements in a multisourcing deal, the reengineering effort must determine how the vendors' different application programming interfaces (APIs) are used in connection to cross-platform information elements. Inevitably, this impacts the company's IT environment.

Internal company politics, too, must be handheld in an ingenious way. It is not unlikely that those doing the reengineering work will encounter negative reactions, even by people who profess that cloud computing is the way to go. Entrenched interests may not only be reluctant to accept a downsizing of their systems and procedures (and budgets) but also try to prolong to infinity the reengineering work.

- Company politics are present no matter what one is doing; that's not news to people who have tried to improve organization and structure.
- Precisely for this reason, I have underlined that *if* reengineering does not get 100 percent support by the board and CEO, *then* cloud computing will end in cloud cuckoo land.

Compromises lead nowhere. A project that is not well done is no project at all. In a well-done reengineering project descriptions of processes and data models address the conceptual and logical dimensions of enterprise information, transforming data formats prevailing in diverse and incomparable legacy systems into a seamless virtual environment (Chapter 4).

The complexity of the job may be increased by the unique characteristics of the user organization's legacy system(s). It is, however, proper to remember that with the Y2K challenge of the late 1990s, those companies benefited from the investments they made to use it as an opportunity to reengineer their IT—and sometimes the firm.

Another issue to be kept in mind is that there is no such thing as an *a priori* success, as some people are professing. But there are *a priori* failures, when the project starts on the wrong foot. In the nearby six decades of computer applications, there has been a swarm of IT project fiascos:

- nearly a third of new IT projects have been *cancelled* before completion, at an estimated combined cost of billions, and
- more than one out of two projects that have been completed were almost 200 percent or more over budget, at an additional cost of billions.

These cases occur regularly in all sorts of companies and all in-house IT projects, and they are due to many factors: lack of senior management involvement, making projects vulnerable; fuzzy project goals, sometimes because of compromises; lack of reengineering; weak composition of project teams in a skills sense; lack of leadership; and senior management's acceptance of steadily slipping time to completion and escalating project costs. Keep all that in mind when thinking about cloud computing.

6.3 The Number One Asset Is Human Resources at the CIO Level

The way an article in the *Daily Telegraph* put it, one of Marshall Montgomery's outstanding contributions before D-Day was his careful meshing of experienced veterans from the Eighth Army* with the keen but green formations that had been training for so long in England and wanted to see action. An old desert hand, Major General G. P. B. "Pip" Roberts found his new headquarters at 11th Armored Division still operating the routines and mess life of the peacetime British army. Without any loss of time he:

---

* Of El Alamein war glory.

- relieved them of such formalities;
- sacked his senior staff officer, a meticulous guardsman*; and
- with Montgomery standing squarely behind him, thoroughly reengineered the organization under his command.

This went hand in hand with reassignments. At the beginning of 1944, all the senior officers were abruptly removed and replaced by others from a quite different world. The exercises and war games, too, changed. Montgomery used his veterans to drill the new recruits to real-life war rather than colonial era (legacy) exercises.

For hours and days at a stretch officers and soldiers of the British army preparing for the invasion of Nazi-held Europe shivered in their tanks on the hills through endless mock attacks and deployments. This had been for them a new experience, but the fact remains that when D-Day came, they did the work that they were sent to do.

Let this be a lesson for all officers and soldiers in the IT department of user organizations getting ready to join the computing cloud. A principle taught by experience is that companies (and persons) who advance faster are successful not because they know so much more in every subject, but because they learned:

- how to exercise and bring themselves up to speed,
- how to formulate the problems accurately, and
- how to channel the needed information and drive for reaching a successful solution.

This is precisely the contribution the Eighth Army veterans made to the joint formations that were learning and looking into what it takes to land at and take over German-held fortress Europe. This is as well the contribution veterans in reengineering and in the transition from the old system solution to the new should bring to the effort, briefly described in Sections 6.1 and 6.2.

Nothing can be achieved without first-class human capital; therefore, the people put in a project should be first-raters. But this is by no means true only of IT projects. A study done by Bankers Trust in the late 1980s, at the peak of its night, documented that the greatest assets of a bank are not the money and other wealth in its vaults but people and people. People its clients and people its employees. I should have rather written "well-trained people," which is a never-ending process because knowledge wears out. It decays if we don't use it. With this in mind, some years ago John F. Kuemmerle, senior vice president/administrator of Guardian Life Insurance Co., remarked that computer people's skills can quickly become obsolete and, to counter that, they should spend a good part of their time learning.

Few companies follow this policy, yet without it the implementation of advanced solutions is going to be defective at best. Kuemmerle's statement about

---

* Who had put a red light over his office door to indicate that he did not wish to be disturbed.

spending a big chunk of one's time learning is valid all the way from the CEO to the CFO, the CIO, his analysts, and programmers. Take onDemand software vs. onPremises software as an example of what needs to be relearned in a different way than in the past.

Traditionally, the policy of company-developed and -owned software allowed the information technology people to deploy applications specific to the ongoing business through custom-made and customized code. The former was developed wholly in-house, and the latter by altering purchased applications packages. A timetable of two to three years was a classic in either case. Quite often,

- bought software was changed so much that at the end it had nothing to do anymore with the vendor's version, and
- this meant a great expense and significant delay in implementation, along with the impossibility of assigning the maintenance to the vendor.

What has been part and parcel of traditional IT culture is no more possible with onDemand software bought from the cloud. OnDemand applications are on rental, and the code sits external to the user organization. Such application routines are shared with a number of cloud customers who will not take it kindly if one of the other users tries to change something (even if it could do so).

Now take the case of a bank that has found an integrative risk management program from one of the cloud computing vendors and thinks about implementing it. Its current IT support for risk control features the ten subsystems shown in Table 6.1. Some are legacy and still batch; others are real-time or can only provide flashbacks in real time.

This has indeed been a real-life case. With bought software the CIO just provided bridges between subsystems, keeping the backbone batch. The batch characteristics prevailed even if some packages which were bought worked in real time.

For instance, the *currency exchange risk* bought software helped the traders in terms of transactions and inventorying of positions. But it did not provide real-time information on counterparty risk (which was batch). For its part, the *interest rate risk* procedure covered only the money market and contributed some information regarding unmatched positions, but this concerned just futures and options:

- swaps associated to longer-term commitments were batch, and
- balance sheet information was updated as of last year.

Say then, and this is a hypothesis, that under these conditions the bank is joining cloud computing. Its first challenge to select vendors should be software onDemand which covers all subsystems in Table 6.1 with real time execution. This, however, is not generally appreciated. To the contrary, most CIOs think of three options:

Table 6.1 Ten Subsystems for Risk Control with a Current Legacy Solution

Applications Programs	IT Status
Counterparty risk	Batch
Interest rate risk	Partially real time
Exchange rate risk	Partially real time
Credit risk (default likelihood)	Batch
Investment risk	Batch
Event risk	Nothing available
Position risk	Real time
Sales conditions risk	Limits only/batch
Funds transfer risk	Batch
Transaction processing risk	Real time

1. buy only infrastructural services from the cloud to relegate the database and its management;
2. forget about cloud computing and continue limping along with the legacy support, which after many years might be improved;
3. engage immediately in thorough reengineering regarding all systems and procedures, evidently including the aforementioned ten risk management subsystems.

The first is a dreadful choice because it combines the worst of two worlds: Paleolithic applications software with patches held together by scotch tape and all of the uncertainties of cloud computing's infrastructure. Anybody choosing that solution should be consulting his or her psychologist.

The second alternative is just postponing the day of truth, and the more that day is pushed out in time, the more expensive and the more complex will become the needed reengineering job. It should be evident that the third solution is the best; the big question, however, is if the CIO can execute it.

Maybe he or she would if he or she gets trained and is careful enough to train his or her people, as John F. Kuemmerle suggested, blending in some Eighth Army veterans from the cloud vendor's enabling services or an outside consultancy. If not, then the CEO should act like Marshall Montgomery, bringing in G. P. B. "Pip" Roberts and firing the old guard. Short of that, you better forget about cloud computing. You will be eaten up alive.

6.4 Promoting Greater Productivity through Reorganization

A different way of looking at the message in Section 6.3 is that computers and communications, as a system, must be learned not in the sense of machines but rather in that of a generic aspect of industrial and cultural life. And it should be updated fast enough, as the facts of real life rapidly change. True enough, the traditional approach is to look at IT as an introvert subject reserved to the system specialist. This is, however, deadly obsolete, and therefore the wrong way.

Technology is an *enabler*; it is not a goal, just like an airplane is not an objective. Computer technology is a *means* for doing specific processing jobs; likewise, the airplane is a means for transportation. Before boarding an airplane we must decide where we want to go. The same is true when we are using technology—new or old. What do we wish to reach?

Say that our goal is to improve the productivity of our firm. Can cloud computing help in this direction? To answer this query in a factual manner, we should return to the fundamentals, looking at what promotes productivity. Such promotion has four components:

- speed of innovation,
- pace of capital investment,
- quality of the workforce, and
- a variable driven by the business cycle.

The first three have longer-term impacts and are the real determinants of ongoing productivity growth under direct control of senior company management. By contrast, the fourth component is exogenous and its impact is shorter term, following a sinusoidal curve.

- In an expansion, productivity takes off as firms use their existing staff more effectively before hiring new workers.
- But as an economy slows, companies don't fire workers immediately. Hence, productivity slows.
- Then starts a sharp increase in unemployment and (in a way, surprisingly so) productivity starts taking off.

For instance, according to published information, U.S. productivity increased by 6.1 percent in July 2009 but not because of new technology, as Alan Greenspan so often said in the 1990s. Instead, in 2009 productivity was promoted by big job cuts, which made the remaining workers and employees work faster. Altogether in the second quarter of that year:

- output per hour increased by 6.4 percent,
- hours worked per person shrank by 7.6 percent, and
- unit labor costs went down by 5.8 percent.*

This was a year of deep financial crisis. What one expects from good governance, and from the able use of technology, is to keep on improving productivity without the assistance of stress conditions. Many companies do so, as shown by statistics provided by William D. Cohan from one and the same company but from different locations (albeit from 1985, but the day is much less important than the huge difference in results):

- Lazard Frères in New York employed 400 people and earned $137,500 per employee.
- Lazard Brothers in London employed 600 people and earned $22,500 per employee.
- Lazard Frères in Paris employed 350 people and earned $20,000 per employee.†

In one of the companies for which I was consultant to the board, a productivity audit revealed a similar one-to-seven difference among the sales engineers. Plenty of reasons may be behind such huge deviations in delivered results, though both management and technology play a good part. Other examples come from the automobile industry. Toyota and a couple of other Japanese companies, like Honda, have consistently exhibited three advantages over Detroit's Big Three:

- fast time to market,
- better quality, and
- greater factory productivity.

The latter is particularly evident in their efficient assembly plants. The steady reorganization and reengineering these factories went through sees to it that they steadily take less man-hours to build a vehicle than their American and European competitors. The score stands for Toyota at less than thirty hours compared to over forty hours for less productive factories. This is representing a cost advantage for the Japanese of up to nine hundred dollars a vehicle.

There is as well the so-called Baumol's disease (named after William J. Baumol of New York University) to account for. Baumol's hypothesis is that jobs in which productivity does not increase substantially over time tend to wind up as part of government. Examples are the postal service, sanitation functions, and the perform-

---

* Data from U.S. Bureau of Labor Statistics.
† William D. Cohan, *The Last Tycoons* (New York: Doubleday, 2007).

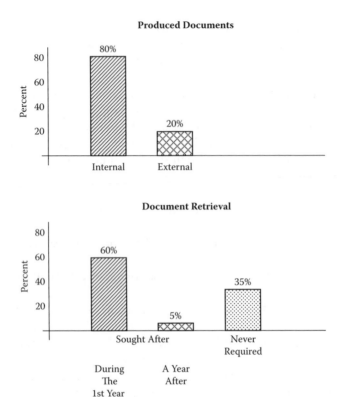

Figure 6.2 Document production and handling of a company for internal and external uses.

ing arts that were once private but came to depend on government funding, because they had not been able to become more productive (recently joined by GM).

At the roots of Baumol's disease lies the fact that as socially useful enterprises cease to become more productive and lose out in the marketplace, the government steps in with funding and eventually takes them on to keep them going. This further demotes the "taken over" products and services into a nonproductive status, which continues living through handouts of public money.

The mismanagement of information has much to do with lower productivity as people spend time in trivia and in searches for documents. Indeed, in spite of huge IT expenses, companies continue producing useless amounts of paper. Figure 6.2 shows some interesting statistics from a study that concentrated on excess paperwork—whether printed or stored on computers:

■ Four out of five documents were for internal consumption only.
■ Over a third of those filed were never required, while a year after their production the share of documents never required rose to 95 percent.

Table 6.2 Efficiency and Effectiveness

Efficiency	Effectiveness
Doing a given job at least possible: • Cost • Time	Deliverables meeting goals in a most able manner

Inefficiency in document handling is a general rule, but it is unevenly spread in an entity. Some parts of the organization are worse violators than others. In a bank, the back office provides an example of urgently needed IT restructuring. One of the major reasons for falling behind in the use of technology is the split in emphasis:

■ front desks get real-time support, while
■ back offices remain with medieval technology.

Theoretically, but only theoretically, efficiency in the use of physical resources, such as IT gear, is not the same thing with the human resources productivity. This is untrue, however, because the two subjects correlate. The same statement is valid for efficiency and effectiveness, whose exact definitions are given in Table 6.2. In fact, they correlate so much that often the two terms are used interchangeably.

It is therefore a legitimate requirement on the side of user organizations that the cloud computing vendor demonstrates how efficiently it uses the physical resources that it provides as a service; for instance, how efficiently the cloud vendor's disk storage is being used.

Today, in the average among IT shops, only 6 percent of server capacity is efficiently used; another 30 percent contains garbage nobody bothered to remove. Cloud computing providers are most elusive in answering questions on how they will be improving these ratios without reengineering the client company and its legacy information technology solutions. Promises have short legs. The user organization:

■ should ask for facts and
■ should have them verified through a hands-on examination.

For all these reasons I would suggest a series of real-life tests of offers by cloud computing providers. As for productivity, let them study the working pattern of *our* company and come up with an offer that qualifies and quantifies productivity improvements. This must become part of the deliverables contractually guaranteed by the service level agreement (SLA; Chapter 5).

The references made in the preceding paragraphs are written in appreciation of the fact that the productivity challenge is present in every enterprise. Cloud computing should never be adopted because of fashion but because of documented results—particularly improvement of factors that count greatly.

A fact always present is that to improve its competitive position, a company needs to significantly increase its productivity. The way an article in the *Economist* had it,* there are plenty of reasons why productivity is kept low:

- regulation of product markets,
- rigidity of labor markets, and
- too much legacy information technology.

Restructuring, and not the label *cloud computing* per se, addresses the reason in the last bullet. It is normal that the user organization should expect significant improvements by way of a more sophisticated use of IT, but these will not come through labels or wishful thinking.

6.5 The Transition from Legacy to Competitive Systems

If cloud computing is chosen by a user organization as its IT solution, whether this decision centers on onDemand software and platforms or extends into infrastructural services, plenty of challenges will face the CIO in the transition from legacy system(s) to the new environment. This is indeed a demanding task, most particularly so if the user organization wants to migrate its database (in whole or in part) to the cloud infrastructure. Because of this, the project must be

- properly planned,
- executed with an iron hand, and
- effectively controlled in all its aspects: quality, cost, and time being at the top of the list.

This transition should be seen as an integral part of reengineering, because it meshes with reorganization and restructuring in practically many of its aspects. Details on how to proceed vary from company to company, and for this reason it has been a deliberate choice to treat the process of transition through a generic approach, leaving to the user organization the task of adapting it to its own circumstances.

A couple of examples from past failures help in bringing the reader's attention to the risks associated with the transition. They also document that when the conversion of legacy systems into new technology is done half-heartedly, or through half-baked methods, the results are a disaster.

In early 1997, after many years and $4 billion spent, the U.S. Internal Revenue Service (IRS) software modernization program descended to hell. The IRS's widely heralded IT project came to an end after extensive criticism from the General Accountability Office (GAO) and the National Research Council. The decision

---

* *The Economist*, October 7, 2009.

to opt out was taken following a revaluation by the National Commission on Restructuring the IRS, which convinced the tax authority to abandon its Tax System Modernization effort.

A GAO report blamed the IRS's failure in the transition to new technology on mismanagement and shoddy contracting practices. It also identified security problems for taxpayers and for the IRS itself. Along with the main project, the IRS system for converting paper returns to electronic form was also cancelled, and the Cyberfile that would have enabled direct electronic taxpayer filing of returns was dropped.

This IRS failure in information technology changeover is by no means an isolated event. Plenty of government agencies and industrial or financial companies have failed both in their transition to new IT systems and in the cohabitation of novel competitive solutions with their legacy infrastructure, for reasons explained in the preceding sections of this chapter.

Among government agencies, for example, the FBI abandoned development of a $500 million fingerprint-on-demand computer system and crime information database, while the State of California spent $1 billion on a nonfunctional welfare database, as well as over $50 million on a new motor vehicle database system that never saw action. The record of manufacturing, merchandising, and financial companies is also spotted with similar failures.

These examples are not written to discourage a changeover to cloud computing but to beg for prudence in the work one does, as well as to bring attention to the sensitive characteristics associated with the transition to a new technology. As a general rule, at least in my experience, legacy systems have three factors of *inflexibility* consistently found when one starts studying at a certain level of detail their conversion:

1. heterogeneous equipment, from mainframes and workstations to databases and networks, as well as incompatible protocols and interfaces;
2. very large programming libraries that contain 10, 20, 30, or more million lines of code—largely Cobol, but also plenty of other languages; and
3. old, poorly documented programs that have evolved in an unstructured manner with extensions and patches, typically written ten, fifteen, twenty, or more years ago.

These millions of lines of code have used different languages that are incompatible with one another (as we already saw that even Cobol is incomparable from vendor to vendor). That's too bad because many programs are mission critical and must work together, which has required bridges and more patches. In addition, in a number of applications incompatible data formats are fed into programs through a data conversion interface.

To make matters worse, the majority of these programs—particularly the important ones—are big and monolithic. Therefore, they cannot be easily adjusted to provide interfaces to onDemand software. As well, it is very difficult, if not altogether impossible, to port these routines to new hardware.

The owners of such old dysfunctional programs are also facing the huge task of their maintenance, which means tracing failures and correcting them. Even if the decision is made to phase them out within, say, two years, in-between maintenance will be very costly and time consuming not only due to the lack of documentation but also because even if the programming routine is still working, practically no one has a clear concept of its exact functionality.

I don't need to insist on the fact that if a cloud vendor, no matter its name, wants to sell the user organization onDemand software written in Cobol, the answer should be a big fat no! Every company should watch out not to stumble backwards into EDP (Section 6.6).*

Apart from other basic reasons for such a statement, the language that we use forms our mind and shapes our thoughts. *If* we buy onDemand software written in deadly obsolete languages, which is the case today with many packages being used by business and industry, *then* our company is losing twice:

■ it is being damaged vis-à-vis its competitors by falling behind in its techno-logical solutions, and
■ it is paying an order of magnitude more than it should for services that employ old, inflexible, low-efficiency, used-up tools.

If we wish to overtake our opponents, we must be much better equipped than they are by employing the best means technology makes available, whether applications are developed in-house or bought. Besides, cloud computing vendors who sell Cobol programs are a disgrace—to themselves and to their clients. This, of course, does not mean that if the onDemand software is written in C++ or Java its introduction into the user organization's information stream will be simple and seamless, but at least it will be worth the effort going into the transition in IT technology.

A similar statement is valid regarding hardware. Chapter 1 brought to the reader's attention that some vendors talk of cloud computing as heralding a return to mainframe, which is patently false. This is a damaging inaccuracy because it leads several user organizations to believe that magic is in the air, disregarding the fact that:

■ king-size storage systems need the ability to scale out that is allowed by servers, and
■ monolithic storage provided by mainframes has become less relevant. Hundreds of thousands of servers are stealing the show.

Rather than being blindfolded by the mainframers, wise CIOs choose hardware vendors with technologies that enable building large, scalable databases with an

---

* Originally, as most readers will recall, EDP meant Electronic Data Processing. In the early 1990s, when Colin Crook radically changed Citibank's IT culture, EDP was used to mean the old culture of "emotionally disturbed people."

efficient power profile and dense recording. Vendors that offer customization and optimization of storage appreciate that a customer will benefit from this solution (see in Chapter 1 the references to Apple and Microsoft, with the latter's two new centers featuring five hundred thousand servers).

Cloud vendors who bet on old technology, such as the fifty-year-old mainframes, are miscalculating because cost savings will be an illusion and bad news has the nasty habit of spreading fast. When it does, the evolution of cloud computing from proprietary platforms will slow down to a drop, as evidence will show that the heralded added value is a fake.

It is bad enough that the mainframe environment is still around after decades of architectural changes and breakthroughs in service-oriented solutions unsupportable by old concepts. Other than conflict of interest, there is really no reason why we should make matters worse by bringing mainframe mentality into the cloud.

Snake oil and medieval practices by the IT's rear guard are common but untrustworthy. The way several information technology projects are conducted reminds me a great deal of medieval medicine. In her book *Pope Joan,** Dona Woolfolk-Cross describes the practice of ninth-century medieval doctors who tried to cure the seriously ill pope:

> The society of physicians sent a dozen of its best men to attend the stricken Pope. They tried a multitude of devices to effect a cure: they brought a fragment of the skull of St. Polycarp for Sergius to touch; they massaged his afflicted limbs with oil taken from a map that had burned all night on the tomb of St. Peter … they bled him repeatedly and purged him with emetics so strong his whole body was racked with violent spasms.

Granted, the ninth century was the darkest of the dark ages. But a similar statement can be made about the use of mainframes and Cobol programs today. "The Ninth Century," Woolfolk-Cross says, "was a time of widespread illiteracy, marked by an extraordinary dearth of record keep." The same is true of medieval information technology today.

6.6 Avoiding the Medieval EDP Mentality

CEOs who are in charge of the company under their watch present a challenge to the old regime of IT by demanding that new solutions are responsive to new realities. A user organization will be lying to itself if it believes that the transition from the legacy to the target system is something painless—whether a public or

---

* Dona Woolfolk-Cross, *Pope Joan* (London: Quartet Books, 1997).

private cloud computing environment. There is one exception to this statement: *if* the conversion is from mainframe mentality to mainframe mentality, *then* the job would look easier (albeit not always so); however, the benefit will be zero and return on investment nil.

It is not only conceivable but also very likely that some cloud computing vendors will try to get the contract by downplaying the need for cultural, structural, and system changes. They will do so to calm the CIO's and his or her cohorts' fears that they have plenty of hard work to do (and if they fail they may lose their job). There is plenty of evidence of this strategy, based on patches—just as there is plenty of evidence that patches fall apart.

The best strategy for CIOs who want to avoid patches and the risk of failure is to look for and find a wholesome onDemand solution, replacing the old incompatible and unmaintainable programming structures with a new and flexible system. The good news is that a dozen years ago Y2K provided excellent precedence to this well-rounded approach to the renewal of a company's programming library. Hence, prior to deciding anything, it is advisable to:

- visit the organizations that have year 2000 experience and
- learn from them, particularly what went wrong and how they corrected it.

In parallel to this, the reengineering/transition program must ensure that all required changes to data formats and data files are done in a serious, comprehensive manner. In this connection, the way to bet is that it will also involve software at the microcode level. To which extent the latter needs to be done will depend on both the present and target systems. No matter what the challenge, data conversion must be reliable and timely.

A wise CIO will never be thrifty with precautions. If the cloud computing vendor suggests electronic file transfer, then the user organization's answer should be that this is nearly the last step—not the first. Methods for the early steps, but for an interim, not permanent solution, are data mapping and data conversion.

- Data mapping works through declarative descriptions written in a domain-specific language.
- These describe how data are mapped from the legacy to the target system.*

This is a rather aged method for data conversion but is still being practiced, and it requires two stages. Compiled by the converter, data mappings cause the new applications database to be updated. A browser will show the relationship between

---

* The data mapping experience started in the early 1990s with a (rather rudimentary) data conversion capability built in C++. This has helped to import legacy data from a mainframe, transforming it on the fly to another database, but the process has been rather cumbersome and inflexible.

information elements, representing the mapping between legacy data and target data. (The alternative had been an emulation approach, which made a PC act like the screen of a stupid terminal with 3270 protocol. This evidently added to the costs and made a mockery out of the power of microprocessors while graphical user interfaces remained rudimentary.)

Another folkloric version of "solutions" pushed by mainframe vendors, and distinguishing itself by falling back to medieval EDP mentality, has been emulation using screen scraping—replacing a terminal screen with graphical representation of data. All counted, this and other approaches still in use add so much disk storage to the mainframes that they lead to system bottlenecks.* Critics would say that the logic of all that is wanting, and experience documents that they are right. However, there is a lack of efficient solutions in that sort of conversion.

The only efficient alternative is to redesign and recast the database—a major job. Moreover, many IT people fail to appreciate the contrast in efficiency between old technology and new technology; yet the difference is striking. Here is an example. Sweden's second largest bank, Nordbanken, started in 1989 to do a loan system written in Cobol and based on DB2:

- the development plan had foreseen six hundred man-years of work, and
- the first subset of deliverables was scheduled to take sixty man-years.

In 1993, four years down the line, when Nordbanken hit the rocks and went practically bankrupt because of bad loans and poor investments, the project in reference was still not ready. Securum, a financial entity set up by the Swedish government, which took over Nordbanken's bad loans and other dubious holdings, did that loan system on a client-server. The procedure was written by one person and required five hundred man-hours. This is less than one hour of client-server programming for one year of highly complacent and featherbedded programming on mainframes.

The reason I bring this example to the reader's attention is that the time of mainframes never lifted in the mind of many IT specialists. In addition, their company's friendly computer vendors want them to stay that way. Therefore, they offer them a cloud computing infrastructure equipped with *their* mainframes. In these cases, nothing changes except that the

- lock-ins will be stronger,
- costs will go significantly up,
- medieval culture will remain unaltered,

---

* In a conference I was lecturing at some years ago one of the mainframe vendors was very proud that some of his customers had 1½ or 2 terabytes of mainframe-based data. What his argument forgot is the fact that mainframe-based connectivity produces very little in end user productivity gains, while costs skyrocket.

- security will notably weaken, and
- reliability will most likely sink.

The reader should also keep in mind the case of IBM going to the edge of the precipice with its mainframes, at the end of the 1980s. The "in" solution at the time was client-servers, and an executive of Goldman Sachs, the investment bank, put his thoughts this way during a meeting we had on Wall Street: "To learn the future, we talk of people who buy the products. What are the customers telling us?"

The Goldman Sachs executive answered his question by stating that a rapidly increasing number of companies were riding the wave of computer downsizing. They were putting their applications on networked workstations, as opposed to the more expensive mainframes, and this called for reevaluation of past investment decisions.

IBM, however, kept in its old track, confident of being a market pacesetter. Then alarm bells rang. On January 9, 1993, it was announced that the company posted a 1992 loss of nearly $5 billion, the biggest in U.S. corporate history so far.

For all the restructurings, personnel shifts, and product initiatives it undertook in the late 1980s, the world's biggest computer maker still resembled nothing so much as a frailing giant unable to extricate itself from the mire of an outdated strategy and culture. Righting the company that had fallen on hard times required a fresh perspective at the top.

The case against John F. Akers, the former CEO, has been that neither he nor IBM's other top executives could believe that their key mainframe business would be eclipsed by smaller machines—despite IBM's own sizable PC, minicomputer, and workstation sales. In the late 1980s and in the mid-1990s, long after it became clear that the cost and complexity of mainframes were making them uncompetitive, they remained IBM's strategic cornerstone.

The first major contribution of the new CEO, Lou Gerstner, has been to avoid a collapse equivalent to those experienced by Wang, Control Data, Tandem, and Prime Computer. Gerstner turned around the Big Blue, but he had to proceed very carefully. In mid-November 1995, his lecture at the Las Vegas computer love affair showed that IBM was still a closed system:

- the belief to the infallibility of the mainframe strategy was not essentially altered, and
- fresh ideas that might have allowed reinventing the company were not permitted to carry the day at fast pace.

The spousing and promoting of the information utility concept demonstrates that the company's top management still did not understand the magnitude of the problem and the speed required to solve it. Only slowly Gerstner found the formula for change, which started with the tough task of saving IBM from itself and required more than a tweak here and a tweak there.

Many user organizations today face a similar challenge with their information technology (and some with their product line). Industry experts suggest that to benefit from cloud computing, they must cannibalize their dependence on mainframes in a steady, managed way. And because the mainframe practices are deeply embedded in their culture, to change dramatically they need someone who makes a fresh start.

A fresh start, however, has no chance when the medieval medicine, to which reference has been made in Section 6.5, permits one to keep on saying that web-to-host access revitalized the mainframes by putting them at the center of the corporate intranet. It is indeed a fact that because of misinformation, pressures by mainframe vendors, and a certain amount of modern IT illiteracy, mainframes continue to be the instruments of choice of backwards-leaning companies. Since the advent of client-server solutions, at the end of the 1980s, the argument has gone roughly like this:

- the client-server architecture is too distributed and a waste of network resources, and
- the best policy is to view the web and Java as a way to return to the centralized approach.

If the client-server was "too distributed and a waste of network resources," think of what cloud computing would be. With these arguments, people who continue living in the past go through what Gartner, a market research firm, calls the *hype cycle*. But after a peak of inflated and unjustified expectations, there comes a *trough of disillusionment*—at least to the company and its shareholders. In the last analysis, no technology is in itself good or bad. It all depends on what people and companies make of it, and what experience teaches is not positive for mainframe solutions.

ANY-TO-ANY PUBLIC AND PRIVATE CLOUDS

Chapter 7

Inside the Cloud of the Competitors

7.1 The Controllability of Computer Applications

The profile of the most important competitors in cloud computing was provided in Chapter 1. Where they position themselves in the cloud's four pillars, in terms of what they offer to the market, was the theme of Chapter 2, which explained the vendors' wares, from onDemand software and platforms to infrastructure and enabling services.

Positioned midway in the book, as the text transits from its emphasis on user organizations to the crucial issues of architecture, security, and reliability in the cloud, this chapter looks inside the offers of a sample of cloud providers. This sample is larger than Chapter 1's dozen, and it also discusses the developing policy of alliances, some of which might be ephemeral, while others become longer lasting.

As the careful reader will recall from the previous chapters, the book's thesis is that the most important advancement with cloud computing, at least so far and in the foreseeable future, is onDemand software and development platforms. The cloud's onDemand facilities offer user organizations a good way to get out of the most dreadful practice in information technology, which lasted for over fifty years: reinventing the wheel and each time making it less round.

Chapters 11 to 13 will present to the reader both the basic notions and case studies on what is on offer in the cloud in terms of onDemand software. However, although buying (or more precisely, renting) the bulk of their needs in programming products online is a wise policy for user organizations, it is not enough. Computer applications have most frequently escaped the notion of *controllability*. Understanding what this means is a prerequisite to appreciating what is offered by cloud vendors, particularly in terms of adding value to onDemand computing routines by way of an ingenious use of platforms (Section 7.2).

Controllability, says Toshiro Terano, professor of information technology at Hosei University, is a technical term frequently employed in control engineering.* It stands for the ability to put a system into a desired state by working on its input variables, processing gear, and the deliverables it provides.

Simply because a product is offered by a reputable vendor does not ensure that the user organization is always able to control it. Often plenty of effort is made in vain: companies fail to be in charge of an uncontrollable product or system—and this is particularly true when technology runs the risk of outpacing human understanding of the way in which the system works.†

Terano's thesis is that looking at contemporary society, one wonders whether people are, or even will be, able to control technology, despite having responsibility for its creation. In the 1950s to the 1970s time frame advances in information technology came at a pace that could be easier understood and controlled, but by the 1980s they showed some new quantum leaps in many fields. Computers and communications enhanced the ability to pool the brains of many individuals. This, however, did not produce a collective link because behavioral issues have been disregarded, and only recently have they come into the realm of systems studies.

It is not always appreciated that because information technology is widely employed, from education and research to daily operations and management decisions, its impact is gradually changing the nature of work. Even our capacity to think is being altered as man-machine systems are used for planning, designing, art, and other creative pursuits. This has two implications:

■ what is inside the cloud of the different vendors (Sections 7.2 to 7.8) will increasingly affect not only the way people work, but also how they live; and
■ the notion of controllability must be extended all the way from company reactions to new technology, which remain exceedingly slow, to the necessary evolution of existing social systems that new technology makes impractical.

For the time being, however, both in the different sectors of industry and in society at large, adaptation to a fast pacing technology is very slow. While it is not clear what causes this delay, the after effect is lack of appreciation of the deeper impact of new technological advances that widen the gap between individual, business, and social responses. Added to this is the fact that when people work with a computer as a partner, their behavior also differs. Until they discover what the

---

* From a personal discussion with Professor Terano at a research meeting in Tokyo.
† See also the discussion in Chapter 10 on the impact of human factors on reliability.

computer is able to do, people refuse to rely on it and act as if they were working alone, but as they learn the computer's capabilities and limitations, they put it to better use. This documents the difference controllability makes.

The other side of the coin is that the more a company advances in its mastery of information technology, the more its operations become dependent on the integrity of the system that it uses. This makes it imperative to understand and critically examine what is on offer. Having done so, and after deciding whether it wants to be inside or outside the cloud, management should be committed to an endless process of upgrading, enhancing, and testing its technology, to effectively meet:

- sophisticated client requirements,
- market and regulatory changes, and
- evolving internal needs for information and knowledge management.

The controllability principle suggests that failure to continue doing so will see to it that the company's business is negatively impacted by advancements in technology, exploited by competitors to gain market share. This is the other side of *technology risk*, which also includes human error, fraud, mismanagement, and natural disasters.

When Lars Thunell was put in charge of Securum (see Chapter 6), he told his people: "If we have a chance to survive, we must keep costs rock bottom and move very, very fast in a fluid market." Then he added: "We must have very sophisticated information technology tools at our disposal."* As the careful reader will recall from Chapter 6, since day 1 Securum's strategy has been:

- choose the most advanced technology,†
- proceed with rapid software development, and
- use IT to improve management decisions, accelerate operations, and lower production and distribution costs.

This has been an excellent example on controllability associated with information technology. But for every good example there are plenty of others that reach nowhere or go sour. One of the biggest and best-known global banks tried for three years and failed to build a "customer base"‡ for its worldwide operations. Here are the lessons learned from that experience, to avoid repeating them with cloud computing:

1. Selected data came toward a center point from databases with incompatible database management systems (DBMSs; which will be common currency with the cloud).
2. Integration of diverse data structures was tedious, costly, error prone, and slow moving.

---

* From a personal meeting with Securum executive in Stockholm.
† Client-servers at that time.
‡ Global customer database.

3. It took about one month to put collected information into useful shape, and by then it was obsolete.
4. Because of that delay and other reasons, the customer base had about 25 percent erroneous information.
5. Due to the high error rate and data obsolescence, the bank's managers and professionals refused to work with the customer base.

As a result, the whole project was dropped sometime after it went live, at great cost in terms of time, money, and human resources. Failures like that dramatize the fact that while technology has been promoted as a means to solve problems, its mismanagement creates more problems than it solves. When controllability takes a leave, cost-effectiveness turns on its head.

This problem is so universal that one will be in the wrong track if he or she spends precious time in arguments for or against cloud computing. The salient issue is not that but one having to do with the controllability of new technology—hence the wisdom of taking a careful look into the cloud of competitor vendors and critically examining how to use their wares, as well as making an honest appraisal of whether or not one is able to be ahead of the curve.

7.2 Platforms Rising: Google Tries to Be a Frontrunner

Google's App Engine, Microsoft's Azure, Amazon.com's EC2, and Salesforce.com's Force are four examples of what the cloud offers in development platforms. They are reasonably priced and therefore well positioned to take away market share from traditional application development solutions. They are also popular, particularly among small and medium enterprises (SMEs), though larger companies, too, are now looking at platforms as an effective way to handle their program development chores.

According to some estimates, of the four main sectors of cloud computing—OnDemand software, platforms, infrastructure, and enabling—development platforms present to the user organization three special advantages distinguishing them from the other pillars of cloud computing:

1. the best means for handholding between cloud providers and user organizations, as a cross-sales interface;
2. logical, indeed necessary, extension of onDemand software beneficiary of the (long-delayed) switch out of onPremises applications; and
3. by 2013 their market will probably be a quarter of the total cloud market, with the latter estimated between $100 and $110 billion.

True enough, today's platforms do not cover all applications, such as personal productivity. But this will most likely change with user requests for greater functionality and as vendors drive to overtake each other in covering a larger part of the market. An example is provided by Google's sprint in prototyping cloud computing by creating a network for university research through *Project Google 101*.

In an effort to keep ahead of its competitors, the cloud provider has as well updated the Google Search Appliance (GSA), its dedicated hardware and software offering for corporate intranets and websites. New features in the GSA 6.0 release include:

- query suggestions, and
- user-generated results.

These allow users to promote certain web pages for a particular query. According to analysts, the company already has some of the wider and deeper cloud computing offerings, including applications like Google Docs, Google Calendar, and infrastructure such as *Big Table*.

Big Table is a multiserver proprietary database system using the company's File Sub System and the so-called Chubby Lock Service designed for a loosely coupled environment emphasizing availability and reliability.* Big Table can also be used as a name service:

- replacing the Domain Naming Service (DNS) and
- translating a storable domain name into a corresponding numerical identifier.

Google says that, moreover, Big Table scales to petabyte storage capacity, distributed over hundreds of thousands of servers. Also, it is designed to accommodate the addition of more servers without difficulty or interruptions to the system's delivery of supported services.

It is not yet clear whether Google's policy of offering certain services free of cost to consumers (with income coming from advertising) will find an echo in bigger user organizations. But the policy of both developing and acquiring applications and tool sets integrating them with its core search and advertising services already bears fruits.

Another interesting offer connected to cloud computing is MapReduce, a distributed computing framework (for a discussion on frameworks see Chapter 11). Its function is to split the processing of large-scale data sets across clusters of computers. As with grid computing (Chapter 1), this is designed to permit a large number of low-end servers to treat large data sets.

Moreover, apart from the software it developed itself and that coming from start-ups and small companies it bought, Google has set up an alliance with Salesforce.com and Adobe. Some analysts look at it as a precursor to a new cloud development landscape that can attract the attention of user organizations.

---

* Google talks of a guaranteed 99.9 percent uptime, still to be proven.

An opinion heard in the market is that this partnership is an acknowledgment that each of its members finds it difficult to put its hand around the global cloud alone. Working together makes sense, as all three companies have been active in driving user organizations and the IT industry toward a wider onDemand solution, away from the PC-centric onPremises approaches identified with Microsoft and other software providers.

Other voices say that Google was obliged to move that way because its Gears is a solution that cannot deliver alone and must be complemented by PC-based development tool kits. Though that might have been a factor, it is no less true that:

■ alliances are a solution companies on the Internet have practiced for nearly two decades, and
■ Google's APIs may be the tip of the iceberg for providing software and services as building blocks for cloud applications.

In addition, by launching a free operating system for personal computers Google is probably targeting Microsoft's client base rather than technology all by itself. Many Internet companies hope to get a piece of the action, which today revolves around Microsoft and its Windows operating system. The first engines running Chrome OS will not be available until late 2010, though netbooks may run ahead of PCs on its initial version.*

It is difficult to see that in the short term alternative OSs will make Windows obsolete and turn browsers into dominant computing platforms, but the new entries will give Microsoft a run for its money. Mid-July 2009, Microsoft reacted to Google's encroachment into its core business with the announcement of a free online version of its Office software to be launched in 2010—a move representing one of the most radical steps yet by Microsoft as it tries to refocus its software business around the Internet and save its income base, as we will see in Section 7.4.

7.3 Salesforce.com and Its Force

In Chapter 1 Salesforce.com was presented as a company whose cloud computing services allow user organizations to share customer information on demand.†
The company started in business by providing worldwide customer relationship management (CRM) software and associated services. Its market is business entities of all sizes and industries.

CRM has been Salesforce.com's first commercial product, and over the years it evolved into a cloud computing onDemand platform, permitting the firm to

---

* Chrome OS will combine Linux, the open-source operating system, with Google's browser Chrome.
† Salesforce.com might have been an excellent investment for patient investors, but its astronomical price/earnings (P/E) ratio of 97 discourages such a move.

increase its attraction to its customer base, enrich its online software solutions, make more defensible its pricing, and develop alliances; for instance, the alliance with Google (Section 7.2), which might significantly improve its fortunes.

According to an analysis by Bank of America/Merrill Lynch, at the end of 2008, onDemand CRM software stood at about 12 percent of the overall CRM market, but this share is expected to double to 24 percent by 2014—in a rising overall demand for customer relationship services. Clearly there are many competitors in this market—Microsoft, Oracle, and SAP among them—but Salesforce's customer base has grown to nearly 30,000 worldwide, and the company has some 650,000 paying subscriptions.*

That's rather impressive in a business life of less than a dozen years. (Salesforce. com was established in 1999, focusing from the start on consumer websites and business applications. The service that it provides is customizable, and the job can be done by the customer alone or with a small amount of help [enabling]. Anecdotal evidence suggests that business users have been attracted by the flexibility of the company's CRM solution, including that of its pricing schedule.)

One of Salesforce.com's competitive advantages is *Force*, its development platform, an offshoot of the vendor's underlying infrastructure. It features an operating system, multitenant database, and applications services. Some experts suggest that Force is a first-class player in the developer tools market:

- featuring relative simplicity and good integration with the firm's onDemand CRM and
- being assisted by the platform's metadata facility, which enables application customization without preserving the core code.

In essence, developers configure the attributes associated with an application's object, storing them as metadata blueprints. These can be accessed through the user interface when end users interact with the application. This metadata-based approach allows user organizations to move to the next version of the platform without disruptions commonly associated with upgrading.

Moreover, Force permits one to integrate applications developed on the platform with other existing routines, to access data in the other systems. It also makes it possible to combine data from multiple sources in a workflow associated with a specific process. This is achieved by means of connectors for:

- ERP routines,
- desktop devices,
- middleware, and more.†

---

* Bank of America/Merrill Lynch, "Salesforce.com," June 4, 2009.
† It also makes feasible integration with third-party applications, including those of competitors: Oracle, Microsoft, and SAP.

In terms of system design, the concept of a layered platform is very interesting, because there are advantages associated with the ability to start at the lower level with what is called secure infrastructure and move up through five layers, each dedicated to a specific mission: database as a service, integration as a service, logic as a service, user interface as a service, and applications exchange.

The system is upgraded through value-added routines. In late 2008 SalesForce.com announced *Sites*, permitting user organizations to expose their Force custom-made applications on public and private websites. This could become a drive of new applications, strengthening the platform's appeal by allowing third-party contributions and by permitting user organizations to be more interactive with their customers.

The profile-driven access provided by Sites facilitates data control over objects and fields made accessible to visitors. Another feature is provided by the *Sandbox* routine, which permits replicating the entire Salesforce.com deployment. As already noted in Chapter 4 in connection to virtual doubles, there are advantages associated with the ability of creating an extra clone that includes all data and customizations.

For example, an interesting aspect of Sandbox is that the vendor's clients can test new customizations or features before rolling them out to their own customers or internal users. The artifact also provides the option to try out different applications on the AppExchange, without impacting live users.

Still another online tool by Salesforce.com, known as *AdWords*, lets user organizations place ads in their CRM environment and also helps them in tracking the success of their online advertising by tracing leads, opportunities, and revenue. This is an interesting feature unavailable in classical CRM software.

The impact of value-added features described in the above paragraphs can be seen through the response of user organizations to surveys concerning the attraction presented to them, and their IT strategies, by onDemand programming products and onDemand platforms. In a late 2008 survey by McKinsey and SandHill Enterprise that involved 857 firms, 31 percent of these firms indicated that OnDemand software and platforms have been the most important trend impacting their business.

Other inputs concur with this finding. A study by Bank of America/Merrill Lynch points out that onDemand is the first successful enterprise business model of cloud computing. It also points out that while the software as a service model has been limited to business applications so far, many more possibilities are open in the future.

Under this aspect should be seen the Google-Salesforce partnership on onDemand cloud products. According to the aforementioned study by the broker: "Google's Application Engine development environment leverages a highly distributed processing architecture with flat file database management. Salesforce.com's *Force.com* development environment, on the other hand, utilizes a shared infrastructure and relational database management."*

---

* Bank of America/Merrill Lynch, "Technology," June 2, 2009.

The way to interpret this statement is that while the goal for both platforms is that of delivering new applications development facilities "as a service" to their customers, their approaches differ. Addressing different market segments through an alliance sees to it that the two complement one another in terms of appeal. Salesforce. com's onDemand offerings focus on transactional business applications, while those of Google aim to capture the market for interactive customer applications.

7.4 Microsoft Is Now on the Defensive

Nearly three decades have passed since Microsoft's blitz in Las Vegas. Today, having attained prominence in the PC, OS, and applications market, but with the classical PC's future in question, the company is on the defensive. What a difference from 1983, when Bill Gates's outfit was one of many software upstarts hardly noticed in the sea of other firms competing in the same market, but it tried hard to come up from under. That year's Comdex* has been an inflection point in Microsoft's fortunes.

- The technical trigger was the prelaunch of Windows, a then nearly unknown PC operating system.
- By contrast, the real event was created thanks to two marketing masterminds, Rowland Hanson and Bob Lorsch, who put in motion the public relations blitz.

"There wasn't a taxi on the Strip not promoting Windows. Stickers were all over the backseats of cabs; the drivers wore Windows buttons," said Jennifer Edstrom and Marlin Eller. "... People couldn't go to bed without Windows." That has been a marketing *blitzkrieg* around a technical product in the making, "Microsoft's competitors were crazed, but Gates and his marketing crew were ecstatic."†

While Windows looked as if it were the focal point, its release was still a couple of years away. Microsoft's strategy had borrowed a leaf out of IBM's book, but for those attending the 1983 Comdex, the marketing blitz was ingenious. In a matter of a few days (and at an affordable cost of $450,000), Microsoft went from being one of many little-known software players to being *the player* in operating systems for personal computers.

On the occasion, Hanson and Lorsch reinvented and refined the concept of consumer product promotion for technological gear, recasting it around a piece of software that became license to riches. Microsoft would manage to keep a near monopoly to that license for over a quarter of a century, in spite of the swarm of challengers that came along with their "open" architectures (Chapter 8).

---

* The computer distributors exhibition, whose Las Vegas annual gatherings started in 1979.
† Jennifer Edstrom and Marlin Eller, *Barbarians Led by Bill Gates* (New York: Henry Holt, 1998).

Only in 2009, as we saw in Section 7.2, Google mounted an assault that might succeed in the realm of cloud computing and got Microsoft worried that if it did not respond in time, it might become another Digital Equipment Corporation (DEC). Microsoft responded with *Azure* (Chapter 1), the brainchild of Ray Ozzie, which—in an effort to protect the current customer base and acquire a new one—takes a hybrid approach: onDemand *plus* onPremises.

This hybrid is a business necessity. Microsoft cannot 100 percent reinvent itself; whether it likes it or not, it has to accommodate its legacy PC products in its cloud computing strategy—hence the deliberate choice that the new services kick in when it comes to new applications launched from the desktop. User organizations are given a choice:

- leveraging the traditional onPremises approach or
- using the new onDemand suite of applications and corresponding platform.

In its way, that policy (also followed by IBM and some other cloud vendors) resembles the two-headed Byzantine eagle, each head looking at a different side. It needs no explaining that a two-headed policy is hardly the stuff for a blitz at the Comdex.* (In 2010 Microsoft finds itself exactly in the position IBM was in the mid-1980s.)

Contrary to the strategy adopted by IBM then and Microsoft now, the companies' own up-starts want to promote a radical change in product line. (In IBM in the 1980s, the up-starts pushed for a PC with Intel Inside and DOS, but the old guard would not abandon its prerogatives—in IBM's case, the mainframes line.) The problem these firms face is that the Byzantine two-headed eagle can split a corporation down the middle.

The pros say that it does not matter because Microsoft is a rich company with a long list of synergies. Lots of prime applications are running through its Client OS, Office, and Business environment; it also features the SQL Server and a tools business. Customers can buy these products in an *enterprise agreement* recognized as subscription, providing a stream of revenues.

This argument has merits, but it is no less true that Microsoft has been generally weak in project management, as attested to by the scarcity of new products and services coming out of its rich software laboratories. There is as well the precedence of the on-and-off fate of Windows, which, over several years in the 1980s, was and was not going to be the company's prime choice for OS. Against this background, Microsoft must now:

- manage in parallel four major development cycles: desktop, server, mobile, and cloud computing;
- do so across dozens of products, which evidently compound the planning and control effort;

---

* Which could not be repeated in duplicate anyway because the rules have changed.

■ balance the Azure functionality in a way that will not hurt the large inventory of classical PC wares; and

■ conduct platform wars with Goggle, Salesforce.com, and their likes, which can work through less complex release cycles with rather minor compatibility challenges.

Coordinating Azure's building blocks with old and new releases will be another formidable task. These include three modules of .NET services: a Service Bus (connecting customers' internal apps to cloud computing), Access Control (providing authorization and coordinating with identity providers), and Workflow (a tool set for interaction among parts of an application).

Other Azure modules are Dynamics Services (targeted at the CRM market) and SharePoint Services (exposing building blocks for applications that focus on content management, business processes, enterprise searches, and collaboration). For its part, Live Services concentrates on the underlying building blocks used by Microsoft to build its Windows Live application. This includes:

■ data synchronization across disconnected consumer devices,

■ instant messaging (IM), and

■ assistance to developers to write proprietary and other applications.*

At the same time, while moving forward with these developments, Microsoft must change its pricing culture. On July 13, 2009, the company announced that it would offer a free, web-based version of its Office suite. It also gave some specifics on its pricing plans for Azure, opening it up to early adopters at its Worldwide Partner Conference in New Orleans.

Users of the free online Office will be able to create and edit documents, spreadsheets, and PowerPoint presentations by using tools they are familiar with, from existing desktop software. While this "free" stuff is only a lightweight version to make it more suitable for use in Internet browsers, the company says that it will provide a fuller service than online rivals such as Google Apps.

True enough, opening the software up to a new audience would significantly expand the Office market in the long term. But, as far as Microsoft's P&L is concerned, it will be reducing its profit margin. This is indeed a good example of the strong and weak points of competition in cloud computing, where newcomers have freedoms that escape the incumbents.

---

* Applications for Azure are written using the .NET libraries. They are compiled to a Common Language Runtime, which the vendor says is a language-independent development environment.

7.5 Amazon.com Leverages Its Infrastructure

Well managed and inventive, Amazon.com is one of the few survivors of the dot-com boom and bust of the late 1990s. The company has been a successful online retailer offering a wide range of products, which it carefully expands in content and appeal. These include books, music, videotapes, computers, electronics, home and garden, and numerous other wares.

Amazon offers an impressive product list as well as handling and shipping to customers, for which it built over the years an impressive infrastructure. According to several opinions that converge in their evaluation of its prospects, the company's entry into cloud computing had a dual objective:

■ to develop a new profitable product line and
■ to get value out of its huge infrastructural developments and expenses.

Because the first bullet connects to its current business, a brief discussion on the company's cultural background will help in better appreciating this duality. Amazon.com aims to be a customer-centric firm where clients—from consumers to business entities—can find anything they may want to buy online. Hence, it continues to expand the range of products and services, emphasizing:

■ global brand recognition,
■ a growing customer base,
■ significant e-commerce expertise,
■ innovative technology, and
■ extensive and sophisticated fulfillment capabilities.

Well prior to cloud computing, the aim has been to launch new e-commerce businesses quickly, with good prospects for success. Therefore, the company's entry into the cloud is a logical extension of the prevailing strategy, with a conceptual framework developed to support it. This approach permits it to:

■ integrate corporate goals with organizational structure and
■ manage without getting a split personality between the interface of strategy and technology.

Critical elements in reaching Amazon's objectives have been not only the recognition of technology as a major business factor but also the role of modern finance, flexibility in decision making, and transferability of competitive advantages across product lines. This has involved a fairly clear perspective of managerial problems, and practical ways to address them, including the development of individual problem-solving skills.

Some cognizant people say that Amazon.com's application of the individual problem-solving skills is more responsible than anything else for its launch into cloud computing. This may be true, but the fact remains that the company has correctly capitalized on its investments and the infrastructure it developed for Web Services. The fact that the latter has been in existence meant it could offer to the market at very reasonable prices.

The *Amazon Web Services* (AWS) facilities offer applications developers direct access to the firm's technology platform on an as-needed basis. Amazon claims that over four hundred thousand developers have signed up, attracted by its web-based computing which also serves small enterprises, because of:

■ its scalability and
■ fast response time (Chapter 10).

The careful reader will remember that Google, too, has made a similar claim about hundreds of thousands of developers. It looks as if a new trend is taking hold in the market. Taken together, these two references suggest that the true nature of the current strategic inflection point (Chapter 3) with cloud computing:

■ may well be a revolution in software development, and
■ this revolution is going to have far-reaching consequences, altering the nature of the software industry as well as the way we look at programming.

Even if only for this and no other reason, Amazon.com should be seen as key player in the cloud, with original ideas that help IT departments and their professionals in modernizing their culture, methods, and practices. By all evidence, this new departure of onDemand advanced development tools brings significant internal efficiency improvements, apart from promoting a sense of utility computing. Aside from that, the company's simple storage service (S3) and elastic compute cloud (EC2) have been among the first to offer databasing and computing in a publicly accessible cloud fashion. The *New York Times* is one of the better-known clients of S3, using the warehousing facilities to run its online archives. (There is a major difference between archiving through the cloud and relegating one's active databases with plenty of sensitive information in them; see Chapters 9 and 10.)

In addition, Amazon's relatively simple database structure, with S3 and EC2, can provide a service for running queries on structured data in real time. What I would ask to have as information, if I were a client of the cloud's infrastructure, is the pattern of response time for queries at Amazon's database. The graph from CALIDA (California Intelligent Database Assistant, of General Telephone and Electronics, GTE) shown in Figure 7.1 provides an example of what all cloud users should require.

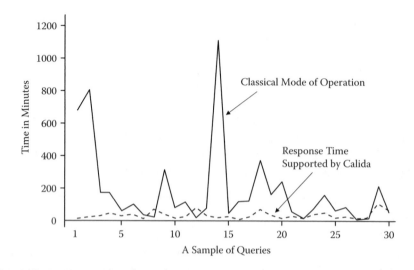

Figure 7.1 CALIDA field results. Response time for complex queries to hetero-geneous databases.

Confronted with a rapidly growing number of queries on accounting charges and their comparison to effective use time, which required access to information elements stored in a variety of incompatible databases and DBMSs, GTE designed CALIDA, an expert system, in the late 1980s. The knowledge artifact significantly improved access time in the aforementioned environment, as attested to by Figure 7.1. Knowledge-enriched database solutions are becoming rather common today; see in Section 7.6 the discussion on EMC's Atmos.

The great importance of response time, and its connection to system reliability, is one of the themes of Chapter 10. Response time is a critical question to be addressed by users to all vendors of the cloud's infrastructural services.

In addition, infrastructural vendors and user organizations should confront the not-so-sexy but critical issue of whether data exclusively for internal users are better stored in the cloud or at the user organization's premises. Statistics from major companies show that roughly 75 percent of paperwork and computer files produced during the year are for *internal use only*—and the majority remains at headquarters.

■ Why should this information be stored in the cloud?
■ What's the cost-effectiveness (and dependability) of such a solution?

The handling of internal paperwork contrasts in a significant way to that of external data relating to business partners, whether clients or suppliers. The latter is characteristically electronic commerce oriented and, as such, is subject to wider distribution—frequently with a financial after effect.

For instance, Amazon's Associative Web Service supports product data and e-commerce functionality, offering website owners and merchants the possibility to leverage their applications. For its part, the Flexible Payments Service (FPS) makes available a set of web APIs facilitating the movement of money between any two entities.

With all that, and most particularly the four-hundred-thousand-user base, it looks to me that Amazon has emerged as a leader in cloud computing. The pundits who say that the mother of all cloud battles will be between Google and Microsoft are wrong. Rather, it will be between the two alliances respectively revolving around Amazon.com and Google.*

7.6 EMC, VMWare, and Virtual Arrays of Inexpensive Disks

It is nobody's secret that since the mid-1990s many companies, particularly the larger ones, have been confronted with rapidly growing storage requirements. The search for cost-effective solutions began in the mid-1980s, as it became evident that use of IT battleships, like DB2 running on mainframes, was offered at an exorbitant cost and had become too inefficient (not to mention the obsolete IMS running on mainframes).† On the other hand, imaginative new approaches like Teradata did not catch the market's fancy.

By the late 1980s redundant arrays of independent disks (RAIDs) challenged the dominance of mainframes and their top-heavy database management systems, as they presented a significantly greater effectiveness at much lower cost. This accelerated in the 1990s with network attached storage (NAS)‡ and storage area networks (SANs),§ which have the advantage of being more sophisticated than earlier solutions. Other RAIDs technology, developed since then, include:

- object-based CAS and
- cloud-optimized COS.

According to their promoters, and a growing number of users, storage area networks can boost the utilization rate of hardware to as much as 80 percent, from about 20 percent in the one-array-per-computer world of directly attached storage

---

* The market also votes that way. The P/E of Amazon is 36, and that of Google 22.
† To answer the operating requirements in response time and contention posed by its public database, which was then the largest in the world, in the late 1980s Dow Jones installed a couple of connection machines—the best available supercomputer at that time.
‡ File-based NAS uses Internet standards to connect processing units to storage arrays; it was originally developed by the network appliance firm.
§ A concept originally developed by EMC.

(DAS). Plenty of competitors entered the RAIDs market besides EMC, including (in alphabetic order): Hewlett-Packard, Hitachi, IBM, and Veritas.

By 2004, within less than ten years, SAN and NAS solutions accounted for more than 60 percent of the (then) $15 billion global storage market, and they have continued gaining market. There are also featured new design advances. For instance, EMC introduced a solution known as *Information Lifecycle Management* (ILM), which is an intelligent version of SAN. With their popularity spreading, servers have been attached not only to one cluster of arrays but to several different classes of storage devices, some high tech and more expensive and others cheaper, more dated, but still popular.

Knowledge-enriched software has been a welcome feature moving data between these devices, as vendors have been trying to improve their cost-effectiveness and at the same time considerably increase their storage capacity. In November 2008, EMC announced *Atmos*, a multi-petabyte information management system projected to assist user organizations in automatically managing and optimizing the distribution of unstructured information across global storage landscapes.

■ Atmos enables Web 2.0 providers and users to build and deliver information-centric services and applications for client computing solutions.
■ According to the vendor, this storage at massive scale is provided with centralized management as well as automated placement and retrieval of information.*

As in the case of Salesforce.com's platform, EMC Atmos benefits from *metadata*, which drive information placement and retrieval. It also provides other data management services like replication and reduplication (see also in Section 7.5 the discussion on GTE's pioneering CALIDA).

The Atmos system uses web services APIs for application integration, provides multitenant support (which allows multiple applications to be served from the same infrastructure), and integrates advancements connected to the virtualization expertise VMware (partly owned by EMC), whose products include:

■ vManage, which runs the virtual infrastructure;
■ vPlatform, a uniform platform for IT infrastructure;
■ vTools, a virtual infrastructure integration tool; and
■ Fault Tolerance and Storage Thin Provisioning facilities.

The company's vCloud APIs and vApps have targeted interoperability among clouds, which presents an interest with hybrid (internal and external) cloud computing solutions (Chapter 1). The vApps employ the Open Virtual Machine Format (OVF) to specify and encapsulate the different components of an application, facilitating the transfer of applications between clouds.

---

* Among its customers are AT&T and eBay.

In 2009 VMware launched a new release of its vSphere (VI4), which reportedly has some interesting improvements over VI3, such as Storage Thin Provisioning, Storage vMotion, Fault Tolerance, and Distributed Power Management. The company's strategy is to position vSphere as an operating system running virtual workloads for cloud computing.

Experts think that VMware, and by extension EMC, has a meaningful technological lead over its competitors in cloud infrastructure. In addition, VMware features a sizable installed base of over 150,000 customers and seems to be well launched to increase its market hold. To do so, it follows a dual strategy, bundling its modules as a part of a product suite while also selling them stand-alone.

VMware has been collaborating with Cisco in connection to the latter's Nexus 1000V switch that will permit network administrators to monitor virtual machines running in the data center. The chosen solution sits between a logical and a physical layer. Under this approach, the network will be aware of virtual addresses, resulting in lower latency as the network will have direct access to data from each virtual engine.

In conclusion, there is plenty of evidence that virtual server approaches will be characterizing future databases, contrary to what some people say, that the IT industry swings back to mainframes. Simply stated, the trend is away from them. To the sorrow of those who like to take wrong-way risk to avoid changing their way of thinking, the information technology industry is clearly moving toward intelligence-enriched virtual arrays of inexpensive disks.

7.7 Wares of Other Cloud Challengers

Back in the 1960s when IBM was the almighty name in the computer industry, reference was made to it and its competitors as "Snow White and the Seven Dwarfs." Also at that time, John Diebold had coined a label: "the BUNCH," which stood for Burroughs, Univac, National Cash Register, Control Data, and Honeywell.

This mid-twentieth-century picturesque history of computing machinery is repeating itself in the early part of the present hundred years. If Google, Amazon. com, Microsoft, and (for RAIDs)* EMC aspire for the role of Snow White, the BUNCH is made by a plethora of names, with no clear choices about who will be ahead as a second layer of cloud competitors.

Some of the companies and their wares for cloud computing reviewed in this and the following section have been briefly introduced to the reader in Chapter 1. Examples are Cisco, Hewlett-Packard, and IBM. Others, like Akamai, are discussed for the first time. The reasons why those already considered reappear is that in the present chapter the products and services they offer, rather than the providers themselves, are the focal point.

---

* Along with EMC I would have included Hewlett-Packard as a top supplier of RAIDs, but the fact that HP competes across the board of cloud services did not permit me to do so.

In addition, in terms of mode of presentation, it has been a deliberate decision to keep it in alphabetic order, no matter the size of the cloud competitor in other business lines. Evidently, some of these cloud providers are big; others are medium sized or small; still others are affiliates of well-known firms. What they share is that all of them seek a piece of the action in the cloud environment.

Akamai Technologies provides global delivery services for Internet content, streaming media, applications, and global Internet traffic management. It also uses technology and software based on algorithms to monitor Internet traffic patterns, providing cloud infrastructure through its Content Delivery Network (CDN).

The company markets cloud-based Application Performance Solutions (APS) serving several user organizations. In fact, it features two versions of APS: Web Applications Accelerator for web-based applications and IP Application Accelerator for applications delivered over different IP protocols.

APS is offered on a subscription basis. One of its better-known applications is that it powers FENICS II, Fujitsu's cloud-based network as a service. It is also employed by onDemand software vendors to provide application performance to their distributed base of user organizations.

Cisco's strategy in cloud computing is to become a one-stop data center solution for user organizations.* In this it capitalizes on its current market for switching equipment, where it has under its wings about 9 percent of the $50 billion in present-day demand. The company's Nexus switch family may well serve the coming generation of data centers, addressing hot issues like:
 – consolidation and
 – virtualization.

The Nexus switch architecture is composed of three main component parts: access switches, aggregation switches, and core switches. Critics say that the architecture is still hierarchical, defined by the core switch. Cisco expects a breakthrough in virtual networking, a theme on which it works with VMware. (An example of deliverables is the Virtual Network Link.)

Like Google, Cisco works with partners: Intel and EMC/VMware in hardware technology; Microsoft, SAP, and Redhat in software; Compugen and Logicalis, which it calls channel partners; and Accenture, Wipro, and Tata in enabling services. Cisco's tactic is to simplify cloud management by offering a bundled solution for switches, servers, storage, applications, and consulting services.

Like other vendors, Cisco approaches cloud computing by means of virtual sessions floating above the network. It claims that its solution will see to it that network managers do not need to be concerned with

---

* Cisco has recently expanded into dozens of new businesses, not only the cloud. Other examples are camcorders and visual systems for sports stadiums.

administration of physical assets, concentrating instead on virtual sessions. Scalability and other crucial issues will be seamlessly managed, according to the vendor.

At the center of Cisco's cloud computing strategy is the Unified Computing System (UCS). Server level innovations include better use of bandwidth (through virtual network interface cards [NICs]) and of memory utilization. The company says that this will reduce the number of servers by improving network and server efficiency.

Citrix's contribution to cloud computing is different than Cisco's, but there is some overlap in market focus. The company reportedly has over an 80 percent share in the remote access market and 10 percent share in the conferencing market. (The conference market is dominated by Cisco/WebEx, with a nearly 39 percent share.)

Citrix' strategy concentrates on application virtualization and desktop virtualization. In its marketing policy it has adopted a subscription type model with flat pricing, offering unlimited use of a monthly fee. The firm's products help connect a variety of applications to a range of endpoints, which may be PCs, laptops, and mobile devices.

Redmond-based *Concur Technologies* is an applications provider. Its software helps companies in setting personalized spending limits for each employee and in steering corporate travelers to preferred hotels and airlines (with which the firm has negotiated discounts or rebates). The services it provides on the cloud come under the envelope Corporate Expense Management (CEM). The company also offers consulting, client support, and training services.

CEM includes the following: Concur Audit, providing expense report auditing services (used in conjunction with Expense); Concur Connect, a global program facilitating communications between travel suppliers and customers; Smart Expense, which automates the creation of expense reports, based on initial travel reservations; Concur Intelligence, providing report creation services and used in conjunction with Travel and Expense; Concur Pay, enabling direct deposit of reimbursable employee expenses (used in conjunction with Concur Expense); and Concur Meeting, a web service for managing corporate registration and travel.

CSC is an IT services company that recently unveiled cloud computing offers. With its Cloud Orchestration it addresses areas such as service level management, remote monitoring, reporting, and auditing. For government customers, it has developed Trusted Cloud, featuring hosted desktop, computing, storage, and infrastructure services with an emphasis on security.

Facebook did not see the light of cloud computing as a social networking company. Pretty soon, however, its wide public acceptance led toward the development of an interesting range of cloud-based application development tools. The initiative it took in enabling plug-in programming routines has been instrumental in creating a novel type of platform.

The Facebook platform permits software developers to write computer programs interacting with core Facebook features, like profiles and friends, by using a proprietary markup language. These applications typically reside on Facebook, but:

- they can also be hosted through partners like Amazon Web Services and Salesforce.com, and
- they can be accessed on Facebook or independently on Internet-connected devices.

The company says that it has well over fifty thousand applications with well over 10 percent of them having more than ten thousand monthly active users. These applications are very profitable, with anecdotal evidence suggesting that in 2009 they generated over $400 million revenue for their developers—largely from advertising.

There are as well collateral applications and revenues. Autonomy, the British search specialist, unveiled Autonomy Interwoven Social Media Analysis to help businesses follow "conversations" about their company or products in Web 2.0. This consists of a series of connectors for its Interwoven content manager that let businesses eavesdrop on social networking sites such as YouTube, Twitter, and Facebook.

Facebook has been a successful enterprise, which cannot be said of *MySpace*, another social networking outfit. In late June 2009, after drastically reducing the size of its American workforce, MySpace slashed its international staff by two-thirds in an effort to adapt to a sharp decline in advertising revenue. Rupert Murdoch News Corporations, which owns the social network website, sparked an intense debate about ending free access to online news content, leaving many observers skeptical that such a plan will work.*

Hewlett-Packard is in a different class than the cloud providers whose wares were discussed in Section 7.7. It has entered into cloud computing through its CloudPoint, which it continues to enrich with new building blocks. The architecture it offers to its customers rests on four pillars:

- intelligence in the client device (including notebooks and smart phones),
- intelligence in the network,
- next-generation data centers, and
- software to provision and manage the cloud.

HP is active in developing all four components, but it is not searching for an all-in-one solution. Instead, it has chosen polyvalent access to cloud services from any device, with emphasis on software scaling. The company concentrates on developing web platforms and services that can be dynamically personalized based on the user organization's location, preferences, and other criteria.

---

* See the discussion on Facebook and MySpace in the Epilog.

HP's advanced research group has developed Dynamic Cloud, which is one of the more interesting initiatives the company has undertaken. Management seems convinced that dynamic services will be able to anticipate and execute searches in cloud computing that will benefit the user organization. Context-aware services will be personalized.

This is not necessarily the approach taken by *IBM's* Blue Cloud, which concentrates on transforming an enterprise data center from localized to distributed computing, across clustered resources. Emphasis is placed on addressing massive, scalable, data-intensive workloads; this is a choice that serves well the company's traditional product line of mainframes.

Announced in November 2007, Blue Cloud has opened several data centers. (There are three in the United States, one for Europe based in Dublin, and one in China, with a second in the making. Others are in the Arabian Peninsula, Vietnam, and Korea.) Known as Data Fields, these centers sell databasing services.

IBM's WebSphere CloudBurst manages individual user and group access. The Hypervisor Edition of WebSphere Application Server software serves in a virtualized hardware environment. A suite of services has been recently released under the Infrastructure strategy (and Planning for Cloud Computing strategy) aimed to bring together business and technical teams for long-term planning and readiness assessment—with the objective of leveraging existing assets, which suggests that change is not in the air.

The company's Design and Implementation for Cloud Test Environments permits user organizations to build a cloud platform within their own IT environment. This is another initiative trying to hold on to the old while putting one foot in the new environment, described in Section 7.4 as the Byzantine two-headed eagle.

As these references demonstrate, though they place themselves in a different framework—the one PC based, the other mainframe centered—Microsoft's and IBM's strategies are very similar in their fundamentals. They cut the tissue of future IT issues with the same scissors, whose one leg is preserving the installed base and the other entering the cloud computer industry in a way that can leave a footprint.

Oracle's strategy regarding the cloud has been that of enhancing its Identity Manager, designed to help businesses improve compliance and reduce fraud. Its latest release enforces segregation of duties (SoD) in a more granular fashion than so far provided, and the vendor considers the enhancements as a contribution to compliance and management control.

If the purchase of Sun Microsystems by Oracle is finalized, the latter will benefit from Sun's cloud computing entries, particularly its Cloud Strategic Planning Service (CSPS). This is a portfolio of offerings designed to help user organizations jump aboard the cloud bandwagon. CSPC works in conjunction with OpenSolaris 2009.06, Sun's latest release providing support for new technologies such as flash storage and virtualization.

Seen in unison, the aforementioned references provide a rationale for the cloud policy of a combined Oracle and Sun. One must also keep in mind that Sun has been one of the leaders in the evolution of open source and, until its acquisition, viewed the cloud infrastructure as an open platform. This contrasts with the position taken by other vendors, whose cloud implementations are proprietary.

By all evidence, there will be a major cultural difference between Sun and Oracle personnel—with the former arguing that many companies and their developers will gravitate toward open systems that allow greater transparency and applications portability. But as we will see in Chapter 8, an open architecture is not necessarily the next big thing in the cloud.

Born in the late 1990s, *Rackspace.com* provides Linux-based Internet hosting services to SMEs worldwide. It offers proprietary software and infrastructure to manage applications for its clients, and its services include cloud sites, cloud servers, cloud files, and Mailtrust. Mailtrust targets smaller firms that don't possess IT resources to manage e-mail.

Rackspace tries to move ahead of the crowd by providing monthly hosting plans, server configuration and deployment, scalable bandwidth options, server maintenance, as well as installation and support for Internet-based applications under select operating systems. Built over time, its wares fall under four headings: sites, servers, files, and e-mail services.

In terms of customer assistance, Rackspace offers monitoring, virtualization, load balancing, data storage, content delivery, and stress testing. Data storage, content delivery, and system management are subject to scaling. Customers may have their onPremises software run by Rackspace hosting through its Cloud Sites offering. Managed hosting supports CRM, ERP, and other applications that can be handled through an Internet browser. Cloud Servers is a consumption-based service based on virtual servers. Its target market is user organizations that prefer to buy and employ for their IT a slice of a virtual infrastructure, from networking to the application layer.

Chapter 8

The Saga of an Open Architecture

8.1 Searching for an Open Architecture

An *architecture* is the art of building a house, a town, a system, or any other artifact involving ingenuity and engineering design, as well as obeying well-defined principles of functionality and proportion. This underlying concept is to meet established functional service goals, including serviceability, maintainability, and future growth requirements. Though, with some exceptions, like the Parthenon and the Coliseum, the architect does not build for eternity, he knows that his artifact may well exceed his own lifetime.

An architecture developed for information technology meets functional service requirements by absorbing and integrating different technologies and their products, as shown through the simple diagram in Figure 8.1. In that sense, as Chapter 1 brought to the reader's attention, an effective architectural solution will serve as a metalevel of the whole aggregate being built. Through its metalevel status, the architecture ensures a framework for more detailed design, aiming to make feasible:

- a holistic approach,
- greater elegance,

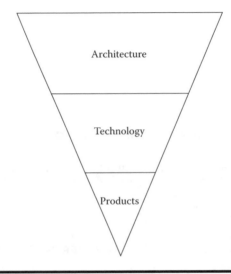

Figure 8.1   The simple philosophy of an architecture as a higher-up level in engineering design.

- higher performance, and
- if possible, a reduced cost per function.

Following up on this definition, the cloud computing's *architecture* will perform as *integrator* of multiple *cloud components* belonging to the four pillars discussed in Chapters 1 and 2. It will also incorporate an important element served by the cloud: the end users' *clients* and their application programming interfaces (APIs). As Chapter 2 brought to the reader's attention, there are different types of clients:

- the now classical workstations and PCs with hard disks;
- thin clients deprived of storage bandwidth, the latter being mapped into the vendor's database infrastructure; and
- mobile clients (often thin type), integrating with fixed clients and networked with the other system resources.

Clients, of client-server fame, are an integral part of a system architecture. They are the final destination of cloud computing services and therefore the visible tip of the iceberg of a user organization's high-level technology model.

Protocols and APIs characterizing the quality of service provided by clients are conditioned by the standards used in architectural design. They may not be open but may be proprietary to a vendor. An example is IBM's System Network Architecture (SNA) of the early 1970s, one of the first to become available in IT.

Or, they may be normalized, typically by a standards organization, and observed by all vendors. For instance, X.25* by CCITT† was an *open architecture*.

While standardization and normalization are, at least etymologically, unambiguous terms, nearly everybody has his or her own view of what the word *open* means when applied to an architecture. Therefore, it comes as no surprise that an open architecture has been given a variety of definitions, with many computer vendors claiming that their solution is "the only one really open." But at the bottom line the true meaning of an open architecture is that of an open *interface* architecture.

This is a simple expression but also a conditional one, because open APIs come in versions: *if* one deducts from that the fact that a cloud computing architecture is not going to be quite open, *then* he or she is fairly near to the truth. This is regrettable, but also understandable, because the results of a truly open architecture are

- wider competition,
- better choice, and
- greater cost-effectiveness.

All three bullets have attached to them attendant benefits for user organizations and implications for vendors; for instance, greater competition and less profits. Therefore, vendor arguments about supporting open architectural standards tend to be light like feathers.

None of the estimated 150 technology firms and other organizations that, led by IBM, signed the *Open Cloud Manifesto* felt they would be obliged to give up their competitive advantages, foregoing the projected market potential and benefits associated with proprietary solutions in the cloud. This is documented by the fact that no matter the manifesto:

- how open the *open cloud* will be has not yet been settled, and
- several experts project the rise of a new proprietary period, before rediscovering the benefits of openness in system standards.

More likely, the coming years will involve a blend of both proprietary and open-source provisioning. A distinct possibility is that traditional software companies will bring to the market some wares that are open (or even open up some of their current products), while traditional computer manufacturers and part of the new breed of so-called open-source firms will adopt a hybrid model in which:

---

* Both SNA and X.25 were network architectures; the first was vertical, monolithic, and hierarchical, and the second layered and horizontal. Their difference is not the subject of this book.
† CCITT was the international consultative committee of the PTTs. In that sense, it also served as an architectural standards body. PTT stands for Post, Telephone, and Telegraph. In France it has often been called "Petit Travail Tranquil" (a small and quiet job).

- they give away a basic version of their produce
- but make good profits by selling proprietary add-ons and the lock-ins that come with them (Chapter 5).

The exercise of control on how open the new programming products and software/hardware packages will be is at best an uncertain business. The only policing force is the user organizations themselves, and these don't work in unison as a pressure group. *If* they were keen to establish and police open cloud standards through an entity specifically instituted, financed, and managed for that purpose, *then* there would be a chance that an open cloud architecture sees the light.

Some people might answer that there already exist cloud computing standards; for instance, for web services, REST; for browsers, AJAX; for markup languages, HTML/XML; for communications, HTTP and XMPP; for data, XML and JSON; for security, OpenID, SSL/TLS, and OAuth; and for platforms, LAMP. Even for virtualization there is OVF. But these are not universally accepted standards, and they have not been projected specifically for cloud computing. Vendors are under no obligation of adherence to them, and there exists a good excuse for not applying them: they are not terribly efficient.

Practically all of them are *déjà vu*, and they predate the advent of cloud computing. Critics would add that fundamentally, this is a not at all exciting heap of initials, most of them pseudostandards in the sense that their observance is rather voluntary, and where there are commitments, vendors have come up with different versions.

As for the *Open Cloud Manifesto*, what it essentially provides is a vague set of principles for companies that are under no legal obligation to observe them. The goal may be that of keeping the cloud platform open and customer-centric, but when agreements and standards are not enforceable, they become useless.

In addition, while behind the manifesto one find names like IBM, Cisco, EMC, VMware, and SAP, other important players, like Amazon, Microsoft, and Salesforce.com, have stayed away. According to anecdotal evidence, this abstention is due not to commercial reasons but to the fact that the cloud computing manifesto itself is in the clouds.

People still believing that the cloud is an open architecture might say that there exists the Open Cloud Standards Incubator (OCSI), to which is connected the Distributed Management Initiative (VMAN). True enough, OCSI has recently formed an incubator to write preliminary specifications that might promote interoperability between:

- the public cloud and
- private clouds within companies and hosts.

If and when that happens, it might enable cloud service portability, but we are not yet there, and it is not going to be available tomorrow. In addition, as the preceding paragraphs explained, it is not enough to obtain adherence. The commitment must be legally binding and policed, which does not seem to be forthcoming.

Neither are the cloud computing hardware and software vendors—as well as the user organizations—the only parties that should participate in standards setting. Telcos are a very important player, at least on the Internet side, but they are absent from the manifesto list, and nobody guarantees that they will join binding norms on a global basis.

In this connection we are talking about broadband Internet, and one should not forget that America, which is its number one user, ranks thirty-fifth in broadband penetration among Organization for Economic Cooperation and Development (OECD) countries. Other jurisdictions are even worse because the telco is still a state monopoly. Last but not least, the big game in normalization will be around 3G and its successors. In the United States, one in four households has now gone mobile, and at current rates the last landline in the United States may be disconnected around 2025.*

8.2 Challenges Posed by Big Systems

Fellow technologists will surely appreciate that any way one wants to measure it, cloud computing will be a very big system. To be successful, engineers and administrators must develop the ability to handle its size and complexity, as well as the dramatic changes and uncertainty it will bring along. Big systems are not small systems that grew over time by outpacing their original technical requirements and utility objectives. Big systems have their own architectural and system design requirements, and these must be fulfilled in the most dependable manner, for the resulting aggregate to perform its mission in an able manner.

Contrarians may say that while the Internet is today a big system, it has not been designed as such. This would be the wrong assumption, because in its original incarnation the Internet has been a defense network projected as a big system. By contrast, other networks and their computing environments that did not benefit from a big system perspective have been characterized by performance bottlenecks due to the traffic they handle, their protocols, and data structures.

The general technology directions envisaged for the second decade of this century stand a good chance to become generally accepted. But the design and administration principles that should characterize them are not yet worked out. This is a handicap because the more widespread a network becomes, the less each of its users owns it or has control over attached devices and their transactions. Particularly in an open network nobody can legislate performance, yet performance criteria are

---

* *The Economist*, August 15, 2009. The quoted article says: "If the telephone network in New York State were a stand-alone business, it would already be in bankruptcy. In recent years it has lost 40 percent of its landlines and revenues have dropped by more than 30 percent."

vital; otherwise, its throughput will degrade, its security will become questionable, and interest to it will bend.

Cloud computing is a big system, and those employing it (whether vendors or user organizations) will be hurt if it exhibits design flaws. With complex systems design flaws arise primarily from the use of conceptual structures that worked well with smaller, simpler, and static aggregates but do not answer the requirements posed by a system that is dynamic and rapidly growing.

To a considerable extent, complex structures have nonlinear behavior, largely due to an increasing stochastic interaction among processes. Individually, all by themselves, the latter might behave linearly, but the aggregate acquires nonlinear characteristics within the larger system context. In addition, under the influence of its players, the impact of the environment within which the system operates changes over time, with the effect that it may discourage or altogether disallow certain services, operations, or actions.

The pros of cloud computing say that there is no such risk because solutions offered by vendors, particularly in the infrastructural domain (Section 8.3), are characterized by *scalability*. According to this opinion, architectural choices that have been made account for *elasticity in the provision of facilities* by means of onDemand provisioning of cloud resources. This is supposed to happen practically in real time on a self-service basis. The pros also add that the cloud has available ways and means for fine-grain performance monitoring.

Considered all by itself, scalability is a nice concept. Not only resources but also applications must scale upward as the number of users and transactions increases, while maintaining contractual response times and throughput rates (Chapter 10). However, the statement that "architectural choices have been made" and that these account for elasticity in the cloud is patently false.

- There has been no grand design for cloud computing and therefore no systemic architectural choices.
- One must not confuse the notion of an open architecture touted by a manifesto with a grand architectural design in a big system sense.

As a matter of principle, there is no doubt that cloud computing must benefit from built-in elasticity, since servers and other resources are automatically shared among thousands of clients. But, at any specific instance there are limits to how much they can scale up successfully to meet higher rates of usage on demand—and these can only be studied through and set by a grand design.

Because of the absence of a *big system* study, what we already know as handy and doable with smaller systems is questionable (at best). The fact that elasticity, and therefore scalability, has economic benefits is in no way in doubt. Vendors, however, will be under constant pressure between:

- overprovisioning, and hence underutilization of expensive resources; and

■ underprovisioning, with disastrous effects on response time, bottlenecks, and reliability.

To make matters more complex, there are other systems variables, like spikes in demand from hundreds or thousands of user organizations that operate online and dearly depend on the cloud's resources. Usage-based pricing, too, may turn on its head, as it will be under the pressure exercised by forces of competition on one hand, and confronted by the risk of overcapacity on the other.*

Anyone with experience in system design is not apt to underestimate the benefits of elasticity in connection to big systems. Unexpected bursts on demand, however, have unexpected consequences. There exist financial, technical, and administrative limits to elasticity. The megacenters of cloud computing infrastructure will be run by people (at least I hope so),† and it is only human to fail from time to time.

I am fully aware that what is written in these paragraphs is controversial. Some of the experts are so taken by the supposed elasticity of cloud resources that they hope user organizations will be benefiting from them without paying a premium in higher cost and in lower reliability. They say that such a facility is an "unprecedented event in IT history." Those who believe in such myths will live to regret it. It is much more likely that the event that is really unprecedented in IT history will be a total system failure, resulting in a deadly blackout.

Another issue that has not yet been paid due attention—and for which there is more wishful thinking than facts—is data compression in a cloud environment. There are today available specialized compression algorithms addressing incremental backups, which can reduce the latter's size and therefore the associated costs. However, backup takes only a part of the storage need to accommodate huge databasing requirement. The lion's share should be available for real-time access, query, updating, and other end user needs—unless one wishes to return to the Paleolithic age of computing with batch processing.

If cloud computing is one day worth its salt, *then* all storage resources should be open online to the richness of oncoming queries, with contractually ensured performance guarantees. Under this condition, the complexity of data structures directly supported by the storage system will make it difficult (though not impossible) to meet user needs the way presently suggested by cloud vendor promises; for instance:

---

* The overcapacity of the global auto industry and shipping industry speaks volumes in this regard.
† The fatal 2009 accident of the Air France airliner from Rio to Paris strongly advises against using models to run the cloud's megacenters. In all likelihood (the nearest thing to an official version), the accident's origins had been an altitude measurement instrument that failed and automatic pilot went berserk. In late August 2009, Air France correctly decided to retrain all its pilots on manual command connected to emergency procedures.

- a great deal of scalability,
- cost-effective resource management, and
- requirements for data durability and other criteria.

Satisfactory answers to each of these bullets must be provided within the context of a big system that is, by necessity, complex and should respond as well to other calls: minimizing overhead, providing resources for virtualization, and optimizing performance. Notice that some of these goals are contradictory, like providing the described functionality through the design, installation, and operation of extremely large-scale commodity data centers at low cost.

Still another challenge confronting cloud computing, from a big system viewpoint, is that the lack of standards (Section 8.1) increases the likelihood of confusion and adds to the difficulty of collaboration among vendors when they will be (unavoidably) confronted with systemic risks, such as regional blackouts and widespread viruses. In addition, the user organizations' confusion will be increased by their fear of being locked in to a big system with protocols and interfaces defined by this or that vendor.

For instance, Microsoft has been winning the battle to control standards for desktops through APIs by rallying independent software firms. Microsoft's "standards" have allowed it to write applications with the knowledge and comfort of a market supported by the software heavyweights.*

Being locked in to a vendor's solution through the lure of cloud computing, the way practiced four decades ago with mainframes (see Chapter 5), is indeed a major worry that, potentially, has huge implications. It may take unconventional action to operate the lock-in, but vendors are inventive and this is not inconceivable. If applications software, databasing, and computing become very profitable services delivered over the Internet, not just one but several vendors will be building cloud cyclops.

8.3 Infrastructure as a Utility

Every dynamic system is characterized by an almost steady expansion, modification, and restructuring. Cloud computing will not be immune to either of these factors. Some vendors say that the transition through the stages of the cloud's expansion will be smoother if they are allowed to observe *architectural freedom* while ensuring good functionality and improving the price/performance of their solution.

The downside of a vendor's architectural freedom is that it does not facilitate the porting of applications between the providers' clouds, even if virtual machine formats encapsulate all components of an application. Virtual machines employed for

---

* This is by no means a criticism of Microsoft. It is just an example. Practically all vendors of computer hardware and software follow that policy; that's why the aforementioned manifesto is just for those who like to believe in miracles.

the cloud's infrastructure are not silver bullets. Apart from their huge overhead (to which reference has been made), they present scheduling concerns particularly for:

- certain types of processes and
- the administration of infrastructural megacenters that are in the making.

As we have already seen, the way providers present the cloud to user organizations is as a seamless utility. What they forget to point out is that because universal standards are by no means guaranteed, moving from one Internet cloud service provider to another could well prove to be much more difficult than switching between mainframes in the old days.

Critics put it this way: "Try to move your My Space profile to Facebook without manually retyping everything and we will talk afterwards." That's a good way of bringing home the difficulties associated with switches in the cloud. User organizations will be well advised to thoroughly investigate the portability issue in the cloud's utility infrastructure before making any commitment.

Another architectural requirement for which the cloud services vendor should provide evidence, to substantiate its claim about an infrastructural utility, is the way in which it handles the applications programming interfaces. This is an issue that links the cloud provider's infrastructural solution to its development platform's characteristics and possible constraints. Plenty of questions cry for an answer:

- Are a few API calls enough to request and configure the virtualized hardware?
- Are there *a priori* constraints on the kind of applications the infrastructure can host?
- Does the vendor's search engine impose any requirements that do not allow seamless access to other vendors' clouds?
- Does the platform being offered permit developers to program whatever routine they want?
- Is there any limitation in the use, or rationing, of computing time in servicing a particular application?
- How exactly do the proprietary automatic scaling and availability mechanisms work?

In connection to the first query, the user organization should look up the *architectural semantics* that describe the behavior of each component part in the broader virtual machine description. Architectural semantics are at a much lower level of abstraction than functional unit semantics and, as such, they assist in effective integration of machine-independent modules.

At the origin of the second question can be found the fact that several designers and developers do not have a hypermedia mind-set, while users don't have the time to recast existing applications when migrating them to the cloud by incorporating hypermedia functionality. Therefore, they depend on the vendor's navigational support, including the ability to:

- import, export, and use any data format; and
- incorporate different hypermedia modes.

In regard to the third query, the user organization's study of a vendor's infrastructural characteristics (and associated platform primitives) should focus on whether they provide support for a collaborative environment—not only in a multiuser sense but also for applications developed in different platforms (multiuser provisions should include concurrency control). Cross-platform facilities are necessary for seamless use of services across vendors' clouds and heterogeneous operating systems. What are the constraints in extending functionality of selected component parts?

The user organization should as well look for a valid answer to the fourth query. A prerequisite to this is to establish *a priori* a technical description of each of its applications entering the vendor's utility landscape, including the (current and projected) resources on which it should run, information elements that it uses, as well as associated frequency and type of access requirements.* (The description of an application's characteristics does not include only guestimated processing time and frequency, but also comments and relationships.)

In replying to the user's request about the polyvalence of his infrastructural utility, the vendor might make reference to his grid experience. This, however, is no proof of lack of constraints. *If* this is indeed the answer given by the cloud provider, *then* the way to bet is that it is conscious of the existence of processing problems.

A similar reference is valid in connection to storage. Cross-cloud services are critical because part and parcel of a well-architectured cloud framework is the user organization's ability to move data in and out of different vendors' systems without delay and at low cost, while also ensuring a high degree of security (Chapter 9) and reliability (Chapter 10).

As the foregoing discussion demonstrates, effective use of the cloud infrastructure raises a number of critical queries that call for accurate answers. In putting together its findings (and vendor's responses) about the infrastructural utility, the user organization may employ a methodology that has been used for intranets and extranets. Two different design approaches can be employed:

- bottom up, which starts by first putting together the infrastructural characteristics within the vendor's cloud; and
- top down, which targets first the choice of applications and definition of their characteristics, using the latter to guide one's hand in the choice of infrastructure.

---

* Input volume and rates, as well as bandwidth, are also important.

While both approaches are architecturally oriented and their aim is to help define a framework with which a valid solution could fit, the approach followed in this section favors the top-down method—hence the basic requirement that has been outlined: to first define the operational requirements and their onDemand routines, in order to quantify and qualify what we want to achieve.

It needs no explaining that knowing what we are after is vital in all human enterprises and therefore in all design work. The most sound way to choosing an information technology environment is to *think first* not only what the applications are but also what are their prerequisites, which must be satisfied through reengineering (Chapter 6). As for the technical prerequisites regarding the cloud infrastructure, which has been raised in this section, these should never be left for "later on" because they will never be ensured postmortem:

- they have to be used at vendor selection time, and
- they must be negotiated and fully guaranteed through contractual clauses, valid at least over seven years.

Even under the most optimistic scenario, the transition to cloud computing could take years or longer to fully play out, because benefiting from it would require reengineering of internal systems and procedures. Any investment advisor worth his or her salt would suggest that the cost of this reengineering has to be recovered over the next five years of a firm contract for cloud services.

8.4 The Cloud's System Architecture and Its Primitives

Up to this point the term *architecture* has been used in a generic sense. Since, however, we have been talking of the provider's cloud offering, there was an implicit reference to *system architecture* and its primitives, as well as to some of the characteristics that govern them. These concerned both the contribution they provide to the cloud aggregate, and their impact on functions and components.

Taken as a group, system primitives make up the facilities supporting the definition of what the cloud infrastructure can or cannot provide. Other elements that assist in defining the system architecture are links, nodes, and interface implementation outlines needed to connect client software with servers; deployment specifications*; and the distribution of computing and storage resources across the global network.

Other definitions qualify the system architecture. These include the nature of software modules used to build service templates, existence of knowledge-enriched

---

* Placing onDemand server hardware and basic software in operation.

interfaces, the nature of modules necessary for scaling and fast response to evolving user needs, and more, for instance:

- architectural principles necessary to reduce the complexity of service support,
- smart routines for wrapping legacy applications,* and
- provision of means to facilitate server-to-server communications.

Furthermore, an important element in the definition of the cloud's system architecture is its modularity, so that software components are designed and execute independently of any other, with each module (when needed to do so) being removed and upgraded without degrading the aggregate's performance.

Still another critical consideration is the presence of embedded facilities allowing each component to be reusable and shared across services, while different resources work cooperatively to perform the cloud's function. The system architecture will also define whether and where there are limits on the number of services or functions that can be performed—or alternatively, geographic and time zone limitations.

User organizations should appreciate that cloud vendors are not equally strong in knowledge-enriched solutions. These are critical because they help in establishing a better technical service to the user anytime, anywhere in the world. Employing an intelligent cloud infrastructure as a base makes it easier to create virtual business architectures (Section 8.5) that address specific customer requirements in areas such as:

- transactions processing,
- cash management,
- payment orders, and
- trust and custody (see also Chapter 13).

If the cloud's architectural primitives and overall system design are ingeniously chosen, *then* customized applications defined by the user organization's business architecture will be able to select and repackage available cloud processes in the form needed for a particular operation or interaction with minimal human intervention. *A priori*, this requires a flexible framework that ensures that individual function processing and service modules can be brought together by means of an object-oriented inheritance mechanism, to execute needed functions. This:

- maximizes flexibility and
- speeds up the execution process.

Knowledge-enriched architectural standards can ensure that all modules pertaining to a given job work together in a coherent structure, creating a processing

---

* With the wrapper acting as a business element server.

model that can be kept in full evolution while serving day-to-day business. (See in Section 8.6 real-life applications involving a financial services architecture that deals with trading, positioning, and risk management, in conjunction with the vendor's system architecture.)

Other system architecture primitives will be scaling up and down computation and storage in a way transparent to the programmer, facilities for modeling based on declarative descriptions of application components, declarative specification of Internet level topology, internal placement details, security chores, and more. System primitives should also provide routable network addresses.

Since the way to bet is that, by following up on current practices, the cloud services will be billed on a *pay-as-you-do* basis, the overall solution requires a cost accounting system, preferably built in since the drafting board. It is very difficult to retrofit it afterwards, because add-ons for timekeeping will be ineffectual as the different user functions and associated supports will be running on virtual machines.

It has also already been brought to the reader's attention that one of the requirements for competitiveness in a pay-as-you-do billing environment is the optimization of the system's performance. This sometimes runs against other goals, such as very low response time (Chapter 10), but generally there is scope for optimization.

Simpler alternatives to pay-as-you-do are subscription agreements negotiated at the time of procurement. Many are based on an *a priori* as-you-do, leading to an estimate of types of needed resources. As an example, roughly 65 percent of wide area networks (WANs) cost comes from high-end routers and the balance from the fiber. The cost of resources depends on choices the vendor made in building its system. Routers made from commodity components provide a lower-cost alternative.

At the system design level, to achieve sought-after functionality at lower cost, for several years some vendors have employed advanced technology like object-oriented databases* and fuzzy engineering. It is a pity that, from what is known, cloud computing providers do not employ in a significant way object-oriented approaches in their system architecture. If they did, they would have found that these permit considerable flexibility in handling user organization requirements by referring to attributes, functions, and instances of a business element or a collection of instances.

In this process, each element triggers another in a domino-like manner, following a path that constitutes a business transaction but in a way influencing potential paths. Processing follows actual paths similar to audit trails through business elements. An actual path contains records of events in the handling of a transaction to its completion. The behaviors and attributes of business element instances essentially constitute programming instances. Eventually these will become *agents*, which may be perishable or permanent objects.

---

* D. N. Chorafas, *Intelligent Multimedia Databases* (Englewood Cliffs, NJ: Prentice Hall, 1994).

In the system solution being described, each server has an interface through which it offers publicly defined services. As members of the system architecture, business element servers act only in response to appropriate messages with different types of services offered through this message-passing interface. For instance, post, advise, and validate are supports enabling the activities of members of the global network.

In addition, administrative services are necessary to manage software instances, such as create, find, and select, needed by the architecture to ensure consistency across servers. Knowledge-enriched artifacts can be instrumental in validating a client software instance's right to request the service. To perform such validation, agents have information like needed attributes.

When a server executes an administrative function at the request of a software instance, it also confirms the entitlement that goes with a valid identity. This wrapper would appear as offering services predefined by the architecture, while using software that translates from predefined services to private services.

In this particular example of a small system architecture (which is by no means a universal practice), each application will be managed as a single unit, although it may have many parts. Cases such as demand deposits, currency swaps, forward rate agreements, custody, funds transfers, and so on are created from parts to serve particular user requirements. (Bank clients, managers, traders, and other professionals are customers of application integrators—the latter being customers of server handlers.)

The reason for including this example in the present section is to provide evidence of the details the user organization's CIO and his assistants should ask the cloud vendor to provide. Prior to committing himself or herself, the CIO should know *which* business and administrative services are being effectively handled—and how. From the user's perspective, the cloud is defined by its system architecture, all the way from clients to databases, computational servers, communications gear, and primitives.

8.5 The User Organization's Business Architecture

The *business architecture* and system architecture are different ball games, yet people and companies tend to confuse the sense of a business architecture with that of a systems architecture. The business architecture must be planned. It is by no means a hill of sand of computers and communications solutions, or whatever resulted from years of haphazard growth.

The practical example in Section 8.6 (from the financial industry) shows what the business architecture should target. Its requirements help demonstrate that system architectures that have been chosen haphazardly lack flexibility to support novel applications, are unable to cope with unforeseen demands, or are outright impeding the firm's ability to deploy new products and services quickly.

Quite often, in the background of such unwise choices is the "favored vendor," who tells the CEO and CIO not to worry because it is offering them a prime solution. That's precisely the spirit and practice described earlier in this book as cloud in cuckoo land. The convergence of data, voice, and video onto a single backbone multiservice network that some cloud providers describe as being *avant garde* is stuff of the 1980s, not of the second decade of this century. Centralized data processing dates still earlier (to the 1960s), while latency control, bandwidth allocation, traffic prioritization, and the like are old news.

Moreover, all that stuff has absolutely nothing to do with the business architecture. By contrast, there is a long list of challenges a business architecture must confront, to enable *our* company to break ranks with the majority of its competitors, and move ahead of them. Take investment banking as an example. Some of the key terms heard in this line of business are *placement power* and *distribution network*.

If we are in the business of originating loans, underwriting or placing securities, and performing other investment banking activities, we must have a distribution network that makes possible the turning over of assets at a rapid pace, by selling them to investors wherever they might be located.* In this context, the chosen business architecture must be characterized by several attributes, key among them being:

- *globality*, adjustable to the fluidity and shifting patterns of worldwide political and economic situations;
- *capillarity*, reaching every corner of our bank's operations, and every potential client, to deliver financial services; and
- *instantaneity*—market prices change in a split second, and if one is a market operator, or investor, one risks major losses if the reaction time is slow.

IT technology is subservient to the business architecture, and the solutions it provides must be sensitive to requirements posed by event triggering, calculation of entitled positions, cancel/amend, operations generated before redemption, redemption transactions, transactions for long and short position redemptions, and, evidently, consolidation of:

- assets and
- risks positions.

Furthermore, the online system must be able to distinguish unsettled trades and open repos, local tax rates, withholding, depot account rates, and other items according to compliance requirements. It should also be in charge of settlement and custodian information, integrating such data with notification and claims management.

While these look like standard banking operations, in reality they are not, because each company has its individuality—partly due to its history, principles,

---

* Placement power is a human, not technological, trait.

and clients with their expectations. Above all stands the firm's strategic plan, and no two strategic plans are the same.

Therefore, the first and most vital element that helps in defining a business architecture is the company's strategic plan. Just like it is not possible to build any long-term structure, whether it is a city, a building, a business division, or a sales network, without some master blueprint, we cannot develop a long-term IT solution without a blueprint that tells us what our objectives are and, by consequence, what we need in supporting facilities. In this sense, the business architecture also assists in ensuring a permanent flexible adaptation of IT infrastructure to:

- ongoing changes in our business environment and
- internal organizational requirements enabling us to confront market forces.

In other terms, the business architecture serves both as blueprint and as framework for steadily improved computers and communications services, including those directed to managers and professionals. This is demonstrated by its products, such as timely, uninterrupted, and increasingly sophisticated service to all end users—and adaptability to corporate and client information requirements, as they evolve.

Along the principles defined in the preceding paragraphs, the business architecture is essentially a master plan for information technology, ensuring that it is able to serve business goals, defining software and hardware requirements within a medium- to longer-term business timeframe, and bringing end users squarely into the picture of evolving IT solutions. For a growing number of companies, the business architecture they adopt must provide a global view of:

- customers,
- products,
- competition,
- risks, and
- profits.

In order to meet these objectives, the business architecture should account for the way in which people are working in each organization position, from the top management level to the lowest level of supervision. This means knowing the company itself, its products, and its competition; analyzing the industry to which it belongs, and the market it addresses; as well as being ahead of the curve of technology—in a business sense.

The business architecture must be flexible and adaptable because information requirements change as fast as products, services, and the marketplace. Such adaptation is never ending because, as many firms have come to realize, if they can't incorporate new technology ahead of their competitors, they will be left in the dust.

A different way of making this statement is that a key objective of the business architecture is to make technology serve *innovation economics*. Companies with experience along this line of reference suggest that attaining such a goal requires two things at the same time:

■ being able to define, and keep on redefining, *our* business architecture as the market environment is in full evolution and
■ providing life cycle management of human capital and technological investments, which promote *our* ability to stay competitive.

This is precisely where cloud computing comes into the discussion. The primitives of the vendor's system architecture discussed in Section 8.4 are needed to satisfy the information requirements posed by the user organization's business architecture, both at the level of partners (clients and suppliers) and inside the firm. The latter should definitely include top management requirements.

The importance of serving top management's decision-making needs has been slow to sip down the organization at the IT level. Part of the reason is the difficulty of defining what must be available, due to board members and CEOs' illiteracy in information technology, to which exist some most interesting exceptions. The number one reason, however, is historical: EDP* has developed as a successor to EAM† chores and kept focusing on the administrative, not the executive, level. This concept filtered into the widening IT landscape.

On the other hand, there have always been exceptional individuals able to move fast, seeing through their policies without allowing slacks to develop. After salvaging Turkey from disintegration, Mustafa Kemal Atatürk replaced Arabic with Latin script. Once he made up his mind, there was no letting go. Steady pressure was exercised not only at the top but also at the bottom. Mustafa Kemal went to towns and villages and talked to the common man. Then, once plenty of people were engaged, reform was carried out within six months.‡

This, however, is not the way the average executive operates (and that's why he is average). Organizations are made of people, and people are often slow in making up their mind, in making decisions, and putting them into effect. This is another reason why the metalayer of a business architecture should act as a catalyst to rapid motion—providing management with the ability to spot opportunities instantly and always keeping in mind that business opportunities are often a by-product of mismatched conditions that are short-lived.

---

* Electronic data processing.
† Electrical accounting machines.
‡ Andrew Mango, *Atatürk* (New York: Overlook Press, 2000).

8.6 Financial Services Applications Architecture: A Case Study

Section 8.5 made the point that senior management can so much better exploit developing opportunities if the company's business architecture is flexible and knowledge enriched, as well as able to process online transaction information, provide real-time position reports, ring alarm bells when risk limits are broken, and handle other important event management activities. The business architecture we adopt should as well specify the level of sophistication of IT applications, all the way to simulation, experimentation, and the evaluation of alternative courses of action.

As Robert McNamara had said, when important decisions are made, the manager must examine all sorts of flavors. Alfred Sloan aptly suggested that for critical decisions we should have at our disposal accurate and timely information that always allows us to reflect and develop dissent.

Timely and accurate (not necessarily precise) financial information is vital because we must always be prepared to retrench, if risk and return projections turn on their head. We should also be able to cope with a multiplicity of financial exposures. The market's rapid pace and global nature require constant attention to:

■ position risks,
■ credit risks, and
■ liquidity risks.

Conceived by Bankers Trust, the *Financial Services Application Architecture* targeted the flexible development of information technology solutions that allow all applicants to collaborate and exchange data (stored on heterogeneous equipment at the lower architectural level) in a uniform way at the middle level and *customized* at the higher level regardless of:

■ location,
■ platform, or
■ data structure.

Known as Financial Services Data Exchange, a custom-made utility operated at different servers, OSs, DBMSs, and transaction processors, bringing together all of the bank's independent applications—and responding in real time to queries and information sharing requirements. At the core of the exchange's design was the ability to allow owners of information to publish it by means of a record broadcast mechanism permitting multiple subscribers to receive it either:

■ in real-time, if they were currently listening, or
■ through the utility's store-and-forward capability.

Being ahead of its time by nearly two decades (since it was designed in the early 1990s) the concept underpinning the Financial Services Applications Architecture can easily be seen as a forerunner of cloud computing, as well as a successful implementation that cloud applications by user organizations should aim to attain even if with twenty years' delay.

In terms of information management, publisher data were differentiated by descriptive tags that made it feasible for subscribers to reference any or all of the information elements through the use of the exchange's remapping capability. This allowed publishers to add or remove data within their publication, without adversely affecting subscribers, since the latter addressed virtual data tags rather than the physical data record.

The Bankers Trust business architecture required, and the system provided, control over who could subscribe to an information source. This gave publishers the ability to preauthorize who could access their information, down to the individual record level. These are examples of checks and balances to which must abide any IT utility, cloud or no cloud, in order to contribute to a dynamic business environment.

The Financial Services Applications Architecture saw to it that because publishers needed only to communicate their information once, they were no longer required to maintain multiple, customized data links to various applications needing such information. This helped to reduce the expense associated with maintenance programmers and their supporting technology. It also assisted in avoiding lots of errors.

Furthermore, the fact that applications communicated with each other using a common utility made it possible to apply advancements in communications technology to a single set of software, rather than having to implement modifications separately at each individual subsystem. This helped to swamp the cost of long-term maintenance, while enabling the exercise of greater control over technology investments.

The flexibility and functionality of the exchange utility designed under business architecture guidelines enabled Bankers Trust to develop, among other key applications, a comprehensive global Risk Management (RM). RM received information in real time from trading systems around the world, supporting an environment that provided *credit risk* and *market risk* exposures, alerting top management when exposure crossed preestablished control limits. This was made available:

- anywhere in the world,
- across all business lines, and
- on trade-by-trade basis, when detail was required.

The business architectures exchange was also used as the underlying transport mechanism of the bank's Global Asset Application. For this purpose, its functionality was extended from purely interapplication data exchange to router action all the way to the end user's workstation (the system's *client* in cloud jargon).

Over time, the fact that the Financial Services Application Architecture had been projected as a flexible and expandable framework made possible its expansion to cover business partner requirements. The bank's customers benefited from the extension of functions reaching them in the form of an interactive financial advisor. This required supporting trading activities as well as information distilling the pricing of complex financial instruments.

The routines incorporated in this particular application were originally developed to support the viewpoint of a trader who operates in several markets and handles a variety of specialized financial products. For starters, each trader's work basically consists of:

- constantly looking for developing opportunities and
- maximizing both the bank's return and those of his or her individual profit center (characterized by specific profit-making scenarios).

Hence, a financial services architecture must be tailored to each trader and serve in the most effective way his or her personalized portfolio management. Well beyond market quotes, this calls for customized information to meet every trader's unique profile and profit strategy. A similar statement is valid for every investment manager. Moreover, a financial services environment must provide market analysis and exposure estimates (associated with limits) to help in monitoring risk and return parameters.

Within the described flexible but focused and personalized applications environment exist atomic business elements comprising interest terms, currency targets, payment orders, commodity options, currency futures, general ledgers, and more. These are combined to form the products the bank sells—from dealing activities to asset management (Chapter 13), mortgage securitizations, account handling, and controlled disbursements. All business functions should be defined in terms of:

- their attributes and
- their behavioral profiles.

Like the example of this business architecture brought to the reader's attention, customization is important not only because many financial products, such as securitization, exotic derivatives, and special purpose vehicles (SPVs),* are complex but also because having specialized modules deal with only a single product (or set) sees to it that no one applications routine becomes overburdened or slowed down.

Last but not least, for management control purposes, sophisticated knowledge artifacts should oversee every trading activity, all traders, and all products. They

---

* D. N. Chorafas, *Financial Boom and Gloom. The Credit and Banking Crisis of 2007–2009 and Beyond* (London: Palgrave/Macmillan, 2009).

must be developed to ensure an overall balance of risk and reward through a flexible and highly tailored approach to meeting trading objectives, and at the same time promote rigorous risk management to avoid following down the drain AIG, Citigroup, and other banks who came hat in hand to the taxpayer to save themselves from oblivion.

8.7 The Architect's Job: Elegance, Simplicity, and Integration

Whether his or her remit is to work at the basic level of the system architecture (Section 8.4) or at the higher-up level of the business architecture (Sections 8.5 and 8.6), the *architect* is a person who bridges the gap between the physical and logical space. He codes his knowledge into structures that are logical but supported by an array of physical components' functionality and dependability.

Architecture is an art rather than a science, and as Marc Chagall, the painter, suggested, "In order to do something substantial in art one has to begin everything from the very start." An artist is one who forever remains within the six days of the world's creation, Chagall said, and from them he draws his paints. Only those six days! After that the world has been created. Master architects aim to create something new rather than to imitate. They do so by targeting three goals in one go:

- elegance,
- simplicity, and
- integration.

Elegance means refinement, grace, usefulness, good taste, culture. Something elegant is fine, tasteful, handsome, comely, well turned out, as well as apt, neat, and ingenious. The chosen architecture must bring an elegant solution to the problem of how to use information technology in the most effective way, helping the business to reach its goals.

Simplicity implies clarity, understandability, straightforwardness, lucidity, intelligibility, and restraint from making things complicated for complication's sake. Something simple is neat, understandable, and comprehensible, but it may also be naïve or elementary. To simplify in a meaningful sense means to clarify, untangle, clear up, explain, streamline. Simplicity also comprises ease of learning and ease of use. The structure of the Pantheon by architect Fidias was elegant but simple.

No better words than *elegance* and *simplicity* can be found to define the world of the larger entity, in which the architect must properly *integrate* myriad components, which may be heterogeneous yet should provide an esthetic functional aggregate. This task of integration must be characterized by completeness, power, and adaptability.

Effective integration means ease of moving between the various component parts and functions of an architectural design (made of hardware, software, and work methods), making them appear similar to the user. This requires a holistic concept, appropriate definition of functionality, ingenious design choices, projections on current and future implementation requirements, and flexibility for meeting them through:

- renewal and
- expansion.

The architect creates a model to map and study the system's design*: the configuration of physical and logical modules, selected details of each, and ways and means used by these modules to interconnect and integrate. It needs no explaining that a sound architectural model must take into account:

- the overall objective(s) of the architecture and
- the way it will embed into its framework chosen models and functions.

Attention should be paid to the concurrency of operations, and since in a dynamic environment the latter frequently change, the architectural solution must provide a platform for experimentation, optimization, and testing. All three are necessary in order to:

- attack cost and complexity,
- accelerate delivery of services, and
- provide security and reliability.

While the most frequent experimentation will concentrate on subsystems, the means available must enable a holistic approach to the evaluation of alternative architectural designs, because a modern system will operate end to end. This is particularly true of big systems (Section 8.2)—and therefore of the cloud—which address a whole partner community, including not only the providers' own business activities and user organizations, but also independent software vendors, system integrators, resellers, and original equipment manufacturers (OEMs), who add value to systems and services.

While the missions of system architects and business architects may superficially seem to be only remotely related, their contributions interlock because of the variety of applications evolving at the side of both vendors and user organizations. A modern bank, for example, is likely to use cloud computing services at two levels,

---

* Many different architectural modeling methodologies have been used. Some map processes to physical resources but have the disadvantage of being single-layer diagrams incapable of handling larger, polyvalent operations.

each with fairly different requirements for system support: the more common and less exciting is that of tactical operations, such as money-in, money-out, and underlying transactions.

Its object is to execute within a structured information environment, as well as assist in improving the productivity of middle to lower management. At this lower level, applications must be attended to with onDemand commoditized software. But as the case study on the Financial Services Applications Architecture (Section 8.6) has shown, the more sophisticated level is that of executive information whose service requirements are different than those of the common level.

The architect must be aware of the fact that at the executive level the value of any IT solution will be judged by its *credibility*, and credibility is established on the basis of the quality, accuracy, and timeliness of *deliverables* that which promote factual decisions and operational excellence. Excuses like "system failures are the cloud vendor's responsibility" will not be looked upon kindly at the executive level.

Quality, cost, security, and reliability of the chosen solution are the reason why I never tire of repeating that business strategy and IT strategy must be established almost simultaneously as one task. The most important product contributed by IT at the executive level is timely information and analytics sustaining management insight and foresight. It is not just technology because technology without tier 1 deliverables means nothing.

Both architects and CIOs should appreciate the fact that information technology has moved outside its traditional setting inside the organization's structured operations, to become a basic support tool to senior management and a key element to relationship management. IT systems should no longer be designed to just handle EAM business. Their primary mission is about business enablement, not business support.

The criterion for *business enablement* is direct contribution to enterprise profits, and this requires a proactive approach reaching all the way to human capital, rather than being limited to machines. To deliver, IT management must also reverse current statistics, which are grim: less than 10 percent of IT budgets is available for new projects; 35 percent of projects come in more than one month late, while another 20 percent never reach anywhere; and 50 percent of IT investments fail to match their intended return. Beyond all this, IT security must be vastly improved—and this should be shown through facts, not words.

Chapter 9

Internet Cloud Security

9.1 Who Owns Whose Information on the Cloud?

On August 17, 2009, the U.S. Department of Justice (DOJ) announced that 130 million credit card numbers were stolen in what was the largest-ever personal data theft. A few days later the DOJ charged a man for identity theft. Albert Gonzalez allegedly stole information on these millions of credit cards from the computers of several retailers, including 7-Eleven.*

Identity theft and plenty of other security breaches do not necessarily happen because of lack of care; a more potent reason is that information thieves are so ingenious. Companies normally apply existing risk assessment tools connected to security capabilities and exercise controls. They use firewalls and other routines, address regulatory and audit issues, develop a backup process (in case the need arises), and demand security safeguards for computers and communications vendors.

But security breaches, including serious ones, continue to happen, even if user organizations integrate security features into their infrastructure and aim to securely manage their information resources. Vendors, for their part, don't cease to announce new offerings of end-to-end security solutions that (supposedly) will work in a fully reliable way (they don't).

Since major security risks continue to happen, the way to bet is that cloud computing is not going to waive them through magic. Neither is it true that security typically improves with centralization of data, due to "greater care" and increased security-centered resources. That's what different vendors tell user organizations

---

* Gonzalez once worked with the Secret Service, helping track down computer hackers.

to sell them cloud computing services, but negative examples from Microsoft, Citibank, and other cases document that such claims are unfounded.

Ironically, the opposite argument is also on the radar screen. Some cloud vendors suggest that security concerns are red herrings thrown by aging chief information officers (CIOs), trying to justify their salaries because they will be out of a job if companies no longer maintain their own big data centers. What that argument hides is that these "big data centers" are just a small fraction of what the big-big cloud represents.

Understandably, security worries raise concerns about loss of control over sensitive information. The argument that cloud providers are able to devote resources to solving security issues that many customers cannot afford is only believable by users who are ready to relegate their security responsibilities just to get rid of them.

■ The cloud and its providers cannot offer, in good conscience, anything better than what current technology makes available, for security reasons, to everybody.

■ By contrast, the cloud increases security concerns; potential security issues grow with very large-scale systems, and with virtualization technologies that are still not too well understood (to put it mildly).

There was a time, which is by now resolutely past, when security concerns were addressed first by a data encryption standard (DES) that was 64 bits long. It was broken and replaced by a 128-bit device (which is also peanuts in security terms). Then came software-supported security, such as firewalls, but with time these became a rather banal commodity, leading firms to add security features like antivirus and antispam, as well as measures to fend off distributed denial of service (DDoS) attacks.

At basic software level one of the great hopes for security/protection has been Kerberos. Kerberos, however, came and went while the security challenges remained. Most of these efforts revolved around the concept that threat protection and access authentication will be enough. They are not. Hence, the move toward what could be described as a richness of security features.

A decade ago it was thought that NASA had found the security elixir. But events proved that its computer security was so vulnerable to attack that hackers could easily disrupt command and control operations, including the tracking of orbiting spacecraft (as a comment in a government report had it). The General Accountability Office (GAO), the investigative arm of Congress, said its teams penetrated NASA systems that process and distribute scientific data and broke into NASA's most vital networks. The GAO picked systems at one of NASA's ten field centers, by "using easily guessed passwords."* Its report concluded that the results of the space agency's work to improve security were exaggerated.

NASA is not alone in exaggerating the effectiveness of its protective measures. Industrial and commercial companies, including computer manufacturers and

---

* *Communications of the ACM*, July 1999, Vol. 42, No. 7.

software firms, do the same. (Intruders broke into Microsoft's well-protected database, as well as Citibank's.) Neither is it a secret that in the general case:

■ data are often left unencrypted on web servers,
■ there is no audit verification after transactions are done, and
■ security management by user organizations is not transparent.

All this has happened prior to cloud computing, and therefore the new environment is not responsible for it. The difference, however, is that so far these were isolated cases—hence more or less contained in terms of damage due to imperfect security. Now we are talking about millions of servers in the cloud with an unprecedented number of accesses by clients. At the core are two critical queries:

■ Who owns whose information in the cloud?
■ Which party has primary responsibility for safeguarding?

Theoretically, the answer to the first query is the user organization. The information elements stored at the cloud provider's site are those of its clients, its employees, and its accounts. If so, this is a flagrant case of absentee management because the least that can be said is that these information elements are not under their owner's direct watch but under somebody else's, that of the cloud infrastructure provider.

This curious reversal of responsibilities (which is accompanied by absentee accountability) brings up the second critical query: Is the provider assuming legal responsibility in case of identity theft, with all damages covered? As far as the cloud infrastructure is concerned, this case has not yet been tested in court, but other evidence from similar cases is disquieting.

In France, in an identity theft case from a bank's database, hackers siphoned out a customer's whole credit line. The bank not only did not recredit the money but also charged its customer interest for his negative balance. A lower court cancelled the interest charges but did not order the bank to credit its customer with the stolen amount, while the account was in its custody (the case is in appeal at a higher court).*

This is by no means an isolated case. Some years ago the Privacy Rights Clearinghouse reckoned that there were roughly 750,000 cases of identity theft a year in the United States alone. Today the actual number of thefts may well be higher, particularly since:

■ many victims do not know how to report the crime, and
■ others do not realize that it has happened until they are hit in the head by the after effects.

---

* There are thousands of identity theft cases in Europe every year. This particular one attracted public attention because of the punitive position taken by a bank against its client, who was also a victim.

Identity theft generally fits a pattern. The perpetrator steals crucial information like the bank account or social security number of the victim, and enough other supporting data, to apply for credit cards, go on a shopping spree, rent an apartment, open a mobile phone account, or take on some other financial obligation. The bills are diverted to a "new" address. Perpetrators may even pay the bills for some time, to raise the credit limit and make a bigger killing later.

At the end of the day, however, when the perpetrator eventually defaults on these obligations, the lawful owner is confronted by a disaster. Is this going to be repeated on a megascale with the cloud? The answer is far from being self-evident. We shall see.

9.2 When Responsibility for Security Takes a Leave, Accountability Goes Along

What Section 9.1 brought to the reader's attention about current lack of security can get more than an order of magnitude more dramatic with the cloud. The way negotiations between cloud vendors and their customers shape up suggests that a user organization suffering severe damage from computer crime, while its database resides at the cloud provider's infrastructure, will also be held responsible for it.

This is a curious twist because the level of security and access to the infrastructural services being offered depends entirely on the enterprise owning the servers. Therefore, the latter should also be legally responsible for security and protection associated with the services it provides. To appreciate why responsibility for security may be taking a leave, user organizations must understand that public cloud systems:

- typically feature access levels that are a sort of free access for all, and
- among subscribers there may also be potential intruders masquerading as legitimate users.

Theoretically, security purposes are served through a set of design principles and gadgets. The first allow us to define a framework for the effective application of technology protecting privacy and security. The second are the gatekeepers. Practically, the nature of the cloud as an open resource* makes it very difficult to police applications and customers by the hundreds of thousands and their whereabouts.

In addition, technology can be a double-edged sword, because design principles promoting security and those advancing the notion of a more effective, more flexible, and less costly system contradict one another. The benefits of effectiveness are numerous, including unprecedented interoperability of business systems and applications. These same benefits, however, work against greater security. There

---

* Though not necessarily as an open architecture (Chapter 8).

exist as well conflicts of interest in a business sense. *If* the cloud makes it easier for consumers and cheaper, too, as the pros say, *then* by significantly increasing the number of accesses, the likelihood of failures and fraud increases, too.

Eventually, everybody would get a "go" at the cloud as many services start being offered for free, supported by advertising (Chapter 1). *If* a cloud-based e-mail service sees to it that one does not have to worry about the bill (though somewhere this is going to hit its limits), *then* the real costs may be opaque, with violations of privacy and security becoming major cost items.

These *ifs* and *thens* are a concern not only to consumers but also to companies. Small and medium enterprises (SMEs) benefit by switching to cloud-based e-mail because accounting and customer tracking supports run inside a web browser. Also, the ability to summon computing and databasing capacity from the cloud, when needed, sounds great, but as the user population rapidly multiplies, security concerns start mounting.

Even if at least some consumers may be happier to trade a bit of privacy for free services, when this "bit" grows in size, they will start having second thoughts. Though people appreciate a free lunch and don't object to listening to the ads, they also like to:

- have control over their personal data and
- be able to amend their profiles, which service providers compile and use to target advertising.

All these personal, technical, and business reasons affect the way people and companies look at security. Beyond that comes the fact that the big bang of the cloud's dimension will make administrative chores extremely complex, if at all manageable. This, too, will work against security.

Neither should the possibility of computer crime by insiders be excluded. Some years ago, an FBI survey on origins of information security risk identified disgruntled employees as the number one reason. Compared to disgruntled employees, hackers did not even amount for half of the insider's cases of information insecurity, as see in the histogram in Figure 9.1.

In terms of frequency of events, according to the FBI survey, hackers were followed by security breaches described as "business intelligence." Spying for business reasons is on the increase, and according to several learned opinions, it will get a helping hand by the cloud.

Compared to the public cloud, a private cloud is better positioned in security terms because it gives the user organization ownership of stored information and full control of how to structure the security service.* Still, the private clouds' wide-

---

* User organizations also have auditing responsibilities according to the Sarbanes-Oxley Act, Health Insurance Portability and Accountability Act (HIPAA), and other regulations.

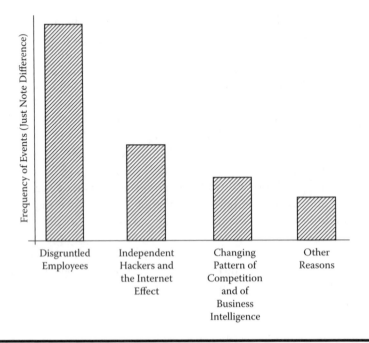

Figure 9.1   Results of an FBI survey on origins of information security risk.

band connections to the public cloud emulate a multitenant environment, while the public infrastructure is under the authority of the service provider.

The reasonable thing to do, in order to confront the challenges posed by this case, is to have all cloud providers and all user organizations (or their associations) get together to establish common standards for security solution under a new *cloud security authority*. This should be a state regulator who has full powers to inspect them, audit them, and police them. This is not even under discussion, leading to the notion that increased potential for fraud is to a large part due to:

- the absence of standard security practices, including their verification on the Internet and the cloud and
- legal and regulatory ambiguity and uncertainty with regard to application and jurisdiction of current laws and regulations concerning online activities.

User organizations, too, must become more realistic about security risks. Today several tend to disregard the fine print of security because they consider databasing in the cloud to be convenient, and they also hope to control their IT costs this way. Of course, there is always a trade-off between security and convenience, operating cost, and certain factors relating to performance. The golden rule, however, is that:

- the level of security required should relate to the operational risk involved, and
- slack in security is essentially lack of care, which means that responsibility takes a leave and accountability goes along.

Such lack of care may well turn out to be very costly in terms of legal risk, all the way from security to compliance (the two issues correlate). In the European Union there is Directive 1999/93/EC on a community framework for electronic signatures, Directive 2000/31/EC on electronic commerce, Directive 97/7/EC on the protection of consumers with respect to distance contracts, as well as a directive concerning the distance marketing of consumer financial services and a directive concerning the processing of personal data and protection of privacy in electronic communications. In the United States there are SOX and the USA Patriot Act.

Both cloud providers and user organizations must account for the cloud's global nature. Many nations have laws requiring the keeping of personal data and copyrighted material within national borders. There are as well states that, for whatever reason, do not like that another country gets access to their legal data or legally protected information. The case of the Internal Revenue Service vs. UBS concerning bank deposits by American citizens was settled out of court in August 2009 and involved forty-five hundred names* (more on government spying in Section 9.3).

The legal risk is most evidently assumed by who owns the information in the cloud, and that party should appreciate that there are no easy answers. As this section has shown, effective protection capability, including intrusion detection, is elusive, and it will continue to be so as cloud computing becomes more complex and cyber thieves continually adapt their techniques to overcome innovations in security.

Additionally, service level agreements have been slow to counterweight new approaches used by hackers and others. Far too often SLAs only loosely define security standards and procedures and surely not to the level of clients, servers, routers, hubs, bridges, concentrators, and firewalls, where the action takes place.

This is surprising to the extent that tier 1 security is a competitive differentiator as well as a business enabler both for cloud providers and for user organizations. It makes sense, therefore, that tightening the nuts and bolts of the security infrastructure should be an inviolable goal of SLAs, though effective solutions should be incorporated at the level of the architectural design.

9.3 Data Fill the Air and Many Parties Are Listening

The very strength of the Internet—its large communications system, powerful search engines, and any-to-any connectivity—facilitates its abuses by

---

* Which in a way has been schizophrenic because on one side Western governments preach and legislate privacy and on the other they violate it.

unscrupulous individuals, companies, and governments. The fact that much of modern business greatly depends on database mining and networked resources intensifies the problem.

The Internet's promotion of anonymity serves a purpose but also fosters abuses. Issues resulting from code breaking and defective surveillance have not yet found fully satisfactory solutions in terms of protection of privacy. To make matters more complex, protection measures have their downside. Digital certificate infrastructures bring up integrity problems, and new challenges have come from nonproprietary free software.

With the cloud the list of problems not in control keeps growing. Individual mobility by lightweight portable devices and sprawling wireless networks has been generally commented on as an important business advance. Somehow forgotten is the fact that wireless networks are notoriously vulnerable to hacking:

- their users will be well advised never to believe they are secure, and
- aware of this, many companies are now worrying about the challenge presented by the growth of wireless networking.

Cloud computing finds itself at the middle of this worry. The concept of mobile and land lines in a networking sense is a commendable objective. But what's its effect on privacy and data security? The dependability associated with existing means for protection is very low indeed,* practically reducing them to simple sources of evidence that "something" is being done.

New, more powerful means of protection employ analytical techniques. Introducers, however, also use similar approaches—and some of these introducers are no kids, but mighty governments and military alliances.

Echelon is a name to retain. It came to the public eye through an early 1999 report on economic espionage from the European Union. This accused Australia, Britain, Canada, New Zealand, and America of using the Echelon military network to spy on international corporations. Equally alarming is that, as the EU stated, intercepted information was passed along to financial and industrial competitors.

Through a combination of spy satellites, sensitive listening stations, and powerful mathematical models, the spy system eavesdrops on just about every electronic communication that crosses a national border—from phone calls and faxes to massive data transmissions and e-mails, including short-wave, airline, and maritime frequencies. Echelon also listens in on most long-distance telecom traffic within countries, including local cell phone calls.

As a system, Echelon is run by the National Security Agency (NSA) from its headquarters at Ft. Mead, Maryland. At the time the aforementioned EU report broke, it was comprised of more than 120 satellites. According to the EU, NSA

---

* Investments in outdated wireless WEP (Wired Equivalent Privacy) become worthless when a hacker can use a so-called point-and-hack tool to expose the network in sixty seconds or less.

deployed software to eavesdrop on nine Internet access points, while a submarine had been used to tap into undersea cables.

Experts say that encryption is no guarantee of security. NSA can probably break crypto schemes with keys almost 1,000 bits long—the reason why 1,028 bits is used by most organizations that are concerned about confidentiality, but this is by no means a sure way to protection.

If the NSA were interviewed on Echelon, it would probably answer that the reason was to squash money laundering, which is said to be the world's third largest business after foreign exchange and oil trading (some estimates put it at between 1.5 and 5 percent of the GDP). But the fact remains that there is surveillance in the airwaves, and heavy telecommunications traffic with the cloud will increase exposure to eavesdroppers of many company secrets.* Whatever fills the airwaves with the cloud is open to code breaking and spying. Ironically, the same is true with hard disks to be supposedly shipped for backup reasons by cloud providers to user organizations (Chapter 2).

Another significant amount of sensitive data is comprised through the loss or theft of devices such as laptops, netbooks, and smart phones. The British Defense Ministry excels in the loss of critical information through the loss of devices carried by its agents (a sort of 007 in reverse). This is a problem to which IT managers contemplating cloud computing have not paid due attention.

Even well-known and popular information transfer media are subject to the law of unexpected consequences; e-mail and instant messaging (IM) are examples. Few people truly appreciate that mature technology has a downside, yet there is plenty of opportunities for intrusion, including by the courts. According to published information, in the short span of a few years up to 20 percent of American employers have had staff e-mail and IM exchanges subpoenaed in court and by regulators.

This did not start last night. Back in 2004 a study by the American Management Association (AMA) and e-Policy Institute documented a significant increase in the use of e-mail/IM in court proceedings. Year on year, in 2003 there were 50 percent more cases than in 2002, while 2002 had a 50 percent increase over 2001. Also, 12 percent of respondents said they had fought workplace lawsuits triggered by staff e-mails.

Worse yet, e-mail is in practical daily use for the transmission of financially sensitive data between companies, because enterprises erroneously believe their e-mail systems are sufficiently secure for that purpose. That's patently false. Failure to appreciate e-mail's lack of security has seen to it that most inter- and intracompany traffic has grown unplanned, from small beginnings into an uncontrollable behemoth:

---

* Though it is hazardous to guess the scale of this problem on the basis of current information.

■ all types of businesses now electronically exchange around the clock an enormous amount of information over the wires, and
■ while the bulk of such transmissions may not be of overwhelming financial value, their content is often confidential, as it contains references to staff details, company products, and prices.

All this talks volumes about security risks arising from future overdependence on the cloud. Telecommunications have been and will continue being vulnerable to a cyber attack. Governments have joined the "bad guys." In early July 2009 North Korea was accused of being behind a cyber attack that shut down the websites of government departments in the United States and South Korea.

According to an article in *The Economist*, initially it was reported that this was the first series of attacks to hit government websites in several countries simultaneously. Officials in both Seoul and Washington, D.C., said they were suffering DDoS overload. Computers overwhelmed with bogus requests for a response sent from infected targets included sites at the U.S. Treasury, Secret Service, and Transportation Department.*

Denial of service attacks occur when a computer forces another to use up to saturation network resources or its own. This may take the form of forcing a host to respond constantly to a barrage of packets so that it cannot perform its formal functions, and neither can it let other packets through. Large information providers have installed filters to identify forged packets often used in denial of service attacks, but there are no ideal solutions.

DDoS attacks are a real and present danger with cloud computing. Warfare, as well as terrorists and other criminals, may cut off the user organization's information lifeline by making IT services unavailable, extorting payments, or taking other measures whose aftereffect is equivalent to a DDoS attack. It needs no further explaining that cloud security is a complex issue whose surface is just being scratched.

9.4 Many of the Cloud's Security Problems Date Back to the Internet

"Maybe it's because of my age rather than anything, that I don't trust Internet security," said a senior British banker during our meeting some time ago. "Intranets and extranets make me feel more comfortable because security issues are under control of the bank and its business partners." Other bankers, too, expressed the opinion that they see few problems in using the Internet for exchange of confirmations because there is no money in it, but the exchange of valuations with counterparties is a different matter.

---

* *The Economist*, July 11, 2009.

While today Internet banking is fairly common, it concerns relatively small private accounts, not big sums. Also, the better-informed investors explicitly request that the banks managing their accounts *not* put them in files accessible through the internet, precisely because they hold the latter's security at low esteem.

The pros answer that a dozen years ago several experts were of the opinion that the business-to-consumer (B2C) segment of Internet commerce would be hampered by concerns about security of payments, potentially fraudulent merchants, privacy of personal data, and cost of accessing online merchants. And they add that all this was too pessimistic; it did not happen that way.

The pros are only half right. Over the years, the largest segments of B2C traffic are issues connected to information on services, reservations, entertainment, travel, and software. Payments and settlements in finance and commerce are made on secure networks because factors such as openness, global reach, and lack of physical contact make the Internet vulnerable. The fact that the credit card is the dominant online payment method sees to it that Internet commerce exposes merchants to potentially high levels of fraud resulting from stolen cards or illegally obtained card numbers. New techniques keep on being developed to deal with credit card fraud, but the security problem is always on the radar screen.

With cloud computing security worries along the aforementioned line of reference increase, because we are no more talking of stand-alone e-commerce operations of the 1990s' sort, but of massive data transfers by cloud providers between hundreds of thousands of servers. It is unavoidable that sensitive financial and personal information will be included in these transfers. Furthermore, the owners of thin clients will have their personal files at the site of the infrastructure provider, which increases:

- privacy concerns and
- the likelihood of identity theft (Section 9.1).

Some years ago, in the United States, the Social Security Administration shut down a website that supplied information about people's personal income and retirement, out of concerns the site could violate privacy rights. After the agency began offering detailed estimates of future benefits on the Internet, security experts expressed the opinion that safeguards were not enough to keep people from obtaining confidential electronic data.

Under the Federal Privacy Act of 1974, individuals are guaranteed access to information the government holds about them. But with social security numbers and mothers' maiden names available in public databases, the government had no way to confirm that the people requesting information on the Internet were the ones authorized to ask for and use such information. This violated the privacy law.

What the previous paragraphs explained is not a one-tantum problem. Practically every day sees a new set of issues in connection to the regulation of databases and networks. They range from proposed new rules for public databases in the interest of privacy, to arguments over cable television's right to electronically scramble satellite transmissions.* Clearly, our society is having difficulty determining:

- just who owns what kind of information,
- how its owner are allowed to dispose of it, and
- what their rights and obligations are in regard to the confidentiality of information they own.

With the cloud, these debates are likely to intensify because, when it comes to information, traditional property rights just don't seem to apply, but all sorts of parties are not in accord among themselves in regard to new concepts and laws necessary for information protection. Such disagreements go all the way to intellectual property's protection (Section 9.6).

As an example of the uncertainties surrounding security on the cloud, a recent meeting focused on the infrastructural solution proposed by a cloud vendor, the speed with which information will move database to database, and the likelihood of interference by an intruder, which could have implications for the bank confronted by this cloud proposal. A central theme of this meeting has been a number of "what ifs."

The reader should know that when internal data become public knowledge, they increase deposit volatility to the extent that many customers maintain accounts on the basis of Internet rates or terms. When changes in deposits and loans of a credit institution are known by competitors, the way to bet is that the bank's client base will be subject to attrition.

The concentration of information in huge databases under the control of cloud infrastructure providers, and massive data transfers over networks, also raises questions on the risk of cyberterrorism. Combined with practically seamless interconnectivity the world over, this creates enormous potential for online disorder and crimes. Banks and other entities are as concerned as states about this likelihood.

Conscience of this threat's potential started in the mid-1990s with the increased reliance on the Internet. In November 1997, the U.S. Commission on Critical Infrastructure Protection issued a report to President Clinton with recommendations based on fifteen months of study of America's vulnerability to a cyberterrorist attack.

The commission concluded that the threat is real. "We are in a new age of threats, and we have to develop new ways to look at them. Waiting for a disaster is dangerous," advised the commission. The underlying thought has been that terrorism is ongoing, and as physical targets have been hardened, terrorists are in search of other avenues. Cyberterrorism is a natural choice because:

- it poses no real danger to the terrorist,
- it is out of the jurisdiction of the country that is menaced, and

---

* There is also confusion surrounding who, if anybody, should audit the Internet.

■ disorders and subversion cost little to deploy and can be launched from a different continent.

Compared to the original Internet threats, cloud computing augments cross-continent attacks by an order of magnitude, as practically all infrastructure providers will have tens and hundreds of thousands of servers in different countries. To optimize the return on their investments, they will be obliged to move huge blocks of data from one center to the other—a process that may as well become necessary for backup reasons.

Even in the simpler environment that it studied in the 1990s, the U.S. Commission on Critical Infrastructure Protection found that with rising computer literacy and a lack of widespread new ethical standards to fit cyber age, any nation—particularly a Western one—is vulnerable. There are plenty of examples of what hackers could accomplish, as another report, issued by the U.S. Commission on Critical Infrastructure Protection, pointed out in connection with cyber attacks.* The list includes:

■ water systems,
■ telecommunications systems,
■ electric power grids,
■ transportation systems,
■ oil and gas infrastructure,
■ storage structures,
■ emergency services,
■ financial services, and
■ government services.

Critical elements of our civilization's infrastructure, such as waste reservoirs, water treatment plants, gasoline depots, and power factories,† are evident sensible targets. Both terrorists and simpler-minded hackers could also disrupt banks, insurance companies, and as international transactions and stock markets. Food processing plants are other possible targets, and the same is true of hospitals and media facilities.

In conclusion, while concerns about cyberterrorism date back to the 1990s, massive databases spread over the globe under the control of cloud providers, and very large-scale data transfers, cast the problem under new light. In addition, there is no silver bullet and no single warning system to protect the cloud from a concerted attack. Government and industry must cooperate, and this means sharing

---

* *Communications of the ACM*, December 1997, Vol. 40, No. 12.
† A Trojan horse command sent to a power station could be as damaging as a bomb.

information and advising each other on advances in security measures. This may give birth to a new industry: *security as a service* (SaaS).*

9.5 Security as a Service by Cloud Providers

Aware of the fact that business opportunity and cloud security correlate, some providers talk about a security architecture they are in the process of studying and establishing. The concept revolves around a malware protection technology that (in cases) is associated with subscription-based services.

No cloud provider, to my knowledge, is today able to ensure total protection through some bundle under the label of web and e-mail security of user organizations, employing tools briefly described in Sections 9.6 and 9.7. Also on offer is a certification service for credit card and debit card payments.

It is not the intention of this text to present an exhaustive list of methods and means but rather to briefly describe what cloud vendors try to do in terms of improving security. As such, I have taken two examples: McAfee and Symantec, which provide security, storage, and systems management to help businesses and consumers with a more dependable handling of their information.† Both offer software and services that intend to protect control information risks related to security and compliance.

McAfee offers a real-time technology known as *Artemis* for onDemand protection, which, in addition to traditional signature-based detection, employs collective threat intelligence based in the cloud. It also includes behavioral analysis to scan suspicious content in real time. Artemis operates in connection with the vendor's ePolicy Orchestrator, aiming to provide:

■ web security and
■ vulnerability management.

Security approaches that rely on signatures go through a cycle of threat discovery, analysis, and protection deployment. There is also available an antimalware blacklist and whitelist used in filtering and behavior-based threat identification methods.

Symantec has added security offerings to its storage as a service cloud infrastructure launched in mid-2007. In early 2008, the company introduced the Symantec Protection Network (SPN), designed to provide web security and storage solutions

---

* The anagram is evidently being confused with software as a service and storage as a service; therefore, the reader must be careful to find out what SaaS stands for when he or she sees it in print.
† These examples will be followed by one on security assessment through an expert system written and used years ago by Livermore.

in the cloud. Through its acquisition of LessageLabs, it also offers a scheme for IM protection.

Most of these approaches and other similar services are directed to the SMEs market. Semantec has also developed Veritas Operations Services (VOS), which targets data centers of larger enterprises. It includes five subsystems:

- Veritas installation assessment;
- storage foundation health check;
- inventory management, which keeps track of license keys;
- patch central, facilitating queries for patches and setting up notifications; and
- error code lookup, including information on cause and resolution.

The cloud industry has a new term, security as a service, and different providers are trying to position themselves in this area of the market. Google recently bought Postini, which has been active in this line of business. (Other companies offering security as a service, apart from McAfee, Symantec, and Google, are ScanSafe and Webroot.)

This market has been promoted by a combination of an increasing threat environment in the cloud and added regulatory requirements, which gave birth to compliance efforts. As they get increasingly sophisticated, security as a service solutions might present an attractive alternative to the traditional onPremises virus and other packages, but it is still too early to make such a statement.

Some experts think that SaaS delivery lends itself well to web and e-mail security, as it provides filtering of unwanted content as well as some measure of protection from viruses, spam, spyware, and other attacks. But it is by no means fail-safe, and neither are all issues connected to security lending themselves to present methods of treatment—though the range of choices, and therefore of threat coverage, is bound to increase.

Indeed, some vendors have started offering wider source code reviews for security applications, a niche that so far has not been particularly explored. All cloud providers and user organizations can benefit by capitalizing on departments that were successful in the past but have been wholly or partially forgotten.

One of them is the expert system for security assessment written and employed by the Lawrence Livermore National Laboratory. The knowledge engineering construct controlled multiple security events by means of a family of e-systems that monitored security alarms, fire sensors, radio communications, and other happenings. Here is a simple example of how the knowledge artifacts worked:

```
IF      <a relevant event "A" has occurred>
        and <event "A" is a member of a class of events that
          imply an intruder>
```

```
          and <an intruder class incident is in progress in the
              same area>
          and <event "A" and event "B" have time and distance
              attributes that imply that they could not have been
              caused by one person>
THEN      <associate the event with the incident; change
              incident class to multiple intruders; create task to
              reassess priority of incident>
```

In its time (early 1990s) this Livermore initiative was outside of the box. (In the late 1980s/early 1990s American Express in the United States and Marks and Spencer in Britain had successfully used expert systems for patterning the behavior of card-holders with the result of significantly reducing theft associated with stolen cards.)

The able use of knowledge engineering can significantly increase perception of individual profiles behind an act. Nowadays airlines are filtering passengers by watching profiles. "There are identifiers of people who have hostile intent that you can pick up," says Kip Hawley, the head of America's Transportation Security Administration. "Our testing indicates an extraordinary high degree of success."

"It doesn't do any good to say, 'this is what I think a terrorist looks like and I think I'm going to frisk him.'" Hawley adds, his thesis being that security measures should not rely solely on machines, however sophisticated, because threats change: "You want it to be as smooth a process as possible, because then the abnormalities pop out."* In cloud computing, however, physical profiles are not available. What is doable is building logical profiles of possible suspects and looking out for those sorts of people.

9.6 Fraud Theory and Intellectual Property

As the examples and references in Section 9.5 have documented, the art of com-puter security has not progressed to the point where a cloud provider can sign a service level agreement stipulating 100 percent protection, or Underwriters Labs can certify that a firewall is absolutely fail-safe. Therefore, with the rather crude tools that are available (Section 9.7), managers have to decide what they are trying to protect and how much they are willing to assume security risks. Down to basics, this is a business issue, not a technical one. *If* it were the latter, *then* fraud theory would have been on its way to providing an answer.

Fraud theory comes in different versions. One of the more interesting and rele-vant to the discussion on protection of information deposited by user organizations in huge cloud databases was evoked in a 1988 U.S. Supreme Court decision. In *Basic Inc v. Levinson*, the court endorsed a theory known as *fraud in the market*,

---

* *The Economist*, June 16, 2007.

relying on the efficient markets hypothesis* (which states that markets are efficient because the same information is available to all players).

Since market prices reflect all available information, argued the court, misleading statements by a company will affect its share price. Because investors rely on the integrity of the price as a guide to fundamental value, misleading statements defraud investors even if:

- they do not rely directly on those statements, or
- they are not even aware of their existence.

In the more than two decades that elapsed since that Supreme Court decision, a similar logic has been employed in criminal cases, and there is no reason why it could not also be used with statements made by cloud providers about their wares being totally safe security-wise. This might permit the weeding out of bogus claims about secure infrastructural services.

Experience on how to go about this task could be derived from well-known examples of bogus Internet-related services; for instance, scam artists promising to set up websites, establish Internet access accounts, or sell computer equipment and delivering inferior goods (or none at all) after receiving payment.

According to the National Consumer Lead, another frequent scam is fraudulent business opportunities, where crooks use unreasonable predictions of profitability to catch people unaware of what is going on. Still another is different fraudulent work-at-home offers that turn out to be fakes. Worse will be the case of an infiltrator into the network of a cloud provider whose aim is to spread misinformation or alter accounting figures.

Here is a real-life example. On August 25, 2000, Internet Wire received a forged e-mail press release, seemingly from Emulex Corp, saying that the company's CEO resigned and its earnings would be restated. Without verifying its origin or contents, Internet Wire posted the message. Several financial news services and websites further distributed it, and the firm's stock dropped 61 percent before it was found that this was a hoax.†

It needs no explaining that semantic attacks of that type will be much more serious in their aftermath when directed against the cloud's infrastructure. Falsifying a user organization's information elements stored in a vendor's databases can have dramatic consequences—from changing balance sheets, bills, and invoices to legal responsibilities connected to altering court documents or rewriting contracts.

---

* The efficient market hypothesis has many pros, even if its foundations are built on sand. It has, however, been discredited by the 2007–2009 deep economic and banking crisis.

† *Communications of the ACM*, December 2000, Vol. 43, No. 12. That same year (2000), the Securities and Exchange Commission charged thirty-three companies and individuals with Internet fraud, many based on semantic attacks such as posting false information on message boards, like the example in this text.

The pros may say only fools would do that, but "what one fool can do, another fool can do too," said Thales, a mathematician and philosopher of ancient Greece. The same thinking goes with crooks. What one crook can do, another can do too—and he can do it even better and in a more damaging way if the opportunity is broader and deeper, as it happens with cloud computing.

Hackers or plain criminals breaking into cloud databases may use their new-found power not for pity theft but for blackmail and extortions, hitting with one stone both the provider and the user organization. Though at this very moment there are no known cases of someone breaking into a cloud database and altering financial accounts, there are no known cases of cloud users and providers doing these sorts of checks either.

Experts say that even if today cyber extortion is relatively infrequent, chances are that it will become more common, because user information held in the cloud infra-structure is so much more valuable and vulnerable. Therefore, both user organizations and cloud providers must have a strategy in place for dealing with such events.

Neither is it unlikely that, as their sophistication grows, cyber extortions may resemble real-world kidnappings. There theft of intellectual property is another case warranting a great deal of attention. Music producers and film makers have been terrified of piracy and work hard to encrypt digital video disks so that only authorized players can read the disks. But the encryption is not hard to break, and pirating is flourishing.

According to some opinions, cyber extortions may one day resemble the wave of music, films, and software thefts that have become legendary, even if several intellectual property rights have been registered on keys and interfaces. Producers hold patents for methods of verifying the legitimacy of software being installed, but hackers hold the upper hand in using stolen intellectual property.

To a considerable extent, the reasons for failure to find a better solution are historical, in the sense that the proprietors don't think outside the box, which is likely to continue with cloud computing. The expectations some software firms still have about their ability to assert property rights in their products were derived from an era in which trade secret licensing was the predominant mode of protecting. The case of software, however, brought a great uncertainty about whether either copyright or patent protection is the way to go. This is not the first time such ambiguity has shown up:

- Copyright has been established to protect literary works.
- Patents have been instituted for technical inventions.

Software is still a different case, and therefore existing legal protection models don't fit—even if it has become common practice in the computer industry to protect intellectual property rights in software through trade secret licensing agreements. Quite similarly, a basically different departure and legal protection scheme will be needed for information elements databased in the cloud.

Lessons should be learned from failures that occurred in the past with intellectual property and software. Back in the late 1970s the Commission on New Technological Users of Copyrighted Works (CONTU), of the U.S. Congress, studied the software protection issue. It recommended use of copyright to provide intellectual property protection for computer programs. The commission noted that copyright was inherently much better suited than trade secret law for the protection of mass-marketed software products.*

However, neither CONTU nor the legislators directly addressed the issue of whether it would be copyright infringement to copy an interface in order to make compatible software, and this opened Pandora's box in copying. Since then, the gap between what is indeed protected and what is not continues to widen, as software becomes polyvalent, complex, and unstuck from underlying hardware devices.

9.7 A Brief Review of Security Measures and Their Weaknesses

The way to bet is that whether they belong to the provider or the user organization, information assets in the cloud will attract hackers and criminals. Different types of threats need to be considered for protection purposes, ranging from confidentiality to integrity and plain theft, with possibly severe after effects. For each threat there are two key issues to think about:

1. the damage that would be done to the organization should a threat be realized, and
2. the greatest gain any attacker could make from his or her action, which gives a measure of its likelihood.

Using the past years as a reference to vulnerabilities, attacks may be directed against computers, communications lines, and electronics devices at large. Or, they may be syntactic, focusing on vulnerabilities in software products and problems associated with protocols, interfaces, and cryptography. Denial of service is another possibility, albeit for different background reasons.

The more sophisticated attacks against information assets will quite likely be semantic, targeting the way users assign meaning to content. There are always people who want to take hold, or at least gain advantages, of other parties' possessions, betting on the unguarded moment and knowing very well that not all doors can be closed at the same time because then there is no business.

The principle of the unguarded door suggests that the danger is proportional to the number of doors, though the relation between doors and the magnitude of

---

* In 1980, Congress passed an amendment to the copyright law to make explicit that copyright protection was available to software.

danger is not necessarily linear. Cloud computing, by its nature, opens plenty of doors, and the traps that are presently set are more or less old and tired. They are not commensurate with the task. Yet, that's what is available, and a brief review of them can serve as a refresher, which might help in avoiding to repeat the same mistakes with the cloud.

One of the first attempts of so-called system security has been password protection and privilege code access intended to secure computer installations at database, record, and field levels. Such access controls were defined by the database administrator (DBA), who determined which users were authorized to view and modify which information elements.

Along this line of reasoning, employees have been encouraged to choose strong passwords and rotate them. Eventually Internet programs contained tens of thousands of common passwords that hackers cracked to break into computer systems. In many companies, internal procedures require new passwords every month or, at the maximum, ninety days, so that by the time the hacker gets the password it will be outdated. That has been a pipe dream.

Keys have been used to authenticate the cryptographic signature of a person or application accessing the computer or network. A cryptographic signature may also be employed as a stronger means of protection than passwords. The problem is that intruders pass through (more on cryptography later).

Keys and passwords have served for access control, but access control also has other aspects. A directory can maintain qualifying information for all persons and applications, detailing behavior and capabilities of objects, as well as security requirements of addressed services. The directory will also contain encrypted passwords for private key systems and for each user, including:

- limitations access to services,
- time windows when access is permitted, and
- restrictions to specific locations (objects, terminals, buildings, and so on).

Part of the directory may be control lists for individual user-application relationships, including the security profile of each relationship, which practically says what a user can do within an application. Other security details that may be in the directory outline session requirements in terms of encryption and authentication, types of security an application or site must support, client-application profiles and relationships, and public key certificates or details of private key relationships. All this is overhead; it is useful but not decisive.

Companies more sensitive than their peers to security challenges have used servers to manage the key distribution process supporting the message authentication and encryption functions. These security servers are part of the network security management system, and they are monitored objects, including status activation/deactivation, backup, recovery, and other functions. Time series provide accurate time stamps to security services. Accurate time-stamping of security-related events helps in tracking attempted security violations and in establishing behavioral profiles.

Cryptography was supposed to provide a security solution that is fair. It did not. Private and public keys, alternatively known as *symmetric* and *asymmetric*, have been used with cryptography. Symmetric key systems work by sharing key pairs specific to given customers and application relationships; the security relies upon both keys remaining secret.

There is a downside with cryptography, even if to many people it is a sort of a magic word for protection, and they treat it as if it were failure-free. Using not only brute force of computing but also information about radiation and power consumption of a device when it executes a cryptographic algorithm (as well as its timing), code breakers have been able to crack open would-be secure tokens. Such approaches have been known as *failure analysis* or side channel attacks. It is possible to break any algorithm based on how systems respond to legitimate errors, and this includes cryptographic algorithms employed by smart cards or as part of secure system solutions.

At times it is not necessary to break the code itself but rather the way it is used. In other cases, it is possible to break the security of a system without cracking its cryptography. This procedure is not new; Alan Turing successfully used it during World War II with Enigma, the German supersecret military code (by capitalizing on the frequency of the "eins").

User organizations joining the cloud should appreciate that crooks can also attack cryptographic codes and systems by analyzing the way different keys are related to each other. Even if each key is secure, the combination of several of them may be weak, and its discovery leads to cracking the supposedly secure cryptographic system. Cryptanalysts have as well taken apart many supposedly secure systems by breaking the pseudorandom number generators used to supply cryptographic keys. The cryptographic algorithms might be secure, but the key generation procedures are not, and the weakest link in the chain is the gate through which to conquer. Practically every algorithm has a weakness.

Cryptographic solutions offer themselves to a greater risk of attack if they are based on industry standards and are specified in a manner that simplifies the interconnection of supply chain systems. This is mitigating technical risk. Standards-based asymmetrical key or public key algorithms are emerging as an appropriate solution to key management for large populations, but they are vulnerable even if they use different keys for encrypting and decrypting data.

In short, vulnerabilities are all over. The common thread connecting different weaknesses of security systems is that all protection methods cluster within an envelope of keys, IDs, cryptography, and the security they are supposed to provide. Code breakers know very well how to look at systems weaknesses and transients, following up with a sneaky attack on what designers did not think should even count.

9.8 Security Engineering: Outwitting the Adversary*

The core of the matter is that defense against an attack on real and assumed rules of behavior in a cyber society has become a crucial issue to be addressed in a fundamental manner. The answer is *security engineering*, but there are two prerequisites to any successful pursuit of that avenue that have not so far been fulfilled:

- new laws and rules have to be established for Internet and cloud living and working, specifically studied for their case, and
- our knowledge on how to make sure security is not broken, even in the presence of a determined and technologically sophisticated *adversary*, must be vastly improved.

The new laws and countermeasures should pay full attention to the fact that in the cloud one deals with invisible adversaries who will do everything in their power to break the rules. As for penalties, they should be established by taking account of the (rather low) probability of catching such adversaries and be weighted on their power to discourage others from doing the same (more on this later).

Some experts think that defending against yet unknown attackers and methods they may invent is impossible. Others believe that the risk can be mitigated through a thorough system design and measures based on highly improved firewalls—not just cryptographic algorithms. Neither of them is right:

- "much better" security is not a product, but a process, and
- to stand a good chance of success, the whole security process must be turned inside out and upgraded through customization and analytics.

Clearly enough, 100 percent success is unattainable, but current security levels are low because the concepts behind them are yesterday's. There is a vast scope for improvement. A good example of search for a better way is the policy now followed by the Recording Industry Association of America (RIAA), which pursues an alternative legal way against online piracy, by following up on individual users of file-sharing hubs.

By late 2009, RIAA had accused eighteen thousand Internet users of engaging in illegal file sharing, demanding settlements of four thousand dollars on average. Confronted with the prospect of a federal copyright infringement lawsuit, almost all settled. These have been soft adversaries of the system. For hard adversaries the penalties must be a lot higher.

Critics point out that if the aforementioned individual parties had stolen a handful of CDs from a department store, they would have faced much lighter

---

* Adversary is a better term than hacker, sniffer, pirate, attacker, or criminal because these are localized, worn-out tags.

penalties (than four thousand dollars). Yes, but the Internet and cyberspace at large is not a department store.

There is a case in the United States where the judge threw out the verdict, saying that he had erred by agreeing to his guidance to the jury "on how they should decide." He went even further, calling the damages "wholly disproportionate" and asking Congress to change the law, on the basis that the adversary was an individual who had not sought to profit from the piracy.

However, at a second trial, which concluded in June 2009, the adversary was found guilty again, and the jury awarded even higher damages: eighty thousand dollars per song, nearly two million dollars in total. One record label's lawyer admitted that even he was shocked. In July 2009, in a different case brought by RIAA against another adversary, the jury ordered him to pay damages of $675,000 for sharing thirty songs.* The rationale of pursuing these cases is

- to make all other Internet users aware that file sharing of copyrighted material is illegal, and
- as this conscience spreads, one can bet that it will impact on file sharing.

Pirating is not a hobby. It is a social offense. A similar concept can be used in taking care of vulnerabilities connected to cloud computing, with identification, customization, and analytics being the first step. There is little doubt that this first phase will result in a depressingly long list of threats and vulnerabilities to consider, but not all of them will be top priority.

A threat presents higher risk if it can be exploited in a way that exposes an asset. *Priority threats* should be cross-referenced with all vulnerabilities to see which combinations produce an exposure. This serves as well for judging that exposure's impact, while its frequency is established by vulnerability statistics. In a way quite similar to that of operational risk studies:

- For high-frequency/low-impact (HF/LI) potential events, currently available security protection methods can be acceptable as an interim approach, until security engineering becomes an established discipline.
- Medium-frequency/medium-impact events are the known unknowns from Internet, which can be used in a scenario analysis to project vulnerabilities in the cloud.
- The salient problem is low-frequency/high-impact (LF/HI) potential events, the unknown unknowns, which are found in the long leg of the risk distribution shown in Figure 9.2.

In conjunction with operating characteristic (OC) curves and confidence intervals, sampling can pinpoint deviations from normal system use. The level of

---

* *The Economist*, September 5, 2009.

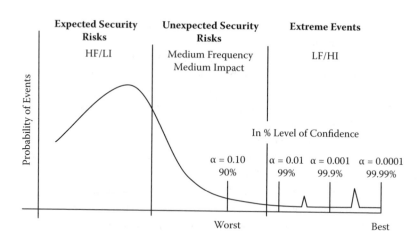

Figure 9.2 Expected security risks, unexpected security risks, extreme events, and security engineering.

confidence for extreme events should be 99.99 percent, which suggests that only one in ten thousand cases would escape attention. This can be reached over a period of time, as a result of analysis and experience.

The way to proceed in studies suggested in this section is assisted through a recent precedence in the banking industry, which has concentrated on identification and monitoring of operational risk, as required by the Basel Committee on Banking Supervision.* Fundamentally, the lack of security is an operational risk of networks, databases, computers, and the cloud.

An analysis along the lines suggested in Figure 9.2 has two merits: discovery and the establishment of priorities. We simply cannot afford to run after all hares at the same time. If we do so, the cloud computing's security will never be improved. We have to proceed in an orderly manner by first focusing on high-impact risks, which could conceivably be realized, however slight the perceived possibility.

Once this is done, we should qualify for each of them the profile of the adversary, with unlikely profiles being at a premium. Then, we should quantify (evidently by guestimating) the benefit an adversary hopes to make from realizing the corresponding threat.

An adversary's potential profit may be greater or less than the cost to the cloud provider or user organization, because of intangibles. Intangibles enlarge the basis that can be used to revaluate the probability of the attack taking place. The probability of the adversary being caught is another important guestimate, ideally guestimated through brainstorming until statistics become available.

---

* D. N. Chorafas, *Operational Risk Control with Basle II. Basic Principles and Capital Requirements* (London: Butterworth-Heinemann, 2004).

Knowledge artifacts should play a major role in this process, not only as guards (Section 9.5) but also as intelligence collectors. The accuracy of guestimates will be significantly improved over time after the intelligence-enriched security system goes into operation and starts learning on the job. New advanced sensor technologies can also help, and the same is true of solutions involving virtual network objects and virtual doubles (Chapter 4).

Through this approach, which enriched with practical experience can be structured as *security engineering*, we will be well positioned for studying appropriate, economically viable countermeasures to reduce exposure:

- increasing the cost of an attack to the adversary (that's what RIAA has done),
- decreasing the damage caused by the attack (by establishing more sophisticated and higher-integrity control procedures), and
- increasing the likelihood of the attack being detected and stopped cold prior to reaching its objective.

To increase the effectiveness of countermeasures, it is advisable to add cultural and behavioral variables, including employee training, understanding and acceptance of the upgraded security procedures, appreciation of the severity of penalties, and other measures of a customized nature to adversary groups (which must first be identified).*

A distributed security architecture must be in place to gather data from the network directly, by searching, capturing, and analyzing patterns of behavior. This approach has a major performance advantage when compared to the centralized bunker alternative, because it is sensitive to local traffic. Using dedicated security subsystems whose data are processed locally does not drain servers and hosts of the network.

In addition to protecting assets, a distributed security architecture can act as a witness in the event that a cloud provider or user organization needs to document a security incident for reasons of internal auditing, an insurance contract, or the courts. (One of the major problems firms encounter in enlisting the help of law enforcement when a computer crime has been committed is their inability to prove that it actually happened.)

Detection and identification of anomalies alert administrators to events and connections that have not appeared before or—if they did—did not ring alarm bells. Learning artifacts, already used in many other cases, can accelerate tuning and shorten the time necessary to deploy a system based on security engineering. They can also help to reduce false alarms, which are unavoidable, whether the system is manual or automatic. As Professor Feigenbaum of Stanford University once commented: the artifact's reasoning capability is secondary; the amount of knowledge we will be able to accumulate is much more important.

---

* D. N. Chorafas, *Chaos Theory in the Financial Markets* (Chicago: Probus, 1994).

In conclusion, the perfect security solution is utopia. This, however, should not discourage us from using the best technology available in new and imaginative ways to position ourselves against threats in the Internet and the cloud that did not exist earlier or, if they did, were much smaller in frequency and impact. Piecemeal solutions aimed at building "a better mousetrap" will lead nowhere. Security engineering is the answer.

Chapter 10

Cloud Reliability, Fault Tolerance, and Response Time

10.1 Business Continuity Management in the Cloud

Etymologically, *business continuity management* (BCM) is the result of critical functions and processes ensuring that a system performs its mission without incidence and that the entity responds to all acts or events in a planned, consistent manner. Business continuity planning is rehearsed through scenario analysis, which:

- targets new, evolving, or projected risks affecting business operations;
- simulates and evaluates the effect of disruptions in information systems support and response time delays; and
- provides a ground for experimenting on effective solutions to every type of BCM disruption entering into the scenario.

The analysis to which reference is made is instrumental in elaborating BCM clauses in service level agreements (SLAs) with cloud computing providers. Sound governance ensures that business continuity studies are part of the evaluation process *preceding* any top management decision in adopting cloud computing, and it also constitutes a factor in choosing cloud providers.

This concern about focused SLA clauses comes over and above previous preoccupations and rules regarding BCM, by boards, CEOs, and supervisory authorities. In the British financial industry, for example, the Bank of England, the Financial Services Authority (FSA), and the Treasury have been concerned with internal control and the institution's resilience, including issues of:

- corporate governance,
- internal auditing,
- liability and interoperability,
- insurance,
- outsourcing,
- supply chain, and
- Internet commerce.

During the last dozen years, one of the major business continuity preoccupations related to the behavior, resilience, and criticality of an entity's technological infrastructure—and for good reason. When in the late 1990s the year 2000 (Y2K) problem caught practically everybody's attention, the Bank of Boston evaluated the aftermath of a Y2K failure. The tests that were done showed that:

- a one-day disruption posed no major problems,
- a two-day disruption required contingency planning, and
- a three-day disruption would have called for considerable damage control.

Following on the heels of this study, the Bank of Boston said the situation was alarming, because a Y2K-engineered three-day disruption was not unthinkable. Its simulated business discontinuity further documented that *if* the bank cannot recover in four days, *then* the fifth day and thereafter, it will be impossible to recover and resume its work. The after effects of lousy risk management in the 2005–2007 time frame and horde of bankruptcies* and near bankruptcies of large, medium, and smaller banks document that in terms of business continuity:

- we no more talk of days, but hours, and
- any disruption in real-time operations can be fatal to the institution.

This has to be kept fully in perspective when planning for cloud computing. Together with security (Chapter 9), lapses in business continuity must be at the top of the list of worries top management must consider. Not only the bigger and medium-sized institutions, but even smaller banks today are (unwisely) engaging in twenty-four-hour trading, which is practically global trading.

---

* From January to late October 2009, over one hundred banks failed in the United States, including some of fair size.

- *Global trading* represents the involvement of a number of different business units in a transaction or package of transactions, with wholesome requirements for risk management.
- *Twenty-four-hour trading* is the means by which a portfolio or a number of portfolios of securities (or other assets) are traded internationally twenty-four hours a day—whether these are proprietary assets or belong to the bank's clients.

Under these conditions, the assurance of business continuity is not an option, it is a must. Many senior bankers say that in the context of twenty-four-hour financial operations, trading is important for two reasons: it brings the bank back to its main role of a financial intermediary, and it places a strategic emphasis where it belongs—in the money aspect of the deal. That's true, but there also exists an often forgotten third major factor. Namely, twenty-four-hour trading poses a horde of challenges, the most important being:

- culture,
- human resources,
- organization,
- information technology, and
- business continuity.

Each of the items in the above list contributes to the assurance that an institution continues to be an operating entity. Business continuity can be disrupted by relatively *normal*, everyday events that present BCM risk and by severe events, or *outliers*, which may be rare but have a very high impact (see Chapter 9 on security).

Business continuity is a vital issue that is not given the attention it deserves. Many companies say that because they want to be very customer focused, they are working to strengthen their IT through outsourcing; quite recently, cloud computing has been given as an example. They also add that "anyway," IT is not part of their core business. This statement is deadly wrong for two reasons:

- in the modern enterprise IT *is* core to any business, no matter what may be its product line, and
- outsourcing is often looked at by senior management as a relegation of responsibilities, and this terribly *weakens* business continuity.

Board members, CEOs, CFOs, CIOs, and strategic planners should appreciate that issues connected to business continuity management are greatly affected by *reliability* (Section 10.2) and *response time* (Section 10.5). While a higher cost of IT does not automatically provide a better BCM, cutting corners lowers reliability and lengthens response time. Here we are not talking about accidents of an unknown nature but about:

■ system crashes and
■ delayed responses from cloud resources, because of contention.

The risks associated with both bullets must be understood in order to be prevented by raising the cost of disruptions and low response to the provider, if need be, to stratospheric levels. Top management should never approve SLA clauses without rigorous study of countermeasures and decisive action to bend the BCM risk curve.

In conclusion, "what if" queries and scenarios must fully analyze the business continuity risks associated with cloud computing and any other outsourcing agreement. Legal experts comb a contract and give a factual opinion on its BCM. Failure to answer ahead of time business continuity questions can lead to a nightmare later on, as problems multiply.

10.2 System Reliability, Human Factors, and Cloud Computing

Reliability is not an ability. It is the probability that a given system will operate without failure over a predetermined time period, under environmental and operational conditions defined in advance. Such conditions must be elaborated on the basis of studies that look at each system component and at the whole aggregate. Derived from weapons systems research, the algorithm for calculating reliability R is

$$R = e^{-t/\bar{T}} \tag{10.1}$$

This is based on the *Weibull* distribution, advanced in 1951 as the best approach for reliability measurements.[*] The variables are $\bar{T}$ = mean time between failures (MTBF), t = projected operational time, for which reliability is computed, and e = Naperian logarithm.

Given the extent to which practically any company today depends on its communications and computers systems for business continuity purposes, anything less than 99.99 percent reliability can end in a disaster. This means that user organizations must pay an extraordinary amount of attention to reliability not only by analyzing statistics but also by incorporating appropriate contractual clauses associated with an outsourcing contract for IT services.

MTBF is based on statistics, and therefore on facts, not hypotheses. Hardware, software, and operational reasons contribute greatly to system reliability. Hence, it

---

[*] D. N. Chorafas, *Statistical Processes and Reliability Engineering* (Princeton, NJ: D. van Nostrand, 1960).

is important to obtain MTBF statistics from the cloud computing vendor. The rule must be "no certified MTBF statistics, no deal."*

With cloud computing we are also interested in the availability of could services. *Availability* is the probability that the system is running without interruption at any point during scheduled time, which is a tough requirement but can be met (Section 10.6). For many companies, particularly those with global operations, the scheduled time for business continuity reasons is twenty-four hours per day, and this practically means that at any time per day must be applied the algorithm

$$\% \text{ Availability} = 100 \times \frac{\text{System Usage Time}}{\text{Scheduled Time}} \qquad (10.2)$$

System usage time (SUT) is also known as uptime, but the latter term is often employed in an ambiguous way. The equation is simple:

$$\text{SUT} = \text{Scheduled Time} - \text{System Downtime} \qquad (10.3)$$

Let me repeat the statement the preceding paragraphs brought to the reader's attention: for the global enterprise, *scheduled time* is equal to twenty-four hours per day. Local companies have a shorter time frame; they should, however, also account for legacy batch procedures (the old technology still alive), which may require twenty-four hours per day scheduled time for business continuity reasons anyway.

A good part of system downtime is due to repair. Therefore, in connection to cloud computing, user organizations must carefully examine what the vendor puts into *system downtime*, because this will define the interruptions of access to the cloud's infrastructure (or onDemand software and platforms, depending on the nature of the SLA). Partial failures will be visible by the user organization only when they affect the *response time*—hence the latter's importance.

One of the arguments used by some cloud vendors is that response time is not important for all jobs because batch processing and analytics that access terabytes of data can take hours to finish. The same vendors, however, also point out that with enough data parallelism in the application, the proactive user can take advantage of the cloud.† There is an evident contradiction. No matter how one looks at it, the argument against response time clauses is nonsense, not just for one but several reasons:

---

* Equally important are statistics on mean time to repair (MTTR). See D. N. Chorafas, *Handholding of Data Communications and Computer Networks*, 2nd ed. (New York: TAB Books, McGraw-Hill, 1991).
† Theoretically, but only theoretically, using computers for a short time costs the same as using computers for a long time.

- Reliability and response time are not negotiable through sales talk.
- There should be no batch with cloud computing, though there may be asynchronous operations.
- High parallelism, if it is indeed supported by the vendor's servers, interests the user organization whose programs support it, which is typically not the case.
- The results of analytical studies must be made available the very moment they are completed, without delays due to system downtime and degradation, or because of a long response time.

Some vendors might say that Equation 10.1 is only good for rockets, which either fly or don't. This is a near-sighted argument. On the cloud, computer power is available online—or it is not, because suddenly the connection is interrupted. While there are many reasons why users may be disconnected from IT resources, as with rockets, in 99 percent of cases the top reasons for unreliability are machine failures and human error amplified by poor management practices.

This suggests that plenty of human factors should come under the magnifying glass of system testing, with the reliability equation serving as an evaluator of the aggregate. Systems testing for reliability is a key element in cloud computing due to the critical issues it can reveal:

- design tolerances and testing parameters must be defined,
- technical knowledge should be on hand to conduct the tests, and
- the reliability measure provided by Weibull's equation should used as confirmation of the vendor's cloud status.

Failures may occur due to incompatibilities of component parts as the cloud expands, untried design, and inadequate knowledge of the way critical parts in the vendor's cloud work. Problems such as personnel training inadequacies and rush jobs or accelerated implementation schedules may well end up with many surprises.

Some of the critical questions concerning cloud reliability can be resolved by expending at the user organization's premises an established failure analysis activity by the vendor (provided there is one). Quality control means should be devised to improve acceptance and rejection methods, as well as to institute stricter discipline than the one prevailing with in-house IT solutions—followed by corrective action.

This is a steady responsibility. Therefore, test procedures for cloud computing reliability must be written to not only check the system under dynamic conditions, but to do this at different sampling intervals. The need for rapid reaction is evident when one considers that business continuity management requires uninterrupted twenty-four-hour operations (Section 10.1).

Time and again in reliability studies, a closer look at the failures reveals that many of the causes are directly traced to human error. Since reliability is a process and a responsibility of people, high reliability requires highly qualified people. Consequently, the user organization must establish:

- specific skill levels,
- people-oriented operational procedures, and
- personnel selection and training practices equal to the task.

The need for eliminating people-caused problems is not new in IT, but the emphasis and management discipline necessary to meet cloud computing reliability requirements is new—requiring a sound methodology and steady practice. Traditional reliability approaches of compilation of failure modes and plotting of failure trends should be beefed up with scenarios and experimentation to flesh out latent or obscure problems.

It is obvious that to improve reliability management, effort must focus not only on the cloud vendor's hardware but also on its software and on the system's overload. All this should be performed in full observance of the quality control axiom, which advocates that product quality must be *built* in to the product, not inspected into it. The same is true of reliability. Shortcuts in testing operations and other practices will leave many deficiencies uncorrected.

Some vendors say that a good cloud computing architecture can take care of quality and reliability problems. This is a false statement. A good architecture, and its supporting infrastructure, may help edit capabilities, customizations, and the leverage of web searches. But quality and reliability are totally different issues. Even the best automatic delivery of documents to users will be interrupted, and the system will underperform if its reliability is not the highest. (More on reliability and availability can be found in Sections 10.6 and 10.7.)

10.3 Case Studies on Designing for Reliability

Quality and reliability, Section 10.2 stated, need to be built in to a product from the drafting board, or they will never characterize it in a positive way. When we deal with structures like the cloud, which is a complex system with many unknowns, the best approach open to us is that of learning from:

- how pioneer designers dealt in their time with novel products and
- what happened after they retired or shifted jobs and lesser people filled their shoes.

One of the giants in engineering design has been Arthur Raymond, of Douglas Aircraft. He and his team created the now famous DC-3,* better known as Dakota, which along with the jeep made an outstanding contribution to WWII victory—

---

* The DC-1 had crashed on landing. The DC-2 had limited success, but it had shown the way to a new design philosophy.

and also served as the flying workhorse all over the world for several decades after the war ended.

Raymond's boss was Donald Douglas, a sharp business mind with rare qualities among the pioneers of flying. After his first success with Cloudster,* Douglas wanted to make an airframe that would be able to provide fast, reliable long-distance travel across the United States and maybe internationally. As a *design goal*, this has striking similarities to the cloud.

In 1932 Raymond was sent to discuss the matter with Charles Lindbergh, who had made the first solo, nonstop transatlantic flight. Lindbergh was also adviser to TWA, the airline Douglas aimed to deal with. Three years later, in 1935, the DC-3 was born. When the Dakota was born, albeit in a small way, so was the notion of mass air travel. The plane:

- shortened the time between destinations and
- was the first aircraft to accommodate enough passengers to be profitable, without carrying mail.

That's the far-sighted design choice cloud designers must make. Arthur Raymond's engineering saw to it that Douglas could hardly keep pace with the orders. Four years down the line, by 1939, the DC-3 accounted for 90 percent of world airline trade. Dakotas continued being built during the war, and many were still widely in service into the 1970s.†

An integral part of Dakota's success was its exceptional reliability. Raymond built highly robust wings into the DC-3, much stronger than would be considered necessary in modern aircraft assumed to have a limited operational life. The airframe was thought to be overengineered, but its trademark became its reputation of being virtually indestructible.

- In cloud computing, I would consider the links and nodes of the network as equivalent to the DC-3's wings.
- The cloud's software will be the equivalent to the plane's motor, which needed a lot more gentle treatment than the airframe itself.

Designed by Raymond with reliability in mind, the Dakota's toughness was generally appreciated, just like cloud computing's toughness should be built in the design phase and appreciated by the user organizations. Eventually, such breakthroughs were followed by other important principles for robust design.

Some were pioneered after World War II by Genichi Taguchi, the Japanese engineer who provided a methodology by which products are made more resistant to failure, by accounting at the design level for variations in environmental and

---

* A biplane claimed to be one of the first aircraft to lift a useful load exceeding its own weight.
† In IT the product to compare to the DC-3 has been IBM's 650.

customer usage conditions. This method relies on experiments, aiming to identify the best designs by applying the principle that *if* robust design principles are applied early enough, *then* companies can raise product quality, get more consistent performance, and increase profile margins.

An example of the contribution by first-class management in achieving a high level of reliability is provided by Hideo Shima, the inventor of the famous bullet train (*shinkansen*). His reputation was such that after leaving the Japanese railway where he was chief of engineering, Shima was snapped up by Japan's National Space Development Agency (NSDA) and became its president until he retired in early 1977.

Under Hideo Shima, NSDA had startling successes; ironically, however, these ended after he retired and second-raters took over. In October 1997, a satellite costing $759 million was lost. By contrast, under Hideo, seven satellites were put successfully into orbit. Reliability was the trick, he said. What he did not say is that human factors made the difference.

Unreliability also hit Japan's bullet trains under the second-raters, who followed Hideo as chief engineers. In 2000, technical problems with the *shinkansen* threatened passengers' lives and shocked the traveling public. In one of the incidents, large slabs of concrete peeled off tunnel walls and slammed into the passenger compartments of passing bullet trains.

Investigation revealed that the concrete was made using beach sand that was not properly desalinated, rather than more expensive quarry sand. With age, such concrete becomes brittle and is easily shaken loose by vibrations of trains racing past at 250 km per hour (155 mph).

Japan Railways blamed the contractors for sloppiness, but experts suggest that the company lowered its own design and inspection standards to save money after it was privatized in the 1980s and lost its government subsidy. This reference is very important because the same can happen on a king-size scale with cloud computing *if* vendors try to save money by:

■ bending reliability standards or
■ assigning the responsibility for quality, reliability, human factors, response time, and fault tolerance to second-raters.

As Section 10.2 brought to the reader's attention, there is nothing more costly than low-quality personnel. In 2000, a chain reaction at a uranium processing plant in Tokaimura, Japan, exposed three workers to lethal doses of radiation and irradiated hundreds more with smaller amounts. This event was the world's worst nuclear disaster since Chernobyl.

Investigation revealed that the company had hired unskilled laborers to do many technical jobs, providing little in the way of training. The factory workers who unknowingly dumped six times more uranium oxide into a mixing tank than they should have were under instructions to break safety rules to save time and money.* There was also a case of outdated equipment—a most frequently encountered condition in information technology, and particularly so in software.

Learning a lesson from the examples that have been outlined, a thorough reliability analysis will address itself not just to normal conditions but also, most importantly, to outliers that may be short-lived but have a great impact. For instance, in electrical engineering the Electric Power Research Institute estimates that 80 percent of the power glitches that wreak havoc on an electronic system last for less than a few seconds, but they happen even if the reliability of the electricity grid has rested at 99.9 percent, which allows roughly eight hours of outages a year. When the industrial economy was built around electric motors and incandescent bulbs, 99.9 percent was more than enough to keep its wheels turning. By contrast, microprocessor-based controls, computer networks, and cloud computing demand at least 99.9999 percent reliability, amounting to no more than a few seconds of allowable outages a year.

Six nines, as it is known in industry jargon, is not even a dream with computers and communications. No cloud computing vendor today offers better than *three nines* (99.9 percent) reliability, which is three orders of magnitude *worse* than what is necessary. User organizations, too, are far from being up to the required reliability standard.

Moreover, six nines is an issue that embraces not only cloud computing vendors and users but also the whole power utility industry. For promises made by cloud vendors to come true, the quality of electrical power must reach *nine nines* (milliseconds of faults a year). Short of that, the so-called digital economy:

- at best, will not have the right quality power to mature, and
- at worst, will start falling apart at its seams.

Let me moreover emphasize that the needed system solution goes well beyond the patchwork employed so far, where various pieces of backup equipment have filled in during outages. Military bases, phone companies, hospitals, and banks deploy lots of generators to ensure that their operations stay up and running for 99.99 percent of the time. But that is a stop-gap approach that still amounts to minutes of outages a year—and it is unfit for cloud computing.

High-tech companies have generators to supplement their power needs, but they also add "uninterruptible power sources" that use batteries to power computers until the generators kick in. That's another patchwork that introduces its own vulnerabilities:

- Batteries are expensive to maintain and do not react instantly.
- Generators do not react fast enough and may deliver dirty power during their functioning.

---

* *The Economist*, March 4, 2000.

Power chips (first developed in the early 1980s) have been seen as the salvation, but nearly three decades down the line they do not deliver wholesome solutions. (They work by splitting a stream of electrical power into tiny packets that can be reconditioned.) To make matters worse, no Arthur Raymond, Genichi Taguchi, or Hideo Shima has yet appeared in the cloud computing landscape—and that, in reliability terms, is scary.

10.4 The Concept of Fault Tolerance in Cloud Computing

In computers and communications the concept of fault tolerance emerged in the late 1960s, as an attempt to produce reliable enough solutions. In the background of the notion underpinning fault tolerance is found a design that keeps on operating, albeit at a reduced delivery level, even after a fault occurred:

- without corruption of data,
- without system timeout, and
- with minimum degradation, for instance, of information services.

From a historical perspective, the first commercially available option of a default-tolerant computer has been Tandem's nonstop system, which became available in 1976. Each attached processor sent a regular message down the bus identifying its uptime status, and by the absence of such a message the operating system detected whether a module had become inoperative. In the more general case, multiprocessor aggregates of a fault-tolerant system can be either loosely or tightly coupled.

The original *loosely coupled* fault-tolerant aggregates consisted of a minimum of two semi-independent processors interconnected by a dual high-speed bus. Each processor ran its own operating system, had its own memory and I/O controllers, and shared multiported peripheral controllers with at least one other processor, as in the tandem nonstop architecture.

Tightly coupled solutions came a decade later, after they became economically feasible following significant improvements in microprocessor technology and the advent of local area networks. The underlying concept has been that attaching independent file servers and gateways on a very high-speed bus capitalizes on system design redundancies and:

- reduces overhead,
- improves the mirroring of information elements, and
- minimizes the instructions required to effect a passthrough from one system to another.

For any practical purpose, what the cloud vendors are proposing to user organizations is a multipolar, tightly coupled system with a wide area network connecting many tightly coupled local area networks and their servers (some of which might be mainframes). This two-layered tightly coupled approach does not come free of cost; it increases the requirements for fault tolerance by an order of magnitude and sometimes much more. It also introduces the need for highly reliable design characteristics:

- six nines system reliability for the cloud, four nines for the user organization, and
- stringent response time requirements as perceived by the end user, carefully monitoring the reasons for response time degradation.

It needs no explaining that these impact in a big way a system solution, affecting its effectiveness, capex, market appeal, cost of operations, as well as associated operational risk and reputational risk. Both the cloud vendor and the user organization must be brought to task in sustaining the cloud's fault tolerance.

In addition, what we are talking about in cloud computing fault tolerance is way above and beyond what in the late 1980s was necessary with client-servers, for instance, making feasible the use of multiported disks, with each drive being connected to the processors through a bus. (More than two decades ago this was a challenging issue because with tightly coupled systems, no pairing or load balancing was required between the individual processors.)

With cloud computing, the focal point of fault tolerance has become *data reliability in the cloud*. Let's look at an example. The way a feature article in *The Economist* had it, in October 2009 "tens of thousands of people with Sidekick smart-phones, for example, lost their address books, calendars, photo albums and other personal data, all of which were being stored in the cloud by Danger, an aptly named subsidiary of Microsoft."*

The aforementioned article also pointed out that a disaster on this scale is unusual, while occasional outages are more common. The "occasional outages," however, may be a minor problem for the smart phone owners, but a major disaster for user organizations whose BCM dearly depends on the cloud.

Let's face it: power outages can create havoc, and the cloud's globalized infrastructure makes them more likely because many countries don't have clean power and are not able to cope with spikes. Moreover, a power failure can snowball, as happened some years ago in Canada. While cloud services can allegedly scale up smoothly, the power system supplying them may not.

Just as worrisome is the usual lack of legally binding clauses in an SLA targeting fault tolerance connected with computers, databases, and network services by the cloud vendor—regardless of location. Not only are fault tolerance clauses

---

* *The Economist*, October 17, 2009.

indispensable, but they should also be reflected into the user organization's business continuity management program when it is updated or upgraded.

Real-time diagnostics help in improving fault tolerance. Both in the vendor's cloud and at the user organization, knowledge artifacts should check for key types of errors or malfunctions, closing down units if a fault is discovered and supporting fail-soft capabilities end to end. This is feasible if the original design accounted for graceful degradation without impairing contractual response time commitments. Cloud integrity is a complex business, and it is calling for sophisticated solutions for:

- diagnosis, detection, and confinement;
- isolation of errors and prevention of further damage;
- repair and replacement of faulty cloud components in a flight*; and
- real-time recovery restoring a stable, consistent system state, for each and every user of cloud computing.

Basically, all these tasks are the cloud provider's responsibilities, and even if the user organization takes appropriate measures, this in no way relieves the cloud vendor of its duties. However, to build up a legal case, the user's IT department must carefully define all issues surrounding:

- cloud disaster management,
- disaster recovery, and
- business continuity management.

It must also steadily train its people by carefully reviewing and analyzing actual case histories involving incidents caused by cloud vendors, other infrastructure providers, natural events, human factors, technological breakdowns, and more. Implementing an improved solution that sustains in the longer-term online business continuity management at a high level of reliability requires a great deal of contingency planning. Cloud computing significantly increases the need for contingency, and this is a job that squarely falls on the shoulders of the user organization's IT, no matter what sort of promises the cloud vendor might make.†

I particularly underline this issue because I know by experience that many companies downplay the need for contingency planning, and they pay dearly for such an oversight. Neither should contingency approaches lead to a dead end because they have been designed for relatively short-term failures in a mainly batch environment, rather than the sort of challenges cloud computing entails.

Complacency is the enemy of contingency. Let me put it this way: a board member of a major company said, "My IT people explained to me that cloud computing

---

* Which has been compared to replacing the tires of a car while running one hundred miles per hour.
† A good way to approach this issue is to compare contingency planning to insurance. Are we buying insurance? Are we angry if we had no accident at the end of the year?

is a win-win situation." That's patently false. For companies spousing that notion, the cloud will be a no-win/no-win situation.

10.5 With the Cloud, Response Time Is More Important than Ever Before

System *response time* is the time the user waits. As such, it is measured from the user's signal to the system that there is work to be done, to the point at which the system begins to present the asked-for information, or computational results, to the user. Within a cloud's operating environment and design structure, response time identifies the prevailing operating characteristics, and it is a function of:

- types, size, frequency, and amount of jobs being treated*;
- contention created by the job stream as well as by the existence of spare capacity and fail-soft procedures;
- input/output characteristics of the system and related issues, such as packet switching, buffering, and virtualization;
- physical and logical capabilities, including those relating to OSs, DBMSs, TPRs, and so on;
- chosen processing mode (interpretation, emulation, compilation), as well as communications and other protocols;
- file access in relation to physical media being used and associated logical supports;
- inherent build-in delays (such as earth to satellite to earth), data transmission, and associated issues; and
- investments made in infrastructure, servers, network nodes, and links, as well as human capital and other critical factors.

The dynamic environment of information technology sees to it that whether we talk of public clouds or private clouds, demand for information services varies every split second. Provisioning a cloud for peak load is a complex job involving the knowledge of user organization(s) and user profiles.

Projections related to the provisioning of cloud computing power must be accurate because loads have to be sustained without violating contractual clauses, which leads to underutilization at other times. The pros who say that cloud computing is efficient because it lets an organization pay by the hour for utilized resources must be themselves living in a cuckoo cloud, because every resource involves costs—and somebody must pay for them. Usually, in all industrial and commercial activities

---

* Including user needs such as formatting and error assist.

that "somebody" is the user, though with the deep financial crisis of 2007–2009 the taxpayers were assigned that role*—but subsidies don't help in the longer run.

Given that the cloud is in its beginnings, there is no "right dimensioning" of resources, because what is right today may probably be too little or too much tomorrow. Whether we talk of a public or private cloud, the party responsible for it will be well advised to plan for a significant amount of spare capacity, over and above what is needed for overhead.

If the cloud's available equipment is nearly 100 percent utilized, *then* queueing theory suggests that system response time will approach infinity. It is not for no reason that well-managed data centers see to it that the *usable* capacity must be kept from 60 to 80 percent utilization.

Cloud computing theorists who say that the pay-as-you-do scheme changes in a radical way the accounting and finance issues that characterized computing for nearly six decades are out of their wits. What has applied with computer rent or lease holds true with utility computing. The bigger and more complex the system, the greater the amount of required overhead in human skills and technology investments to make it tick.

While it is unquestionably true that cloud or no cloud, the common critical element in all enterprises is the ability to control the cost of services, the fact that computer resources are sitting idle at the data center is not the only reason for high costs. Human resources sitting idle at executive desks and trading desks because of long response time classically involve higher costs by an order of magnitude.

Documented through practical examples, these references lead us to the need to factor in the response time whenever we talk of cloud computing or, indeed, of any other solution involving computers and communications. Dr. Michael Stonebraker and Dr. Wei Hong, of the University of California at Berkeley, have proposed a pragmatic algorithm for optimization of return on investment in regard to information technology:

$$\text{Cost Function} = \text{Resource Consumption} + (W * \text{Response Time}) \quad (10.4)$$

where W is a judgmental factor, valuing response time over the cost of resources. If end user time is expensive, then W can be equal to 5 or more. At an executive level W may be greater than 10, while for clerical work it may be between 1 and 2.† Every time the response time increases, so does the total cost of the provided solution, no matter what the cloud theorists may be professing.

Moreover, as the preceding chapters have underlined, the cloud's system response time should be employed by the user organization as a contractual gatekeeper. The

---

* Salvaging through trillions and against their best judgment the self-wounded mammoth banks and motor vehicle companies.
† If the current huge (and irrational) discrepancy in salaries and bonuses is accounted for, then the range of variation of W will be in the hundreds.

careful user will recall that this book has emphasized the need to base the SLA not just on cost but also on the twin pillars of:

■ high reliability and
■ very short response time.

For the sake of both cloud providers and user organizations, the clauses specifying short response time should not be monolithic but escalate between 80 percent of responses being subsecond (but quantitatively expressed) and a little higher level for the next 10, 7, and 3 percent. In addition, the user organization should require that the resulting profile of response time is reevaluated with the cloud vendor every month, to flash out cases where the slightly higher response time falls at the level of executive desks and trading desks. *If* this is found to happen, *then* contractually guaranteed immediate corrective action should be taken by the cloud vendor at its expense.*

One can never blame himself or herself for leaning to the side of caution. The degradation of Internet access time (at least in some countries) provides enough evidence that something similar may well happen with cloud computing. Here is, in a nutshell, what has been observed. Until mid-1995, at least in most European countries, Internet access was nearly excellent. But as the number of users increased, it slowed down because of:

■ the many users accessing the system and
■ the growing number of accesses per user.

Besides this problem, which broadband Internet promised to solve, in a systems sense Internet servers presented queuing problems, to which were added updating problems by some providers. Who does not learn lessons of the past is preparing to repeat the same mistakes.

Internet experience may also be a test bed for political problems. Not only have a number of government-run telcos obstructed the Internet's spread, but they have also found it difficult to agree on what to do with cross-border hackers. In Amsterdam today there are computer wizards selling their services in a "rent a hacker" market. This has had several security after effects, and similar cases may spread with incalculable consequences in cloud computing.

10.6 Improving the Availability of Cloud Services

Section 10.2 defined availability as the probability that the system is running without interruption at any point during scheduled time. It also provided two equations

---

* And repetition of this case should lead to severe penalties.

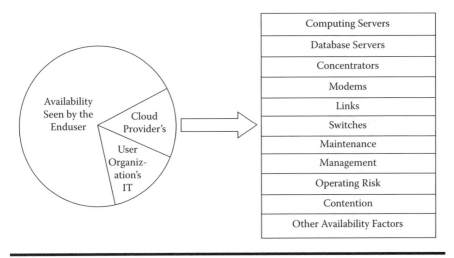

Figure 10.1 With cloud computing, availability has two reference timeframes instead of one.

for the measurement of availability and cautioned against the use of creative statistics by means of manipulating fail-soft incidents and systems response time.

All devices attached to a cloud computing solution weigh on its availability, and the same is valid of their sustenance and management. As Figure 10.1 shows, the cloud vendor's environment includes computing servers, database servers, links, switches, and much more. Individually and in unison, the system's availability is conditioned by those devices: hardware, software, and lifelong maintenance (Section 10.7).

Because resources are shared, the operating environment and the system's contention play a major role in terms of availability perceived by end users. System management practices leave a visible footprint, an example being hot swapping and live insertion, which evolved from expensive, special solutions upgrading mainstream design features.

Providing hot-swapping features on a bus interface makes it feasible to repair a faulty or damaged component without having to shut down the system. Live insertion for repair assumes that when a module goes out the machine can detect the failure, take the affected module offline, replace it with a standby, and then notify the system administrator that the failure occurred.

Key to this approach is both a redundancy that enables one to perform at least some system functions through alternative components, and intensive employment of intelligent software for diagnostics. Design-wise, in client-server and similar solutions, most hot-swap features are fully integrated with the operating system and with the application environment.

- Hot swapping builds upon the system specifications,
- High-availability design adds the layer of dependability.

■ The use of knowledge engineering artifacts redefines the method by which the operating system acts on impending insertion or extraction of a module.

The reader should, however, notice that critical to this solution are knowledge-enriched diagnostics that permit one to automatically detect the presence or absence of a fault, leading to dynamic reconfiguration able to accommodate needed changes, then proceeding through software intelligence to make hot swapping possible. Smart software must monitor, even anticipate, adverse events and be satisfied with the failure's removal.

The problem is that a great lot of user organizations moving or contemplating to move to the cloud are still in medieval times as far as advanced technology is concerned. While one can argue that a user organization behind the curve can benefit from the cloud vendor's expertise in improving system availability, this is only partly true because its internal IT will simply not be in charge.*

Still, a close collaboration between the vendor and the user in improving availability through network intelligence helps—provided the vendor provides ample and qualified training for user personnel. Experience from industrial floor automation and telecommunications helps in moving in the right direction, as in these instances:

■ System solutions have targeted nearly 100 percent uptime.
■ Nearly half of factory automation designs require hot swapping.

As it has happened with factory automation, administrative automation systems are now in search of uninterrupted service solutions for business continuity reasons. Among the better-managed companies, the race is on to create highly competitive solutions that can offer customers system reliability well beyond what was available in the past, but we are not yet there.

According to Pareto's law, a small number of system components will be responsible for a large number of failures. Therefore, the preceding paragraphs promoted the use of intelligent software so that error-prone and failure-prone devices are tracked individually through detailed statistics, flashed out, and swiftly replaced. User organizations contemplating cloud computing services are well advised to group together their efforts in this domain, just like banks did in the early years of this century in order to:

■ understand the nature of and
■ get hold of operational risks.†

---

* As an old proverb has it, pity the fellow who cannot scratch himself and waits for others to scratch him.
† In 1999 the Banking Committee on Banking Supervision required that banks keep capital reserves for operational risks. Until then, the concept of op risk was foggy, and to be in charge of the issue, many banks grouped together in a common effort to clear up what op risk is and collect statistics.

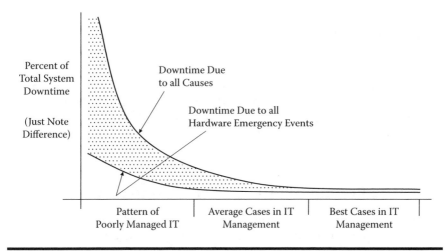

Figure 10.2 Management practices play a very significant role in the improvement of system availability.

Not only hardware but also software, system management practices (including operational risk), and environmental factors should be handled according to Pareto's law. Subsequently, they should be monitored, measured, and analyzed for:

- establishing cause and effect and
- tightening the margins of variation that result in system downtime.

Based on actual operational statistics, Figure 10.2 dramatizes the role played by a first-class system administration in improving overall availability. Detailed statistics based on steady monitoring and widespread use of knowledge artifacts are powerful tools in the hands of system administrators, but they are not always used, let alone properly employed.

Detailed runtime availability statistics are most essential to the configuration of a reliable online system able to meet application requirements, as well as measure the impact of component failures on every application. Each failure and each error condition must be subjected to careful analysis, with the failures themselves carefully classified into:

- catastrophic,
- major, and
- minor.

Systems and procedures as well as statistical tables from WWII military standards are among the best available tools today, in terms of contributing to the improvement of cloud availability.* Also helpful are operating characteristic (OC) curves by individual component, with categorization by aftereffect (for instance, data damaged or not damaged).

All this is written with the understanding that detection of the nature, frequency, and extent of failures is critical, and it must be based on analytics, not on guesswork. Subsequently, it should be used in conjunction with telediagnostics and telecontrol. Apart from flashing out weak links and components, this will make the steady online maintenance so much more effective.

10.7 The Premium for Life Cycle Maintainability

The first six sections of this chapter have explained why cloud computing reliability, availability, and response time are so important for timely, accurate, and uninterrupted provision of cloud services. This section will explain the importance, goal, and content of life cycle maintainability, which, like reliability, rest on inherent design characteristics imbedded at the drafting board of a system and of each of its component parts. In fact, more than maintainability, the target is *sustainability*, and this includes not one but three overlapping processes:

- *maintainability* proper is the extent to which preventive maintenance can be performed without degrading availability;
- *repairability* refers to the speed with which a component failure can be detected and fully corrected; and
- *recoverability* identifies what happens at the after-correction time of a component failure, specifically the speed with which system facilities can be restored, including recovery of data damaged as a result of failure.

For any information system, this whole range of activities is a life cycle process, with particular emphasis placed on two items: *baby failures*, which occur when the system comes alive, and *wear-out failures*, which invariably show up toward the end of its useful life.

As shown in Figure 10.3, between these two milestones in a system's life cycle, there is, more or less, a cruising period, which should in no way be interpreted to mean that maintainability should be relaxed. This being said, preventive maintenance required for various components (and classes of components) varies widely, depending upon their nature, type, and design characteristics.

For instance, a unit without moving mechanical parts needs less preventive maintenance than one with moving parts, such as a disk drive. Still, the first requirement for proper maintenance of hardware is that the component is designed for

---

* Such as MIL-STD 105A, available at the Government Printing Office in Washington, D.C.

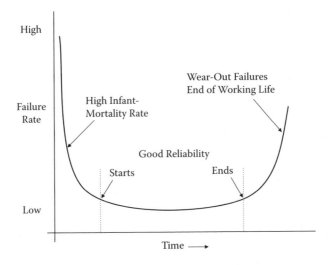

Figure 10.3 Natural and man-made systems have baby failures and wear-outs. Our goal should be high reliability.

preventive maintenance. Cloud or no cloud, a basic rule for preventive maintenance in IT is that the entire system will not be stopped in order to perform it.

Since the cloud must operate continuously, preventive maintenance has to be performed without a disrupting effect. As the previous sections brought to the reader's attention, administration-wise, this is assisted by the use of agents* and a feedback reporting system able to project the next likely failure(s). Smart diagnostics were not born last night; they date back to the late 1980s, though many user organizations still don't make use of them.

Diagnostic routines must be able to run in the normal job stream without disrupting the entire system, capitalizing on logs of component behavior and on analytics that pinpoint units that need immediate care. By examining such a log, expert systems would identify devices' behavior in regard to the limits of their tolerances—projecting trend lines that might break such limits. This is critical to life cycle maintainability for all four basic system classes:

- hardware,
- software,
- protocols and interfaces, and
- operational.

Hardware malfunctions and outages are far from being the number one reason for worry. In a cloud computing environment, software and protocol failures may

---

* D. N. Chorafas, *Agent Technology Handbook* (New York: McGraw-Hill, 1998).

range from a programming screw-up to a single bit error leading to a protocol blow-up. In the case of Amazon.com, on July 20, 2008, a single bit error leading to gossip protocol unavailbility resulted in an outage of up to eight hours.

Correspondingly, failure in authentication services is an operational malfunction. Also in connection to operational risks in a cloud environment, there have been data transfer bottlenecks, bugs in the realm of large-scale distribution and access of files, as well as other mishappenings affecting performance in a negative way. My approach to the problems associated with these examples is not mainstream. I consider them to be

- part of the cloud vendor's operational risk and
- subject to the realm of life cycle maintainability of its systems and procedures.

Operational malfunctions, like performance issues, can prove highly costly. It is normal that for business reasons vendors use general purpose servers, and they depend on virtualization across their infrastructure to optimize the resources pool, but this sometimes collides with the objectives of user organizations—particularly demands posed by those applications that are mission critical.

In conclusion, reliability and business continuity correlate among themselves and with life cycle maintainability. Even assuming that a cloud computing vendor can guarantee 99.9999 percent availability, which is way above what is commercially available today, this would imply almost one hour of downtime in a year.

Statistically speaking, this one-hour outage might never occur for some customers, but it will be quite a bit higher for others. These are not issues that are given due weight by companies looking at the cloud, yet they can dearly affect their business and therefore their reputation.

CASE STUDIES ON CLOUD COMPUTING APPLICATIONS

Chapter 11

Open-Source Software and onDemand Services

11.1 The Advent of Open-Source Software

Classically software* has been divided into two distinct classes: *systems* and *applications*. The operating system (OS), database management system (DBMS), and tele-processing routines (TPRs) are examples of systems software. Applications routines constitute the other class; they interact with the computing devices through system calls, invoking a predefined function.

This has been the traditional approach, which, however, in many cases has resulted in a coarse-grain customization of system resources and therefore in sub-optimization in the use of available computing facilities. This underutilization of both machines and programmer skills has been particularly pronounced with homemade programs, which were the only ones available in the first dozen years of computer usage.

By the late 1960s came to the market off-the-shelf software that could be bought by user organizations as a commodity. The first packages addressed the more wide-spread applications (at that time), such as accounting. During the 1970s other

---

* The word *software* was coined during the 1958 conference, in Philadelphia, of the Association of Computing Machinery (ACM). Another term born during the same event is *operating system*.

applications domains had also been well served by commodity software. A good example is computer-aided design/computer-aided manufacturing (CAD/CAM).

The 1970s as well experienced a renaissance in software development methods with computer-aided software engineering (CASE). The 1980s saw significant strides in software sophistication through expert systems. Among user organizations, Bankers Trust and, at the vendors' side, DEC and Xerox have distinguished themselves with new technological strides. Xerox PARC research center has been famous for inventing things (but also for not being able to profit from them).

Everything counted, these developments, combined with the use of off-the-shelf software, significantly improved the utilization of human resources for programming routines—but only up to a point. The reason for failing to do better is that user organizations fell in love with their legacy system. In terms of applications programming, only 20 percent or so of human resources have been invested in developing new software. The other 80 percent sank in the maintenance of decades-old legacy routines. With awful misallocation of human resources, packages were supposed to correct this maintenance ensured by the vendor. But bad practices among user organizations did away with this benefit, as they tried (often unsuccessfully) to customize the onPremises bought software to their crumbling procedures—rather than doing precisely the inverse.

The changes user organizations have been doing to the commodity software they purchased are not only irrational, time-consuming, and very costly but also self-destructive. Early in this century, a study by the Gartner Group found that three years after being purchased, 70 percent of enterprise management packages are neither fully implemented nor meeting the goals of their users.

This negative performance attests to the poor management of software, and the resulting difficulty of supporting new solutions, as well as to the slowness with which some IT departments work, and their wrong way of handling their expected deliverable. New software implementation may be undermined in many ways: through inefficiency, slow-moving projects, and "not invented here" arguments, as well as by the aforementioned manipulation of onPremises packages:

- to make them fit archaic organizational procedures or
- improve upon what is offered in the market, with regrettable results.

It comes, therefore, as no surprise that since the first years of this century, the more clear-eyed companies have shifted their software strategy from in-house development and proprietary massaged packages to the *open-source* business model. Vendors who make their living from computers, communications, software, and IT services have also been shifting their policy toward becoming open-source providers; those who do so appreciate that if they don't, they may be in trouble. But is open sourcing really a new departure in applications routines or a commercial gimmick that:

- gained ground during and after the dotcom boom as a way to cut costs?
- became a catchword to hook up clients for paying services?
- is at risk of becoming a passing glory or a fad?

To answer these questions, we need to return once again to the 1950s, at the beginning of the computer industry and the early commercial and industrial applications. In these formative years, companies such as Univac, IBM, and Bendix, to name but a few, kept close to their chest their design specs and machine language code that conditioned programming. There were, however, many computer experts asking for standardization that would have allowed the *portability of programs* between computers, lowering by so much the barriers vendors raised: the vendors' answer to the standardization argument has been that it had no place in a young industry in full evolution.

There was truth in this argument. More than that, however, there has been the belief that it would be foolish to open up and allow rivals to steal one's edge. This became a vendor policy that got amplified with protocols, APIs, search engines, and other subsequent developments. In hardware, standardization eventually came with "Intel inside," largely the result of Intel's commercial thrust.

By nearly monopolizing the market for microprocessors, Intel's designs transcended the manufacturers of computer equipment and their edge—at the core of computing machinery. Other computer manufacturers, like AMD, objected, but there is scant evidence that the market at large or the government paid attention to their claim that a monopoly is bad for everybody.

In software, the now obsolete Cobol provided an early, but very poor example of standardization in programming languages.* This has been very poor for two reasons. First, because each computer vendor saw to it that its compilers made source and object programs incompatible on the different competitors' equipment. At the OS end, Unix, too, finished by having incompatible versions. The better example of an operating system able to run on multisourced equipment is Linux (more on this later).

The second reason why Cobol is a very poor example of a universal computer language lies in its deadly obsolescence. We don't use any more hardware of the Univac I and IBM 705 crop. Why should we be using a commercial language designed in 1957 by Codasyl—and therefore by a committee that had no soul to blame and nobody to kick.

Would it be correct to see the recent trend to open-source software as a revolt by users against vendor monopolies and programming language obsolescence? The case of users having had enough with vendor monopolies is true in connection to OS. Installing Linux in the late 1990s was a gesture of defiance against Microsoft's domination of the software industry and most particularly of the PC OS market.

---

* Prior to Cobol, Fortran (for tran(s)IT) was much more successful as a design of a scientific language.

By adopting an open operating system, standard user organizations became independent of vendors and their hard sales but not for long. IBM and Oracle, among others, threw their weight behind the Linux OS in part to join the bandwagon and in part to weaken Microsoft. Many critics have questioned whether vendors—indeed any vendor—are truly committed to openness. Commercial reasons caution against it.

Programming language obsolescence is, by contrast, a strong argument promoting open-source software, along with the onDemand benefits when compared to onPremises. As Chapter 1 brought to the reader's attention, whether called onDemand software or software as a service (SaaS), the on-rent model incorporates the maintenance chores that have been classically consuming up to 80 percent of programming skills available in a user organization. It also provides a much more sophisticated routine in practically real time, which cautions most strongly against in-house developments.

11.2 An Era of Partnerships in onDemand Software

Just like the advent of off-the-shelf commodity software during the late 1960s and early 1970s, the twenty-first century's onDemand software targets the areas of greater market thrust in terms of applications. This strategy of reaching the most ample possible market is further promoted through partnerships. An example is Salesforce.com's partnership with Google:

- offering Salesforce's CRM programs to Google's customers,
- reselling Google apps to Salesforce customers, and
- aiming to capture the market dominated by Microsoft's onPremises productivity suite (MS Office).

The fact that Salesforce's customers can use Google apps when they log into Salesforce.com results in a seamless suite for personal and business productivity. This enhances the business of both partners. A prerequisite to such collaboration has been that Salesforce integrated its CRM routines with Google AdWords to create a seamless marketing-to-sales environment.

The attraction exercised by a vendor on the online market increases almost by the square of good products it has on offer. Mid-October 2009 Google said that Rentokil Initial, a pest control and parcel delivery entity, would roll out its (the vendor's) online applications to its army of thirty-five thousand people.* This will be a first in terms of a company's commitment involving a mid-five-digit number of employees.

---

* *The Economist*, October 17, 2009.

The principle of sharing a common ground and mutual interests prevails with other partnerships. Companies entering into an applications software partnership are capitalizing on the added value the one can offer to the other. This offers a good way to come up from under the *give-away* policy, which started in late 1990s with the Netscape browser offered as a bait. The zero cost to the user was a one-off event, and while he or she was not paying for the browser, he or she was paying for the attachments.

The business plan is that companies that give a product away get paid in a nontraditional way. On that premise, Netscape deviated from the classical pay-as-you-buy model. By adding value, onDemand vendors profit from a line of services connected to the original product that permit the vendors to make money even if the product is free or sold below cost. Gillette more or less is giving away the razor, but it makes money on the blades.

Other mechanisms for generating profits out of being generous with the original product are service agreements, maintenance fees, options, and upgrade fees, as well as income from the steady flow of new features. This is by no means reserved to the software business. Cellular phone companies are nearly giving away the handset to get a steady stream of service revenue—and that's only a start.

By all evidence, *mobile convergence* will present great business opportunities. At present, Apple's iPhone is by far the market leader in smart phones (with over 30 million units being sold), but other vendors are assaulting this lucrative market. In October 2009 Microsoft released a new version of Windows for smart phones. Google's answer is the Android OS, which is gaining momentum.* Some experts predict that it may overtake the iPhone within three years.

Hybrid markets aside, ingenious pricing of onDemand software, including upgrades, can provide a steady revenue stream. As we have seen in Chapter 3, Salesforce.com's CRM editions—Group, Professional, Enterprise, and Unlimited—scale up enterprise CRM applications for sales, service, and marketing, along with additional functionality, depending upon the edition. In terms of added value, the unlimited edition also includes Mobile and Sandbox (a testing environment). By contrast, lower-priced professional and enterprise editions limit the custom applications but can get access to Salesforces' Mobile for a fee.

What these applications have in common is scalability in modes for computation, storage, retrieval, and communications. Business partnership in onDemand software must share this scalability model, or at least ingeniously use virtualization to hide the implementation of how different routines are multiplexed and shared. Indeed, according to some opinions in the coming years, different utility computing offerings will be distinguished by the

---

* In October 2009 it received the backing of Verizon.

- level of abstraction presented to the programmer and
- level of management of the available resources, so that to the user the service seems to be seamless.

The better and more promising onDemand software partnerships are commercial enterprises guided by market size, not by the goal of building a better mousetrap. There are also joint efforts aimed at building more integrated approaches able to accommodate a large number of dynamically interacting end users where future interrelationships among them cannot be

- properly understood,
- thoroughly planned, or
- anticipated in the longer term.

It is only reasonable to expect that as at least some partnerships favor open source, and as this becomes more professional, its appeal will significantly increase. In the early days, most open-source programs consisted of routines free of charge written by volunteers who collaborated online. This pattern has changed.

Nowadays established companies have joined the bandwagon, while at the same time start-ups that had in their early years opted for open source grew and became well known. Red Hat is the world's biggest independent open-source firm, with annual revenues of nearly $800 million at the end of 2009. Other software companies and partnerships specialized in value-added solutions beyond an open standard.

To enhance the salesability of onDemand software designers, vendors and business partners pay a good deal of attention to two factors: agile user interfaces and costs. Customers have come to expect better interfaces than those already available, and usability is key to adoption. Cloud vendors are increasingly designing their software with users in mind, and tend to be much more customer oriented than in the past. As a result, enterprises and their end users are benefiting from more user-friendly applications, apart from the fact that the cost curve has bent.

Traditionally, since the advent of personal computers in the late 1970s/early 1980s, significant cost reductions have been associated with hardware; now the day of lower cost but more functional software has come. Combined with the introduction of new devices, this translated to an ideal scenario for the cloud: lots of Internet access with a need to offload application processing and storage. Let me repeat this reference: with fierce competition in the onDemand market, software is joining hardware in the downsizing of prices, and this fits nicely the current market mood, as with the severe economic and credit crisis of 2007–2009, many firms are keen to keep in check their IT budget.

Cost, however, has not been the only reason for open source's popularity. As Section 11.1 explained, a growing number of users appreciate that it offers more flexibility than proprietary programs. Beyond this is the fact that the licenses for proprietary programs often include restrictions on how they can be used.

The better-managed vendors have taken notice of the evolving cost consciousness among user organizations. Intuit, for example, employed the onDemand delivery model to appeal to cost-conscious consumers, as well as small and medium enterprises (SMEs). The company ranks just behind Salesforce.com as the second largest player in onDemand software:

- offering various products like TurboTax, QuickBooks, and QuickBase and
- leveraging their functionality by means of connected services like Homestead and Digital Insight.

To integrate its customer offering, Intuit markets its QuickBase as an online database of business offerings hosted in its data centers. It also treats customers signing up as business partners, providing its Partner Platform to build applications, also making available a back-end infrastructure as well as hosting user management, integration, and billing services.*

This is an example of a framework featuring the various layers required for developers to create onDemand applications and market them to the large base of some 4 million SME Quickbook customers. The adopted solution also leverages QuickBase and Adobe's open-source Flex framework to build a range of Internet applications.

11.3 Frameworks, Platforms, and the New Programming Culture

Intuit's Partner Platform is one of the recent developments of frameworks, a concept dating back to the 1990s. The original idea was to provide programming solutions based on data objects and presentation objects, with the latter shared among many workstations (see also Section 11.4). In this sense:

- object-sharing becomes the basis for building computer applications, and
- security, integrity, and transactional constraints are at work to protect shared data objectives.

Every framework provider has his own design solution. Down to the basics, however, there exist two alternative ways of looking at a framework. The broader one is to consider it an infrastructure that consists of domain-wide reusable software. This is projected in a way that allows it to integrate other reusable and ad hoc modules, in order to answer the requirements of a specific job.

---

* Intuit has structured a subscription-based revenue sharing plan with developers that involves no up-front costs and charges developers only when they generate revenue.

The alternative way of looking at a framework is as a set of classes that embody an abstract design for programming a family of related problems. By extension, framework-oriented programming is the exploitation of object-oriented integrative structures. The three main linkages used between data and presentation objects can be expressed as

- value,
- structure, and
- transaction.*

Typically, these linkages can be adaptable, implying that a value in the presentation object can be updatable in the data object. But a linkage can also be volatile; a value can be changed by another application, and that change is reflected in the presentation object.

Structure linkages and value linkages resemble one another when maintaining consistency between presentation and data objects. By being active, scrollable, and updateable, structure linkages affect application design.

Transaction linkages are associated with a transaction as committed by the database system, with visibility as perceived by a user manipulating presentation objects. The aim is that changes in data objects continually match changes in presentation objects.

While the foregoing notions are not new to the software industry, as of recently they are being extensively employed due to the realization that they constitute a prefabricated structure, or template, of a working program. Application frameworks have come of age because they provide good support for other elementary functions, encapsulating a group of closely related classes, making it possible for the developer to work at a higher conceptual level of software design.

- This approach significantly improves programmer productivity and software dependability (Section 11.5).
- The framework itself sits in the background supporting the developer's effort.
- The focal point shifts to interactions among object types with which the designer, analyst, and programmer are working.

This permits major improvements in developing and testing programming routines, as well as a better understanding of software reusability criteria. Reduced maintenance is another advantage. Such functionality has generated developer interest, and it has served third parties' drive to create a swarm of software products.

An example on the implementation of notions described in preceding paragraphs is Google's Web Toolkit, enabling a growing number of applications to run

---

* Another consideration is the mechanism for resynchronizing the presentation and data objects.

on the browser online or offline. Users can write extensions and leverage Google services such as Maps, Calendar, Earth, and Gadgets.

Since 2008, when Google unveiled its new facilities allowing users to access its data centers, BigTable and Google Files System (through the Google App Engine), the company benefited both directly and indirectly through third parties. The online development platform made available to users tools to write and launch their own programming routines, leading to new subscriptions:

- the App Engine gives access to Google's web architecture, making feasible scalable applications able to handle a large number of users, and
- by sharing their infrastructure programming framework with outside developers, Google facilitated the development of quite competitive applications, when the latter are compared with existing software.

Another example is Adobe's AIR, which it presents as *de facto* platform for Internet applications. The company has made progress in furthering its runtime environment and created ways to monetize it. In early 2009, AIR reportedly registered 100 million downloads. In a partnership agreement, Salesforce.com actively promotes AIR to its developers, and Google is pursuing an open-source alternative with Dears that is complementary to AIR.

These recent examples brought to the reader's attention are practical manifestations of the primary purpose of frameworks and platforms: to assist human resources by building a user-friendly software environment behind which hardware details are hidden. As an added advantage, this is improving their efficiency. Emulating the notions characterizing an operating system, modern development platforms are:

- general purpose,
- interactive, and
- multiuser oriented.

Interfacing all the way to the basic software framework enables a higher level of code and design than what is practical otherwise. Theoretically this could be done through fourth- and fifth-generation language code generators, but these are based on procedural programming techniques and cannot easily provide the necessary infrastructural and design guidance.

By contrast, such guidance is made possible through the use of platforms. In short, this is a facility that helps to extend the entire scope and concept of flexible, reusable software solutions—from developing applications to their renovation, restructuring, and maintenance.

The wisdom of complementing onDemand software through the use of platforms is further documented by the fact that these are designed to support the execution of various processes currently—and with a reasonably high throughput. Supporting concurrent execution of programs also requires advanced operating system features to coordinate the partitioning of resources among the programs, as well as do dynamic partitioning at runtime. This responsibility is assumed by virtualization. As already stated in Chapter 2, virtualization is a machine-oriented process. To the contrary, the mission of the framework (or platform) is user oriented, providing designers, analysts, and programmers a higher level of abstraction for application development.

This duality of approach—framework and virtualization—comes none too soon. As hardware technology evolves, it is not really feasible to predict well in advance where information system support can be usefully extended. The uncoupling of the development environment from the underlying hardware makes it feasible to virtually extend the computers and communications aggregate the way developers think best. Another advantage of interfacing frameworks to systems functions is that this allows extensions:

- without upsetting the current applications environment
- or having to write entirely new kinds of device drivers for every application.

This is particularly important as a number of research projects reveal that in many programming systems, roughly half the code involves fixing or working around problems and obstacles posed by configuration issues. Moreover, modern platforms permit developers to revise their applications at a more rapid pace, without having to interact directly with hardware and the operating system primitives.

11.4 Finding Better Ways to Build IT Services

In essence, what onDemand software and cloud platforms provide is a better way to build products and services based on the most recent advances of information technology. This is particularly important when the components of services are neither local nor locally controllable, which is a characteristic of globalization.

Another requirement by modern industry that the use of Cobol (God forbid) and other obsolete languages cannot satisfy is the nesting of IT services, which has become a must, as one function is increasingly depending on another. While not universally appreciated, this is one of the basic reasons behind the quest for open software.

The need for nesting will increase significantly during the coming years. By consequence, when the service designer finds that already existing services are not under his or her control (since someone else may own them) or are incompatible with the environment in which he or she works, he or she will be frustrated. This is an adversity that:

- increases costs,
- lengthens lead times, and
- works against software dependability.

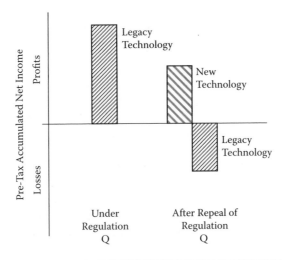

Figure 11.1 Impact of technology on profit and loss, before and after deregulation.

Programming efficiency calls for both open solutions and runtime supports that identify service change, as well as for tools that effectively respond to the designer's actions, like real-time version control.

For instance, in the highly competitive market of private banking (Chapter 13), many financial institutions say that their strategy is focused on wealthy clients, with services designed primarily for them. But the technology they use is far from providing the full range of "best of breed" customer services they advertise. Their legacy applications simply cannot support top-class abilities in marketing, innovation, product design, privacy,* and, most importantly, risk control.

As far as the renewal of legacy programming libraries is concerned, onDemand software and the use of platforms are a gift from heaven. My research, however, documents that many user organizations, particularly the bigger ones, forego these benefits because they don't wish to change their crumbling IT culture. Instead, they enter (or try to enter) the cloud from its weakest link: the infrastructure.

The result is loss of competitiveness. When Regulation Q (of the U.S. banking industry) was repealed, a study by Bank of America established a *technology analysis* model. Shown in Figure 11.1, this documented that with Regulation Q banks could make good money from a client account even with old technology. By contrast,

---

* A large part of the failure to providing privacy is old technology, which is unable to overcome the lack of security that comes with the swarm of digital information about people and assets. See also Chapter 9.

- post–Regulation Q, competition became intense, and
- a bank has been losing money with old technology, counted in terms of pre-tax accumulated net income from client accounts.

The facts of life document the need for adapting to one's era and the requirements it brings along. Under legacy approaches, when the sophistication of IT services for products, clients, and internal operations increases, slow and limited tools become counterproductive. What is needed is a means able to provide product and client management with quick responses, which can be effectively done with object-oriented solutions supported through frameworks.

Section 11.3 made reference to Intuit's Partner Platform and its objects but did not elaborate on the wealth of functionality built into object-oriented programming. Briefly defined, an *object* is an instance (or a class) and a basic runtime entity. A *class* is the abstraction of shared characteristics; among others these include:

- inheritance,
- encapsulation and signatures,
- data abstraction,
- procedural abstraction, and
- metarules, constraints, equilibration.

Other important functionalities benefiting the users of object-oriented approaches are polymorphism, reusability, distributed concurrency, interoperability, dynamic binding, integrative ability, message passing, behavior monitoring, extensibility, versioning, referential integrity, query relevance, hypermedia, and semantic modeling.

All these are unknown facilities to legacy programming languages and one of the basic reasons why they are deadly obsolete. (Another fundamental reason for not using them is low productivity.)* Unfortunately, object-based programming is also uncharted territory for many analysts, programmers, and CIOs—not to mention CEOs and board members. No wonder, therefore, that in these companies information technology continues being medieval.

To bring about a renaissance, computer programming must use object-oriented paradigms treating each individual transaction as a set of behaviors, containing both process and data. In platforms like Intuit's, this set of behaviors is encapsulated into an independent object, so that it can be

- reused easily in a modular fashion and
- recombined to support different business activities.

---

* "Today programming in Cobol is a criminal offense," a professor of information technology taught his students at Zurich's Technical University (ETH). The year of that statement was 1988—think of 2010!

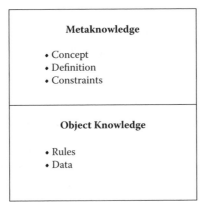

Figure 11.2   Metaknowledge is metarules and metadata.

Critical to this approach, and cornerstone to the new programming culture, is the concept of *meta*. Meta provides a conceptual interface between a man-made system (thus an artifact) and a real subject by means of a higher-up layer of control and command. The service of conceptual modeling is demonstrated by providing a two-way road between:

- generalization (hence induction) and
- a generative way of producing instances.

Along this frame of reference, *metadata* are data that describe, or help to interpret, other data. *Metaknowledge* is higher-level knowledge. A *metapredicate* controls the inference processing mechanism. Contrasted to metaknowledge, *object knowledge* is a more basic level, such as a usual description. Object knowledge forms a layer below metaknowledge, as shown in Figure 11.2. Stated in different terms, metaknowledge is based on the aims and intentions of a computer user. It differs from object knowledge in the sense that it describes the controls on object knowledge.

We can structure metaknowledge in a very flexible way to meet specific goals, for instance, permitting intelligent database management systems to:

- contain opinions on each object and
- include concepts for managing logic databases.

Another function supported by means of a metalayer is that of *metaphors*; these are ways of describing what the computer is doing, as contrasted to what people do. A metaphor alludes to action such as sending a message or providing an interface with common technology. *Constraints*, too, form part of metaknowledge.

In these few simple paragraphs (keeping them simple has been a deliberate choice), the reader finds all he or she needs to know to start understanding the background of modern software development platforms. By employing them, the distributed implementations of business elements become a network of objects whose services are made available to the application(s) serving end users—whether these are the company's own professionals or its business partners.

11.5 The Case of Software Dependability

The discussion on frameworks and platforms will be incomplete if due attention is not paid to software dependability. This is a most crucial issue that CIOs and developers must definitely address. Handling it in an able manner requires a return to the origins of programming complex systems, to appreciate some fundamental notions.

In his seminal book *The Mythical Man-Month*, Fred Brooks says that the difference in attention and complexity between (what was in the 1960s) an application program and a programming product is practically equal to an order of magnitude. Though Brooks referred to OS 360 as a programming product, off-the-shelf software (since the late 1960s) and more recently onDemand software are programming products, too.

Indeed, even with the (rather simple) applications programs of the 1950s and early 1960s, error detection, localization, and correction have been 100 percent the programmer's responsibility. Debugging is as old as the first programming routines ever written. But the concept of *software dependability* largely evolved in the 1970s with CASE (Section 11.1).

CASE tools provided some automated support for development activities, including specification, design, implementation, testing, and maintenance. Subsequently, new CASE versions used for the generation of programming routines provided workbenches and tool sets that not only supported a number of related tasks, but also created environments able to:

- encompass the program development process and
- enhance the analyst's/programmer's ability to test for dependability.

As these references document, the technological part of the software dependability challenge is a problem that goes back a long time. Its origins lie in fault tolerance. Without this concept, and what it implies in terms of controls, software dependability is weakened, even if it contains supposedly dependable programs. An application:

- may contain embedded bugs that escaped testing and
- be subject to misuses that exceed the coverage of fault tolerance.

For instance, procedural weaknesses can completely undermine the programming routine's intended robustness. The human part of the equation is always perplexing, because it is very difficult to anticipate all possible human errors. This does not necessarily mean that the human component is inherently unreliable, but rather that the whole system of software development and usage leaves much to be desired.*

Therefore, with software, as with every other man-made system (see also Chapter 10 on hardware reliability), one of the important challenges facing us is to be able to develop dependable aggregates out of less dependable components. This is especially important when the solutions we provide have to rely on the behavior of people whose dependability is not certain.

Clearly, software dependability is an issue of universal concern to all tool developers, and there is no unique best method to ensure it. However, there exist some best practices associated with program construction and testing activities, which we will discuss.

For starters, poor software dependability has always been a major negative in computer processing, and it is much more so today in a rapidly expanding environment of computer usage, ranging from very small devices to very big systems (Chapter 8). Whether they like it or not, user organizations have to undertake proper, systematic, and consistent program dependability evaluation, including:

- details of software releases,
- Severity of malfunctioning,
- application's area of manifestation,
- subsystem and workstation area of manifestation,
- date and time of problem registration, and
- type and effect of corrective action.

User organizations need a wealth of statistics for tracking the dependability of programming products (evidently including onDemand software, onPremises, and internal developments). Software failure analysis should be planned in a way to facilitate detection and monitoring, as well as lead to better mastery of the system.†
Moreover, cloud computing requires greater detail in steady monitoring to capture not just local but also end-to-end software problems.

- To concentrate on what is important, as a start it may be wise to drop minor faults and target high-impact failure rates and severe faults.‡
- The process chosen for steady validation must be consistent with the principle that software dependability growth models are considered applicable only when an operational profile is run.

---

* For instance, the C++ draft standard is more than seven hundred pages, and it is revised three times a year. Nobody can keep track of these changes in a dependable manner.
† This method has been traditionally applied during the validation phase of in-house testing.
‡ Provided, of course, that the proper preparatory work of a clear distinction between major/severe and minor faults has been made.

Other organizational conditions concerning the distribution of software failures have to do with the analysis of interfailure times. This requires a distinction between systematic and random failures, with the elements of each group classified according to their impact frequency and duration.

Particular attention should be paid to cross-platform software products, as failure rates might vary by platform. While it may be the right choice to avoid developing separate platform-specific versions of programming routines for each operating system, a cross-platform development strategy poses its own requirements of steady watch.

Clear goals as well as time and effort are needed to create a dependable cross-platform management system. This is an indispensable overhead, its wisdom documented by the fact that tailoring even small amounts of code to specific platforms can create a programmers and logistics nightmare—particularly in managing it afterwards. There is no free lunch.

Vendors, user organizations, and developers should appreciate that minimizing platform-specific code through cross-platform techniques involves its own challenges. For instance, it means developers should write code that does not incorporate any interfaces or programming tricks specific to a particular operating system. Another requirement is that of relatively low level programming conventions and interfaces that are common across the different platforms.

A clear aftereffect is foregoing many existing platform-specific APIs and programming conventions. These have been usually incorporated to enable programmers to write code that runs faster or handles graphics in a better way than code using lowest-common-denominator interfaces, or they have been implanted to lock in user organizations (Chapter 5). Therefore:

- Cross-platform usage and software dependability are two distinct goals to be pursued one at a time, not together.
- Mixing them will result in confusion and in an inordinate increase in the amount of errors; a better policy is to look at software dependability in a sense of vertical integration.

Classically, program testing is done by developers on each executable component, before release. Integration and system testing are performed (or at least should be performed) by an independent group. Validation with the customer is done by the vendor, based on a prespecified set of acceptance tests. These three phases should be integrated.

In addition, software dependability should be under steady watch. Properly designed agents can make a significant contribution to it by way of monitoring runtime. They can monitor, measure, and record the behavior of every programming routine, and derive future expected behavior as a function of its current behavior.

This approach is critical to the effort of detecting vulnerabilities that cannot otherwise be localized. As software increases in complexity and operates cross-platform, it is becoming impossible to analyze its dependability without structural and functional means and careful watching at runtime—which should be performed by knowledge artifacts.

11.6 Auditing the Conversion to Software as a Service

Since Chapter 1 the reader has been warned that converting from the current system to cloud computing is not easy because it involves cultural, political, organizational, and technical challenges. Chapter 6 explained the need for reengineering the organization, but it has been left to this chapter to discuss auditing the conversion to cloud computing—particularly to onDemand software. To help in understanding the focus of auditing, Figure 11.3 positions onDemand software in the middle of a layered architecture.

- The layers below have for decades been commodity modules, developed and sold by computer manufacturers and software vendors.
- The three layers above it are the produce of the company's internal developers, even if some value-added applications could be bought as a programming product.

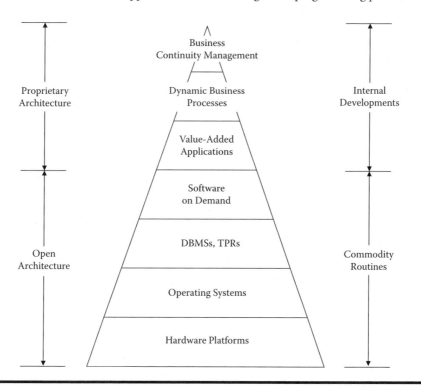

Figure 11.3   onDemand software as a service is an architectural mid-layer capitalizing on web browser facilities.

Let's take as an example a company that bought onDemand software to manage its workflow, leverage its data, and provide its people with the ability to work collaboratively on intranet sites, but—as it so often happens—it could not rid itself of legacy programs. The chosen cloud software key features have included:

- document sharing,
- meeting workspaces,
- shared calendars,
- document libraries, and
- office routines.

This onDemand programming product provided archiving, continuity, and filtering functionality to existing e-mail and electronic communication services; a repository for e-mails and interactive messages for archiving purposes; and routines to assist in fulfilling compliance requirements.

Among end users, some criticized the fact that the encryption facilities of the onDemand software were not satisfactory in regard to e-mail policy violations. Other users, however, praised the overall suite, emphasizing the office communications functionality, which provided cloud-based instant messaging. This enabled real-time person-to-person communication through text, voice, and video, and it also supported remote access to presence awareness and distribution lists.

The audit confirmed that the office suite of the onDemand software indeed includes useful features, such as interactive applications/desktop sharing, whiteboard tools, and active speaker video switching. Through it, end users accessed, edited, and stored files, synchronizing outlook calendars as well as tasks and contacts. The onDemand software also featured a web-based front end for managing from within a browser the workspace and associated database elements.

The results of the audit were less positive in terms of planning the changeover to onDemand software. Internal politics saw to it that the first subsystem of legacy programs subject to conversion had been the legacy office routines, even though a brief feasibility analysis revealed that the transition would face as its main obstacle the lack of interfaces to accounting and other subsystems (the company's back office functions had to be part of the transition as well). This choice was made despite the objections of the newly appointed CIO.

Nor could the onDemand software integration be effectively done without adequate interfacing with several other legacy programs, given their age, incompatibilities, and patches. Ironically, one of the critiques of the conversion plan was that modules of onPremises software, bought some years earlier to support an "unprecedented" simultaneous access to corporate data, had been literally:

- squeezed into the company's legacy system and
- held by patchwork (a frequently used, but wrong, approach).

As a result, the onPremises package did not do away with the monolithic applications development paradigms of earlier years. It also created more problems, one of them being the added complexity in introducing the onDemand software. Quite similarly, benefits said to have been derived from the onPremises package, like better exploitation of corporate information elements, were nonexistent. A mezzanine layer that might have supported this functionality had been simply set aside.

The old CIO, who had in the meantime retired, defended his changeover plan by saying that it was inconceivable that "he and his staff could roll out improvements at this speed made feasible through that mezzanine software." Neither did he believe that the traditional approaches of in-house program developments should be discarded because of buying some packages. His critics answered that the retired CIO was for more than a decade at the bleeding edge behind his time and always tended to be skeptical of the deliverables of new software technology.

The new CIO wanted to change that policy so that the company could benefit from onDemand programming products and platforms. To support his argument, he pointed out that much of what is now available on demand in the cloud comes from consumer technologies such as IM, which typically make employees more productive. But there was internal resistance to going along that way.

Provided that the new CIO had been given a free hand, his game plan had been to create through onDemand software core capabilities that define the specification of service elements that are highly configurable and tailorable. This would have ensured that:

■ costs for creating products and services are kept down, and
■ operating costs could be reduced over time, by integrating newer, more cost-effective technologies and workflow processes.

Correctly, the new CIO maintained that successful information technology implementations are dependent on the capabilities of the core system to allow integration of real-time end-user-centric data and processes. The best-managed computer shops, he said, appreciate that notion, while it is alien to those who continue living at the age of electrical accounting machines (EAMs).

The new CIO also wanted to create a company interoperability laboratory as a means of testing the hardware and software technologies, including those obtainable in the cloud. He looked at the lab as a corporate resource, largely driven and shared by the end users who play dual roles as:

■ IT service consumers and
■ company service providers, within the context of their functional responsibilities.

The lab was also supposed to serve as a repository for corporate technology assets, like reusable software objects and libraries, as well as the authority defining and enforcing requirement for open systems interoperability. This would have helped to redefine the way the firm worked with its business partners.

Company politics vetoed such plans. They also brought up opinions contesting the new CIO's authority. At least one of the IT department heads came up with a statement that in the case of IM and some kinds of file sharing, viruses or spyware could come into the corporate network from the outside, which unaware employees could ship inward and outward.

This security risk was a red herring, but it did kill a couple of projects in the making, in spite of the fact the new CIO answered that he did not consider the risk as being serious enough to warrant staying behind in technology. He did, however, face a bottleneck in the use of human resources, as the large majority of analysts and programmers were utilized to keep the legacy system running, and because of the economic crisis, the company was not hiring new staff.

Postmortem, another audit made at the board's request by an independent expert demonstrated that a large part of the corporate information system being kept on a legacy solution made matters more complex, not easier, for all concerned. The kinds of constraints the legacy system imposed to the renewed smaller part that underwent transition to onDemand software proved to be a severe handicap.

The audit also found that much of the difficulty in providing a quick transition to the use of onDemand software was accentuated by a (rotten) policy established under the old CIO: the IT organization was not in the habit of doing the necessary restructuring work. Yet, the latter had to be performed in an able manner because the firm's computer park included plenty of heterogeneous equipment, incompatible operating systems, installations in multiple geographic locations, and rather scant attention paid to reliability and availability.

11.7 Software Piracy Might Enlarge the Open Source's Footprint

Media and information technology are two domains suffering the most from a wave of global piracy. It matters little that this is illegal, as different jurisdictions condone the practice or look the other way as software pirates operate and enrich themselves.

There is, however, an interesting finding that should be brought into perspective. As the amount of software on personal computers being pirated continues rising, statistics available on software piracy reveal a growing share of open source. According to a report by the Business Software Alliance, a trade group, it hit 41 percent of total software being used, just short of the 44 percent paid for.*

Of this amount, a rather surprising 15 percent is open source, and hence theoretically free. The piracy rate is high in countries where sales of PCs are growing

---

* *The Economist*, May 16, 2009.

fastest. In some jurisdictions like that of Georgia, an estimated 90 to 95 percent of all software is unlicensed. By comparison, in Western Europe, a third of all software is unlicensed, and while the rate seems to be lowest in America, still as much as 20 percent of software is pirated.

Quite interestingly, in recent years in the BRICs (Brazil, Russia, India, China) software piracy has dropped sharply, though the practice has not disappeared. Nobody can say for sure if open-source software contributed to that result, but there is little argument that it has had an aftereffect on the computer market.

According to some opinions, the fact that open-source software attracts pirates is evidence that its wave has come a long way from its antiestablishment origins, to embrace users who did not want to be locked in to proprietary vendor products, or inflexible vendor contracts based on proprietary solutions. One of the forces propelling open-source efforts has been the wearing out effect of patents, as new programming languages have significantly increased the speed at which software products can be developed and marketed.

Piracy set aside, another fact behind open software's acceptance is that companies no longer perceive free programs as riskier. This has two aspects: the dependability placed in their regard and relief from the fear of using routines whose developer might have violated somebody else's intellectual property.

Taken together, all these reasons have been instrumental in bringing to bear a much more pragmatic approach by the user community toward open-source software. Increasingly, a key criterion is whether the savings in licensing fees for proprietary products outweigh the additional costs in manpower to integrate and operate the free programming alternative.

Companies that know how to count dollars and cents (which means the best and therefore the minority) also use as a criterion whether they can built added value upon the facilities provided by open-source software*: integrating the new software into the existing system, interfacing to ensure seamless operation, adding value through differentiation at a higher level, and thereby personalizing the application to the end user.

Through this approach, open-source software is expanding its footprint in recent years as the technology evolves and benefits to user organizations become more evident. Ironically, the pirating of open-source software assists in the expansion of its footprint, and the same is true of add-ons, such as agents and other sophisticated artifacts, which amplify its reach and appeal.

Open-source software needs knowledge engineering artifacts to promote its mobility. Nowadays, there is no reason why the location of where the code resides must be tied to the location of where the code will be executed. True enough, that assumption could also be heard with legacy software, but in essence it was an

---

* This is not at all the same with manipulating and changing the base program. An added-value layer is welcome, while massaging the programming product is pure stupidity, if not malfeasance.

outgrowth of opposition to the concept that everything stays put: IT shops could only run code that was locally resident, as in the 1950s. Today, by contrast:

- code can be stored at any location, and
- this is a fundamental concept underpinning onDemand solutions.

Agents can propagate the code to the machines where it is required on an as-needed basis while the application runs. This way, systems functionality can be swiftly changed in response to end user requirements. The basic premise is that until applications run, the local system's code need not be resident. It will be imported *as needed*. The set of things the computer can do must not be determined *a priori*, provided:

- the processing environment is fluid and dynamic, and
- it changes in response to application requirements as defined ad hoc by the end user.

The careful reader will recall the reference already made in this text that agents can cover larger and diverse implementation domains, accounting for a great deal of the difference between medieval legacy concepts in IT technology and its cutting edge in the twenty-first century. A direct aftermath of the strategic inflection points discussed in Chapter 3 is that application life cycles have collapsed. Top-tier organizations do appreciate that the tools to manage the new environment should reflect the disposable nature of software. Past is past.

Usually, companies whose state of mind still favors older technologies would benefit less by spousing open sourcing. There are also sectors of the computers and communications business where software development is capital-intensive, products take a longer time to come to market, and they remain on sale for years. Robotics for the manufacturing industry is an example, where open source cannot be powerful or reliable enough for heavy-duty usage.

Last but now least, some experts think that an open, standards-based network could give birth to a thousand new companies. Others are not so sure because they believe that most entities are not prepared to put up the needed preparatory work in order to make good on that opportunity—or simply, internal politics complicate matters an awful lot (Section 11.6). Plenty of organizational effort is necessary to get diverse technologies functioning seamlessly and reliably, but by far the number one factor for "good" or "bad" is top management. The bottleneck is always at the top of the bottle.

Chapter 12

Leadership in Logistics

12.1 Logistics Defined

Today, the term *logistics* is largely associated with the management of the flow of goods and materials through an organization: from raw materials to finished goods. While this might sound a simple enough process of moving things around, in reality it is very complex, and it is becoming increasingly so as customers demand more finely tuned services, while high technology and use of the Internet open up new ways of servicing customer requests.

Logistics underpins the industrialization of production and distribution and enables coordination of human activities. But it is wrong to associate the term logistics only with these processes and those described in the preceding paragraph. At its origin is a Greek word meaning a *calculator* as well as *accountancy*. Webster's dictionary defines logistics (noun, singular) as the branch of military science having to do with moving, supplying, and quartering troops.

Webster's has a reason for promoting this definition because since antiquity logistics has been the art and science of supplying armies and fleets, then the biggest assemblies of human planning efforts, with the supporting services required to carry out their mission. Logistics, therefore, predates the industrialization of production and distribution, and closely associates its meaning to that of effective administration.

Many historians believe that Alexander the Great would have been unable to move in to and conquer the heart of Asia, if it were not for the support Greek logisticians provided him with. Today multinational companies and supermarket chains clearly depend on logistics, as they command more people and materials than Alexander the Great ever did in his far-away expeditions. Therefore, Webster's definition is too narrow and needs to be extended in two ways:

■ in breadth, to encompass not only military science but also that characterizing all sectors of the economy, and
■ in depth, to include prognostication, computation, planning, accounting, and controlling—all vital activities, compared to the red blood cells of an enterprise.

As companies de-leverage, reengineer, and take out the waste from their assembly lines and supply chains, logistics is being paid very close attention—from seeking to eliminate excess weight to handling more cost-effectively goods and services. Business needs logistics as much as an army needs generals. It requires a well-balanced and optimized decision system for ensuring:

■ the availability of the right people and the right goods,
■ the fact that they are in the right place at the right time, and
■ the evidence that all this is happening at the right cost.

Peter Drucker has pointed out that a good part of the problem faced by the American armed forces in the early months of the Korean War was due to the fact that procurement and inventory policies—therefore logistics—were in bad shape. To make matters worse, for the next ten years this has been followed by countless studies, but things got no better. When Robert McNamara was appointed Secretary of Defense, he challenged the traditional measurement of military inventory based on:

■ total dollars and
■ total number of items in procurement and inventory.

In an application of Pareto's law, McNamara identified those items that consumed more total procurement dollars—some 4 percent of the inventory. He also focused his attention on a small group of items, another 4 percent, which accounted for 90 percent of combat readiness. Since some of the items in reference belonged in both categories, the crucial list came to about 6 percent of the total when measured by numbers, but a large share of total procurement when measured by value.

In a show of leadership (and discipline) in logistics, McNamara saw to it that these items had to be managed separately and with attention to *minute detail*. For the rest, which account neither for the bulk of the dollars nor for essential combat readiness, he applied *management by exception* through probabilities and averages— increasing by so much the effective decisions on procurement and inventory management.*

---

* Peter Drucker, *The Effective Executive* (London: Heinemann, 1967).

In business and industry, too, one reason for the leadership of Japanese car plants has been that they were pioneers of modern logistics: running just-in-time inventories (JIT; Section 12.5), applying fast flow replenishment (FFR) methods, experimenting on the best place for a warehouse to serve shops spread over the whole country, and, most importantly, paying a great deal of attention to quality.

Sam Walton, of Wal-Mart fame (Section 12.4), used an aerial inspection method for choosing the location of his stores, starting with intelligence and confirming the statistics he gathered by flying over a target area as an experienced pilot. Other supermarket chains, too, and their suppliers have been at the sharp end of the logistics process. A good example comes from the frozen foods business.

- Faulty delivery patterns cause overstocking and cost big money.
- Suboptimization leaves empty shelves and disappoints customers.
- Delays and other mistakes take the chill from frozen foods, making them disastrous.

Throughout the goods industry, changes that swamp delivery delays have dramatic implications for companies. Those whose monitoring and control system is less than perfect fall by the wayside. Distributors who are operating by rule of thumb are unable to face the business challenges that loom in the market, and eventually they are wiped out.

All these references point to the fact that the need for a first-class logistics is widespread. Tough problems exist, from production, inventorying, and transportation to sales, requiring imaginative approaches for their solution. Which is the optimal route for trucks to take from a warehouse, to make deliveries to widely distributed stores? How can we account in a dependable way for road-mending delays, fog predictions, and perpetual traffic jams?

Many chief operating officers (COOs) pose the following question to themselves: Can we address the problems posed by integrated logistics in a way that makes sense in a highly competitive environment? Can we do so by building the system that we need? The answer to these queries is definitely yes—provided the COO decides to improve his or her company's effectiveness and has the necessary skills and tools.

The decision to push through significant improvements in logistics is his or her own—the skill he has to hire, train, and manage. The tools are those of reengineering (Chapter 6) and software, and the latter can be bought on demand. These include, but are not limited to, customer relationship management (CRM; Section 12.2), enterprise resource planning (ERP; Section 12.3), and supply chain management (Section 12.4).

The cloud provides at an affordable price a golden horde of programming routines and associated services for better logistics. This is vital to the modern enterprise. Siemens, the big German mechanical, electrical, and electronics engineering firm, claims that software has been a basic ingredient in its business revolution.

Siemens has more software developers than Oracle or SAP, and this software is embedded in its trains, machine tools, and factory automation.

The company's CEO calculates that as much as 60 percent of his or her firm's sales now involve software. This shift in emphasis has been promoted by the company's strategic inflection toward electronics during the 1990s. Today some 90 percent of its development in machine tools is in electronics and related hardware. A similar reference is true for cars. Today, a BMW and a Volkswagen are a network of computers.

12.2 Customer Relationship Management

Promoted with Internet commerce, CRM software helps companies manage their customer base, keeps track of customers, and targets them with new products or price offers to stop them from defecting. This is essentially a self-service software solution that helps the enterprise using it in several ways.

An example from telephony would be that instead of setting up a DSL connection by sending an engineer to the customer's site, the telco does the same job more effectively, and at lower cost, by installing the equipment in its central office—switching, through software, the customer line to DSL automatically. The same approach can be followed to automate the configuration of new services, provide technical support, make it possible for businesses to order and configure new network services, and more.

As Internet commerce gained weight among consumers and in the business community, onPremises customer relationship management routines became popular because firms sought to understand their online customers, and serve them better than at lower cost, by implementing an increasingly more efficient solution to:

■ manage customer relationships,
■ integrate business processes and data streams, and
■ increase the ways and means for exploiting such information.

In a holistic sense, customer relationship management procedures are inseparable from those targeted by enterprise resource planning (Section 12.3). In a credit institution, for example, CRM addresses itself to the task of efficiently managing front desk processes associated with the customer, including marketing, sales, service, and handholding. Correspondingly, ERP will address back office processing and distribution chores, seamlessly linking planning premises to the clients' IT. A sophisticated CRM would:

■ produce customer intelligence that can be used effectively in targeted marketing and
■ improve the analytics underpinning decisions made in investing the company's human and other resources (Chapter 13).

An integral part of CRM software is better campaign administration across all channels by using customer intelligence to personalize marketing campaigns. Another target is to efficiently disseminate valuable customer intelligence to all people that need it. This assists in optimizing the supply chain (Section 12.4) by exploiting information uncovered through analytics.

Plenty of CRM software is available on demand, but its deliverables are so much better when the user company's procedures are first class. To reach the goals expected of it, CRM software should:

■ track incoming and outgoing customer communications,
■ flash out types of customer-initiated events, and
■ register responses to business-initiated communications in a way that can be effectively exploited.

What is essentially sought after through a CRM solution is the ability to incrementally increase customer account visibility, linking front desk transactions with back office ERP and legacy transaction processing in a way that permits getting the most out of the supply chain. This can be instrumental in closing the *intelligence gap* that today exists in most firms.

Behind the reason for analytical business processes, I am suggesting, is the need for integrating and investigating data streams to understand business partner activity, as well as behavior, over time. Also, there is the need to evaluate the effectiveness of operational processes such as marketing and service support. This enables a company to move toward personalizing products and their sales procedures in a way able to promote:

■ customer value and
■ customer loyalty.

With these objectives in mind, many versions of onDemand CRM software offer customization possibilities. Through them, the user organization can support individual customers' personalization while maintaining the CRM's multitenant polyvalence.

To increase their CRM's market appeal some vendors target both the cloud and the off-the-shelf commodity programs market. For instance, Microsoft's Dynamics CRM provides traditional CRM services, including customer management and marketing analysis, on both onDemand and onPremises offerings. Microsoft has two versions of Dynamics CRM, differing in offline data management and storage:

■ Dynamics Professional Plus permits users to take data offline, since the product supports a web server and database server running locally in a client-server mode.
■ Dynamics CRM 4.0 is onDemand, an outgrowth of an earlier version (CRM 3.0) featuring increased scalability for the web. It also runs a Microsoft Outlook client.

Other companies follow a different strategy. Rather than competing head on with the big boys, RightNow Technologies has found a niche in the customer service segment of the broader CRM market. This is in the knowledge-intensive call center, empowering its clients' customers to find answers to their questions effectively using web-based self-service.

RightNow approaches this market by offering three CRM solutions: The core one includes features like multichannel contact center, web and voice self-service, self-learning knowledge base, e-mail response management, custom analytics and reporting, as well as integration with other enterprise planning processes. The other two routines promote sales and marketing services:

■ RightNow Sales integrates forecasting, quote generation, opportunity status, and contact management.
■ RightNow Marketing targets the automation of marketing activities with information management and resource optimization.

SAP is selling onDemand software in the CRM and human resources (HR) markets, as stand-alone and in conjunction with its Business by Design (BBD) product. The latter is supposed to address all major application software aspects for small and medium enterprises, including ERP, CRM, HR, and so on.

These are only a few examples of a large array of offerings. The fact that so many vendors are competing in the cloud's onDemand CRM market can be interpreted to mean that this market is vibrant—which is true. But at the same time, the integration with legacy programs and with other cloud programs is by no means straightforward.

For instance, CRM-ERP aggregation presents problems associated with heterogeneity of vendors and their wares. Many more differences are present when integrating CRM software with a user organization's legacy systems. Among the difficulties that are typically encountered are

■ data quality issues,
■ multiple incompatible sources for same information elements,*
■ complexities of misaligned windows of data availability,
■ problems associated with achieving a single customer view, and
■ the lack of a methodology for a common approach to the effective integration of all feeds.

One of the proposed solutions has been an *information portal* making it feasible to subscribe, access, publish, and understand business information that is in principle heterogeneous. This portal is supposed to act as a single-user interface to all information and applications, as well as to business intelligence tools and analytics. The feedback received to my queries left some doubt on its effectiveness.

---

* And what to do with them.

Other problems have to do with limitation of CRM software, particularly in pattern analysis. Several companies using onPremises or onDemand customer relationship management start complaining that given the development they experience in their business, its level of detail is not up to the required standard. Telecoms, for example, need more than cumulative data. They want to know the traffic pattern of *social networks*, and they are no more satisfied with the number of calls a client makes.

In the background of this need for information lies the fact that two people, each using the network for three hundred minutes per month, may have radically different profiles. The one may call two or three parties only, while the other may speak to thirty or more parties.

All important in a social network is to know who receives more calls, because this helps to identify individual customer behavior, serves in mapping the social context of communications, assists in evaluating (indeed computing) access and interconnection costs, and provides a basis for distributing sales and administrative costs. Well-managed firms use that input to make factual estimates regarding cost of goods sold and profit and loss (P&L).

12.3 Enterprise Resource Planning

The term *enterprise resource planning* essentially stands as a collective reference to various suites of business software able to support an internal and external information structure. The latter addresses business partners, and its objective is to plan and control production, inventories, purchasing, just-in-time manufacturing, personnel, and financials, as well as to provide status information on customer orders.

Given this polyvalence of functions, it is reasonable to think that many different routines integrate into an ERP programming product. One of them has been manufacturing resource planning programs, which primarily address internal or local functions like in-plant production management. ERP distinguishes itself from programming routines written for a more limited domain through an effective business partner connection that permits:

- sharing common data and
- covering a whole range of operations in real time.

As with CRM, with ERP there is a learning curve for all users regarding both the software per se and its functionality. This software takes in the latest orders and planning forecasts from the assembly lines, calculates minimum component stock to meet production targets, and sends order plans to suppliers. It also interfaces with other programs to monitor ongoing orders against those planned, adjust component stocks, and help in managing a number of variants. Still another function is to answer queries in terms to the status of execution of sales orders. As these references demonstrate:

- ERP maps processes, not functions;
- it can help in engineering a just-in-time supply chain (see Section 12.4);
- its pass-through capability is instrumental in strengthening business partner relations; and
- its functionality helps in integrating many formerly discrete island processes.

But the able use of commodity ERP software requires a lot of preparatory work. To get commendable results, practically each process associated with ERP must be properly analyzed, reengineered, and streamlined. Also, proper linkages have to be designed and implemented with a number of other applications, like CRM.

One of the questions many people are asking is How long would the implementation of ERP take? There is no one-size-fits-all answer to this query, but in principle it is sound management that Pareto's law dominates the timing of ERP deliverables. The complete implementation of an integrative ERP solution can take from three months to two years in total, with intermediate deliverables every one to two months.

Admittedly, three months to two years is a wide range, which is due to a number of reasons internal to the user organization. These range from available skill and know-how to effectiveness of project management, homogeneity or heterogeneity of computer environment and of data sets, attention paid by top management on getting results, the prevailing return on investment (ROI) culture, and internal IT policies in working hard on deliverables.

Another factor affecting the timing of ERP deliverables is whether users collaborate in detailing the quality of service the ERP project must observe—doing so at the very start of the project rather than asking for changes when the project is in progress. It is a basic rule in IT that projects that are being altered, interrupted, or rescheduled because of inserting new requirements at a later day are destined for failure.

The vendor's technical knowledge and support to the user organization evidently contribute to the success of ERP's implementation. Practical supply chain applications are indeed a challenging issue, but first-class project management can be instrumental in maintaining a rapid timetable as well as in obtaining quality deliverables.

The reason why I particularly insist on this issue is because while there are many ERP vendors, not all of them have sufficient applications knowledge. The fact that business is good in the domain of cloud ERP software has brought in players with thin experience in the applications market. According to estimates, the ERP business presently stands at the $45 to $50 billion level,* with nearly 90 percent in onPremises packages, and the balance in onDemand ERP software. This is the part that is rapidly growing.

---

* This estimate includes not only pure ERP but also add-ons, like Enterprise Asset Management, Financial Management, Manufacturing/Operations, Supply Chain, and Human Capital Management.

NetSuite provides an example of a firm offering onDemand integrated ERP, CRM, and e-commerce programs. Like Salesforce.com, NetSuite is a pure cloud company, marketing its software solely on a hosted basis with subscription pricing. The particularity of this suite is its approach to front desk and back office applications for the SME market. Competitors like SAP focus primarily on the high end of the mid-market and on larger firms.

Like other suite offerings, NetSuite's ERP is modular in nature. The company has also introduced a platform for independent software developers and an online marketplace for third-party applications known as SuiteApp.com. This is a policy to be watched, because other cloud providers, too, plan integrated offerings.

Over the next two or three years, practically all ERP vendors will be confronted with the need to scale up resources to handle a much larger user community and to provide their customers with ways for seamless access to their distributed databases. Another challenge is that of the end users' mobile access to CRM/ERP systems.

If salespeople can input an order straight into a mobile phone or other portable device, *then* there is no rekeying to be done and the error rate will be lower. Also, their timely order input can activate other parts of the CRM/ERP aggregate, such as inventory planning and supply chain management, permitting executives at headquarters to:

- check in real-time inventories and sales for a particular region, by units and/or value; or
- compare current orders to salesperson quotas; and
- identify the most profitable customers for appropriate handholding.

Mobile access can see to it that the benefits of a company's enterprise software need not be restricted merely to people in the office. Mobile executives and salespersons can be given access to decision support data and mine databases while in the field, in a two-way communication. This, however, presupposes a modeling methodology and appropriate tools that:

- make it possible to experiment on goals prior to settling on them;
- help in evaluating the implementation, increasing its clarity; and
- provide benchmarks against which are measured obtained results.

Modeling also permits the prioritization of the use of ERP functionality, which is very important because, as statistics show, while two out of three user organizations tend to employ all the facilities provided by ERP, the balance only select some routines, most frequently financial accounting. These firms underutilize the ERP software.

Underutilization is a regrettable policy because everything counted, the ERP software and its implementation don't come cheap. The cost of organization studies and implementation chores comes above that. Studies that focus on cost-effectiveness suggest that user organizations spend 200 to 800 percent more money to develop the ERP applications environment than what they paid for off-the-shelf or cloud software.

12.4 Wal-Mart: A Case Study in Supply Chain Management

The successful extension of ERP applications toward an intelligent supply chain is not just a matter of substituting some of the legacy routines by onDemand software. The whole solution must be architectured, and the way to bet is that there exist prerequisites and should be milestones in going from "here" to "there."

There is no better way to demonstrate what well-managed companies can achieve with modern technology than a case study. Wal-Mart has been chosen as an example. This is a company with more than four thousand suppliers who have access to its warehouses and are jointly responsible for managing the merchandiser's inventory and shelf stock, down to the detail of individual store level.

The good news about this warehouse-based cooperation is that it has greatly reduced inventory levels, therefore saving lots of money and making the giant retailer more responsive to changing market conditions. Wal-Mart's sophisticated services are being imitated by other merchandizing organizations, but many of the latter are handicapped by their legacy systems, which were developed decades ago in a relatively stand-alone manner. Typically, legacy routines are focusing on non-integrated functional areas, such as marketing, inventory, and accounting—and discrete island approaches are an ERP graveyard.

To the contrary, Wal-Mart's case is a leading example of how a company redesigned its logistics to fit its business strategy and market and how its efficiently managed warehouses became a key to corporate success. The company collects detailed and focused sales data at all of its stores, supercenters, and wholesale clubs, maintaining those information elements in its very large database in a way readily accessible to authorized users.

By means of real-time database mining and assisted through models, company management can monitor sales not only through past statistics but also via data streams at the checkout counter. Mathematical models for FFR help to restock shelves before a product is sold out. The sense of these references is that model-based marketing campaigns, JIT inventory, and fast flow replenishment are not just manufacturing success stories. They are global examples of thousands of ahead-of-the-curve business practices made possible by the able use of technology.

Knowledge-enriched models are instrumental in analyzing *trends* and *patterns*. Using this analysis, Wal-Mart makes decisions about markdowns, replenishment, and inventory in minutes, not days. The end result is a hard-earned reputation for exceptional customer service that ranks Wal-Mart above its competition in the American consumer satisfaction index, as reported in *Fortune* magazine.

Analysis is part of the company's business strategy above and beyond CRM, ERP, and other software. The merchandiser is known for rigorously analyzing daily cash register receipts and for working with suppliers to avoid building up inventory. It does its own forecasting of consumer demand through its collaborative forecasting and replenishment (CFAR) system and offers a standardized way for suppliers to work together on forecasts across the Internet.

As a practical application, Wal-Mart records every sale in its over twenty-three hundred stores in the United States in a large database used for honing its market strategies. It uses database mining not only to master its marshalling yards channeling goods to its stores, but also to effectively promote its sales effort.

By organizing all the exchanges on an electronic bulletin board, Wal-Mart makes it possible for each party to review related messages and append new ones. There are thousands of forecasts, one for every product in every store for fifty-two weeks into the future; for example, weather analyses to gauge how bad the hay fever season will be. With CFAR software, the business partners exchange a series of written comments and supporting data, including:

- details for a future sales promotions and
- analysis of past sales trends and customer behavior.

Technology serves Wal-Mart by abiding by the retail industry adage "retail is detail." The same is true of any business. But for big companies this means a massive amount of detail that, when it is properly classified,* monitored, audited, and mined, helps buyers and suppliers:

- discern changes in customer trends,
- track inventory to minimize costs,
- manage merchandise assortment, and
- evaluate profitability while the business is running.

To achieve these results, Wal-Mart has created the world's largest commercial data warehouse, designed to handle detail and develop a more intimate understanding of its customers. On the inventory management side, the company's massive processing and storage capacity means that it can track merchandise volume and movement not only in the United States but also in each of its stores and clubs in countries abroad.

The objective that has been achieved is to manage the stores as individual locations with specialized needs, providing a merchandise assortment uniquely tailored to the preferences of the customers that each store serves. And as already mentioned, suppliers can access this information to help Wal-Mart buyers:

---

* D. N. Chorafas, *Integrating ERP, CRM, Supply Chain Management and Smart Materials* (New York: Auerbach, 2001).

- be in charge of inventory and
- identify site-specific opportunities at neighborhood retailing.

As this case study documents, efficient management did not come to Wal-Mart just by buying CRMs, ERPs, and other software. The company has done a great deal of preparatory work describing processes, their interactions, and their relationships with organizational functions; identifying in qualitative and quantitative terms expected results during the whole life cycle of a given process; and integrating a large number of concepts expressing functional, informational, organizational, and resource views.

This is tantamount to effectively managing a flexible business architecture, where many interactions take place between subsystems, as discussed in Chapter 8. It is precisely because of these reasons that in the migration from discrete island approaches of the 1980s to an intelligent supply chain, the necessary reengineering effort affected the whole user organization. The lesson is that senior management and the CIO should not be hypnotized by the vendor's kind words that "My CRM/ERP software can do:

- opportunity management, enabling collaboration among sales teams milestones."
- territory management, which helps in defining administering, analyzing, and changing sales territories."
- global forecasting, giving executives visibility into their sales pipelines and into future product and service trends."
- account and contact management, providing a 360-degree view of each of the customers and much more."

Maybe the onPremises or onDemand software can do all that and even more. But the problem is not really there. Instead, it lies in the fact that *if* the preparatory steps outlined in the Wal-Mart case study are not properly executed, *then* there will be no successful transition from the old to the new IT environment.

Cloud or no cloud, an effective change from ERP processes of the 1990s (let alone from legacy routines) to new, much more sophisticated models cannot be achieved without reengineering (Chapter 6) and a sound methodology. My experience has been that benefits derived from tools for process analysis are directly proportional to the methodology we adopt and follow. That's why the Wal-Mart case study is so important.

An orderly approach is even more critical when we contemplate the integration of all enterprise processes, in terms of activities, organization, information, and resources, into a wholesome integrated model of corporate functions. The methodology we choose should provide a background able to handle business processes in a way that optimizes organizational and information solutions.

In conclusion, the migration from earlier CRM and ERP approaches to the new intelligent supply chain calls for a significant amount of architectural planning to create the preconditions—not just the technical platform—able to meet future business needs. While a fair amount of technology fixing and rapidly executed troubleshooting might provide temporary relief, it will not create a valid answer to the evolving business needs because much will be left to the fire brigade.

12.5 Just-in-Time Inventories

According to anecdotal evidence, Toyota began the development of what has become known as the *just-in-time* system, prodded by one of its employees who, over a period of time, kept asking why there should be so much inventory on stock. A first release of the (then) new method became available in the 1960s, providing evidence that the concept underpinning it is far reaching. Simply regarding JIT as a policy of inventory reduction is seriously underestimating its importance:

- JIT has changed the fundamental economics of manufacturing, and
- it altered the basis of competition in many industries, particularly in companies where management is in charge.

To appreciate the value of the just-in-time concept and its reach, the reader should know that there are three different levels of inventory accumulation in a manufacturing industry. The first is that of raw materials coming into the factory. The second is semimanufactured goods stored between machine shops, the so-called banks, and it is usually composed of inventories that will be used by the next shop in line. The third is that of finished goods, which pile up in the warehouse until they are shipped.

All three are subject to just-in-time inventory management. But, as always, there are prerequisites. Raw materials and banks must be very closely coordinated with production planning and control. Short of that, the machine shops will remain idle. Right scheduling is at a premium, and it must involve a very close collaboration among typically distinct departments in manufacturing, in terms of:

- timing of operations and
- quantity of production.

By contrast, the coordination necessary for JIT inventory management is between purchasing, materials delivery, sales and merchandizing operations (if other than the manufacturing), and wholesalers, retailers, and clients who will receive the goods. Because the customer firm, too, is interested in JIT or (more precisely) fast flow replenishment, coordination must be supply-chain-wide.

In this connection the use of ERP software helps in answering questions about the status of execution of customer orders. ERP routines, however, don't manage

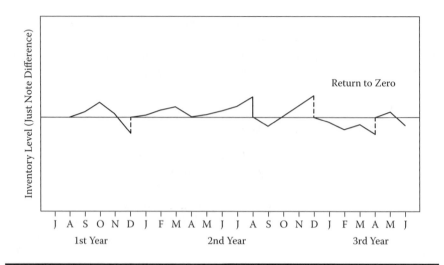

Figure 12.1   Return to zero JIT for product A (from a real-life application).

inventories; they question and inform. Moreover, both ERP and just-in-time logistics require a most significant preparatory work, starting with:

- recognizing and identifying all products and their component parts, down to the last detail*;
- updating in real time the bill of materials of every product and immediately alerting scheduling (and if necessary stopping production);
- having in place a system of standard costs and cost control accounting, to track inventory excesses and report them; and
- using real-time technology, including models, to ensure that a "zero line" is observed, which means a predefined level of planned inventory followed item by item.

Based on a real-life application, Figure 12.1 gives an example of how this method works. The preparation necessary to reach the zero line result and immediately adjust production has been significant. A sophisticated model for inventory planning and control must specify the customer service level as a percentage of orders, and this should be accomplished within a target lead time that is very short.

Traditional statistics, the way manufacturing and merchandising firms keep them, are not helpful. For each item, all the way to its most basic components, management must establish a level of fulfillment of client orders at 99.9, 99, or 95 percent level of confidence, which corresponds to inventory unavailability, or $\alpha =$ 0.1, 1, and 5%. The 5 percent is no good but might in some cases be admitted for

---

* D. N. Chorafas, *Integrating ERP, CRM, Supply Chain Management and Smart Materials* (New York: Auerbach, 2001).

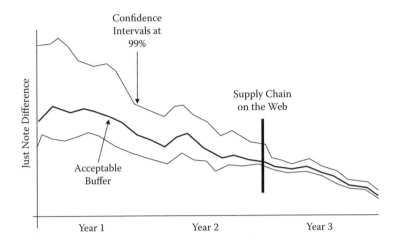

Figure 12.2   Trend line confidence intervals in inventory management and the temporarily acceptable buffer.

nonessential items, or those of high cost and rapidly declining demand. By choosing a level of confidence for inventory management:

■ an operating characteristics (OC) curve can be used in inventory optimization item by item, and
■ this OC curve is ingeniously employed to help in combining the likelihood of servicing with the corresponding inventory costs.

Not only the establishment of confidence intervals is very important, but also, as Figure 12.2 demonstrates, these must be steadily decreased over time. This is doable by tuning the quality of production scheduling and JIT, but once again, it is an issue requiring considerable effort and senior management commitment.

A highly innovative evolution in inventory planning and control is the switch from build-to-inventory to build-to-order manufacturing. This has produced a new and efficient manufacturing/merchandising environment, which led to:

■ improved competitiveness,
■ reduced order cycle times,
■ much lower inventory costs,
■ market share gains, and
■ quality improvements across product lines.

Build to order, however, has its prerequisites. It requires lots of prognostication, organization, and self-discipline, which is not characteristic of all firms. Another prerequisite is the decision to deliver value to the customer, including the policy of making the customer a partner in the cost savings.

To appreciate the impact of just-in-time solutions, it is appropriate to recall that this inventory management system was born out of the need to develop a better way for manufacturing, swamping the results of complexity and customization on inventory increases. In Toyota's case, the challenge consisted in building automobiles of many different kinds in small volumes but with high cost-effectiveness to overcome the disadvantage inherent in a smaller company size. (At the time Toyota was smaller than Nissan, its key competitor in Japan.)

As it developed, the JIT system included *level scheduling,* a process in which product schedules are progressively refined in the months prior to their execution. This permits a master production schedule to be done way ahead of time, while the final production schedule is usually frozen for two weeks to one month. During this period no changes in the schedule are permitted.

Time level scheduling procedures make it feasible to prepare and refine a master production plan a year prior to its becoming actual. This master schedule serves for capacity planning as well as for coordination with suppliers—being released through ERP. A middle schedule is prepared three months prior to the date of production, with the estimates of the volume of manufacturing for each model (or other target item), with the understanding that in the next round of estimation the volumes will not be changed.

As an example of how Toyota's manufacturing strategy, and JIT technology, has helped the firm to perform much better than other companies, J. C. Abegglen and G. Stalk Jr. use Yanmar Diesel.* In 1975, the Japanese economy was in deep recession, and demand for Yanmar's diesel engines and farm equipment was severely depressed; so were profits. Toyota was caught in the same recession as Yanmar, but Toyota was profitable.

Postmortem, Toyota management credited its ability to weather the recession to the efficiencies of its unique production system and the economies that it made possible. Recognizing these facts, Yanmar began a crash program to convert to JIT, which is an excellent example of reengineering, and the results have been very positive:

- total factory labor productivity almost doubled,
- work-in-process inventories shrank by between 66 and 80 percent, and
- production volume required for the factory to break even fell from 80 percent of capacity to 50 percent.

I have seen these effects and associated statistics repeated in a number of other companies for which I have been a consultant to the board. A project done not too long ago compared earnings per share with days of supply in inventory. Five different firms participated in this project. What came out of it is presented in

---

* James C. Abegglen and George Stalk Jr., *Kaisha. The Japanese Corporation* (New York: Basic Books, 1985).

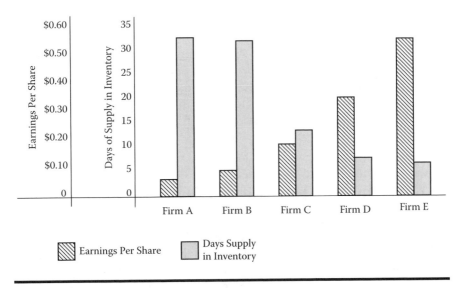

Figure 12.3   There is a negative correlation between earnings per share and days supply in inventory.

Figure 12.3, and the statistics are smashing. Companies contemplating similar projects should appreciate that nowadays:

- This is not a technology problem, because onDemand software is available on the web (albeit not the meticulous models a firm might require).
- This is a problem of sound governance, management culture, organization, and reengineering (Chapter 6), which not all companies are willing or able to put forward.

The senior management of manufacturing firms and merchandising companies should understand that *if* they want their company to be competitive in the global market, *then* they cannot afford lavish inventories that cost greatly and weigh heavily in profit and loss terms. Orders have to be filled within a couple of days or a few hours.

The electronics industry provides an example. Notebook computers are shipped out in one day; CD-ROM drives are shipped in three or four hours after the order is given. *Response time* has overtaken low-cost labor as the number one competitive advantage.

The reader should however keep in mind that "building a better mousetrap" is no business that can go on forever. The relationship between *cost* and *effectiveness* is not totally linear, and at an inflection point a "still better approach" can turn against the firm.

With its recall of more than 9 million cars experiencing brake failures, Toyota provides the best possible example on such an event. For many years the company was renown for its quality, but eventually *quality* took the back seat, *cost cutting* gained the high ground, and *business risk* soared.

Lulled by past glories from the time the company was a renown quality producer, top management failed to appreciate that *risk is a cost*. Lehman Brothers, Citigroup, Washington Mutual, Royal Bank of Scotland and plenty of other financial institutions have fallen in the same trap. At Toyota, as in the big banks, the high cost of "more risk and leverage" overtook other savings. Eventually this turned the reputation of the Japanese auto manufacturer, of its JIT and of its gimmicks on their head.

12.6 Machine-to-Machine and RFID Communications

According to many experts, materials technology is the real wealth of nations. This is not a recent concept. It has been the hallmark of civilizations stretching back eight thousand years to the Bronze Age, and today's priorities are no different.

Our civilization effectively uses an impressive array of metals, alloys, and ceramics, and it employs a larger number of highly diverse machines and final products. Without silicon that is more than 99.999 pure, there would have been no computer chips, cell phones, and fiber optic networks.

There is no a reason why the machines and products we have built should not be communicating among themselves in a fully integrated environment. This requires sensors, antennas, data, and networks, as well as understanding what it takes to affect machine-to-machine, product-to-racks, and intertransport vehicle (or warehouse) communications.

Machine-to-machine (M2M) communication is one of the recent developments in technology, following the deliverables of a seminal project at MIT. Several enterprises have been applying it, and others have undertaken trials. Many made M2M deployments based on GSM, GPRS, and 3G. Down to the basics, M2M is designed to:

- track objects,
- record utility usage,
- monitor machine performance, and more.

In Britain, Yorkshire Water uses GSM-based M2M to monitor remotely chlorine levels in drinking water, the level of water in tanks, and the performance of pumps, as well as to check up on leaks. Vodaphone uses M2M for telemetry, including remote alarm systems monitoring and remote meter reading for utilities.

Promoters of sensor networks point to the growing use of radio frequency identification (RFID) tags as evidence that embedding tiny wireless devices in everyday items makes commercial sense. Such sensor networks are impacting burgeoning data streams, posing the question of what we will do with all this information; JIT and FFR are part of the answer. The RFID tags:

- are the size of a small grain,
- do not contain a battery, and
- are woken up by a pulse of radio energy.

Such energy is absorbed and used to power up a small chip and transmit a response that is usually an identification (ID) number. Also known as low-frequency ID (LFID), such tags are now employed, among other users, by retailers for inventory control. Wal-Mart and Tesco are examples.

In 2004 Wal-Mart required its top one hundred suppliers to have LFID tags by January 2005, with electronic product codes (EPCs). The company took this step on the belief that through them it will significantly improve its inventory management. It also pointed out that, on average, a person today deals with one hundred bar codes per day—and bar codes have become an inefficient old technology.*

Such sensors are inexpensive, and they can be installed quickly and easily. Also known as smart dust, because they are as small as a grain of sand, they should be looked at as an evolutionary process at a time when nearly everything seems to include shape memory alloys (which change shape according to the temperature), and piezoelectric materials that mechanically deform when an electric field is applied.

These materials are said to be "smart" because they can be employed to sense and respond to the environment. Smart materials are not limited to solids. Liquids can be smart too, finding their way into all sorts of devices, from cars to digital cameras. (The term *smart fluid* is generally applied to fluids whose properties can be changed by the application of an electrical or magnetic field.)

One of the engineering applications under development is sensor-based wireless communications linked to monitor stresses on aging bridges to help decide maintenance priorities. On October 26, 2009, the U.S. government put in the budget $4.6 billion to develop *smart grids* of power supply. The premise is that the old technology of current grids must be significantly upgraded to be able to answer society's power transmission needs.

All fields of activity are open to upgrades. Among smart dust applications connected through wireless communications is agriculture. Approaches have been tested to tell farmers when to irrigate and harvest grapes to produce premium wine.

Smart dust solutions can also assist in monitoring forests for fire-prone conditions and in providing early fire detecting and reporting. The applications domains widen as technology develops sensor nodes the size of postage stamps powered by very small lithium batteries. The principle is that:

- sensors need only enough power to communicate with their neighbors, and
- messages can easily be passed along to a more powerful computer-based control station for management use.

---

* Like mainframes and Cobol programs.

An ambitious experiment on smart dust is that involving an 885-foot oil tanker, Loch Rannocj, operated by BP. The tanker has been outfitted with 160 sensors that measure things like vibrations in the ship's pumps, compressors, and engines, passing on their readings using wireless links. The goal is to use the sensor network to predict equipment failures, and test the robustness of its deliverables for wider use.*

The company is also considering using smart dust type sensors in some forty other projects, binding together sensor networks to bridge the gap between more classical information systems and the real world. BP has also put sensors in its trucks to monitor not only their routes but also driver behavior. The pros say such sensors are needed for safety reasons. Critics respond that they are invading privacy.

The real downside of these solutions lies in hardware reliability (Chapter 10) and software dependability (Chapter 11). The issue is hot, but system-wise there exist doubts because not enough experience is yet on hand to allow documented opinions. Some worries, particularly those connected to software failures, come from the motor vehicle industry. The policy of embedded auto electronics is becoming a classic; however:

■ software problems are in their way of reaching epidemic proportions, and
■ dealers are very often unable to trace the causes, particularly those of intermittent error messages.

For example, a brand new Citroen spent a full three months back with the dealer following sudden and unexplained battery drain, intermittent failure of the telephone and entertainment systems' voice control, and failure of some of its warning instruments. Many other examples have come up, along similar lines.

Lawyers have been involved in messy, unpleasant cases in which there are no winners. Research by the German Center for Automotive Research (CAR) points to electronics glitches as the main reason why cars with embedded electronic gear break down. Last but not least, there are communications problems connected to straight-through processing (STP)† due to uneven network bandwidth supported by vendors and to huge differences in the technology status of user organizations.

12.7 Challenges Presented by Organization and Commercial Vision

The good news is that the Institute of Electrical and Electronics Engineers (IEEE) has drawn up a standard communications protocol, called 802.15.4, for the tiny

---

* Years ago Veritas, the Norwegian ship certification entity, had developed a similar solution based on expert systems but without the benefit of smart dust.
† D. N. Chorafas, *The Real-Time Enterprise* (New York: Auerbach, 2005).

sensor devices discussed in Section 12.6. The ZigBee Alliance, an industry group, hopes its ZigBee standards will popularize 802.15.4 in the same way that the Wi-Fi Alliance popularized another IEEE standard, 802.11, known as Wi-Fi.

Protocol standards are crucial because the logistics environment evolves very fast, and for competitive reasons companies need rapidly updated data, along with the ability to capture information services from all sides of a transaction. This information includes elements pertaining to products that are intermediated and shipped to customers.

While protocols have to be standardized, business transactions are not. Still, companies may well find onDemand software in the cloud matching their operational needs but find problems arising from an uneven preparedness of business partners in executing online transactions. These differences make the communications systems asymmetric.

That's unsubstantiated. Though seamless online access, pass-through linkages, high functionality, and low cost are worthy goals, from one company to the next, system solutions vary widely. In addition, global applications must confront the fact that network technology provided by telcos is not always the best. The use of legacy routines is another bottleneck. Only those system solutions that are state of the art, integrated, functional, reliable, and flexible have competitive advantages and favorable cost factors associated with them. Internally, a great deal of the results of reengineering depend on how the work is organized, the skill available to design and implement advanced solutions (and hence the availability of human capital), and top management's readiness to support such a project.

A different way of saying this is that there are challenges presented by organization and commercial vision. OnDemand software for a first-class logistics solution may be available in the cloud, but is *our* company ready for it? Several issues lie behind this query: some are managerial, like *commercial vision*, while others are organizational, for instance, *supply chain restructuring*.

The need for supply chain restructuring has been already discussed as a must. This is important to every company, and it is even more so when two or more firms combine their supply chains. In early 2000, for example, Sears Roebuck and Carrefour announced that they combined their purchasing on the Internet to the tune of $80 billion. This affected the supply chain not only of the aforementioned two firms but also of their suppliers:

- fifty thousand companies sold goods to these two retailers, and
- those not ready to face the restructuring challenge ran out of luck.

This is by no means a once-in-a-lifetime example. Plenty of firms are in the process of combining their supply chains. Entities in the health care industry, for instance, are joining forces to squeeze costs out of purchasing. Johnson & Johnson, Abbot Laboratories, and others have entered into such agreements.

The need for reengineering is underlined by the fact that online shopping environments are increasingly characterized by choice, complexity, and information overload. Search engines facilitate access to valued information on goods and services, while many firms make money by leveraging the power of the Internet to provide almost unlimited expansion of the search space.

Buyers expand their search space through search engines, but the prerequisite is that of an organized universe aggregating a large number of suppliers and the myriad items in which they deal. The matching of buyers and suppliers becomes so much more effective when both parties have a commercial vision.

Underpinning *commercial vision* is client focus and the ability to understand the client's needs, answering them in the most effective way. This should be done in an environment of client intimacy. Part of the effort to meet and continue meeting customer requirements is a steady innovation in products and services.

Along with reengineered supply chain chores, *innovation*, or the ability to create business ideas and drives, is a most critical element of business success. It enables the core product lines of *our* firm to differentiate themselves from their competitors in a way that the customer will return time and again for more products and services.

In the 1960s and early 1970s, when IBM had reached its high water mark in the computer industry, more than 75 percent of its fast-growing annual business was coming from its existing client base. But management of a lesser quality took over the reigns, the company was slow to adapt to the minis and maxis by falling in love with its mainframes, and by the 1980s the customers drifted away, which nearly ran the company to the ground.

This is by no means an exceptional happening. For many decades the legendary watchmakers of Switzerland were so good at their craft, and so widely admired, that they owned a remarkable 65 percent of the world market for all types of timepieces. The drift started in the late 1960s, and by 1980 the Swiss share of the market plunged below 10 percent. The Japanese de-creamed the world's watch market, and Seiko became synonymous with a quality timepiece.

A similar story took place with German cameras. Zeiss and Leica were the world's quality standards, but they failed to move with their time and lead the market in its switch. Nikon, Olympus, Pentax, Conica, and other Japanese camera makers became masters in innovative products, designed and sold them at an affordable cost, and took the world's camera market away from the traditional German makers.

Without a doubt, advances in information technology and the restructuring of the supply chain are very important. But without commercial vision and steady innovation, the solution will be like the projected Nabucco pipeline, which seems to have solved several problems—except for where to find the gas it is supposed to carry and sell to Europe.

Every company also faces its own technological challenges, an example being the *architectural semantics** needed to integrate the supply chain within the realm of a holistic IT. This is important inasmuch as embedding metalevel semantics would allow onDemand programs to attend to their implementation and execution. They would also enable the CIO to cope with changes needed for adaptation of interface programming, making the code easier to manage.

Companies with experience enabling them to express a factual opinion say that architectural semantics are a powerful means for describing the exact behavior of each component routine in the broader system description. They may include, for example:

■ order of phases in the pipeline,
■ conditions under which data are placed on a given bus, and
■ stages of transformation undergone by a given support function.

In conclusion, the business change a company is seeking, the long-term direction it is pursuing in technology, and management decisions necessary to substantiate both of them should be part of a grand design that starts with strategy, proceeds with market analysis, focuses on logistics, and uses technology as the enabling agent. Architectural semantics will be instrumental in keeping the developing infrastructure flexible and adaptable. They will also guide the CIO's hand in choosing the best onDemand facilities, among the many available in the cloud.

---

* In terms of hierarchy of supported functions, architectural semantics are at a lower level of abstraction than functional unit semantics. As such, they assist in the effective integration of system-independent modules, which is typical of onDemand software.

Chapter 13

High Technology for Private Banking and Asset Management

13.1 Cloud Software for Private Banking

To a substantial extent, the banking industry today is clear on what the emerging technology will be. What is still a puzzle is how to choose and use this technology to increase business opportunities, control risks, and better profits. As with any other endeavor, the results must be visible. One should not let them hide for eternity.

Customer relationship management, asset selection and rotation, and steady risk control are the pillar on which rests a successful implementation of IT in private banking. "This is not a computing problem, it's a database mining problem," said Gordon Bell in the course of our meeting in San Francisco, adding that existing software can help for tracking purposes, even if it has been developed for other reasons.

Cybercrash, for example, was developed for small amounts, but it can track everything, including the $20 billion JP Morgan Chase loaned to Worldcom. The good news for the banking industry is that many computer programs needed for private banking are on demand in the cloud as part of customer relationship management (CRM). Examples are

- *product catalog*, enabling one to manage catalogs of products and services, as well as to access pricing information;

- *asset management*, permitting one to track the different financial products customers have purchased; and
- *data quality management*, which ensures that customer, product, and pricing data are available, valid, and free of duplicates.

Cloud vendors are interested in fulfilling the information technology needs of private banking, because this is a burgeoning industry pregnant with competition. These needs can be better appreciated by briefly discussing private banking goals, services, and procedures. This is a sector of the financial industry that addresses itself to high-net-worth individuals* and, in cases, to middle net worth.† All told, this is big business that continues to grow.

Despite the financial upheaval of 2007–2010, the expectation is that the ranks of the rich will continue to expand. A bird's-eye view from some selected countries is given in Table 13.1. According to some estimates, the projected rate of growth stands at about 9 percent a year in the next four years.‡ Whether this projection will materialize depends on the economy.

The private banking industry has been affected by the crisis. Turmoil in the financial markets has swamped the value of assets managed by private banks, while their clients are buying fewer investment products and are switching accounts when news or rumors that a bank may be in trouble comes to the market. Banks that lost droves of high-net-worth individuals have but themselves to blame, because their risk appetite scared them away.

Private banking is an industry very sensitive to quality of service *and* to good news/bad news. Not only the trustee's risk appetite but also volatile markets have a double impact on institutions that depend on private banking for their earnings. Fee income is taken as a percentage of assets under management, and it falls as asset values shrink, client activity tends to disappear,§ or clients move their accounts to another bank.

The net result is that fee income shrinks, and this is compounded by the fact that a bank's cross-departmental services also suffer. There are two reasons why other businesses, like loans taken by private banking clients, also move south. Those with a high-risk appetite, particularly in Russia, Asia, and the United States, take loans to invest in the market in the upswing. But in a downturn, that line dries out.

Just as relevant is the case of private banking's extension into commercial banking relationships. This is characteristic of small and medium enterprises (SMEs),

---

* Defined by the banks as persons or households with more than one million dollars under asset management (excluding their homes). Worldwide there have been a little over 10 million prior to the economic and banking crisis of 2007–2009.
† People and families with $500,000 and $1 million under asset management.
‡ From 2003 to 2007 there was an 11 percent growth rate.
§ Examples are what has happened to banks with heavy losses, like RBS, UBS, and Merrill Lynch. Afraid of what would happen if their wealth manager collapsed, several clients have chosen to shift assets to other institutions.

Table 13.1   High-Net-Worth Households[a] (with more than $1 million under asset management)

Country	Percentage of All Households
United States	4.1
Japan	Est. 3.0
Britain	2.4
Germany	Est. 1.5
China	Est. 0.1
France	Est. 1.2
Italy	Est. 1.2
Taiwan	Est. 2.4
Switzerland	6.1
Brazil	Est. 0.6
Netherlands	2.0
Belgium	3.0

[a] Statistics presented in the Financial Times of June 18, 2008, rounded up to two significant digits and with gaps filled in by order of magnitude (est.). Among countries not featured in this table, in the UAE, 6.1 percent of households are millionaires; Qatar, 5.2 percent; Kuwait, 4.8 percent; Singapore, 3.8 percent; Taiwan, 3 percent; Israel, 2.7 percent; Ireland, 2.4 percent; Bahrain, 2.2 percent; Saudi Arabia, 2.1 percent.

particularly family-owned businesses that don't like to deal with large investment banks. The private bank often has close relationships with the owners of these firms, all the way to financing them and their enterprises.

Because these relationships tend to increase in complexity, computer support is vital. As the previous chapters brought to the reader's attention through practical examples, there is no lack of accounting and client management software available in the cloud on demand. In the CRM domain alone, the private banker can find a wealth of programming products to serve his or her requirements, particularly so routines valuable in sales automation; for instance,

- *workflow programs* that help in customizing sales and marketing documents;
- *collateral management*, which provides a valuable repository for the most recent versions of sales and marketing information;

- *list management*, assisting the private banker in customer leads, contact information, and business handling; and
- *marketing analytics*, which permit studying the impact of marketing campaigns, determining those activities generating the most revenue, and measuring the results of marketing spending.

Software, however, is only a high-power tool. The most key ingredient is personality traits. *If* the personal banker does not have the personality, training, and drive to gain the customer's confidence, and if he or she is bothered by the customer's visits and queries, *then* no matter how rich the onDemand software is, it would not close the gap. As Demosthenes, the ancient Greek orator, said over 2,300 years ago, *in business what counts is confidence*, and confidence is built by:

- a person's personality characteristics;
- quality of service, where onDemand software helps; and
- skill as well as attention to detail and risk management.

Many high-net-worth individuals have made their fortune in their lifetime. They did not inherit it. Therefore, they prize the preservation of their capital. Risk control is of paramount importance—a statement equally valid whether we talk of investments in stocks or in bonds. Bankers follow a similar concept with loans. The goal with investments (equities, bonds, other commodities) is to get back the capital with appreciation and interest (with bonds) or dividends (with equities). With loans, the same criteria prevail in getting back from the borrower the capital and receive the agreed upon interest. That's what *creditworthiness* is all about.

This brief description of what it takes to be successful in private banking helps to identify for the reader the type of action private bankers need to take to fulfill their duties in an able manner. As already mentioned, nearly all of the necessary computer programs can be obtained in the cloud on demand (though sometimes this is poorly used). How well or how poorly the private banker will perform is a matter of leadership. It is not necessarily the cloud vendor's problem.

13.2 Leadership Is Based on Fundamentals

In business and industry, there are two types of leadership. The one is so-called charismatic leadership, which is full of promises and lots of glitz and glamour, as well as the ability to sustain them over time (quite often through smoke and mirrors). Luck helps, but this is only one of the inputs. The other type is *leadership based on fundamentals*. The person who follows it puts in place the firmest policies, ensuring that these are customer friendly, and elaborates a strategy to which he or she will stick. This person leads by example, which he or she takes to the people and says, "This is me and my company. This is who we are, and this is what we stand for. I can tell you what we are doing and I can prove that it upholds investor value, and that it is effective."

Speaking from personal experience, the best bankers are those basing themselves and their carriers on fundamentals. They take risks, but they know and understand the risks they take, putting limits to them and watching them carefully. Those peoples' behavior is best explained through two pieces of advice. They come from George Moore, a former chairman and CEO of Citibank, who, when in the late 1960s he chose Walter Wriston as his successor, gave him the following advice:

■ On growth policies: "Be brave to scare Chase,* but not so brave to scare me."
■ On facing challenges and coping with them: "If we do not have troubles, we would not have any high priced people around to solve them."

That's not the sort of advice one will find on demand in the cloud. By contrast, what can be found online are tools to improve management effectiveness, provided one has management skills to take advantage of them in the first place. For instance, routines for business analytics can be used either as a banal means to produce tables nobody cares to look up, or as a trigger for immediate action.

In addition, the reader should notice the shift taking place in the IT industry. Originally, the demand was dominated by accounting routines and then by transaction processing. While transaction handling is still strong, a growing share of the demand for computing resources is now spearheaded by the demand for understanding customers and their buying habits—as well as for factoring in human behavior and restructuring supply chains (Chapter 12). These activities generally come under the label of *decision support*.

The good news for private banking, asset management (Section 13.3), and decision support is that significant libraries of onDemand mathematics software exist. All sorts of companies can use cloud computing to perform business analytics on an onDemand basis.† End users don't have to wait months or years until an overloaded (in a programming and maintenance sense) IT department can answer their requests.

This is one of the best examples of the change brought about by the cloud and its positive aftereffect. Online software, which is ready in use, is a great help in promoting leadership based on fundamentals. Lee Iacocca's‡ business philosophy was that all business operations can be reduced to three words:

■ people,
■ products, and
■ profits.

---

* Chase Manhattan was then the leader in the U.S. financial market, whose position was challenged by Citibank.
† Mathematica and MATLAB® are two of the companies present in the cloud with excellent analytical tools.
‡ Of Ford and Chrysler fame.

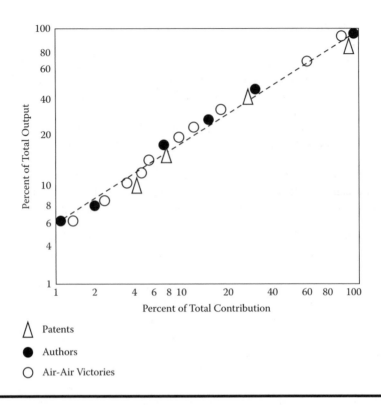

Figure 13.1 Contribution to final results.

onDemand software is available to help people manage products and customer relationships, leading to better profits. In a globalized environment of unprecedented competition, business success depends a great deal on analytics. The CEO and his or her immediate assistants want to know who are the best performers among the people working for them—because they appreciate that in terms of end results, a small group produces a high multiple of what all the others deliver together. As documentation, Figure 13.1 presents statistics from three areas: patents, authors, and air-to-air victories in World War II.

When he was running General Electric, Jack Welch held annual Session C meetings during which he personally evaluated the performance of GE's top echelons of several hundred managers. These meetings included general managers of major business units, as well as senior engineering, manufacturing, sales, and marketing executives. The goal was to extend GE's boundaries by:

■ evaluating careers;
■ linking bonuses to new ideas, customer satisfaction, and sales growth;
■ promoting cost cutting and efficiency; and
■ spending billions to fund "imagination breakthrough" projects.

Leadership has been based on fundamentals. The onDemand human resources software today available in the cloud would have provided assistance, but would not have changed the need for leadership. Other CEOs don't have the stamina to get through long, gruesome meetings like that.

This is not meant to downplay the role of analytics. Analytics helps in leveraging knowledge and in providing better-documented answers to queries. onDemand sales and marketing modules assist well-managed companies in improving the marketing of their products and services.

Manufacturing companies and banks have for decades spent princely sums on computing and data management systems, but when second-raters ran the firms, General Motors, Bear Stearns, Lehman Brothers, and plenty of other companies failed. Evidence has been provided by the fact that risk management has been underfunded, and credit decision making was divorced from analytics.

Clean longer-term historical data on credit histories and credit events were not necessarily required in the past. To a considerable extent demand for data to support decision making emerged from the requirements of active portfolio management rather than from Basle II's reporting requirements. At most banks, demand to record and maintain obligor risk ratings only arose in the last decade. Even today, few banks have systems in place to measure recovery rates from the collection of nonperforming loans and their borrowers.

This failure has been cultural, managerial, and technological at the same time. Data are the main problem, but also programming products for in-depth analysis were scarce—particularly timely and sophisticated in-house developments. Data constitute 80 percent of the challenges confronting the management of any firm, and it takes years to build rich databases. To begin, one has to start, and therefore better start, with onDemand analytics than accumulate more delays waiting for internal programming developments.

Moreover, some onDemand software for credit analysts has been equipped with systems for recording assumptions that permit a qualitative reflection. But the cultural challenge must be confronted. Today too few banks understand the real economics of the business of extending and investing in credit, as the subprimes' bubble and bust of 2007 documented.[*]

In the globalized economy, no single bank's individual experience can provide statistically significant credit risk samples upon which to vet detailed default frequencies and recovery rates. Banks need to commingle their data to reach sufficient sample densities. The cloud does not offer that. What it offers is the processing routines that help in getting started as well as in appreciating the kind of data that need to be collected.

---

[*] D. N. Chorafas, *Financial Boom and Gloom. The Credit and Banking Crisis of 2007–2009 and Beyond* (London: Palgrave/Macmillan, 2009).

13.3 Cloud Software for Asset Management

Asset management and private banking (Section 13.1) overlap in some of their functions. The former is much broader since it concerns institutional investors and the banks' own fortune. Every company must manage its assets in an effective manner, and this entails a flow of both daily and longer-range decisions regarding:

- asset allocation by instrument and market,
- country and currency in which investments are made, and
- the structure of portfolios and their effective risk management.

Every asset manager must establish, follow, and steadily recalibrate an asset allocation strategy. He or she also needs state-of-the-art tools to support his or her research and decision, as well as provide steady position management capabilities.

Networks, databases, computing engines, and software are second in importance only to skills, but at the same time, asset management firms have to watch their cost base—hence the interest in onDemand software. Here is a short list of programming routines available in the cloud:

- *Asset allocation* permits the determination of optimal allocation of assets to achieve targeted investment goals. Stocks of different countries, bonds in different currencies, and money market instruments are covered.
- *Bond systems* are designed to help in managing and evaluating risks for debt instruments, options, and futures based on a spot yield curve.
- *Equity systems* cover individual stock and stock market indices, allowing one to screen issues in accordance with investors' objectives.
- *Forex systems* support currency exchange and other functions, like currency options trading, hedging of forex exposure, and foreign exchange forecasting.

Some vendors specialize in front office chores; others are more oriented toward back office requirements. The front desk is where fund managers and the financial markets meet, and is thus an important depository of asset management information. Ideally, a front office system must ensure that its users have immediate access to all necessary data sources, including prices, interest rates, exchange rates, and more.

Quite crucial is the ability not only to interface in real time with information providers but also to allow traders to create their own display as it best suits their decision profile. Sophisticated internal models (when available) help in decision making through experimentation on different positions by performing analysis and simulation in connection to a variety of hypothetical situations.

This functionality should be embedded into the trading system's architecture. A simple schema of a typical asset management system is shown in Figure 13.2. One of the value-added building blocks allows the assets manager to experiment in reordering investment plans for his or her assets. The processing of order and

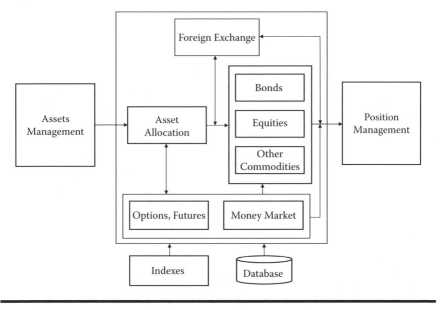

Figure 13.2   Building blocks of a basic assets management function.

contract data is the work of the back office, and the cloud's offers of onDemand software include:

- balance sheets,
- profit and loss statements,
- legal financial reporting, and
- attribution of portfolio performance by fund manager.

Also available are internal accounting management information systems furnishing information on portfolio positions by product, market manager, and strategy—after thoroughly analyzing assets and liabilities. *If* the institution operates internationally, *then* this system should be extended to cover forms corresponding to various accounting standards and compliance procedures coexisting in the global landscape.

Most prized are routines that permit experimentation on hedging asset positions in a cross-country, multicurrency sense, as well as programs allowing one to assess the management performance of assets (and each assets manager's individual results), analyze in absolute terms and in conjunction to limits, and provide a cross-sectional analysis of commodities and markets where investment products are at play.

In terms of value differentiation, the software a user organization would like to have, including knowledge engineering artifacts, is important, enabling it to seize opportunities as they develop, including emerging markets. Investments in emerging markets shares have been on the rise due to diversification of investor preferences. Fund distribution by country, currency, and commodity on the basis of expected risk and return, as well as investment restrictions in each market, is assisted by onDemand programs such as:

- *asset analyzer*, assessing the efficiency of the present portfolio and recommending likely improvements;
- *market trend analyzer*, able to evaluate the global stock, bond, and currency exchange markets from various angles;
- *basic information provider*, which gives for equities the beta coefficient (sensitivity to index), dividend yield, price/earnings, and other issues critical in each market*; and
- *experimental allocator*, enabling the user to simulate likely results from plans for allocating assets on the basis of individually specified rates of return or indices.

Value-added software will support interest rate and exchange rate projections for each market, as well as trends in credit risk, market risk, and political risk. Exposure and degree of correlation must be measured and integrated into the model, and the same is true of conditions restricting investment, such as the regulations for pension funds. (For example, in several jurisdictions regulations for pension funds require that stocks should not account for more than 30 percent of invested funds, or that bond investments must feature better than A– credit rating.)

Programming products are also necessary for currency exchange risk, which is a critical issue in the global market. Forex market rates can be estimated, employing purchasing power parties. In the case of simultaneous investment in foreign-currency-denominated bonds and stocks, the system must provide the assets manager with necessary information to help decide on crucial ratios in order to hedge investments; for instance, between:

- bond futures and options,
- stock futures and options, and
- Forex futures and options.

Information on the volatility of each of the indices that are underlying the original assets, estimates of dividend schedules, and interest rate information are vital. By utilizing these elements, the analysis of various situations and of market issues, made by the asset manager, becomes better documented.

Also important is accurate and swift price analysis. To price options, most programming products use Black-Scholes and binomial models. When it comes to the pricing of American type options, they usually take into account the premium aris-

---

* Also for bonds, average coupon rate of an index on the basis of currency, average ultimate yield, average duration, and credit risk.

ing from the fact that options can be exercised at any time before expiration, which is not the case with European options.

In conclusion, the onDemand software to be chosen must supply information for all forms of trading needed for price analysis; short-term strategies such as hedging, arbitrage, and option strategies; and long-term strategies like portfolio management. Alternative models of analysis should be used for each important product, as this assists in risk evaluation. One size fits all is not advisable.

13.4 Cloud Technology Can Improve Fund Management

One of the senior executives who contributed to the research project said in the course of our meeting: "We tried to push technology in fund management, but people don't pay attention. We showed asset managers what they can do with expert systems, but we were somewhat disappointed to see that the question 'What can high technology do for me today that it did not do five years ago?' was never asked."

According to the opinion of another banker, "Somehow in a significant number of cases, particularly in some countries, the urge to use technology is not there. Even institutions that employ traditional technology don't make it as sharp as it should be. One of the ironies is that quite often the guys looking for the best use of high tech are the people who don't really need it that much because they deal in small amounts, not in hundreds of millions dollars under their management."

Both opinions are based on facts. Many people in the financial industry don't seem to be motivated to use high technology to their company's advantage. Much more is done in accounting than in analytics. Electronic order books can automatically match purchase and sales orders. And while some exchanges, such as Frankfurt, London, and New York, continue to use floor trading, electronic systems are now taking over important support functions at these locations, too.*

Banks that have allowed themselves to fall behind in the employment of high technology where it counts the most say (as an excuse) that the extensive use of IT systems creates high fixed costs. But at the same time, they develop their own software for trading and processing, which is exactly where the high costs lie.

By contrast, the choice of onDemand software is a much more cost-effective way to proceed, saving money that can be deployed in analytical studies. onDemand software should be a must for the basic functions of trading, accounting, payments, and settlements. There is plenty of evidence to document that fully electronic trading and integrated settlement could be ten times cheaper than traditional procedures.

---

* As "dark pools" have demonstrated. This is not, however, a subject of the present book.

Allow me, however, to add a word of caution. Even massive cost benefits alone do not guarantee success in the longer term. As I never tire of repeating, the key to continuing effective use of technology is in reengineering the organization as well as in hiring, training, and retaining key staff able to:

- manage uncertainty,
- control risks,
- observe limits,
- deal effectively with very creative accounting,
- understand and manage the role of the technology as gatekeeper,
- keep on being creative and high performing over time.

Another contributor to better results in fund management is to develop reward and incentive systems that are not counterproductive (as the big bonuses proved to be in the 2007–2009 crisis) but consistent with the changing motivations of professionals. Senior management must keep under close watch the organizational culture and ensure the incentives remain positive.

An integral part of this challenge is how to better communicate with, inspire, and guide professionals to create a more highly motivating work environment. Senior management has a significant role to play in this effort because it is part of the relationship between innovation, motivation, change, and uncertainty that haunts all financial (and many other) organizations. To provide the appropriate guidance, the board and CEO must be able to answer for themselves and their employees questions such as:

- What will the asset management business model look like in five years?
- What activities should each asset manager see as his or her core competencies?
- What level of technology investment and associated skill will be required to support the business?
- How much onDemand software should be bought to avoid delays and unnecessary costs in implementation?

To perform these obligations in an able manner, senior management often finds itself confronted with resistance to organizational change, some of it coming from IT, as well as with a fair amount of company politics. CEOs should nevertheless appreciate that with competition what it is, the company simply cannot afford to continue spending hundreds of millions per year on legacy systems. That is precisely why onDemand software and platforms offer a great opportunity.

Senior management will also be wise to examine and find by itself that long and complex programming routines are not only very costly and time-consuming, but also failing to satisfy end user demands. A number of reasons lie behind this statement, some of which have been already brought to the reader's attention in connection to legacy programs:

- lack of a customer-centric view that characterized old solutions but today is antibusiness;
- focus on plugging the gaps rather than delivering a streamlining business functionality that provides a competitive edge;
- absence of a common architecture across multiple channels of activity;
- inability to adopt a holistic, proactive core systems strategy that satisfies the shifting asset management objectives;
- high development and maintenance cost of legacy systems; and
- the still present batch processing, which handicaps decision making in trading and fund management.

All of these reasons caution against the use of legacy technology in banking. Not only is onDemand software cost-effective, but as a recent survey in Western Europe pointed out, four-fifths of the participating institutions were not satisfied with their core banking systems. These were so old and inflexible that they had become an impediment to the delivery of strategic objectives.

"While it is an onerous task, it is vital that we modernize," said one of the bankers who responded to my research. Several other people had a similar reaction. It needs no explaining that it is useless to complain about a system that does not work. Corrective action must be enlightened, focused, and swift. "I do not meet my managers to tell them what to do," said Jack Welch, GE's former CEO, in a conference, "but to make sure that they do it NOW!"

13.5 Criteria of Success in Asset Management Technology

There are two ways of measuring success or failure. The one most favored by managers, investors, and bankers is to look at profit figures. The other is to account for and evaluate not just one but several factors behind profits, such as skills, products, and the market, with technology the next in line. As far as the asset management business is concerned, there are also other top performance indicators to account for:

- net new money under management;
- invested assets, their preservation, and their growth; and
- gross margin on invested assets (in basis points).

Behind all these indicators lie reputation, human capital, customer handholding, prestige, opportunity analysis, and the fine print of risk control in financial transactions. (Technological criteria are discussed later on.)

Chance could play a role in asset management but not year after year. The third and fourth straight years of profitable investment performance provide a foundation for differentiating the assets managers' results. Depending too much on one's "good fortune" breeds complacency, which leads straight to downfall.

The bottom line is that companies (and their professionals) must be on alert today if they plan on being here tomorrow—and technology is an integral part of this alert status. Clear-eyed executives appreciate that the onslaught of technologies has changed the way we do business. Because of, rather than in spite of, technology, a skilled and knowledgeable workforce is key to ensuring *our* company's ability to compete in the marketplace.

In fact, true commitment to ongoing development of our ability to compete may be *the* distinguishing factor that sets us apart from the crowd, and technology has a role to play in this differentiation. Figure 13.3 presents a general schema of technological support in asset management. A mark of distinction is the sophistication of software entering into every one of the blocks in the diagram.

As a minimum, but only as a minimum, the people working in fund management need software for monitoring positions, measuring exposure, and making

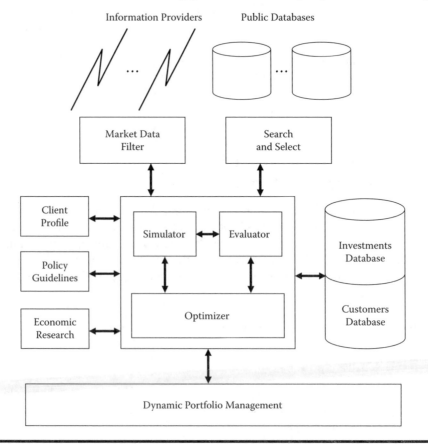

Figure 13.3   General schema of technological support in assets management.

investment decisions (or recommendations depending on the type of client contract). This is fundamental in all endeavors having to do with control over assets and liabilities. Examples of business solutions currently available on demand include (in generic terms):

- a comprehensive banking functionality for wealth managers and account managers covering portfolio valuation, information positions, online messaging, and account statements;
- creditworthiness evaluations for debt instruments (a higher level), requiring credit exposure computation, limits specification and monitoring, and netting agreements;
- other necessary routines including collateral handling, such as the calculation and updating of collateral requirements, the revaluation of positions coupled with real-time feeds, trade/custodian reconciliation, and rehypothecation.

Browser-based position management applications must be deployed portfolio-wide, to provide comprehensive real-time risk measurement by account, product type, topology, and institution-wide basis. Equally important is marketing management facilitating demographic and other segmentations, activity tracking, and database mining all the way to personalized processing.

Middleware facilities are also necessary, integrating a variety of front desk and back office operations. Both administrative chores and CRM marketing routines are offered in the cloud by different vendors, and they increasingly feature value-added enhancements. For example, Google AdWords:

- lets customers place ads in its CRM environment and
- helps track the success of their online ad spending by tracing which ads and keywords generate leads and opportunities.

Also available on demand are asset management dashboards, and software supporting campaign management that assists in planning marketing chores, managing a variety of online and offline initiatives and campaigns, and analyzing the performance of these different initiatives.

For instance, e-mail marketing provides tools to plan and execute e-mail campaigns targeted at personal banking and asset management prospects and customers, including an integrated response helping to measure the results of e-mail campaigns. Still another example is auto-answer e-mail, which automatically sends tailored personalized responses to customer inquiries based on the nature of the inquiry.

As these references document, there is no lack of functionality in onDemand software, and financial institutions that do not use it have only themselves to blame for that failure. The wealth of programming routines available in the cloud is one of the most basic criteria of success in asset management technology—and it is available to everybody.

Critics may say that all this hides the downside, which lies in the fact that there is no proprietorship attached to such programming routines. That's true, but it is no less true that all companies purchasing them don't use them in the best possible way—while at the same time, nothing forbids them from developing some sophisticated, proprietary add-ons.

As the careful reader will recall from previous discussions on onDemand software (Chapter 10, etc.), the biggest challenge in using what the cloud has to offer is how to push forward an environment that, left to its own devices, becomes institutionalized and lethargic. That's bad because returns greatly depend on an ongoing synergy between:

- insightful product marketing and
- leading-edge technology to support it.

There is by now plenty of evidence to document that the old cookbook approaches to IT solutions do not work in competitive environments like asset management. The best way to benefit from technology is to keep the spirit of innovation alive. This is written in full appreciation of the fact that sustaining a dynamic technology environment may not be easy, but it is a must.

One of the criteria of success is how scalable is the solution, as well as in which way new technology is introduced into assets management, for instance, rapid implementation, size of global coverage, immediate and visible functionality gains, minimum or no operational disruption. Another criteria of success is production improvements. To appreciate this last statement, the reader must know that 50 percent of fund management costs are spent on something that is practically overhead, and it is a direct result of the fact that scant attention is paid to how to get top results from IT.

In conclusion, able approaches should aim to ensure that the main players, including asset managers, personal bankers, and technologists, are contributing to the necessary synergy between fund management and technology without being distracted from their primary disciplines and responsibilities. However, as it has so often been brought to the reader's attention, this is a cultural and organizational problem—not a technology problem.

13.6 Functionality Specifics Prized by the Experts

There is little doubt that some of the software functionality an asset manager would like to have will not be found on the web, because it has no particular appeal to the broader market. This is precisely the role of added-value modules a company must develop in-house. Still, there is a big difference between trying to do everything (which is the most widespread practice) by reinventing the wheel and developing only what is necessary to be ahead of the crowd.

An example of analytical, knowledge-enriched software to be developed in-house is the one hunting for *anomalies* in the market, essentially in the pricing of financial instruments. Let me better explain this issue by giving some background.

The financial hecatomb of 2007–2009 has discredited the efficient market hypothesis, which states that because information is being immediately disseminated, and every player is getting plenty of it, the market is efficient. Quite to the contrary, the market is inefficient. Therefore:

- there exist pricing anomalies, and
- one can strike gold when he or she finds them and exploits them.

Much of the gold can be mined when other investors agree with the finder's discovery and make his or her fortune by backing his or her judgment, albeit with some delay on the finder. Such market anomalies, however, are passing phenomena. They disappear as fast as they appear. *If* they lie around gathering dust, *then* they have no value, though they do occur.

George Soros, for example, is known to have thrived on anomalies. From 1969 until October 1987, Soros achieved a 350 times increase in the value of the Quantum Fund. The way he put it in an interview with *Fortune* magazine: while bargains no longer predominated, "a search quickly turns up stocks selling for less than a company's breakup value."*

This is an anomaly often encountered in the stockmarket but not always exploited. (Carl Icahn is another investor who thrived on breakup value.) Other anomalies are more difficult to identify. To locate them, one must subject assets, liabilities, and cash flow to rigorous analytics, combining fair value, risk management, and interest-rate-related product management to flash out cases where:

- assets and liabilities are mismatched,
- cash flow matching of assets and liabilities happens only under restricted conditions, or
- assets and liabilities have sensitivity to interest rate changes beyond the normal case because they are highly leveraged.

If an institution is in the business of originating loans, underwriting or placing securities, and performing other investment banking activities, *then* it must have a distribution network that makes it possible to turn over assets at a competitive pace and price, by selling them to investors wherever they might be located. This distribution network should be characterized by certain key attributes embedded into the enterprise architecture:

---

* *Fortune*, September 1987.

- *globality*, including the monitoring of fluidity and shifting patterns of worldwide political and economic situations;
- *capillarity*, reaching every corner of operations, every potential investor, and delivering the financial service he or she desires; and
- *instantaneity*—if one is a market operator, or investor, one risks major losses if the reaction time is too slow.

Another area where more sophisticated solutions than those to be found as a commodity are necessary is *product liability*. During the coming decade, *litigation* based on product liability will, in all likelihood, be the single most common pitfall dug by regulatory violations, breaches of intellectual property laws, employee conduct, contractual failures, shareholder actions, and product liability.

In 2000, Sotheby's, an international auction house, and UST, a chewing tobacco firm, saw their credit downgraded because of some publicized antitrust violations. Beverly Enterprises was hit for violating America's complex Medicare billing practices. American Home Products was downgraded following a $12.3 billion settlement, stemming from its production of a diet drug that cleared federal safety hurdles but was later found to be dangerous. A better-known product liability case is that of asbestos. These are operational risks.*

Still another domain prized by experts is *experimentation*—not only examining alternatives but also subjecting financial conditions and market twists to stress testing until they reveal their secrets. Analytical techniques include duration, matching, horizon immunization, and multiperiod immunization of assets and liabilities to develop a *perception value*.

Cloud or no cloud, the required highly sophisticated software is not generally available. The same is true about programming routines supporting experimentation on profit and loss (P&L) calculations along the lines shown in Figure 13.4, including the ability to enlarge the array of investment factors entering into an optimization.

- *Experimentation* and *optimization* are keywords in this frame of reference.
- Both have a great deal to do with the fact that the main objects of computing are foresight, insight, analysis, and design. It is not the automation of numerical calculation or the legacy data processing chores.

One of the main objectives in experimentation is to keep exposure under close watch, while at the same time assuming risks, because without risk taking there is no profit. Keeping risks under lock and key requires worst-case analysis to provide an estimate of what might turn into a major loss—immediately judging whether this is affordable. Among other issues, experimentation should target:

---

* D. N. Chorafas, *Managing Operational Risk. Risk Reduction Strategies for Investment Banks and Commercial Banks* (London: Euromoney Books, 2001).

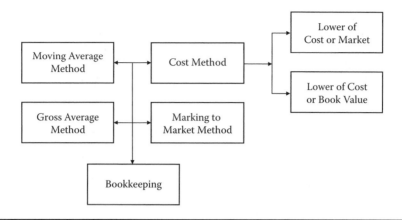

Figure 13.4   Alternative methods for profit and loss calculation, which should be used simultaneously for experimentation reasons

- ■ trading and investment hypotheses and
- ■ market moves that are unlikely but plausible events.

Experimentation is not limited to decisions, because not every catastrophy or near catastrophy is due to bad judgment. Errors, too, can create havoc. On December 12, 2005, the malfunctioning of the trading system at Tokyo Stock Exchange (TSE) prevented Mizuho Securities from quickly canceling a botched trade. With this, the number two Japanese bank faced a stock trading loss of $333 million, the result of an error committed by a broker inputting an order for *J-com* shares. The order was to sell 610,000 shares for 1 yen each, instead of selling 1 share for 610,000 yen.

If the Tokyo Stock Exchange's order canceling system had functioned properly, the amount lost would have been much smaller. Getting wind of the error, Mizuho rushed to buy back a majority of the trade, but 96,236 shares (more than six times the number outstanding) had to be repurchased from investors. A case against TSE went to court, and the court decided that the party responsible was Mizuho.

There have always been exceptional individuals able to move fast and see through their policies. Mustafa Kemal Ataturk favored replacing Arabic with Latin script. Once he made up his mind, there was turning back; the pressure was on not only at the top but also at the bottom. Mustafa Kemal went to towns and villages, and talked to the common person. Then, once engaged, reform was carried out within six months.*

This, however, is not the way the average executive operates. Organizations are made of people, and people are often slow in making decisions and even more so in putting them into effect. Therefore, the metalayer of an enterprise architecture

---

* Andrew Mango, *Atatürk* (New York: Overlook Press, 2000).

should act as a catalyst to rapid motion, providing management with the ability to spot opportunities instantly, and always accounting for the fact that business opportunities are often a by-product of mismatched conditions that are short-lived.

As Alfred Sloan, of General Motors fame, aptly suggested, we should have at our disposition accurate and timely financial information. This is vital because we must always be prepared to withdraw from a position if our product does not meet with its established objectives. We must also be able to cope with a multiplicity of risks. In finance, the market's rapid pace and global nature require constant attention to:

- position risks,
- credit risks, and
- liquidity risks.

In conclusion, a thoroughly studied and well-implemented information technology for asset management is very important because, together with skill and expertise, it multiplies the effectiveness of a company with its customers and in the market. This cannot be achieved using the traditional data processing of yesterday. The best policy, therefore, is to buy onDemand software and create a layer of added-value functions that provides *our* firm with a competitive advantage.

13.7 Institutional Investors, High Net-Worth Individuals, and the Cloud

Banks that expect a steady stream of fees and transaction income from private banking and institutional investors* must be aware that both populations put them under steady watch in regard to their practices, fees, and the results they deliver. Institutional investors have:

- the clout to negotiate a contract with the fund manager prior to signing it and
- the policy to watch over the shoulder of the bank assuming asset management responsibilities, checking up on whether deliverables correspond to promises that have been made.

One famous case is that of a major British pension fund that obliged Merrill Lynch to make up with its own money for the difference between what was contractually required as an annual return and the net return on investment (ROI). The latter had failed to match the contractually agreed upon amount.

The particular attention bankers paid to pension funds and other institutional investors dates back to the early 1960s. By the late 1980s the market of high-net-

---

* Institutional investors are pension funds, university and other endowments, and insurance companies usually managing large sums of money.

worth individuals joined that of institutional investors, as it attracted a great deal of attention because it grew much faster than the global economy. During the first seven years of this century it increased at an estimated 9 percent per year, and though the turmoil in financial markets bent this curve, it is currently in the process of again picking up speed.

At the same time, however, the effects of the 2007–2009 economic and banking crisis have shown how exposed investors can be. University endowments that (wrongly) adopted a policy of high leverage, and bet their shirt on an upswing of the economy, lost 25 to 30 percent of their net worth. Wealthy people who relied on leverage to enhance their capital and income have been badly burned.

In the aftermath, the credit crisis raised questions about private banking and asset management operations. It also reopened the debate about the benefit of combining deposit taking with private and investment banking. The larger issue is whether expected benefits from leveraged positions are outweighed by the risk run by investors.

Banks that watch better than others over exposure and care to know more about their clients and their investment goals have built *profile analyzers*. A customer profile expert system includes modules that evaluate risk aversion, the client's rate of income and income tax, as well as how he or she evaluates the prospects for interest rates and exchange rates. The system also evaluates the client's time horizon.

Other modules are a *professional advisor* to assist the account manager; tools for *choosing*, in a documented manner, investors for new banking products; a means to *test and prune* the client's position; and a *learning tool*, for new account officers. These modules also integrate different products and services, giving the account manager a complete frame of reference to improve customer handholding.

Beyond that are modules that allow the investment advisor or asset manager to incorporate into a *customer mirror* other important client relationships in order to determine information needed but missing from the customer file and more accurately isolate investment type problems. A most important contribution to sound asset management is made by the analysis of risk factors. Credit risk provides an example.

Credit risk is the oldest exposure in the banking industry. It appears when the customer takes the loan, not just when the loan goes sour. Hence, in any loans book there is latent risk that leads to an asymmetry in capital reserves. Executives motivated by credit risk only at the time of bankruptcy aren't worth their salary and bonus. "I am a risk manager by profession, and my job is to see to it that when everybody earns money for our bank, he or she does not wreck the edifice by taking inordinate risks," said one of the executives who participated in the research leading to this book.

Credit risk management is not an exact science. As Jesus Surina of Banco de Espana aptly stated,* the mistakes on credit risk control are made in good times, by failing to account for assumed exposure. They are not made at the time the loan

---

* Basle II Masterclass, organized by IIR, London, March 27/28, 2003.

becomes damaged goods, and the answer to this problem is a steady watch regarding borrowers' creditworthiness through expert systems.

Well-managed banks follow this approach, with credit risk dynamically measured counterparty by counterparty. Investments, too, are exposed to credit risk, as well as to market risk and more. ROI is a good yardstick that requires first-class IT support.

Apart from other uses, formal ROI representations can serve as moveable stand-ins for physical assets, enabling the simulation of hypothetical situations in order to explore a range of possibilities. This makes feasible the evaluation of property representations resulting from projected investment strategies while keeping in mind the need for:

◼ limits to credit risk and market risk,
◼ the overriding consideration for flexibility, and
◼ the importance of preserving the managed assets.

Good investments are fundamentally under steady watch because of market dynamics, new information, changes in the nature or magnitude of risks, updates of assumptions, discovery of errors, and other reasons—some of which are unpredictable and impossible to anticipate but hit in the most inopportune moment.

Therefore, as Section 13.6 brought to the reader's attention, investors and asset managers must learn to experiment and portray solution trade-offs. First, they must be able to prioritize portfolio design problems and determine where to concentrate their efforts.

Much can be learned in this respect from engineering. To successfully develop a complex product or system, project managers decompose the design problem into smaller subproblems, which in turn may be further decomposed. Development teams are then assigned to each design problem or subproblem, with the project manager:

◼ coordinating the overall engineering design and
◼ aiming to achieve an integrated final product that meets specifications, is cost-effective, and has great market appeal.

These are not the types of jobs that can be done by paper and pencil. They have to be performed in a steady and analytical manner. It is no means by accident that, as already mentioned in the Foreword, 54 percent of the total investment in equipment in America is in IT (compared to 30 percent in 1980)—and of this, nearly half is in software (compared to 12 percent in 1980).* As these statistics document,

---

* *The Economist*, October 24, 2009.

- the evolution toward onDemand software is one of necessity—it is not an option, and
- cost and long delays aside, there are simply not enough qualified people to write in-house the programs that have become the alter ego of competitiveness and market leadership.

Without a doubt, not every programming product necessary to fulfill the applications requirements described in this section will be found in the cloud. This, however, should not discourage using onDemand software. Instead, it suggests the wisdom of learning how to add value through onDemand platforms—in order to develop modules that bring *our* company ahead of its competitors.

In conclusion, the mastery of a long list of issues—some client oriented, others functional, and still others technological—is the basic ingredient of sound asset management. Technology plays a critical role, but by far the top factor is people. Therefore, the salient problem of CEOs and boards is not to be for or against the cloud but to profit from what is available and decide on what kinds of people and critical skills are needed to maximize this profit.

Technology is not a goal per se, and the cloud falls under this dictum. Whether we talk about logistics or asset management, IT is an enabler that under certain conditions assists in being in charge of operations and in providing a sense of achievement. As Peter Drucker once said, "Effectiveness is a habit."

Epilog: Technology's Limit

The technology you have is not the one you want.
The technology you want is not the one you need.
The technology you need is not the one you can obtain.
The technology you can obtain is not the one you can afford.

These four lines encapsulate a whole lot of technology's limits to which many boards, CEOs and CIOs are turning a blind eye. Unwisely, since Day 1, with computers and information systems the limits and risks associated to technology, and most particularly to new technology, have been confined to the rubbish bin.

Etymologically, the word *risk* derives from the Italian "risciare" which means to dare. Daring, and therefore risk, is a choice—not a fate. By risk we understand is the chance of injury, damage or loss; a hazard. But at the same time risk is the most vital ingredient of opportunity. What many people fail to appreciate is that:

- The doors of risk and return are adjacent, and indistinguishable.
- Technology is a game of risk; no policy, engineering design or model can eliminate that element.

It is he who uses the opportunity but is in charge of the risk best who wins. The qualification and subsequent quantitative expression of loss or harm ought to be proportional not merely to the impact of an event, but also to its probability of occurrence. The problem is that the existence of many unknown makes such probabilities pure guesswork. Yet experience teaches that even the most improbable events may become a reality. This Epilog examines two domains where the limits of technology and risks associated to it are being felt:

- Big data, and
- The consumerization of IT.

Big Data Law

For a large number of entities, including a wide range of business enterprises as well as government departments, the proliferation of data makes them increasingly inaccessible and therefore obscure. What there is consumed by overabundance of information is rather obvious: Information consumes the attention of its recipients, said in 1971 Herbert Simon, an economist. Simon concluded that:

- A wealth of information is counterproductive.
- It creates a poverty of attention.

There is no better documentation of Simon's statement than the fact that units of measurement and sizes of digital counts have been increasing by leaps and bounds, as shown in Table 1. Like Moore's Law which in the early 1970s described the rise in cost/effectiveness of semiconductors and microprocessors over the decades that followed, a yet unnamed *big data law* is that;

- The amount of digital information increases by an order of magnitude every five years.

Over the last two decades data is widely available, but this has not been matched by our ability to extract knowledge out of it. Moreover, a vast amount of data is shared in a multidimensional way among different entities brings to bear problems

Table 1   Units and Sizes of Digital Data Counts

Unit	Size
Bit (b)	A binary digit
Byte (B)	8 bits; basic unit in computing
Kilobyte (KB)	1,000, 10^3, or 2^{10} bytes
Megabyte (MB)	10^6, or 2^{20} bytes
Gigabyte (GB)	10^9, or 2^{30} bytes
Terabyte (TB)	10^{12}, or 2^{40} bytes
Petabyte (PB)	10^{15}, or 2^{50} bytes
Exabyte (EB)	10^{18}, or 2^{60} bytes
Zettabyte (ZB)	10^{21}, or 2^{70} bytes
Yottabyte (YB)*	10^{24}, or 2^{80} bytes

* Added in 1991.

of consumerism of IT (section 3). Primarily this is personal data originating with a simple transaction, but:

- Leading to complex interrelationships, as well as to serious privacy concerns.

Big data has become both a novelty and a headache; an example of high tech's deliverables and of technology's limits. Its sheer magnitude poses unprecedented storage and handling challenges. Anecdotal evidence suggests that in one year alone: 2005 (latest year of which semi-reliable estimates are available) mankind created 150 *exabytes* (billion gigabytes). The way a guestimate has it,

- In 2010 mankind would create 1,200 exabytes, and
- This represents a 800-percent increase in a mere 5 years.

From where comes all this mass of data? What does it *really* serve? Why did it get out of hand? are most legitimate questions. Wal-Mart, the global retail chain, and Nestlé, the world's largest food company, offer examples.

Wal-Mart operates 8,400 stores internationally and reportedly handles more than one million customer transactions *every hour*. These are fed into databases estimated at more than 2.5 *petabytes* (million gigabytes). That number becomes more overbearing by accounting for the fact that Wal-Mart's two million employees and millions of customers, too, must be databased and this information needs to be steadily processed creating intermediate data storage requirements.

It is fairly obvious that this leads to enormous challenges of data storage. There are as well rapidly growing requirements of analysis—spotting patterns and extracting useful information. A new term *data exhaust* has been coined to identify data that is a byproduct of transactions, but can be effectively recycled to:

- Provide a more focused identification,
- Reveal business opportunities,
- Bring attention to opaque trends,
- Improve customer service, and
- Assist in product innovation.

There are also the more classical data processing chores of handling clients accounts, upkeeping financial records, serving in supply chain and inventory management. More advanced solutions are enabling suppliers to see the exact number of their products on every shelf of every store—which is an example of data exhaust as a utility.

Big companies want to have a complete overview of when and how their products are selling, because this enables management to better control the stocks, reduce costs, and keep dynamic the business model of retailing. Nestlé needs this model to be in charge of a sales network handling more than 100,000 products in 200 countries and using 550,000 suppliers.

We are still at an early stage of this development. Nomadic (mobile) computing will exaggerate the big data problem, creating new major challenges in terms of management and of technology. Evidently, also of storage. Limits and risks range:

- From privacy and security (Chapter 9),
- To the reliability of storage devices and of big data systems (Chapter 10), and
- To solutions able to store big data over time, fallback procedures, associated costs, and management issues.

For the time being at least, factual and documented system solutions are not on hand. But there is hype. For example, the European Commission* recommended that Google, Microsoft and other cloud infrastructure providers should limit data storage to 6 months. Just like that.

It needs no explaining that this blanket sweep of databases is an impossibility, but the "recommendation" also shows how little politicians understand the implications and problems of storing massive data in the Cloud. And not only the politicians.

Another "solution" for digital files, this one advanced in the United States, is to have *expiry dates* associated to information elements—which is easier said than done. First, because the retention of data over time is a legal and legislative requirement which varies by jurisdiction. Second, because it is not whole files that would be deleted at expiry (though that might happen as an exception) but fields—hence, parts of files.

The case of companies which have organized their databases in a way enabling them to effectively apply expiry dates, without risk of unwanted or unlawful deletions, is indeed rare. Even the observance of privacy principles, which is a more straightforward operation, is spotty. In 2003 when a new law in California required companies to notify people if a security breach compromised their personal information, companies had trouble complying with its requirements.†

Important as they may be, new demands such as expiry and security breach (an ill-defined concept‡) would not be effective without policing. Regulators must require all companies to undergo an annual information privacy-and-security audit

---

* Governing body of the European Union.
† Not only people and companies should be given access to and control over the information held about them, including whom it is shared with, but also they should have a veto on additions and deletion of data concerning them. Even if this is the letter of the law, it takes a miracle to implement it in a mass society and its big data.
‡ Breach of exactly which information element in a client file, by whom, under which conditions?

by an accredited organization, similar to financial audits for listed companies by certified public accountants. Such an audit:

- Should be a "must" if ever a policy of expiry dates was adopted, and
- It has to be accompanied by criminal prosecution for wrongdoers on charges of contributing to the *entropy* of the nation's (or the world's) information system.

For those of us who were active in information technology at its beginning, in the early 1950s, the hope was that computers will help in keeping paperwork under lock and key (which has never happened), and in bending the curve of *entropy*. Entropy means disorganization.*

Now with big data measured in petabytes, exabytes and eventually zetabytes, and yottabytes (Table 1) precisely the opposite takes place. The entropy of information has escaped control, and entropy leads to lack of patterning, while data exhaust and analytics are tried as medicines to provide some sort of negative entropy.

Few people realize the deep and further out implications of big data. At corporate level, entities with big data structures often find that half or more of their records are obsolete or duplicated†, and of the remainder about one-third are inaccurate or incomplete—often leading to double-counting. It needs no explaining that many professionals and managers do not trust the information on which they have to base their decisions. Several say that:

- IT was meant to make sense of data, but quite often it just produces unfocused information.
- Therefore, instead of providing an answer to their problem big data contributes to overcrowding and confusion.

In addition, intentional or even accidental deletions from databases may turn people into non-persons. Companies, too, might suffer from the same syndrome. What happens if the technology stops working altogether, or there is a major malicious attack with system-wide consequences?

Such cases have major impact. In January 2000 the torrent of data pouring into the US National Security Agency (NSA) brought the system to a crashing halt. The agency was "brain-dead" for three-and-a-half days, said General Michael Hayden, who was then its director. Hayden added that "Our ability to process information was gone."‡

---

* Information measures are used to evaluate an organization, since organization is based on the interaction among parts.
† Triplicated and quadrupled is not unheard of either.
‡ The Economist, February 27, 2010

By large majority users at individual, corporate and government level do not come to grips with big data risk. Improving the performance of existing technologies is a good idea, but far from answering the core of the problem. Fallback solutions must be radical, independent of the failing system, available on split second notice, and effective.

Ways have to be found to stop entropy's drift towards zetabytes and yottabytes because of entropy. And the effect of the mass society on big data must be reversed. Widespread social networking practices suggest that this is not in the wind.

The Consumerization of IT

In February 2010, Facebook celebrated its sixth birthday, and together with it the fact that in this short span of time it became the second most popular site on the internet (after Google). In fact, it got Google running by launching Buzz, a social-networking system for sharing messages, images and video competing with the likes of Facebook and Twitter.*

A month later, mid-March 2010, Facebook overtook Google to become America's most popular website. Figures for the week ending March 13, 2010 have shown that the social networking site accounted for 7.1 percent of US internet traffic, compared with Google's 7.0 percent. (Still with revenues of $23.7 billion in 2009, Google remains the more profitable of the two.)

Facebook's race to the stars has been impressive, but it would be wrong to think that social networking has only a positive aftermath. Office work seems to suffer. A survey of British employees by Morse, a technology firm, found that 57 percent of staff use Facebook, Twitter or other social-networking websites for personal purposes during office hours. Moreover,

■ By so doing they are sometimes divulging sensitive business information,† and
■ This practice ends up with the average worker spending almost one working week a year on such sites.

Another complaint is that that social networks were not designed for businesses, the way spreadsheets and other popular programs have been. Employees using them at work hours cannot even pretend of serving their firms. Rather, they become part of a growing trend which has become known as the *consumerization of IT.*

The trend to consumerization is documented by the fact that subscriptions have been growing by leaps and bounds. With a guestimated 350 million users at the

---

* A much smaller but growing competitor. The name comes from its service. It lets members send out short, 140-character messages called "tweets."
† The Economist, October 31, 2009

time of its sixth birthday, Facebook has left behind MySpace, which itself features an impressive 250 million membership.*

The case of Facebook versus MySpace is instructive because it describes the dilemma faced by social networking companies as aftereffect of their success. Originally, MySpace grew rapidly as a site focused on members' musical interests; then it became a more eclectic network but as it expanded:

- It spent too much time chasing revenue, and
- Too little improving its online offerings, to the point that it is bleeding users and advertising.

This is precisely one of the key challenges faced by social nets. Their's is a balancing act. They need to both drive up membership as fast as possible, and experiment with ways of raising money to fund long term growth which is investment-intensive. But there are risks in trying to kill two birds with one well-placed stone:

- Pushing too hard for revenue in the short term, has unwanted consequences on the network's followship.
- Such a policy drives away users, and it undermines the enterprises because both advertising and membership collapse.

Another wrong strategy by social networks is arms twisting of their clients, all the way to violations of privacy. In December 2009 Facebook caused a storm of protests from privacy groups, and its own "dear clients." This came as it unveiled plans to simplify its privacy and security controls.

At the eye of the storm has been its decision to make more data from individuals' Facebook profiles available by default to anyone with access to the internet. The reaction to this unwarranted invasion of privacy was so strong that some privacy groups filed a complaint against Facebook to the Federal Trade Commission. They argued that the recent changes to its privacy policies and settings violate federal law, and asked for corrective action.

Prior to the aforementioned change of policy, the only data about individuals publicly available were their names and regional or national subnetwork (within Facebook) they belonged to. The change in privacy policy meant that far more information is put on show automatically, even if users could change their default privacy settings to restrict access to some of it.

Facebook is not alone in confronting privacy hurdles. In early 2010 Google moved to contain a firestorm of criticism over Buzz. When it introduced its new social network, as its answer to Facebook and Twitter, Google hoped to get the service off to a fast start. But after Buzz was added to Gmail, users found themselves with a network of "friends" automatically selected by the company.

---

* MySpace was bought by News Corp. in 2005

- What Google viewed as an expedient move, stirred up a lot of angry critics, and
- Many users complained of an invasion of their privacy, faulting the firm for failing to ask permission before sharing their personal data.

The notion to which led Facebook's and Google's snafus, is that with wide-spreading social and other networks there is no permanent way to guarantee endus-ers privacy. Neither is it easy to exercise control over all the digital information that exists about them, as changes in policy have unexpected consequences. Somewhere, somehow there is the risk a change in policy will leak out information which vio-lates privacy rules and makes users angry.

If social networking is now judged as being part of the consumerization of IT, *then* cloud computing too can be seen as part of the same trend. Both social net-works and cloud computing allow all sorts of information services to be delivered on the internet. And privacy is not the only challenge with the rapidly growing importance of internet based communications. Security concerns by businesses lacking the means to confront them, is another problem.

A wave of sophisticated computer attacks has been draining bank accounts of small and medium-sized enterprises (SMEs). Security experts say that the latest ver-sion of a relatively recent but widely distributed criminal tool will worsen the losses among American banks and their customers from computer intrusions facilitated through the internet.

To appreciate the magnitude of the problem, the reader should know that in the third quarter of 2009 falsified electronic transfers in the US were about $120 million—more than 300 percent the level of two years earlier. This represented a most significant increase in fraud.*

In France, fraud statistics have not been too good, either. In 2009 there were 2.5 million cases of fraud—half of them in internet commerce. The average cost stood at euro 130 ($176) per case of fraud, to a total of Euro 325 millions ($439 million).†

This was spreading theft of money is far from being the only worry connected to a wanting internet security. Mobile applications are becoming a game-changer for enterprises, which can use them to implement services faster and more cheaply. Their downside, however, is less security.

Mobile apps are very popular with business users who rush to adopt a simpler personal productivity software, as opposed to more complex enterprise suites which, by and large, require integration. But like PCs in the 1980s, mobile apps escape company control and "IT departments are very concerned about security and data

---

* Financial Times, March 8, 2010
† M6 TV, March 21, 2010

protection," says Andrew Gilbert, executive vice-president for Qualcomm's Internet Services division.*

NATO, too, is highly concerned about security from internet intruders and "Trojan" programs.† On March 4, 2010 Anders Fogh Rasmussen, NATO's Secretary General, warned that new threats to the alliance may come from cyberspace and cannot be met by lining up soldiers and tanks. In an apparent reference to terror groups and criminals working through networks, Rasmussen said there are several international actors who want to know what's going on inside NATO "and they also use cyberspace to achieve their goals."‡

It's all part of IT's consumerization. Therefore, of technology's limits and of technology's risks.

---

* Financial Times, February 12, 2010
† Law enforcement officials, who made combating Zeus and other "Trojan" routines a priority, said hundreds of thieves are running such operations—particularly focused on small businesses because they have larger bank accounts and less robust electronic security. But military gear, too, is subject to Trojan attacks.
‡ The former Danish prime minister was speaking in Helsinki on the sidelines of a NATO seminar on increasing co-operation in crisis management around the globe.

Index

ML   1/11